TIME IN GROUPS

RESEARCH ON MANAGING GROUPS AND TEAMS

Series Editors: Elizabeth A. Mannix and
                    Margaret A. Neale

RESEARCH ON MANAGING GROUPS AND TEAMS
VOLUME 6

TIME IN GROUPS

EDITED BY

SALLY BLOUNT

Stern School of Business, New York University, USA

2004

ELSEVIER
JAI

Amsterdam – Boston – Heidelberg – London – New York – Oxford – Paris
San Diego – San Francisco – Singapore – Sydney – Tokyo

ELSEVIER B.V.
Sara Burgerhartstraat 25
P.O. Box 211,
1000 AE Amsterdam
The Netherlands

ELSEVIER Inc.
525 B Street, Suite 1900
San Diego,
CA 92101-4495
USA

ELSEVIER Ltd
The Boulevard, Langford
Lane Kidlington,
Oxford OX5 1GB
UK

ELSEVIER Ltd
84 Theobalds Road
London
WC1X 8RR
UK

First edition 2004

Library of Congress Cataloging in Publication Data
A catalog record is available from the Library of Congress.

British Library Cataloguing in Publication Data
A catalogue record is available from the British Library.

ISBN: 0-7623-1093-6
ISSN: 1534-0856

∞ The paper used in this publication meets the requirements of ANSI/NISO Z39.48-1992 (Permanence of Paper). Printed in The Netherlands.

CONTENTS

LIST OF CONTRIBUTORS

Deborah Ancona	Sloan School of Management, Massachusetts Institute of Technology, USA
Caroline A. Bartel	Stern School of Business, New York University, USA
Gail Berger	Chicago, IL, USA
Sally Blount	Stern School of Business, New York University, USA
Allen C. Bluedorn	University of Missouri-Columbia, USA
Jeanne Brett	Kellogg School of Management, Northwestern University, USA
Ya-Ru Chen	Stern School of Business, New York University, USA
Kathleen M. Eisenhardt	Department of Management Science and Engineering, Stanford University, USA
Josette M. P. Gevers	Department of Technology Management, Eindhoven University of Technology, The Netherlands
Karen A. Jehn	Social and Organizational Psychology, Leiden University, The Netherlands
Steven J. Karau	Department of Management, Southern Illinois University, USA
Janice R. Kelly	Department of Psychological Sciences, Purdue University, USA
Byron A. Kirton	David Eccles School of Business, University of Utah, USA

Katie Liljenquist   Evanston, IL, USA

Elizabeth Mannix   Johnson Graduate School of Management, Cornell University, USA

Victoria Husted Medvec   Kellogg School of Management, Northwestern University, USA

Frances J. Milliken   Stern School of Business, New York University, USA

Margaret A. Neale   Graduate School of Business, Stanford University, USA

Gerardo A. Okhuysen   David Eccles School of Business, University of Utah, USA

Mara Olekalns   Melbourne Business School, University of Melbourne, Australia

Christel G. Rutte   Department of Technology Management, Eindhoven University of Technology, The Netherlands

Jeffrey Sanchez-Burks   Institute for Social Research, University of Michigan Business School, USA

Rhetta L. Standifer   University of Missouri-Columbia, USA

Wendelien van Eerde   Department of Technology Management, Eindhoven University of Technology, The Netherlands

Mary J. Waller   A.B. Freeman School of Business, Tulane University, USA

Laurie Weingart   Graduate School of Industrial Administration, Carnegie Mellon University, USA

Mary Zellmer-Bruhn   Curtis Carlson School of Management, University of Minnesota, USA

TIME IN GROUPS: AN INTRODUCTION

Sally Blount

... all things come to be and pass away in time.

Author Unknown

As philosophers have long observed, human experience can only be understood across the landscape of time (see Turetzky, 1998, for a review). Yet organizational research has traditionally paid little attention to time as a construct (Ancona, Goodman, Lawrence & Tushman, 2001). Within the groups and teams literature, the study of time has received periodic spurts of attention since the 1950s. The earliest contributions took place within psychology with the study of problem-solving groups in the laboratory. Work on interaction process analysis by Bales and colleagues (Bales, 1950a, b; Bales & Strodtbeck, 1951; Borgatta & Bales, 1953) and Tuckman's (1965) developmental model of "forming-storming-norming-performing" are prominent examples from this line of research (for a review, see Mannix & Jehn, this volume).

In the 1980s, several authors began to examine group temporality, taking context into account. Consider, for example, Moreland and Levine's (1982) work on group formation stages; McGrath and colleague's (McGrath, 1991; McGrath & Kelly, 1986) work on social entrainment; Gersick's (1988, 1989) work on mid-point transitions, and Eisenhardt and colleagues' (1989; Eisenhardt & Bourgeois, 1988; Eisenhardt & Tabrizi, 1995) work on the speed of decision making in top management teams. The 1990s saw another wave of development with research on time pressure and deadline effects (e.g. Karau & Kelly, 1992; Parks & Cowlin, 1995), organizational norms regarding time (Perlow, 1999), and how patterns of behavior, such as decision-making, negotiation and conflict,

Time in Groups
Research on Managing Groups and Teams, Volume 6, 1–7
© 2004 Published by Elsevier Ltd.
ISSN: 1534-0856/doi:10.1016/S1534-0856(03)06001-8

unfold over time (Jehn & Mannix, 2001; Mannix & Loewenstein, 1993; Mannix, Tinsley & Bazerman, 1995; Okhuysen, 2001; Waller, 1999; Weingart, 1992).

As this brief overview shows, the study of time in groups is alive and well. Yet because these contributions have been published in disparate books and journals across the past 20 years, it is our sense that their impact has not been fully realized. No integrated set of readings or unified perspectives has emerged. Thus, the goal of this volume, and the conference upon which it was based, was to consolidate, integrate, and build upon the past 20 years of research on the role of time in groups. Our motivating question is this: What is it that we now know about group temporality, and what should we be exploring next? A call for papers went out in the summer of 2001; a two-day conference was held in May 2002 at Stanford University; papers were submitted for publication in spring 2003.

CENTRAL PREMISES

Conference presentations covered a broad range of topics. For example, Brett, Weingart and Olekans presented work that examines patterns in how group negotiations unfold over time; while Chen, Blount and Sanchez-Burks explored how group status structures influence how members align the pace of their tasks within a group. Zellmer-Bruhn, Waller and Ancona initiated the study of how groups can use pauses in work cycles to break out of embedded routines; while Medvec, Berger, Liljenquist and Neale sought to examine how organizational work groups can avoid the pitfalls of short-term time pressure in decision making.

Yet even amidst this diversity, several themes emerged across the presentations. These commonalities serve as starting points for approaching the study of time in groups. Most notably, all contain *the premise of extra-group context*. Groups and teams do not operate in isolation. A group's many stakeholders – customers, suppliers, upper-level decision makers, and competing work groups – create an extra-group context that imposes temporal demands on a group. These demands can take the form of externally-imposed deadlines for producing deliverables; ongoing cycles of repetitive events and interdependencies, such as buying seasons and fiscal years; background cadences and rhythms, in terms of economic cycles and general rates of technological progress. Even nonroutine events can jolt a group's equilibrium; such as technological breakthroughs, earthquakes, member arrivals and departures. These demands intimately affect how a group understands, interprets, and conducts the timing of its work. As Ancona and Chong (1996) have emphasized, organizational work groups naturally align themselves to match the pace of recurring events that surround them in the organization and the external environment. The work of Waller (1999) has also shown that nonroutine events that occur outside a group, too, shape group temporality and effectiveness.

A second commonality of the chapters is *the premise of group member heterogeneity*. Groups are composed of diverse individuals, who vary not only in terms of demographic characteristics, such as age, gender and ethnicity; but also in terms of their expertise, training, experience, and work motivation. As a result, members vary in how they perceive, understand, and value time. Some members may work slowly and methodically, others quickly and more recklessly. Some may attack tasks one at a time; others may juggle multiple tasks simultaneously. Some may seek resolution quickly; others may like to ponder decisions over longer periods of time. Thus, individual-level differences in tendencies such as time urgency (Conte, Landy & Mathieu, 1995), temporal perspective (Zimbardo & Boyd, 1999), time awareness (Francis-Smythe & Robertson, 1999a, b), and need for closure (Kruglanski & Webster, 1996) can affect how each member interprets, understands, and uses his or her time on behalf of a group. How groups resolve the temporal asynchrony that member heterogeneity introduces is critical to successful performance (Bartel & Milliken, this volume; Blount & Janicik, 2002; Waller, Giambatista & Zellmer-Bruhn, 1999). Further, the most successful work groups are likely to be those that have the ability to synergistically leverage these differences (Eisenhardt, 1989).

A third foundation is *the premise that the process of group interaction itself produces temporal stimuli*. These temporal stimuli may include the establishment of temporal norms, rhythms and routines. Roy's (1960) classic work on banana time epitomizes the way in which ongoing groups naturally segment their time in recurring "chunks" over time and develop accompanying rituals for behavior within different time segments. But group task processes also create temporal outcomes, including, for example, relationship and trust building between members, the development of task procedures and shared mental models, and the production of group-based decisions and other task outputs. Schein (1992) and Barley (1986), among others, have elucidated how the nature of a group's task (e.g. production vs. accounting) affects group temporality. However, Perlow's studies of multiple software teams (1999) have also shown that group temporality is idiosyncratic and unique to each group, not simply a reflection of a group's task demands.

CONCEPTUAL CHALLENGES

In sum, the study of group temporality requires a multi-level perspective, that is, the extra-group level, (including both extra- and intra-organizational influences), group and even coalition levels, and individual member level. Therefore, this research lens faces several conceptual challenges. **First, the study of group temporality requires considering time and time-related constructs as both independent and dependent variables**. For example, as an independent variable, the passage of time affects the nature of work habits, intra-group relationships, communication patterns and norms, as well as task performance. As dependent variables, the emergence of temporal norms, shared cognitions about time, and repeated work patterns within groups are themselves phenomena worthy of study. Further, as dependent variables, time-relevant constructs can be studied as moderators and mediators of other group-based outcomes. For example, Gevers, Rutte and van de Vlien (this volume) postulate that the development of shared cognitions about time within a group will affect group performance across time.

Second, group temporality is experienced by groups and their members at multiple levels of aggregation**. Thus, good theory building regarding group temporality must consider not only the traditional levels of analysis problem (Rousseau, 1985), but also the issue of time scale (George & Jones, 2000; Zaheer, Stuart & Zaheer, 1999). On one end of the spectrum are the micro-level phenomena, such as might occur within a 1-minute, 15-minute, or 1-hour time segment within a group. On the other end of the spectrum are the macro-level phenomena, such as might occur across weeks, months, and years. The temporal phenemona encountered at each level are quite different. At the micro-level, issues of coordination, speaking turns, cognitive load, information disclosure, cognitive integration, and affective reactions are the focus of study. At the macro-level, the role of the environment and the outcomes of group processes (e.g. trust and relationship networks, status differentials and power dynamics, and transactive memory structures) are focal.

In sum, the study of group temporality is conceptually complex and spans a vast array of potential topics. It incorporates multiple levels of analysis, multiple types of constructs, and spans multiple time scales. As Ancona, Goodman, Lawrence and Tushman (2001, p. 660) have noted, organizational researchers do not yet have a "rich set of theoretical and methodological tools" for studying time-based phenomena. There are both practical reasons for this (e.g. proper causal theory-building is difficult (Mitchell & James, 2001), and reliable statistical methods for testing time-based hypotheses are not always available); and institutional forces that block the development (e.g. time-based research may challenge existing findings based on static analyses). Still, there is a need to push for more research in this direction. A time-based perspective opens up new avenues of research in areas that have traditionally been studied as nontemporal issues. Further, as the chapters contained in this volume show, time-focused research is intrinsically interesting and important for better understanding the behavior of groups and their members. Human experience can only be understood across the landscape of time.

BOOK STRUCTURE

This book contains eleven more chapters, which we have grouped into four categories. These include the study of: (a) group processes across time; (b) group synchrony and task alignment; (c) the effects of time pressure on group performance; and (d) group temporality in organizational research.

The papers in the first category address the temporally emergent nature of group processes, such as relationship building, trust, information exchange, consensus building and performance. The papers in the second category focus on the study of how groups align their activities over time. Here, papers that examine both how groups align the timing of their outputs to meet the temporal demands of external constituents and how individual members internally align the timing of their tasks to synchronize with each other.

Our third section hones in on the problem of time pressure that emanates from the ever-accelerating demands of organizational life. These papers examine how short-term time pressure puts stress on group members' cognitive functioning and how those effects influence short-term performance. Finally, we close with two papers that seek to integrate this volume's perspective on groups within a broader organizational context – highlighting key convergence points and posing questions for further study by organizational groups scholars.

When taken altogether, this volume attests to the fact that study of group temporality is flourishing; a broad body of shared knowledge and frameworks is now in-place. Yet, the topic is clearly vast, and we have only begun to under-stand its complexity. These papers lead the way in highlighting new directions and questions.

REFERENCES

Ancona, D., & Chong, C. (1996). Entrainment: Pace, cycle and rhythm in organizational behavior. In: L. L. Cummings & B. Staw (Eds), *Research in Organizational Behavior* (Vol. 18, pp. 251–284). Greenwich, CT: JAI Press.

Ancona, D. G., Goodman, P. S., Lawrence, B. S., & Tushman, M. L. (2001). Time: A new research lens. *Academy of Management Review, 26*, 645–663.

Bales, R. F. (1950a). A set of categories for the analysis of small group interaction. *American Sociological Review, 15*, 257–263.

Bales, R. F. (1950b). *Interaction process analysis: A method for the study of small groups.* Cambridge, MA: Addison-Wesley.

Bales, R. F., & Strodtbeck, F. L. (1951). Phases in group problem-solving. *Journal of Abnormal and Social Psychology, 46,* 485–495.

Barley, S. (1986). Technology as an occasion for structuring: Evidence from observations of CAT scanners and the social order of radiology department. *Administrative Science Quarterly, 31,* 78–108.

Blount, S., & Janicik, G. (2002). Getting and staying in-pace: The "in-synch" preference and its implications for work groups. In: E. A. Mannix, M. A. Neale & H. Sondak (Eds), *Research on Managing Groups and Teams: Toward Phenomenology of Groups and Group Membership* (Vol. 4, pp. 235–266). Greenwich, CT: JAI Elsevier.

Borgatta, E. F., & Bales, R. F. (1953). Interaction of individuals in reconstitued groups. *Sociometry, 16,* 302–320.

Conte, J. M., Landy, F. J., & Mathieu, J. E. (1995). Time urgency: Conceptual and construct development. *Journal of Applied Psychology, 80,* 178–185.

Eisenhardt, K. (1989). Making fast strategic decisions in high-velocity environments. *Academy of Management Journal, 32,* 543–576.

Eisenhardt, K. M., & Bourgeois, L. J. (1988). Politics of strategic decision making in high-velocity environments: Toward a midrange theory. *Academy of Management Journal, 31,* 737–770.

Eisenhardt, K., & Tabrizi, B. N. (1995). Accelerating adaptive processes: Product innovation in the global computer industry. *Administrative Science Quarterly, 40,* 84–110.

Francis-Smythe, J. A., & Robertson, I. T. (1999a). On the relationship between time management and time estimation. *British Journal of Psychology, 90,* 333–347.

Francis-Smythe, J. A., & Robertson, I. T. (1999b). Time-related individual differences. *Time and Society, 8,* 273–292.

George, J. M., & Jones, G. R. (2000). The role of time in theory and theory building. *Journal of Management, 26,* 657–684.

Gersick, C. (1988). Time and transition in work teams: Toward a new model of group development. *Academy of Management Journal, 31,* 9–41.

Gersick, C. J. (1989). Making time: Predictable transitions in task groups. *Academy of Management Journal, 32,* 274–309.

Jehn, K., & Mannix, E. A. (2001). The dynamic nature of conflict: A longitudinal study of intragroup conflict and group performance. *Academy of Management Journal, 44,* 238–251.

Karau, S. J., & Kelly, J. R. (1992). The effects of time scarcity and time abundance on group performance quality and interaction process. *Journal of Experimental Social Psychology, 28,* 542–571.

Kruglanski, A. W., & Webster, D. M. (1996). Motivated closing of the mind: "Seizing" and "freezing". *Psychological Review, 103,* 263–283.

Mannix, E. A., & Loewenstein, G. (1993). Managerial time horizons and inter-firm mobility: An experimental investigation. *Organizational Behavior and Human Decision Processes, 56,* 266–284.

Mannix, E. A., Tinsley, C., & Bazerman, M. H. (1995). Negotiating over time: Impediments to integrative solutions. *Organizational Behavior and Human Decision Processes, 62,* 241–251.

McGrath, J. (1991). Time, interaction, and performance (TIP): A theory of groups. *Small Group Research, 22,* 147–174.

McGrath, J. E., & Kelly, J. R. (1986). *Time and human interaction: Toward a social psychology of time.* New York: Guilford.

Mitchell, T. R., & James, L. R. (2001). Building better theory: Time and the specification of when things happen. *Academy of Management Review, 26,* 530–548.

Moreland, R., & Levine, J. (1982). Socialization in small groups: Temporal changes in individual-group relations. In: L. Berkowitz (Ed.), *Advances in Experimental Social Psychology* (Vol. 15). New York: Academic Press.

Okhuysen, G. A. (2001). Structuring change: Familiarity and formal interventions in problem solving groups. *Academy of Management Journal, 44,* 794–808.

Parks, C., & Cowlin, R. (1995). Group discussion as affected by number of alternatives and by a time limit. *Organizational Behavior and Human Decision Processes, 62,* 267.

Perlow, L. A. (1999). The time famine: Toward a sociology of work time. *Administrative Science Quarterly, 44,* 57–81.

Rousseau, D. (1985). Issues of level in organizational research: Multi-level and cross-level perspectives. In: B. M. Staw & L. L. Cummings (Eds), *Research in Organizational Behavior* (Vol. 7, pp. 1–27). Greenwich, CT: JAI Press.

Roy, D. (1960). Banana time. *Human Organization, 18,* 158–168.

Schein, E. H. (1992). *Organizational culture and leadership* (2nd ed.). San Francisco, CA: Jossey-Bass.

Tuckman, B. W. (1965). Developmental sequences in small groups. *Psychological Bulletin, 63,* 384–399.

Turetzky, P. (1998). *The problems of philosophy: Time.* New York: Routledge.

Waller, M. (1999). The timing of adaptive group behavior. *Academy of Management Journal, 42,* 127–137.

Waller, M. J., Giambatista, R. C., & Zellmer-Bruhn, M. (1999). The effects of individual time urgency on group polychronicity. *Journal of Managerial Psychology, 13,* 244–256.

Weingart, L. (1992). Impact of group goals, task component complexity, effort and planning on group performance. *Journal of Applied Psychology, 77,* 682–693.

Zaheer, S., Albert, S., & Zaheer, A. (1999). Time scales and organization theory. *Academy of Management Review, 24,* 725–741.

Zimbardo, P. G., & Boyd, J. N. (1999). Putting time in perspective: A valid, reliable individual-differences metric. *Journal of Personality and Social Psychology, 77,* 1271–1288.

PART I:
GROUP PROCESSES OVER TIME

LET'S NORM AND STORM, BUT NOT RIGHT NOW: INTEGRATING MODELS OF GROUP DEVELOPMENT AND PERFORMANCE

Elizabeth Mannix and Karen A. Jehn

ABSTRACT

Early efforts in the study of groups had an inherently temporal dimension, notably work on group dynamics and the related study of phases in group problem solving. Not surprisingly, the majority of work linking time to groups has focused on team development. By contrast, work on team performance has tended to take the form Input-Process-Output, in which the passage of time is implied. There is rarely a discussion of how processes might be affected by timing. We suggest ways in which the two literatures might be brought together. We review models of group development and group performance, propose ways in which temporal issues can be integrated into performance models, and conclude by raising questions for future theory and empirical investigation.

INTRODUCTION

Until quite recently, time has not been a major focus in the organizational behavior literature. That is changing, however, as the calls to include time in our theoretical

Time in Groups
Research on Managing Groups and Teams, Volume 6, 11–37
Copyright © 2004 by Elsevier Ltd.
All rights of reproduction in any form reserved
ISSN: 1534-0856/doi:10.1016/S1534-0856(03)06002-X

thinking have begun to draw attention (cf. Blount & Janicik, 2002; Bluedorn, 2002; Bluedorn & Denhardt, 1988; Butler, 1995; George & Jones, 2000; McGrath & Kelly, 1986; Mitchell & James, 2001). Empirical work has been building in volume, examining temporal issues such as pacing and patterns of interaction (Gersick, 1988, 1989), social entrainment (e.g. Ancona & Chong, 1996; McGrath, 1991), deadline effects (e.g. Karau & Kelly, 1992; Parks & Cowlin, 1995), organizational norms regarding time (Perlow, 1999), and how patterns of behavior, such as decision-making, negotiation and conflict, unfold over time (Jehn & Mannix, 2001; Mannix & Loewenstein, 1993; Mannix, Tinsley & Bazerman, 1995; Waller, 1999; Weingart, 1992). Indeed, both the *Academy of Management Journal* (Barkema, Baum & Mannix, 2001) and the *Academy of Management Review* (Goodman, Ancona, Lawrence & Tushman, 2001) have recently published special issues on *Time*.

Interestingly, a great deal of this recent attention has been focused at the group level of analysis (cf. Ancona, Okhuysen & Perlow, 2001; Harrison, Price, Gavin & Florey, 2002; Waller, Zellmer-Bruhn & Giambatista, 2002). Temporal issues affect groups in a variety of ways. For example, Moreland and Levine (1982) have defined the stages of group formation as members enter and exit over time, affecting team composition and factors such as the goals, norms, and power structure of the group. As teams mature, they must manage the scheduling of internal task activities and interpersonal patterns of behavior within the group (McGrath, 1991; McGrath & O'Connor, 1996). Deadlines come into play, as groups must finish projects "on time" (Parks & Cowlin, 1995) and often in synch with external activities of the firm (Ancona & Chong, 1996, 1999). Teams may also be asked to respond to nonroutine external events, such as environmental shocks or unexpected crises, within a certain time frame (Waller, 1999).

Not surprisingly, perhaps, the majority of work linking time to groups has focused on team *development*, attempting to describe the stages or phases of group experience and tended to be less concerned with team *performance* (cf. Bales, 1950; Tuckman, 1965). By contrast, work on team performance has tended to take the form *Input-Process-Output*, in which the focus is on the final product or performance of the team and the passage of time is inferred, but not explicit (cf. Hackman, 1983; Hackman & Morris, 1975; McGrath, 1964). While process is directly linked to performance in these models, there is rarely an explicit discussion of how processes might be affected by timing or might pass through specific phases (for an exception, see Marks, Mathieu & Zaccaro, 2001). Because scholars of organizational behavior tend to be interested in task-performing groups, we suggest in this paper ways in which the two literatures might be brought closer together. We review some models of group development and group performance, present some of our own research, propose ways in which temporal issues can be brought into performance models, and conclude by raising questions for future theory and empirical investigation.

MODELS OF GROUP DEVELOPMENT AND PERFORMANCE

Classic Models

Perhaps the best known model of group development was proposed by Bales and his colleagues over fifty years ago (Bales, 1950a, b; Bales & Strodtbeck, 1951; Borgatta & Bales, 1953). Interaction Process Analysis (IPA) is the group observation and coding technique that was developed based on Bales' theory that problem-solving groups are continuously faced with two sets of concerns: instrumental and expressive. Instrumental concerns are task-oriented and cycle through three stages: (1) orientation, or the gathering of information; (2) evaluation of that information; and (3) control, or decision-making. Expressive concerns, by contrast, are socioemotional and cycle back and forth through positive and negative. When groups focus on the task, that is, instrumental activity, it causes strains for the socioemotional aspects of the group. As these strains increase, there are attempts to counter-balance them, resulting in a cycle of both positive and negative socioemotional activity throughout the life of the group.

In terms of group development, Bales proposed that as groups progressed, the relative rates of each of these categories would change. Orientation should be highest at the beginning and decline as work progresses; evaluation rises toward the middle of the session, then declines; and control is low at first, but rises steadily toward the deadline. At the same time, expressive acts cycle through positive and negative, steadily rising over time. However, they remain relatively infrequent compared to instrumental activity and positive acts are predicted to predominate toward the end of the task.

To test these propositions, Bales built an elaborate coding scheme including 12 categories (6 instrumental; 6 socioemotional) based on this theory. The instrumental categories include passive and active subcategories (asks vs. gives orientation, opinion or suggestion), while the socioemotional categories include positive and negative subcategories (agree/disagree; tension build-up/release; group solidarity/antagonism). It is important to note that the IPA coding scheme and theory were developed together, making it difficult to separate them. In addition, it is assumed that all group behavior fits into one, and only one, of the 12 categories. There is no "other" category, implying that every action serves either a task or a socioemotional function and that no behavior can serve both functions simultaneously. As McGrath (1984, p. 143) notes, the tight links between Bales' theory and coding scheme are both a "boon and a bane," and make it very difficult to use IPA to test anything other than Bales' theory. In addition, most of the groups studied by Bales focused on solving a particular problem within a single session. These assumptions make the study of longer-term groups dealing with complex problems, in which performance is measurable and evaluated, nearly impossible. Another coding scheme, known as SYMLOG (Bales, 1979), was created to address some of these issues. However, it suffers from some of the same issues and its complexity has limited widespread adoption.

Despite these drawbacks, one of the major tenets of IPA – the existence of instrumental vs. expressive activity – has remained at the center of most theories of group development. In addition, the search for a pattern of interaction, broadened to encompass longer group interactions, became the focus for other scholars of team development. Tuckman (1965) proposed the best-known theory of group development with his "Forming-Storming-Norming-Performing" Model. Tuckman's work began with the study of therapy groups, and later applied it to T-groups, as well as groups in labs and natural settings. Each of his four stages includes a task-related component and a group-structure component – similar to Bales' IPA. Thus, *forming* involves testing and orientation for the group structure and the task; *storming* includes intragroup conflict and emotional response to the task demands; *norming* includes the development of group cohesion and the open discussion of the elements of the task; and *performing* involves the development of functional roles and the development of task insights.

One of the problematic issues with both Bales' and Tuckman's models is the extent to which teams actually progress through particular phases in a specified order. In addition, one might ask whether all phases are critical to group development and, perhaps most importantly for our purposes, whether all phases are critical for group performance. Some scholars have clearly questioned and even rejected the phase approach, arguing that theories of innate, concrete phases in groups are not adequate (cf. Bell, 1982; Mintzberg, Raisinghani & Théorêt, 1976; Seeger, 1983). Poole (1983a, b; Poole & Roth, 1989a, b) was one of the first to systematically argue against innate or unitary phases in problem-solving groups. His empirically-based model proposes that decision making groups will follow multiple sequences, including cycles and recycles of the same steps, as well as substantial periods of unorganized activity. His contingency-multiple sequence model suggests that while some groups do experience the normative unitary sequence, other groups go through complex cyclical phases in which certain activities are continually revisited (such as conflict or solutions). Factors such as the type of task or the complexity of the group structure can affect the actual sequence of group activity, the amount of disorganized activity, the number of interruptions or breaks in activity, as well as the number of cycles the group experiences. Poole's work has suggested a movement away from attempts to characterize group development as an unvarying sequence of stages or activities, proposing that more insight may be gained from an examination of broader *patterns* of group interaction.

Recent Developments

One such approach has been proposed by Gersick (1988, 1989), in which temporal phases emerge as bounded eras within each group, without being composed of identical activities across groups and without the phases necessarily progressing in a hierarchically set order. In Gersick's work, groups involved in a creative, problem-solving task acting under a deadline tended to perform more effectively when they experienced a punctuated shift at the midpoint. That is, high performing teams tended to stop work, notice the elapse of time experience a noticeable paradigm shift in which they adopted new perspectives on work and completed or dropped initial agendas. Interestingly, this shift took place at the midpoint regardless of the total time of the group task.

Recently, Waller, Zellmer-Bruhn and Giambatista (2002) have examined the punctuated equilibrium model in groups with changing deadlines. They found that all groups steadily increased their attention to time as deadlines drew nearer and that groups with changing deadlines paid significantly more attention to time than groups with stable deadlines. In addition, both types of groups experienced a task transition at or near the midpoint of the allotted time – although they did not significantly increase attention to time at the midpoint. In related work, Okhuysen and Waller (2002) have conceptualized time pacing as a "semi-structure." Semi-structures were originally discussed by Brown and Eisenhardt (1997, p. 28) and are described as "... frameworks in which some features are prescribed or determined (e.g. responsibilities, project priorities, time intervals between projects), but other aspects are not." Semi-structures are templates that help members make sense of uncertain tasks without locking them into formalized stages. In essence, they are tools that provide flexible arrangements through which groups can organize their work. Interestingly for our purposes here, Okhuysen and Waller (2002) argue that the punctuated equilibrium is best viewed not as a group development model, but rather as a task progress model, with a focus on task performance processes over time.

The punctuated equilibrium model does link temporal patterns to outcomes; however, it is not a fully elaborated model of group performance. Perhaps Gersick herself says it best in arguing that, "... ultimately, the midpoint itself is not as important as the finding that groups use temporal milestones to pace their work and that the event of reaching those milestones pushes groups into transitions" (1988, p. 34). A more elaborate model, directly focused on the relationship between time and performance, was proposed by McGrath (1991). McGrath's Time, Interaction and Performance Model (TIP) assumes that groups have multiple functions, including task production, member-support, and group well-being (see also Hackman, 1983). In addition, all group activity includes one or more of four modes of activity: Inception and acceptance of project (goal choice); Solution of technical issues (means choice); Resolution of conflict (policy choice); and Execution of performance (goal attainment). The TIP model does not assume that all modes are required, nor is it assumed that all teams go through all modes for all tasks. Rather, behavior in workgroups shows many forms of complex temporal patterning, raising issues of scheduling, synchronization, time allocation, and entrainment.

McGrath and his students conducted many tests of the TIP model, several of which are reported in volume 24 (3) of *Small Group Research* (McGrath, 1993). These articles report a 13-week study of student groups engaged in a variety of tasks (cf. Arrow & McGrath, 1993; Gruenfeld & Hollingshead, 1993; McGrath, 1993; McGrath, Arrow, Gruenfeld, Hollingshead & O'Connor, 1993; O'Connor, Gruenfeld & McGrath, 1993). Generally, their results revealed that as groups gain experience with each other, they tend to routinize their behavior (see also Gersick & Hackman, 1990). Therefore, changes in group composition, task structure, or technology resulted in at least some disruption to the flow of activity. For example, membership changes actually improved performance on complex tasks, possibly because such changes tended to be accompanied by a reduction in general conflict levels or by the addition of new members with differing perspectives (Gruenfeld, Martorano & Fan, 2000). In addition, they found that in time periods for which conflict was higher, performance tended to suffer (cf. McGrath et al., 1993).

To summarize, while we have learned a great deal about the interaction sequences some groups might experience, many questions remain. Strong tests comparing multiple models of group development have yet to be done. While the movement away from set and unified phases or stages toward broader patterns of interaction seems fairly well agreed upon, it is not yet clear what patterns of group interaction are universal or to what extent they are contingent on certain features of the group interaction. In addition, the link between these patterns and actual team performance remains unclear.

As a next step, we review some classic as well as more recent models of team performance and examine to what extent the sequence of interactions might affect team performance. Interestingly, some of the key work in this area was done by a social psychologist who later worked extensively on the temporal issues in team development – Joseph McGrath. We begin with his classic I-P-O model of team performance, developed more than 40 years ago (McGrath, 1964).

TEAM PERFORMANCE MODELS

Classic Models

For many of us, the reason that we are interested in temporal patterns has to do with their link to group performance. Unfortunately, most models of group performance have not explicitly included the temporal dimension. While the Input-Process-Output (I-P-O) link implies a time sequence, the process component is often aggregated, eliminating the opportunity to examine emergent phases. In general, processes (e.g. communication, conflict) are viewed as mediating mechanisms, linking group inputs (e.g. diversity, skills) to outputs (e.g. performance, satisfaction) (see Goodman, Ravlin & Schminke, 1987, and others cited below for reviews of group effectiveness models).

In the I-P-O model introduced by McGrath (1964), the group interaction process is discussed as a single construct that influences team performance. (Process is defined as the interaction among members.) Early work failed to specify the multiple types of interaction and how they may affect performance. The interaction process is seen as one (black) box. Interaction process was defined as all observable interpersonal behaviors (Hackman & Morris, 1975), a definition that doesn't easily lend itself to empirical research and predictive models. Later reviews (e.g. Guzzo & Shea, 1992) include examples of these interpersonal behaviors, such as information exchange and influence attempts.

Many factors of the group and its members influence this interaction process; these are called inputs, which were initially theoretically divided into three categories: individual-level factors (e.g. member skills, attitudes, and personality variables), group-level factors (e.g. group structure, group size), and environment-level factors (e.g. task characteristics, reward structure) (Hackman & Morris, 1975; McGrath, 1964). While the focus theoretically was on inputs that group members bring to the group (e.g. personality attributes, skills, demographic characteristics, experience), the initial empirical work showed that characteristics of the group task as an input consistently influenced the group interaction process (Carter, Haythorn, Meirowitz & Lanzetta, 1951; Deutsch, 1951; Hare, 1962; Morris, 1966; Talland, 1955). In 1975, Hackman and Morris determined that the critical inputs for examination were group composition, norms, and task design.

More limited in the early work, however, was the delineation of group interaction processes. In fact, the research mainly focused on one process in problem-solving task situations, the weighting of solution proposals generated by team members (e.g. Hoffman, 1961; Hoffman & Maier, 1964; Kelley & Thibaut, 1954). A later model of process loss introduced by Steiner (1972) provided researchers working with the I-P-O framework a method by which to identify a variety of group interaction behaviors related to coordination and motivation (e.g. Latane, Williams & Harkins, 1979; Shiflett, 1979). However, Hackman (1987) and others (Hill, 1982; Michaelson, Watson & Black, 1989) in reviewing I-P-O models criticized research that followed Steiner's process loss construct because, according to Hackman, there was no provision made for "process gains" which might evolve from the interaction of the group members. Hackman introduced examples of contributing processes to group synergy such as commitment, collective learning, and planning. He went on to specify four stages for creating work teams: (1) prework; (2) creating performance conditions; (3) forming and building the team; and (4) providing ongoing assistance. However, he did not link these stages to the theory or variables of the I-P-O model.

Gladstein's (1984) research is some of the first work using the I-P-O framework to more fully delineate and theoretically specify the seemingly black box of group process and relationships to group performance. She defined group process as "the intragroup and intergroup actions that transform resources into a product" (Gladstein, 1984, p. 500) and focused on open communication, supportiveness, conflict (lack of), discussion of strategy, weighting individual inputs, and boundary management. Her initial findings related to satisfaction and self-rated effectiveness as outputs (no effects were found for objective performance), indicating that intragroup processes significantly increased subjectively rated effectiveness.

Recent Developments

While Gladstein's work (1984) more fully specified the intragroup processes component of the I-P-O model, the empirical examination of inputs to this process is disappointing. Her theoretical model is quite elaborate as far as inputs are concerned, but empirically focuses on only one category of inputs – group structure – leaving out other factors such as diversity or group composition. This is not surprising given that early work on the I-P-O model also focused on group structure and even a smaller range of variables than Gladstein's, namely, group size (cf. Guzzo & Dickson, 1996; Hackman, 1987). While the early I-P-O models of McGrath (1964) and others included both the number and characteristics of group members, most empirical work focused on group size as an input factor that complicates coordination and motivation (Guzzo & Dickson, 1996).

More recently, reviews and empirical work of group process and performance have focused on team member heterogeneity as a critical predictor of group interaction processes (Jackson, May & Whitney, 1995; Jackson & Ruderman, 1996; Jehn, Northcraft & Neale, 1999; Levine & Moreland, 1998; Williams & O'Reilly, 1998). In fact, this is one area in which there seems to be a natural opening to integrate temporal and I-P-O models, given that what members bring with them to the group is, by definition, during an early stage in the group's life or before the group is even formed. Thatcher and Jehn (1998) provide a model of member differences over time that takes into account individual characteristics such as race and values that are present before they even enter the group. The next stage is also pre-group in that members know they will be working with others of certain characteristics. They begin to form views and, unfortunately, stereotypes of members before interactions begin. Once the group has formed the interaction processes influence both individual's views of themselves (individual identity) and of their group (group identity), which recent work has shown to influence other team processes (e.g. communication, conflict) and team outcomes (Brewer, 1996; Dovidio, Kawakami & Gaertner, 2002).

An often ignored aspect of I-P-O models is training and intervention to influence a team's activities. Process interventions are theorized to reduce process loss within the group (Hackman, 1987). Hackman and Morris (1975) noted that the influence of behavioral norms in the group as an input to group processes sets expectations about how to approach the task being performed. They suggest that the most effective way to influence or revise norms is through process consultative techniques or training interventions. The classic I-P-O models conceptually include norms and training interventions, often as inputs (Goodman et al., 1987), but empirical work on this aspect did not arise until quite recently (Marks, Zaccaro & Mathieu, 2000; Mathieu, Heffner, Goodwin, Salas & Cannon-Bowers, 2000). For example, recent empirical work by Marks, Sabella, Burke and Zaccaro (2002) focuses on developing shared team-interaction mental models which allow more efficient coordination and increased back-up behaviors such as helping, coaching, and giving constructive feedback. This recent work, however, does not address the issue of timing of the training and its resultant behaviors.

A final point in combining the reviews of stage and I-P-O models of team interaction is the focus on a specific process variable, team conflict. Most previous models and empirical work have focused on positive group interaction processes such as coordination and communication, only mentioning negative processes as such process loss, but not specifying a model incorporating both negative and positive group processes. Conflict is one variable that is briefly mentioned in past conceptual and empirical work (e.g. Gladstein, 1984; Guzzo & Shea, 1992), but not often specifically studied or studied in relation to positive processes as well (cf. Levine & Moreland, 1998).

In summary, a review of I-P-O models makes it clear that an integrated model of time, process and performance becomes very complicated very quickly. It can probably be said that the static I-P-O model is very well developed and a delineation of which variables should be included in such a model is fairly well agreed upon. However, what variables will be most important in different settings and for different tasks is not at all clear, although variables such as team heterogeneity, conflict, and trust have been keenly focused on in recent work. In addition, adding the temporal component is starting to force scholars to consider factors such as what occurs before the group forms as well as after it disbands, to consider more carefully the difference between processes (e.g. communication) and states (e.g. trust) and to address issues of causality and cycling within the "transformation process" of the black box in more rigorous ways.

In the following sections we summarize the results of two studies that attempt to address several of these issues. In both studies we focus on specific aspects of conflict within teams, their inputs or antecedents, as well as the interplay and effects on positive group processes such as trust and respect. This will allow us to use past theorizing on group development that also mentions conflict in general as an important stage in a group's life (e.g. Tuckman's "storming"), but does not link it directly to positive processes or effectiveness. Specifically, our first study focuses on dimensions of group member heterogeneity (e.g. values, member demographics) and how they influence team effectiveness in an effort to combine theories of group development and team performance to predict stages of group interaction over time. The second study adds the effect of a team process intervention and examines the timing and effectiveness of subsequent behaviors and changes in team norms.

TEMPORAL PATTERNS, PROCESSES, AND OUTCOMES IN GROUPS

Study 1: The Temporal Nature of Conflict

Conceptual Overview

Our first study was designed to focus on the types of conflict experienced by teams over time and how those patterns of conflict affect other team processes (e.g. communication, competition) as well as team performance (Jehn & Mannix, 2001). We also explored the potential effect of certain antecedents, or inputs, to conflict – notably that of group value consensus. Thus, we attempted to bring together some of the variables commonly described by I-P-O models of group performance and also include an exploration of temporally-related processes and phases. Conflict is an awareness by the parties involved of discrepancies, incompatible wishes, or irreconcilable desires (Boulding, 1963). Based on past research (Amason & Sapienza, 1997; Cosier & Rose, 1977; Guetzkow & Gyr, 1954; Jehn, 1997) we categorized conflict into three types: relationship, task, and process conflict. Relationship conflict is an awareness of interpersonal incompatibilities, including affective components such as feeling tension and friction. Task conflict is an awareness of differences in viewpoints and opinions pertaining to the group's task. Finally, process conflict is defined as an awareness of controversies about how task accomplishment will proceed.

Cross-sectional studies using one-time measures show that relationship, or affective, conflict is detrimental to individual and group performance, member satisfaction, and the likelihood the group will work together in the future (Jehn, 1995; Shah & Jehn, 1993). In contrast, moderate levels of task conflict have been shown to be beneficial to group performance in certain types of tasks, as teams benefit from differences of opinion about the work being done (Bourgeois, 1985; Eisenhardt & Schoonhoven, 1990; Jehn, 1995; Shah & Jehn, 1993). Of the three conflict types, process conflict is the least examined. Recently, Jehn, Northcraft and Neale (1999) found that groups who continually disagreed about task assignments were unable to effectively perform their work. Similarly, Jehn (1992) found that process conflict was associated with a lower level of morale, as well as decreased productivity in groups. Thus, it may be that when a group argues about who does what, overall levels of satisfaction and performance are reduced.

In this study, our primary aim was to examine the link between certain patterns of conflict and performance. The question, however, remains: Once we understand the connections between conflict and performance, is it possible to predict which groups will be more likely to exhibit these beneficial patterns of conflict? One answer may lie in the configuration of values and the subsequent atmosphere that result among the group members. As such, we also examined the values members brought with them to the group, defining *group value consensus* as the extent to which the potential members had similar values regarding work. We reasoned that when group members had similar values, beneficial patterns of conflict would be more likely to emerge, as would other positive patterns of group interaction. However, we also recognized that too much similarity might make it difficult for groups to engage in any conflict at all, possibly limiting the level of constructive or task conflict (cf. Jehn, Northcraft & Neale, 1999).

Prior to forming the groups, we measured individual-level values using O'Reilly, Chatman and Caldwell's Organization Culture Profile (OCP, 1991). The OCP is an instrument that can be used to identify the central values of individuals and to assess how intensely the values are held and the consensus among group members (cf. Chatman, 1989, 1991). The OCP consists of 54 items sorted by a Q-sort technique into nine categories ranging from very important to very unimportant. Example items include being careful, being innovative, and sharing responsibility. We then computed the consensus among group members on the 54 items, resulting in a measure of group value consensus.

Using project teams composed of part-time MBA students, we studied the patterns of the three conflict types in 51 groups during a semester. The groups worked as consulting teams on projects involving the strategy formation and implementation in an actual firm. For example, one team helped a locally-run coffee shop establish and implement a marketing strategy to compete with the national chains in the city. Another team worked with a Fortune 500 company to analyze its managerial information system. These projects comprised more than 50% of the students' grades for this semester course. Teams spent an average of 10.8 hours per week together on the project and 20.6 hours total per week of individual time.

The task included problem identification, information collection and analysis, and making recommendations and implementation suggestions. It also included attending organizational meetings and conducting interviews with employees and managers. The participants reported bi-weekly on their group interactions by completing individual questionnaires and group worksheets. The project culminated in a final report to the consulting client and to the professor. Output, or performance, was measured by ratings of the report by two independent raters. Points were awarded by the two independent raters for thoroughness of problem identification (0–10 points possible), accurate problem analysis and conclusions (0–10 points possible), and appropriate recommendations to the firm and actual firm presentation (0–10 points possible). Students were aware of the point breakdown prior to completing the task.

Conflict Patterns and Group Performance

Our findings revealed that higher group performance could be differentiated by a particular pattern for each of the three conflict types. High-performing teams were characterized by process conflict that started out very low, but increased somewhat at the midpoint, and again toward the deadline. Relationship conflict also started out low, remained low at the midpoint, but increased slightly toward the deadline. Perhaps the most interesting finding was the pattern of task conflict, which started out at moderate levels, rose at the midpoint, and dropped back down toward the deadline. Given the differentiating effects of task and relationship conflict, the results also provide some verification for Bales'(1950a, b) separation of instrumental, or task-focused, processes and expressive, or socio-emotional, processes. In addition, while past theorizing on stages of group development does not specify patterns of high performance, our results are consistent with Tuckman's (1965) model that includes the "storming" stage as being necessary before the "performing" stage of a group. The pattern is also consistent with Gersick's (1998, 1999) theory that the midpoint is a crucial time. In our high performing groups the midpoint was characterized by concentrated debate and discussion of the task. This seemed to allow groups to adopt new perspectives, leveraging the synergy provided by moderately high, but not overly high, levels of task conflict. To reach high performance, groups were then required to follow-through with consensus and implementation of the task goals, which is represented in our findings by a decrease in task conflict after the midpoint.

Low performing groups, by contrast, actually experienced a dip in task conflict during the middle time block. In addition, they experienced a high degree of task conflict right before the project deadline, when it was likely to be more destructive than helpful. The same low-performing groups also exhibited an escalating pattern for relationship conflict. This dual rise may reflect the negative cycle that can develop between task and relationship conflict. In these groups, task conflict may have been misperceived as personal criticism and interpreted as relationship conflict (Amason, 1996; Brehmer, 1976; Deutsch, 1969). If this occurs over time, the a steady rise in both task and relationship conflict may result, as well as a performance loss rather than gain.

In addition to measuring conflict as a dynamic variable, we also explored the potential antecedents of different conflict patterns as inputs to group interaction processes, focusing on *group value consensus* as an input variable. We measured each subject's values before they began work in their teams, thus any value consensus within a team was a chance occurrence. Our results revealed that group value consensus predicted low levels of task, process, and relationship conflict at the middle and later phases of group interaction, however, there were no significant relations between group value consensus and conflict in the early stages of interaction. The timing of the relationship between group value consensus and conflict also seems to imply that value consensus may take some time to play out in groups – the effects not emerging until the team was well into its task. Given that a similarity of values is not an immediately obvious type of similarity within a team, this is not terribly surprising and seems consistent with past theories of group development. For instance, Tuckman's (1965) norming stage, in which values regarding the task are discussed and consensus about task strategy is reached, is one of the final stages before performing (and comes after storming). The effect of group value consensus is also likely to depend on other factors, such as the level of interdependence required by the task or the complexity of the task itself.

In addition, group value consensus made it less likely that teams would have any sort of conflict – even constructive conflict. This presents a dilemma: How to compose groups that will have moderately high levels of task conflict, as well as low levels of relationship conflict? These dilemmas are indicative of teamwork, according to Bales' focus on dynamic opposition of processes and, later, Berg and Smith's (1987) theorizing on group paradoxes. One answer may be found in the results for the several other group process variables that were included here for exploratory purposes.

Drawing from I-P-O models, we included measures of team trust, respect, open communication, and cohesiveness to complement our examination of negative group processes such as conflict and competition. We found that during the middle time range, both relationship and process conflict were positively associated with low levels of trust and respect; by contrast, task conflict was positively associated with open communication. Thus, in groups with high value consensus it may be possible to enhance constructive task conflict through norms that favor open communication. Thus, a more intricate view of multiple group interaction processes, the interplay among them, and their antecedents and consequences is needed than has been provided by either past I-P-O models or stage models of group development.

Conclusions

In sum, we believe that Study One demonstrates that static investigations of team interaction tell only part of the story. Consider how our results and their interpretation would have been very different had we used a one-time measure of conflict. We might have concluded that low performing groups have very high levels of all types of conflict throughout the group process, while high performing groups have moderate amounts of conflict with little differences between the levels of task, relationship, or process. By looking at patterns over time, it is possible to see that *when* certain interactions take place may matter as much as *what* sorts of interactions occur.

It is also important to note that there were a number of limitations to this study. In Study One we admittedly focused on one specific process variable (conflict) and one specific input variable (value consensus) despite our exploratory inclusion of other group process variables (i.e. trust, competition, respect, communication). To what extent other process variables change over time, or result in patterns that predict team performance, is unclear, but we do have some clues given the present study's findings. We also were limited by the task itself. We do not know if these results transfer to other types of tasks that might be either more routine or even more creative. Thus, concluding that a unitary phase model exists – even for conflict patterns – is certainly premature. These issues led us to conduct a second study with a different sort of task and time frame, and to measure an additional set of input, process and output variables over time.

Group Processes and Emergent States

Conceptual Overview

As in our first study, we focused on the team interactions of MBA students. In this case we used 2nd year full-time MBA students, participating as part of a Negotiation elective. In addition, we focused in more detail on inputs, measuring four types of team diversity (gender, age, ethnicity and functional background). In addition to measuring group value consensus, we also asked subjects to what extent they *perceived* that their team members had similar work-related preferences and values to themselves. We were interested in distinguishing the effects of objective vs. perceived factors, as well as considering that perceived similarity might affect processes early in the interaction, while objective similarity might play a role at a later point.

In terms of processes, we considered a recent model of temporally-based team process in which processes are distinguished from emergent team states (Marks, Mathieu & Zaccaro, 2001). Emergent states are not interactive processes (e.g. conflict and communication) but are instead qualities of a team that represent member attitudes, values, and motivations (e.g. collective efficacy, trust, cohesion). Emergent states are products of team experiences (including team processes) and may be viewed as both inputs as well as proximal outcomes. Emergent states may be malleable over time, affected by team processes. Therefore, a team of strangers may begin with low levels of trust, but as they interact over time, a state of high (or low) trust may emerge. This state can become relatively stable, but may also change given new information or behavior. The distinction between processes and states seems especially important when considering temporal issues in teams. As such, we measured processes (communication, task procedures) as well as states (trust and respect), selecting variables that our exploratory analysis in Study One revealed as important. Given past theorizing and recent research in I-P-O models, we also included an additional team input – a group process intervention.

As in Study One, our output measure was a final written report prepared by each team. We expanded the evaluation of this output measure by scoring the report's level of integrative complexity (Tetlock, 1991; Tetlock & Hannum, 1983). Integrative complexity is rated on a scale of from one to seven. A score of 1 indicates that a paper displays only one perspective. A score of 2 suggests more than one perspective may exist, but the second perspective is not explicitly stated. A score of 3 indicates that the paper fully develops both sides of an issue, treating each as equally plausible, but does not address the tension between the two. A score of 4 implies that the paper fully describes two or more perspectives, highlights the tension between them, and suggests a potential resolution. A score of 5 indicates that the perspectives are fully presented, a tension exists between the views, and a partial resolution between the perspectives is presented. A score of 6 implies that the paper displays a complete plan towards resolution. A score of 7 indicates that the paper displays the highest level of complexity and integration; the team fully understands the intricacies of an issue and suggests a resolution of perspectives in a comprehensive plan. Using this measure also allowed us to expand the conceptualization of group effectiveness of traditional and recent I-P-O models that often focus only on satisfaction and group productivity as measures of group effectiveness.

The sample for consisted of MBA students enrolled in a 12 –week Managerial Negotiation Course. Early in the course they were randomly formed into 28 teams of three members each. The teams participated in a multi-round negotiation simulation that took place in three separate meetings over the length of the course (Adam Baxter/Local 190 developed by Valley & Medvec, 1996). This simulation is based on the Hormel negotiations and subsequent strike that took place in the 1970s and 1980s. Several components of this team interaction were graded, comprising 30% of the students' final course grade. Round 1 took place in week 5 of the course and included 2 stages: a 90 minute preparation session with the three team members, followed by a 90 minute negotiation in which two teams met and tried to resolve their differences. This first session is arguable the most complex of the three, involving several qualitatively described issues with integrative potential. Round 2 took place during week 7, and involved a fairly simple distributive task taking 30–45 minutes. Finally, Round 3 took place during week 10, and is similar in complexity to Round 1. Questionnaires were completed following Rounds 1, 2 and 3, as well as following the end of the course (week 12 – when the final paper was also turned in). Following the final negotiation the real facts of the Hormel negotiations and subsequent strike were revealed and discussed in class.

As an additional input variable, half of the teams were given a "team effectiveness" intervention prior to the Round 1 Negotiation. They received a short (20 minute) lecture on team effectiveness, which included a discussion of the potential assets and liabilities of teams (Maier, 1967). In addition, they were given an "Effective Teams Checklist" which stressed the benefits of constructive, task-based conflict, and the detriments of personal, relationship-based conflict. The checklist included 8 statements, such as, "Recognize that disagreements within your team can lead to a more innovative solution," "Disagreements should not cause hard feelings," "Consider facts and opinions that do not support your own ideas." Teams given this intervention were urged to use this checklist in their preparation and interaction. The remaining teams were given no team intervention or instructions.

Antecedents to Group Processes and Emergent States

Several differences between this study and Study One emerged immediately. First, no significant effects on process or performance emerged for either task or relationship conflict. Process conflict, by contrast, revealed several interesting patterns. In addition, group value consensus was not a significant antecedent, however, team members' *perceptions* of value similarity did predict several interactions patterns. These findings, as well as other patterns of interest, are described below.

We began by looking at the relationship between input variables (team composition and intervention) on group processes and emergent states during the first round of interaction. We reasoned that the links between these antecedents and initial processes should lead to subsequent emergent states and, ultimately, performance.

Two types of diversity – age and ethnicity – decreased the level of open communication and increased conflicts regarding how to approach the task (process conflict) during Round 1. Groups with higher age and ethnic diversity were also more likely to report greater dissimilarity of values among group members (whether or not this was actually true as measured by the OCP). Functional diversity, that is the diversity of the work background of the team members, also increased the perception of this value difference. Interestingly, gender diversity had no effects of any of these variables.

The team effectiveness intervention did ameliorate some of these effects, as groups that experienced the intervention had more open communication during Round 1. There was also a direct effect of the intervention on emergent states and processes in Round 2 – increasing trust and respect, while decreasing process conflict and increasing process conflict resolution.

Patterns of Group Processes and Emergent States

The majority of our analyses examined the relationships between the group processes and subsequent emergent states in Rounds 1, 2 and 3, as well as the overall levels of performance and satisfaction following the final interaction. We looked for patterns that might be linked to superior, or inferior, performance. As described above, we focused on integrative complexity as a measure of performance. This measure captures the extent to which the negotiators understand how and why they had performed as they did and whether they understood the causal links between their behavior and their outcomes in a complex and balanced manner.

In terms of the dynamic model of performance, the factors that predicted integrative complexity were relatively limited. Neither task nor relationship conflict had significant effects. Indeed, the remaining variables had significant effects only during specific time periods. Specifically, perceptions of value differences and open communication in Round 1, which in turn led to high levels of trust, respect, low levels of process conflict, and high levels of process conflict resolution in Round 2, predicted high integrative complexity scores at the end of the course. Note that is was perceptions of value *differences* – not similarity – that increased performance (Perhaps this makes sense given the performance metric of integrative complexity, which requires a diversity of approaches). Regarding antecedents to higher performance: Functional diversity had a direct effect on increasing integrative complexity, as did perceptions of value *differences* among group members (these two variables were also moderately correlated).

Interestingly, final levels of satisfaction (measured at the end of the course) were predicted by somewhat different patterns. Higher satisfaction was the result of higher levels of respect and trust and lower levels of process conflict in Round 2, as well as higher levels of trust and respect in Round 3. Thus, process and states measured more recently (in Round 3) had more impact. Functional diversity, measured before Round 1, also had a direct effect on increased satisfaction among group members. However, unlike performance, satisfaction was also increased by perceptions of value *similarity*, as well as by the team effectiveness intervention.

Conclusions

Our results suggest that certain process patterns – beginning with open communication and leading to low levels of process conflict, high levels of process conflict resolution, trust and respect – can lead to higher levels of performance in certain types of intact teams. It is, of course, interesting to note what did not predict performance. While we cannot draw definitive conclusions from null effects, they do point out interesting quandaries to consider in future research. First, several variables that have been important predictors of performance in similar studies did not emerge here – that is, task and relationship conflict, actual group value consensus, and group cohesiveness – to name a few. In addition, several variables that were significant predictors of performance only achieved significance during certain time periods. That is, open communication in Round 2 and 3 did not affect final performance, nor did trust, respect, process conflict or its resolution in Rounds 1 or 3. So, at least in this task, it seems that certain processes are time dependent and that it is also relevant to consider when certain states emerge and how long their effects may last.

Another interesting result concerns the effects of antecedents to process and performance – both in terms of diversity and in terms of value similarity. Focusing first on the latter, in study two the similarity of values was measured both objectively as well as perceptually, but it was also manipulated by the team effectiveness intervention. In effect, the team effectiveness intervention can be viewed as a manipulation of values – leading to similarity. Unfortunately, we do not have a multi-faceted set of value measurements from study one, so it is difficult to generalize. In addition, it is not the case that the effectiveness intervention increased perceptions of similarity regarding values. In fact, both the team effectiveness intervention, as well as perceptions of dissimilarity regarding team values, had direct positive effects on team performance. Such a result leaves open the question of how perceptions of dissimilarity and instructions regarding team interaction affect team performance (if not solely through communication, trust, respect, and process conflict). Thus, we are left asking what are the conclusions we can draw and what are the relevant variables to consider when studying group interaction and performance over time?

CONCLUSIONS AND FUTURE DIRECTIONS

There are a number of differences between the results of the two studies we present. The tasks performed by the teams in each study are quite different, and the time they spent interacting with one another varied. The subjects themselves are different in terms of age and demographics, experiences and responsibilities. Based on their position in school, they have different pasts as well as futures with one another. The studies took place in different universities, with varying norms and cultures. To what extent do these differences matter and to what extent can we draw reasonable conclusions from the results of both studies that we have presented remains to be determined. It does seem, however, that there is a clear link between inputs, temporally-based phases, and outputs. Group values (whether measured or manipulated) seem especially important, perhaps most so in setting up expectations for subsequent interactions. Conflict appears in both studies – although in study one it is task conflict that really seems to differentiate low from high performing teams, while in study two it is process conflict (and its resolution). Process variables (such as communication) matter – and should be distinguished from emergent states (such as trust and respect). However, to what extent processes lead to emergent states and to what extent that pattern is cyclical is yet to be determined.

In some ways, our conclusions are not dissimilar to what other scholars such as Poole (1983a, b), Gersick (1984) and Okhuysen and Waller (2002) have concluded. There do seem to be patterns of interaction that teams experience – whether these patterns are called decision paths, punctuated equilibriums, or semi-structures. Poole has gone down the path of complexity, presenting multiple possible decision paths and focusing on the unique patterns of individual group interactions (cf. Poole & Roth, 1989a, b). By contrast, Gersick has opted for simplicity, focus on one break-point in the pattern of group interaction as most important (cf. Gersick, 1989). Which is the "right" choice?

Perhaps it would be best to take this opportunity to bring together what we seem to know and then to create an agenda for future scholars. We can all agree that the I-P-O link is very complex, especially once the time dimension is added, however, it is difficult to find many scholars (including ourselves) that have studied the temporal dimensions of the I-P-O model with systematic rigor. If indeed, as we argue, the I-P-O model is a useful starting point and framework for systematic temporally-based research, then we as scholars must force ourselves to raise and to pursue a number of issues. I-P-O models, while fairly inclusive, do not specify how to conceptualize or operationalize critical variables, especially those that are affected by time. For example, on the input side, team heterogeneity is discussed as everything from functional differences, to racial and ethnic differences, to value differences. All too often, when empirical work is conducted, it is not acknowledged that these are similar types of diversity. However, there is excellent theoretical reasoning suggesting that this is not the case (cf. Bartel & Milliken, this volume; McGrath, Berdahl & Arrow, 1995). Some empirical evidence is beginning to build that different types of team diversity lead to different interaction processes as well as outcomes (cf. Jehn, Northcraft & Neale, 1999; Pelled, 1996; Pelled, Eisenhardt & Xin, 1999). For temporal researcher, it is also important to look at how some times of heterogeneity, such as value- or information-based differences, may lessen as teams work together over time (cf. Moreland & Levine, 1982). Thus, even something as seemingly fixed as "diversity" might change over time. Another example comes from the "P" component of the I-P-O model. Variables that are commonly considered process variables, such as trust, are actually better considered to be emergent states and likely to be the result of certain processes (such as open communication) rather than processes themselves. They are likely to change over time and be part of causal loops (Marks, Mathieu & Zaccaro, 2001). So, for example, it might be important to look at the recursive relationship between certain types of diversity, social identity and trust. This raises the important and tricky issue of determining causality in other than clean, linear pathways. By adding the temporal component, it is likely we will find more cyclical and recursive patterns, but we have to be looking for them. Thus, by including the temporal component, what variables are included and how they are measured and modeled is likely to need much more careful consideration.

Another issue for temporal researchers harkens back to one of McGrath's (1964) most important admonitions – to take the task seriously. It is clear from the two studies we presented that the task matters – both in terms of the task typology and its duration. A myriad of other examples can be found. For example, Weingart (1992) found that task complexity influenced group performance by affecting the effort exerted by team members, as well as the amount, quality and timing of their planning. Jehn (1995) focused on task routineness and task interdependence in her research, finding that each moderated the impact of conflict on task performance. Models such as McGrath's task circumplex (McGrath, 1984), Laughlin's group task classification (Laughlin, 1980; Laughlin & Ellis, 1986), or Hackman and Morris' (1975) task types force us to more carefully think through the importance of temporally-measured variables and the potential generalizability of our empirical results.

The same issues arise when looking at the context in which the group is embedded. Ancona and Chong's (1996, 1999) work focuses on pace, cycles and rhythm as key aspects of the *environment* that exert influence on team interaction and performance. They urge scholars to study the temporal context of teams by examining the entrainment of team behaviors to external influences. This external focus also begs the question of the broader context of the team and the team members (cf. Zellmer-Bruhn, Waller & Ancona, this volume). In any temporally-based project is becomes clear that we have to consider what occurs before the group forms and what the future hold for group members. How well do team members know each other – have they worked together before (cf. Hinds, Carley, Krackhardt & Wholey, 2000)? How does the team form, and at what point do members leave, the team disband (cf. Arrow, 1998)? Are team members anticipating future interactions, thus changing their current interactions, strategies or goals (cf. Mannix, 1994)? All these questions force us to expand the boundaries of our research to uncover previously latent, but organizationally and contextually important variables.

In any temporally-based research, the question of what time periods are critical, and how to measure those periods, becomes important. One key question revolves around the unique nature of "time period 1." To what extent does the first meeting have a critical impact on subsequent interactions? As Bettenhhausen and Murnighan's (1985) classic work found, norms can develop extremely quickly in newly formed teams. Team members rely on scripts and schemas to anticipate and interpret interactions, and when those scripts are divergent the first meeting can be especially critical. This has been most recently of interest to scholars studying virtual teams, in which the first meeting, or "launch" has been theorized to be critical to subsequent success (cf. Gibson & Cohen, 2002). Critical moments or breakpoints might also occur at other moments in a team, such as the midpoint (Gersick, 1988, 1989). However, recent empirical work has also put limits on the punctuated equilibrium model, raising the question of what other critical moments occur in teams, depending on the context, task, time pressure, or other conditions (cf. Lim & Murnighan, 1994; Okhuysen & Waller, 2002). Of course, this also begs the question of how to determine when time periods begin and end. Does it make sense to measure variables in equally-time spaced sections (such as every 10 minutes), or to portion the interaction into segments based on % of interaction (e.g. 1st 10%, 2nd 10%, etc), or to divide the interaction into unequally-timed segments based on theoretically- and contextually-driven categories (e.g. first meeting, mid-point, delivery). Measurement issues abound in temporal research, and solving these difficulties is likely to take multiple methods – both quantitative and qualitative. Excellent advice on dealing with time and method can be found in Kelly and McGrath (1988) (see also Weingart, Brett & Olekalns, this volume).

Finally, all these factors bring us back to the question of theory. The ultimate question is: Can we move away from static snapshots and adapt our theories of group input, process and performance to include the dynamic passage of time? So, with considerable homage to Joseph McGrath (1986), who has inarguably been the inspiration for so much of the work on group development *as well as* group performance over the last four decades.

TEN CRITICAL NEEDS FOR THEORY, RESEARCH AND PRACTICE

(1) To carefully consider and define the type of measures we use – for independent variables (such as "diversity" or "values"), process variables (such as "trust"), and dependent variables (such as "performance").

(2) To make a serious attempt to resolve the question of temporally-based causality.

(3) To take seriously the role of task-type and task demands.

(4) To consider the context (organizational and otherwise) in which the team is placed.

(5) To take seriously the importance of history and prior interactions of the team and the team members.

(6) To take seriously the role of future and subsequent team interactions.

(7) To consider the special role of "Time Period 1" – the first interaction.

(8) To disentangle critical incidents and break-points from less critical occurrences.

(9) To understand how to measure any temporal period – especially in terms of determining whether phases have begun and/or ended.

(10) To put more emphasis on theory, and by doing do, filling in the "black box" of process.

REFERENCES

Amason, A. (1996). Distinguishing effects of functional and dysfunctional conflict on strategic decision making: Resolving a paradox for top management teams. *Academy of Management Journal, 39*, 123–148.

Amason, A., & Sapienza, H. (1997). The effects of top management team size and interaction norms on cognitive and affective conflict. *Journal of Management, 23*, 496–516.

Ancona, D., & Chong, C. (1996). Entrainment: Pace, cycle and rhythm in organizational behavior. In: L. L. Cummings & B. Staw (Eds), *Research in Organizational Behavior* (Vol. 18, pp. 251–284). Greenwich, CT: JAI Press.

Ancona, D., & Chong, C. (1999). Cycles and Synchrony: The temporal role of context in team behavior. In: E. Mannix, M. Neale & R. Wageman (Eds), *Research on Managing Groups and Teams* (Vol. 2, pp. 33–48). Stamford, CT: JAI Press.

Ancona, D., Okhuysen, G., & Perlow, L. (2001). Taking time to integrate temporal research. *Academy of Management Review, 26*, 512–529.

Arrow, H. (1998). Standing out and fitting in: Composition effects on newcomer socialization. In: M. Neale, E. Mannix & D. Gruenfeld (Eds), *Research on Managing Groups and Teams* (Vol. 1, pp. 59–80). Stamford, CT: JAI Press.

Arrow, H., & McGrath, J. E. (1993). Membership matters: How member change and continuity affect small group structure, process and performance. *Small Group Research, 24*, 334–361.

Bales, R. F. (1950a). A set of categories for the analysis of small group interaction. *American Sociological Review, 15*, 257–263.

Bales, R. F. (1950b). *Interaction process analysis: A method for the study of small groups.* Cambridge, MA: Addison-Wesley.

Bales, R. F. (1979). *SYMLOG: A system for the multiple level analysis of groups.* New York: Free Press.

Bales, R. F., & Strodtbeck, F. L. (1951). Phases in group problem-solving. *Journal of Abnormal and Social Psychology, 46*, 485–495.

Barkema, H., Baum, J., & Mannix, E. (Eds) (2001). Special research forum: A new time [Special Issue]. *Academy of Management Review, 45*.

Bell, M. A. (1982). Phases in group problem-solving. *Small Group Behavior, 13*, 475–495.

Berg, D. N., & Smith, K. K. (1987). *Paradoxes of group life.* San Francisco: Jossey-Bass.

Bettenhhausen, K., & Murnighan, J. K. (1985). The emergence of norms in competitive decision-making groups. *Administrative Science Quarterly, 30*, 350–372.

Blount, S., & Janicik, G. (2002). When plans change: Examining how people evaluate timing changes in work organizations. *Academy of Management Review, 26*, 566–585.

Bluedorn, A. (2002). *The human organization of time.* Stanford, CA: Stanford Business Books.

Bluedorn, A., & Denhardt, R. (1988). Time and organizations. *Journal of Management, 14*, 299–320.

Borgatta, E. F., & Bales, R. F. (1953). Interaction of individuals in reconstitued groups. *Sociometry, 16*, 302–320.

Boulding, K. (1963). *Conflict and defense.* New York: Harper & Row.

Bourgeois, L. J. (1985). Strategic goals, environmental uncertainty, and economic performance in volatile environments. *Academy of Management Journal, 28*, 548–573.

Brehmer, B. (1976). Social judgement theory and the analysis of interpersonal conflict. *Psychological Bulletin, 83*, 985–1003.

Brewer, M. (1996). Managing diversity: The role of social identities. In: S. E. Jackson & M. N. Ruderman (Eds), *Diversity in Work Teams: Research Paradigms for a Changing Workplace* (pp. 47–68). Washington, DC: APA Press.

Brown, S., & Eisenhardt, K. (1997). *Competing on the edge: Strategy as structured chaos.* Boston, MA: HBS Press.

Butler, R. (1995). Time in organizations: Its experience, explanations and effects. *Organization Studies, 16,* 925–950.

Carter, L. F., Haythorn, W., Meirowitz, B., & Lanzetta, J. (1951). The relation of categorization and ratings in the observation of group behavior. *Human Relations, 4,* 239–254.

Chatman, J. (1989). Improving interactional organizational research. A model of person-organization fit. *Academy of Management Review, 14,* 333–349.

Chatman, J. (1991). Matching people and organizations: Selection and socialization in public accounting firms. *Administrative Science Quarterly, 36,* 459–484.

Cosier, R., & Rose, G. (1977). Cognitive conflict and goal conflict effects on task performance. *Organizational Behavior and Human Performance, 19,* 378–391.

Deutsch, M. (1951). Task structure and group process. *American Psychologist, 6,* 324–325.

Deutsch, M. (1969). Conflicts: Productive and destructive. *Journal of Social Issues, 25,* 7–41.

Dovidio, J. F., Kawakami, K., & Gaertner, S. L. (2002). Reducing contemporary prejudice: Combating explicit and implicit bias at the individual and intergroup level. *Annual Review of Psychology, 53,* 137–163.

Eisenhardt, K., & Schoonhoven, C. (1990). Organizational growth: Linking founding team, strategy, environment, and growth among U.S. semiconductor ventures, 1978–1988. *Administrative Science Quarterly, 35,* 504–529.

George, J., & Jones, G. (2000). The role of time in theory and theory building. *Journal of Management, 26,* 657–684.

Gersick, C. (1988). Time and transition in work teams: Toward a new model of group development. *Academy of Management Journal, 31,* 9–41.

Gersick, C. (1989). Marking time: Predictable transitions in task groups. *Academy of Management Journal, 32,* 274–309.

Gersick, C. J., & Hackman, J. R. (1990). Habitual routines in task-performing groups. *Organizational Behavior and Human Decision Processes, 47,* 65–97.

Gibson, G., & Cohen, S. (Eds) (2002). *Virtual teams that work.* San Francisco, CA: Jossey-Bass.

Gladstein, D. (1984). Groups in context: A model of task group effectiveness. *Administrative Science Quarterly, 29,* 499–517.

Goodman, P., Ancona, D., Lawrence, B., & Tushman, M. (2001). Special topic forum on time and organizational research [Special Issue]. *Academy of Management Review, 26*(4).

Goodman, P. S., Ravlin, E., & Schminke, M. (1987). Understanding groups in organizations. In: L. L. Cummings & B. Staw (Eds), *Research in Organizational Behavior* (Vol. 9, pp. 121–173). Greenwich, CT: JAI Press.

Guetzkow, H., & Gyr, J. (1954). An analysis of conflict in decision making groups. *Human Relations, 7,* 367–381.

Gruenfeld, D., & Hollingshead, A. (1993). Sociocognition in workgroups: The evolution of group integrative complexity and its relation to task performance. *Small Group Research, 24,* 383–405.

Gruenfeld, D., Martorana, P., & Fan, E. (2000). What do groups learn from their worldliest members? Direct and indirect influence in dynamic teams. *Organizational Behavior and Human Decision Processes, 82,* 45–59.

Guzzo, R. A., & Dickson, M. W. (1996). Teams in organizations: Recent research on performance and effectiveness. *Annual Review of Psychology, 47,* 307–338.

Guzzo, R. A., & Shea, G. P. (1992). Group performance and intergroup relations in organizations. In: M. D. Dunnette & L. M. Hough (Eds), *Handbook of Industrial and Organizational Psychology* (pp. 262–313). Palo Alto, CA: Consulting Psychologists Press.

Hackman, J. R. (1983). A normative model of work team effectiveness. Technical Report #2, Group effectiveness research project, School of Organization and Management, Yale.

Hackman, J. R. (1987) The design of work teams. In: J. Lorsch (Ed.), *Handbook of Organizational Behavior* (pp. 315–342). Englewood Cliffs, NJ: Prentice-Hall.

Hackman, J. R., & Morris, C. G. (1975). Group tasks, group interaction process, and group performance effectiveness: A review and proposed integration. In: L. Berkowitz (Ed.), *Advances in Experimental Social Psychology* (pp. 1–56). New York: Academic Press.

Hare, A. P. (1962). *Handbook of small group research.* New York: Free Press.

Harrison, D., Price, K., Gavin, J., & Florey, A. (2002). Time, teams, and task performance: Changing effects of surface- and deep-level diversity on group functioning. *Academy of Management Journal, 45,* 1029–1045.

Hill, M. (1982). Group vs. individual performance: Are N+1 heads better than one? *Psychological Bulletin, 91,* 517–539.

Hoffman, L. R. (1961). Conditions for creative problem solving. *Journal of Psychology, 52,* 429–444.

Hoffman, L. R., & Maier, N. R. F. (1964). Valence in the adoption of solutions by problem-solving groups: Concept, method, and results. *Journal of Abnormal and Social Psychology, 69,* 264–271.

Jackson, S. E., May, K. E., & Whitney, K. (1995). Understanding the dynamics of diversity in decision-making teams. In: R. A. Guzzo & E. Salas (Eds), *Team Effectiveness and Decision Making in Organizations* (pp. 204–261). San Francisco: Jossey-Bass.

Jackson, S. E., & Ruderman, M. N. (1996). *Diversity in work teams: Research paradigms for a changing workplace.* Washington, DC: APA Press.

Jehn, K. (1992). *The impact of intragroup conflict on effectiveness: A multimethod examination of the benefits and detriments of conflict.* Unpublished Doctoral Dissertation, Northwestern University Graduate School of Management, Evanston, IL.

Jehn, K. (1995). A multimethod examination of the benefits and detriments of intragroup conflict. *Administrative Science Quarterly, 40,* 256–282.

Jehn, K. (1997). A qualitative analysis of conflict types and dimensions in organizational groups. *Administrative Science Quarterly, 42,* 530–557.

Jehn, K., & Mannix, E. A. (2001). The dynamic nature of conflict: A longitudinal study of intragroup conflict and group performance. *Academy of Management Journal, 44,* 238–251.

Jehn, K., Northcraft, G., & Neale, M. (1999). Why differences make a difference: A field study of diversity, conflict, and performance in workgroups. *Administrative Science Quarterly, 44,* 741–763.

Karau, S. J., & Kelly, J. R. (1992). The effects of time scarcity and time abundance on group performance quality and interaction process. *Journal of Experimental Social Psychology, 28,* 542–571.

Kelley, H. H., & Thibaut, J. W. (1954). Experimental studies of group problem solving and process. In: G. Lindzey (Ed.), *Handbook of Social Psychology.* Reading, MA: Addison-Wesley.

Latane, B., Williams, K., & Harkins, S. (1979). Many hands make light the work: The causes and consequences of social loafing. *Journal of Personality and Social Psychology, 37,* 822–832.

Laughlin, P. (1980). Social combination processes of cooperative problem-solving groups on verbal intellective tasks. In: M. Fishbein (Ed.), *Progress in Social Psychology* (pp. 127–155). Hillsdale, NJ: Erlbaum.

Laughlin, P., & Ellis, A. (1986). Demonstrability and social combination processes on mathematical intellective tasks. *Journal of Experimental Social Psychology, 22,* 177–189.

Levine, J. M., & Moreland, R. L. (1998). Small groups. In: D. Gilbert, S. Fiske & G. Lindzey (Eds), *Handbook of Social Psychology* (4th ed.). New York, NY: McGraw-Hill.

Lim & Murnighan, J. K. (1994). Phases, deadlines and the bargaining process. *Organizational Behavior and Human Decision Processes*, *58*, 153–171.

Mannix, E. A. (1994). Will we meet again? The effects of power, distribution norms, and the scope of future interaction in small group negotiation. *International Journal of Conflict Management*, *5*, 343–368.

Mannix, E. A., & Loewenstein, G. (1993). Managerial time horizons and inter-firm mobility: An experimental investigation. *Organizational Behavior and Human Decision Processes*, *56*, 266–284.

Mannix, E. A., Tinsley, C., & Bazerman, M. H. (1995). Negotiating over time: Impediments to integrative solutions. *Organizational Behavior and Human Decision Processes*, *62*, 241–251.

McGrath, J. E. (1964). *Social psychology: A brief introduction*. New York: Hold.

McGrath, J. E. (1984). *Groups: Interaction and performance*. Englewood Cliffs, NJ: Prentice-Hall.

McGrath, J. (1991). Time, interaction, and performance (TIP): A theory of groups. *Small Group Research*, *22*, 147–174.

McGrath, J. (1993). Introduction: The JEMCO workshop – Description of a longitudinal study. *Small Group Research*, *24*, 285–306.

McGrath, J. E. (1993). *Small Group Research* [Special Issue], *24*(3).

McGrath, J., Arrow, H., Gruenfeld, D., Hollingshead, A., & O'Connor, K. (1993). Groups, tasks, and technology: The effects of experience and change. *Small Group Research*, *24*, 406–420.

McGrath, J. E., & Kelly, J. (1986). *Time and human interaction: Toward a social psychology of time*. New York: Guilford Press.

McGrath, J., & O'Connor, K. (1996). Temporal issues in work groups. In: M. A. West (Ed.), *Handbook of Work Group Psychology* (pp. 25–52). New York: Wiley.

Marks, M. A., Sabella, M. J., Burke, C. S., & Zaccaro, S. J. (2002). The impact of cross-training in team effectiveness. *Journal of Applied Psychology*, *87*, 3–13.

Marks, M. A., Zaccaro, S. J., & Mathieu, J. E. (2000). Performance implications of leader briefings and team-interaction training for team adaptation to novel environments. *Journal of Applied Psychology*, *85*, 971–986.

Marks, M., Mathieu, J., & Zaccaro, S. (2001). A temporally-based framework and taxonomy of team processes. *Academy of Management Review*, *26*, 356–376.

Mathieu, J. E., Heffner, T. S., Goodwin, G. F., Salas, E., & Cannon-Bowers, J. A. (2000). The influence of shared mental models on team process and performance. *Journal of Applied Psychology*, *85*, 273–283.

Michaelson, L. M., Watson, W. E., & Black, R. H. (1989). A realistic test of individual vs. group decision making. *Journal of Applied Psychology*, *74*, 834–839.

Mintzberg, H., Raisinghani, D., & Théorêt, A. (1976). The structure of 'unstructured' decision processes. *Administrative Science Quarterly*, *21*, 246–275.

Mitchell, T., & James, L. (2001). Building better theory: Time and the specification of when things happen. *Academy of Management Review*, *26*, 530–547.

Moreland, R., & Levine, J. (1982). Socialization in small groups: Temporal changes in individual-group relations. In: L. Berkowitz (Ed.), *Advances in Experimental Social Psychology* (Vol. 15). New York: Academic Press.

Morris, C. G. (1966). Task effects on group interaction. *Journal of Personality and Social Psychology*, *5*, 545–554.

O'Connor, K., Gruenfeld, D., & McGrath, J. (1993). The experience and effects of conflict in continuing workgroups. *Small Group Research*, *24*, 362–382.

Okhuysen, G., & Waller, M. (2002). Focusing on midpoint transitions: An analysis of boundary conditions. *Academy of Management Journal*, *45*, 1056–1065.

O'Reilly, C., Chatman, J., & Caldwell, D. (1991). People, jobs, and organizational culture. *Academy of Management Journal, 34*, 487–516.

Parks, C., & Cowlin, R. (1995). Group discussion as affected by number of alternatives and by a time limit. *Organizational Behavior and Human Decision Processes, 62*, 267–275.

Pelled, L. (1996). Demographic diversity, conflict and work group outcomes: An intervening process theory. *Organization Science, 7*, 615–631.

Perlow, L. (1999). Time famine: Towards a sociology of work time. *Administrative Science Quarterly, 44*, 57–81.

Pelled, L., Eisenhardt, K., & Xin, K. (1999). Exploring the black box: An analysis of work group diversity, conflict, and performance. *Administrative Science Quarterly, 44*, 1–28.

Poole, M. S. (1983a). Decision development in small groups II: A study of multiple sequences in decision making. *Communication Monographs, 50*, 206–232.

Poole, M. S. (1983b). Decision development in small groups III: A multiple sequence model of group decision development. *Communication Monographs, 50*, 2321–2341.

Poole, M. S., & Roth, J. (1989a). Decision development in small groups IV: A typology of group decision paths. *Human Communication Research, 15*, 323–356.

Poole, M. S., & Roth, J. (1989b). Decision development in small groups V: Test of a contingency model. *Human Communication Research, 15*, 549–589.

Seeger, J. A. (1983). No innate phases in group problem solving. *Academy of Management Review, 8*, 683–689.

Shah, P., & Jehn, K. (1993). Do friends perform better than acquaintances? The interaction of friendship, conflict and task. *Group Decision and Negotiation, 2*, 149–166.

Shiflett, S. (1979). Toward a general model of small group productivity. *Psychological Bulletin, 86*, 67–79.

Steiner, I. D. (1972). *Group process and productivity.* New York: Academic Press.

Talland, G. A. (1955). Task and interaction process: Some characteristics of therapeutic group discussion. *Journal of Abnormal and Social Psychology, 50*, 105–109.

Tetlock, P. (1991). An integratively complex look at integrative complexity. Paper presented at the 99th Annual Convention of the American Psychological Association, San Francisco.

Tetlock, P., & Hannum, K. (1983). *Integrative complexity coding manual.* Unpublished manuscript, University of California, Berkeley.

Thatcher, S. M., & Jehn, K. A. (1998). A model of group diversity profiles and categorization processes in bicultural organizational teams. In: E. Mannix, M. Neale & D. Gruenfeld (Eds), *Research on Managing Groups and Teams: Composition* (pp. 1–20). Grenwich, CT: JAI Press.

Tuckman, B. W. (1965). Developmental sequences in small groups. *Psychological Bulletin, 63*, 384–399.

Waller, M. (1999). The timing of adaptive group behavior. *Academy of Management Journal, 42*, 127–137.

Waller, M., Zellmer-Bruhn, M., & Giambatista, R. (2002). Watching the clock: Group pacing behavior under dynamic deadlines. *Academy of Management Journal, 45*, 1046–1055.

Weingart, L. (1992). Impact of group goals, task component complexity, effort and planning on group performance. *Journal of Applied Psychology, 77*, 682–693.

Williams, K., & O'Reilly, C. (1998). Demography and diversity in organizations: A review of 40 years of research. In: R. Sutton & B. Staw (Eds), *Research in Organizational Behavior* (Vol. 20, pp. 77–140). Greenwich, CT: JAI Press.

BAUBLES, BANGLES, AND BEADS: MODELING THE EVOLUTION OF NEGOTIATING GROUPS OVER TIME

Jeanne Brett, Laurie Weingart and Mara Olekalns

ABSTRACT

Understanding how dyadic negotiations and group decision processes evolve over time requires specifying the basic elements of process, modeling the configuration of those elements over time, and providing a theoretical explanation for that configuration. We propose a bead metaphor for conceptualizing the basic elements of the group negotiation process and then "string" the beads of behavior in a helix framework to model the process by which group negotiations evolve. Our theorizing draws on the group decision development literature (e.g. Bales, 1953; Poole, 1981, 1983a, b; Poole & Roth, 1989a, b) as well as on the negotiation process literature (e.g. Gulliver, 1979; Morley & Stephenson, 1977). Our examples are from our Towers Market studies of negotiating groups.

INTRODUCTION

A negotiating group is a particular type of decision making group. It consists of three or more parties who can be single individuals or teams of individuals, although in our Towers Market example they are single individuals and throughout this chapter we refer to them as group members. Members of negotiating groups

Time in Groups
Research on Managing Groups and Teams, Volume 6, 39–64
Copyright © 2004 by Elsevier Ltd.
All rights of reproduction in any form reserved
ISSN: 1534-0856/doi:10.1016/S1534-0856(03)06003-1

are interdependent in the following ways: (a) members' interests (reasons for their positions) on a set of multiple issues are in conflict; and (b) the pattern of their conflict of interests is such that there is no a priori majority coalition that cuts across all issues. Negotiating groups have what McGrath (1984, p. 96) calls a mixed motive task structure, which means that each member's behaviors affect their own and others' outcomes and that no member can achieve as good an outcome by unilateral action; each needs the cooperation of others.

Negotiating groups are different from most of the groups that have been studied in the group decision development literature. One cannot assume, as is common in that research (Poole & Roth, 1989b), that the group goal will be more important to members than their individual goals, that group members have the same goal (the best group decision possible), or that the possibility of some members benefiting individually and asymmetrically from the group's decision is unimportant.

The group decision development and the negotiation process literatures do share two assumptions about group members and negotiators that are important to our theorizing. The first is that individual group members' and individual negotiators' behavior is goal directed, that is individual group members and negotiators choose their behaviors to serve the function of goal accomplishment; the second is that effective goal accomplishment requires meeting certain functional requirements dictated by the task and doing so in a particular order (Poole, 1983).

These two assumptions underlie the two major themes of our chapter. Motivated behaviors are the fundamental elements around which we construct a framework for thinking about group process. They are the beads that we will string into the necklaces that represent group process. Our discussion highlights the unique insights available from studying behavior in terms of *acts* of individual group members, *sequences* of two group members' interactions, *phases* of multiple coherent acts involving multiple group members, and *breakpoints* that signal transitions. Functional order, instantiated via sequences, phases, or breakpoints, is the structure of the evolution of the group process. Our necklace metaphor and helix model of group process present a richer, more nuanced, and more flexible conceptualization of the evolution of group decisions than previous rational model conceptualizations (e.g. Bales, 1953) which posit that behaviors evolve in particular functional sequences. Although rational models have been debunked by empirical research (Poole & Roth, 1989a, b) they have not been satisfactorily replaced.

CONCEPTUAL FRAMEWORK

Think of the behaviors that group members may exhibit as a set of multicolored beads. In the set are some duplicate beads, some similar beads (varying in shade or shape), some very different beads, and some unique beads. These behavioral beads are the fundamental elements of motivated behavior in group negotiation. We are going to string these behavioral beads into a multi-strand necklace that when twisted together forms a helix that represents the group process. The result will be a framework for conceptualizing the structural elements of group negotiation processes.

There are two elements to our framework. The first is the *content* of the behavior. Here we are interested in group members' behavioral choices and the goals motivating those choices and present a typology of motivated behavior in group negotiations. This can be represented by the process of "sorting" the beads by color (strategic orientation) and composition (strategic function). The second element of our framework is the *behavioral unit* to which the content is assigned. Here we are interested in individual acts, sequences of interaction, phases of coherent action, and acts that break up coherent action, or the structural elements of group negotiation process. This we can think of as the configuration of our beads.

Behavioral Content: A Typology

Table 1 presents our typology of motivated behavior in group negotiations. This table is derived from our most recent research on group negotiation behaviors (Weingart, Brett & Olekalns, 2002) in which we identified two integrative strategies (labeled "integrative information" and "value creation"), two distributive strategies (labeled "distributive information" and "value claiming"), and two breakpoints (labeled "closure" and "process").

The rows in Table 1 are identified by strategic function and can be distinguished by the shape of the beads; perhaps those in row 1 are round, those in row 2 are square and those is row 3 are triangular. The information behaviors in row 1 include both asking for and providing information about group members' positions and interests. This information facilitates decision making by providing insight into group members' desires and needs. The action behaviors in row 2 direct the group toward a particular decision. The breakpoints in row 3 are distinct behaviors that redirect the negotiation.

The columns in Table 1 are identified by strategic orientation and distinguished by the color of the beads. Distributive behaviors in column 1 (say, green beads) promote self-interests. Integrative behaviors in column 2 (say, purple beads) promote own and others' interests simultaneously. Distributive and integrative strategies are the core building blocks of negotiation behavior (Walton & McKersie, 1965). Essentially no one studying negotiation behavior ignores these two strategies (e.g. Donohue, Diez & Hamilton, 1984; Olekalns & Smith, 2000; Putnam & Jones, 1982b; Weingart, Hyder & Prietula, 1996). The information-action distinction, however, comes from our own research where we have used empirical grouping or

Table 1.   A Typology of Negotiation Strategy and Examples of
Negotiation Tactics.

Strategic Function	Strategic Orientation	
	Distributive	Integrative
Information	**Distributive Information** • positions • facts	**Integrative Information** • priorities • needs • interests
Action	**Value Claiming** • substantiation • threats • power use • bottom-line • single-issue offers	**Value Creating** • packaging • tradeoffs • creative solutions • multi-issue offers
	Procedural Orientation	
Breakpoint	**Closure** • time checks • recognize similarities	**Process** • reciprocity • moving on • vote

clustering techniques to classify negotiators' behaviors independent of outcomes (Olekalns & Smith, 2000, 2001a, in press; Weingart, Brett & Olekalns, 2002; Weingart, Thompson, Bazerman & Carroll, 1990; Weingart, Prietula, Hyder & Genovese, 1999).

Behavioral Units

The behavioral units or structural elements of the group negotiation process are acts, sequences, phases, and breakpoints. In subsequent sections we define each of the structural elements, relate each to our typology of motivated behavior, and discuss the unique insight each unit of analysis provides into the process of group negotiation.

Acts
An act is the verbal, paraverbal, or nonverbal behavior of an individual group member. We study verbal behavior and define an act as beginning when the person

starts speaking and ending when the person stops, either because she has finished or has been interrupted. In negotiation research, motivated acts are frequently called tactics. Group members use a variety of tactics, and we are particularly interested in tactics such as the examples in the cells of Table 1. Each bead in our metaphor represents a tactic.

Focusing on the relative frequencies of strategic groups of tactics allows us to test hypotheses about individual behavior in negotiating groups. For example, we have looked at group members' social motives, their use of the information and action strategies in Table 1, and their individual outcomes (Kern, Brett & Weingart, 2003). We can also test hypotheses about group differences. For example, we have looked at the motivational composition of groups, the groups' use of the four strategies in Table 1, and the group's decision (Weingart et al., 2002). In general, focusing on the relative frequency of strategies allows the researcher to investigate an array of multi-level questions relating individual differences and contextual variables to strategy, and strategy to individual and group level outcomes.

Sequences

Relying on group members' acts as the fundamental building blocks for studying evolutionary processes over time ignores the important point that group decision-making is a decidedly social interaction and that stable social structures are built not of individual behaviors but of repeated behavioral sequences or interacts: pairs of acts and their associated responses (Weick, 1969). One group member's tactical behavior provides the stimulus for another group member's tactical response. The second group member's tactical behavior provides the stimulus for a third group member's response, which may stimulate the fourth group member to weigh in, or stimulate a further response from one of the previous speakers. At its most basic level, social interaction in groups is a series of dyadic interactions. Even when a tactic is addressed to the group as a whole, it is one member who responds first, and that member's response will shape how the process develops. Both group decision development (Poole & Roth, 1989a) and negotiation researchers (Donohue, 1981; Putnam & Jones, 1982a) have treated sequences as the fundamental building blocks of social interaction and used repetitions or frequencies of sequences in terms of type and content to reveal stable patterns of social interaction. In our metaphor sequences are represented by two beads fused together.

Studying sequences can reveal how the group process builds toward an agreement or breaks down into disorganization (Poole, 1989a). The social validation of strategy that occurs when one party confirms the strategic behavior of the other by matching it with a tactic from the same strategic group increases the likelihood that other group members will choose tactics from that strategic group. While matching signals a willingness to follow a strategic lead, mismatching signals unwillingness to follow and provides an opportunity for strategic redirection (Brett, Shapiro & Lytle, 1998). Thus, sequences are useful in uncovering conflict among group members and can reveal efforts to change the strategic direction of the group.

Sequences also can be used to answer questions in the group context that are irrelevant in dyads. For example, does reciprocity develop as a group norm or do some members of the group engage in reciprocity while others do not, and with what consequences. Reciprocity among a subset of group members may provide evidence of coalition formation and predict a group decision that is based on majority rule.

Prior negotiation research identifies three types of sequences in dyadic negotiations: reciprocal, complementary, and structural (also called transformational) (Olekalns & Smith, 2000; Putnam & Jones, 1982a; Weingart et al., 1990). These sequences differ in the level of change that they introduce in strategic orientation and strategic function. In discussing these sequences, we treat a change in strategic orientation as more disruptive to negotiation processes than a change in strategic function: When negotiators change strategy but maintain orientation, they are essentially fine-tuning an existing approach. However, when they pair strategies of different orientations they are signaling a departure from the immediately preceding framing of the problem.

The different types of sequences can be represented in our metaphor by the fusion of same or different colored and shaped beads. Table 2 illustrates these three types of sequences using the strategic typology from Table 1. Because of their infrequent occurrence and their role in signaling breaks with a long-running orientation, we do not include breakpoints in this typology.

Table 2.   Examples of Types of Sequences.

	Types of Sequences		
Initial Behavior	Reciprocal	Complementary	Structural
Integrative information (InfoI)	InfoI → InfoI	InfoI → Create	InfoI → Claim
			InfoI → InfoD
Value creating (Create)	Create → Create	Create → InfoI	Create → InfoD
			Create → Claim
Distributive information (InfoD)	InfoD → InfoD	InfoD → Claim	InfoD → Create
			InfoD → InfoI
Value claiming (Claim)	Claim → Claim	Claim → InfoD	Claim → InfoI
			Claim → Create

Note: In structural sequence column, top example in each cell shows change in both strategic orientation and strategic function; bottom example in each cell shows change in strategic orientation only.

Reciprocal Sequences

Reciprocal sequences reveal that group members are choosing tactics that reinforce each other's strategic orientations or strategic functions and suggest that group members (or at least the two involved in this sequence) agree with each other's construction of strategic direction. Examples include sequences in which one group member makes a threat and the other makes a counter threat (tactics from value claiming); when one group member offers information about interests and the other offers some in return (tactics from integrative information); when one group member provides facts and another matches with more facts (tactics from distributive information); or, when one group member makes a multi-issue proposal and another counters with a variation of that proposal (tactics from value creating). Note that questions and answers within the same strategic orientation are also considered reciprocal tactics in this typology; a request for information about a group member's priorities that is answered is an example of reciprocity of integrative information. Returning to our analogy, reciprocal sequences string together beads of the same shape and color.

Complementary Sequences

Complementary sequences indicate that group members are maintaining their strategic orientation even if they are changing strategic function. Column 2 in Table 2 illustrates complementary sequences. An example would be when one group member shares some information about preferences (tactic from integrative information), and another integrates that information into a multi-issue proposal (tactic from value creation). Another example would be when one group member provides factual information (tactic from distributive information) and another answers with threats (tactic from value claiming). These sequences string together beads that have the same color but are shaped differently. These sequences are likely to influence the group process in a way that is similar to reciprocal sequences, by providing social reinforcement for a self vs. self-and-other focus. Unlike reciprocal sequences, they redirect the negotiation from action to information or from information to action. Also unlike reciprocal sequences, they generate some uncertainty about the negotiation process because they do not match strategies exactly.

Structural or Transformational Sequences

Structural sequences are composed of tactics from incongruent strategies. For example, group members may block a destructive conflict spiral by responding to a threat (tactic from value claiming) with a question about priorities (tactic from integrative information). Or, they may signal their refusal to follow another's strategy by answering a multi-issue proposal for agreement (tactic from integrative information) with a threat (tactic from value claiming). Column 3, Table 2 illustrates structural sequences.

The key feature of structural sequences is that they disrupt the strategic orientation of the negotiation, affecting a move from an integrative orientation to a distributive one or from a distributive orientation to an integrative one. They may also simultaneously be used to signal a shift in function. Structural sequences always change the color of the beads in the necklace; they can also change the shape of those beads. Negotiators in dyads use structural sequences to reorient a negotiation strategically (Brett, Shapiro & Lytle, 1998; Olekalns & Smith, 2000), and it seems likely that group members can use structural sequences for the same purpose. Group members who would benefit from no agreement may use structural sequences to disrupt the development of an orderly process (Poole, 1989a).

Phases
Phases, in both the group decision development and negotiation literatures, refer to coherent chunks of activity that form when parties repeat tactics or sequences from the same strategic group (Holmes & Sykes, 1993; Poole, 1989a). Phases can be thought of as extended periods of reciprocity, that is a string of two or more similarly colored and shaped beads.

Phases signal the emergence of social structure (Weick, 1969). For example, a reciprocal integrative information sequence followed by a functionally complementary integrative-distributive information sequence might be called an informational phase. A focus on phases differentiates coherent and disorganized activity, allowing the researcher to ask questions about social interaction like, "How much coherence is necessary for group members to reach individually and/or jointly satisfying outcomes?" "Can a group negotiation process be sabotaged by introducing disorganized activity?" "Can a group negotiation be salvaged by introducing coherent activity?" "What factors encourage coherent vs. disorganized activity?"

Poole and Roth (1989a) suggest the following rules for parsing a group decision process into phases: Phases should be fairly short runs of similar sequences, but long enough to establish meaning. Phases should be allowed to vary in length. Phases should be able to distinguish periods when there is no single coherent activity. Phases should have clear well-defined boundaries. In their own research, Poole and Roth begin with a string of data at the sequence level of analysis where each sequence has already been assigned to a phase type based on the function of the sequence. They consider triplets of sequences moving forward one sequence at a time. They define a phase as beginning when they encounter three sequences in a row from the same phase type and ending when they encounter three sequences in a row of different phase types. Three sequences in a row from different phase types define the beginning of a disorganized period that continues until terminated by three in a row from the same phase type. Poole and Roth (1989a) indicate they chose three interacts assuming that several interchanges were necessary to demonstrate coherence, but that three was a small enough "window" to allow shifts in focus to surface.

Breakpoints
Studying the relative frequency of behaviors and strategies, or of sequences, or of the length and frequency of phases, takes the perspective that what parties spend the bulk of their time doing is what is important strategically in a negotiation or a group process. A breakpoint approach suggests something different: that it is the spaces between phases or the events that punctuate the dominant approach that are important to the group or negotiation process. Unlike other analyses of negotiation processes, breakpoints focus us on differences in process rather than similarities.

There have been several different conceptualizations of breakpoints in the group development and negotiation literature. Breakpoints can be turning points that signal a transition from one strategy to another (Poole, 1983b), for example, at the boundary between different phases. Such breakpoints are well captured by episodic models that define phases as uninterrupted runs of tactics chosen from the same strategic group (a short string of similarly colored beads), and breakpoints as phase shifts either to a different coherent phase of strategic activity or into disorganization. Our metaphor would show phase shifts as changes in color between short strings, and disorganization as a series of beads of unrelated color. Phase shifts break into periods of coherency and in doing so provide a mechanism for changing the group dynamic (Baxter, 1982). Druckman (1986) for example, suggests the following as turning points: when parties realize they have an overlapping bargaining range so agreement is possible, when parties realize they agree on an interpretation of the problem, when parties reach agreement on a framework after periods when negotiators realize that no progress is being made, or when they recognize a threat to further talks and move the negotiation toward settlement. DeDreu (in press) provides a theoretical explanation:

> When parties impasse they have the time to reflect on their current strategies; they realize current practice may lead nowhere, and they face the cost of not reaching an agreement. Desire to better understand the task and the opponent increases, and high levels of epistemic motivation translate into higher levels of problem solving behavior, more sophisticated information processing, and greater probability of finding an integrative agreement.

Breakpoints may also be critical incidents that interrupt the negotiation or group decision-making process and move it toward or away from agreement. The key feature of breakpoints is their relatively infrequent occurrence: Strategies or events gain salience and impact the negotiation process because they are "rare" (Olekalns & Smith, 2000, 2001a). These types of breakpoints would be represented in our metaphor by beads of special and different color and composition, a striped macaroni shaped bead for example. We have been particularly interested in investigating process and closure tactics as breakpoints (Brett, Shapiro & Lytle, 1998). Major breakdowns of civility and emotional outbursts are also likely to be critical breakpoints. Our interest in critical incidents as breakpoints is because they redirect the group's attention from its primary task of reaching a decision to the secondary task of managing the process. Okhuysen and Eisenhardt (2002), for example, report that attention switches to process provide windows of opportunity to adjust group process and improve knowledge integration. Jett and George (in press), writing about work interruptions, point out that interruptions cause people to notice discrepancies between what is occurring and what should be occurring. They say that such events interrupt automatic processing of task related information and motivate people to actively and deliberately search for and analyze information about the discrepancy.

There has been so little research on breakpoints, that the first question is whether successful and unsuccessful group negotiations have different breakpoint profiles. Our own research (Olekalns, Brett & Weingart, 2002) leads us to believe that when all group members are cooperative they can reach agreement without reliance on breakpoints. When group members' motivations are mixed, breakpoints may be the factor that distinguishes between a group reaching an agreement and an impasse.

Breakpoints, whether defined as critical phase shifts or critical events, occur infrequently, and subsequently are ignored when researchers focus on the relative frequency of tactics, sequences, or phases. Identifying breakpoints requires special techniques that capture low base-rate phenomena. Some researchers count strategic transitions between phases (Poole, 1983b). Others code sudden departures from a pattern of give and take (Druckman, 2001). Researchers may ask negotiators or decision makers who have been videotaped to review their tape noting critical or unexpected events that made them change their strategy, changed their impression of the other party, affected their relationship with the other party, or the outcome (Olekalns & Smith, 2001b).

Modeling the Evolutionary Process of Group Negotiations

Now that we have organized our beads by color, composition, and configuration, we need a model for stringing the beads together. We turn first to an analysis of the utility of the rational evolutionary model. Then, we introduce our own punctuated helix model of the evolution of group negotiation.

Theory suggests that our necklaces should reflect the rational model beloved of textbooks and economists. Rational models, for example, Bales' group development model (Bales & Strodtbeck, 1951) and Morley and Stephenson's negotiation model (1977), consist of a set of rather long phasic strands of activity dropped one after another in a specified functional sequence (Poole, 1983a). Rational models assume that the group decision or negotiation task imposes certain functional requirements and further that these functional requirements must be met in a prescribed order, if the task is to be completed successfully. Bales' three phase decision making model (orientation, evaluation, control) and Morley and Stephenson's three phase negotiation model (distributive bargaining, problem solving, decision-making) resemble models of the progression of logical thought: problem definition, search for alternative solutions, selection of and commitment to a choice (Dewey, 1910). They are also eerily reflective of low context, linear, Aristotelian logic (Hall, 1976).

Poole and Roth (1989a, b) make a strong argument that rational models of group decision development are normative and part of group members' "cultural stock" of common sense. Holmes and Sykes (1993) suggest that people use such normative models in negotiation to "gauge progress, predict what will happen next, and focus their efforts." Whether or not rational models accurately represent what groups do when they make decisions or negotiate, they do provide a normative foil against which to compare other models.

Given the evidence that decisions and agreements do not meet the standard of rationality (Janis, 1982; March & Olsen, 1976; Neale & Bazerman, 1991; Pruitt, 1981), it is in some respects surprising that rational models continue to be the dominant normative standard for decision development and negotiation process. The reason seems to be that the research that has debunked rational models is input-output research, not process research. In the negotiation context, for example, research shows that negotiators' agreements are suboptimal, and that their understanding of the other's priorities is incomplete (Thompson, 2001). Such results imply that negotiators' fail to take full advantage of the middle problem-solving phase of Morley and Stephenson's rational model, but they imply nothing about the validity of the model's progressive assumptions. Certainly "lazy" models (Poole & Roth, 1989a) in which decision makers and negotiators sub-optimize process at each stage of decision making or negotiation better represent what people do, but they still assume that logical progression of functional phases.

There is good evidence that neither all groups nor all negotiations follow the rational evolutionary model. Poole (1981, 1983a, b) and Poole and Roth

(1989a, b), after conducting a series of studies of group decision development, concluded that the rational model of problem identification, analysis, solution, confirmation is not the dominant model for decisions. Rather, they found that most groups follow different and more complex models. A solution-focused model best characterizes one set of their groups: these groups eschewed rational problem definition and analysis and focused on solutions. Some of these groups ended their sessions with solution confirmation, as predicted by the rational model, but others exhibited a more complex pattern switching between solution and confirmation behavior throughout their sessions, suggesting that elements of the decision were being resolved one by one (sounds like negotiations) or that there were repeated, failed attempts to confirm the group decision. Other groups followed more complex developmental patterns cycling between problem analysis and solution behaviors from two to seven times. These groups exhibited a halting, spiraling evolution toward their decisions, as opposed to the smooth progress predicted by the rational model.

Recall the three-phase, rational model of negotiation identifies stages of distribution, problem solving, and integration. Pruitt and Lewis (1975), in contrast, suggest a variety of single-phase models concluding that some negotiators focus primarily on distributive tactics (e.g. column 1, Table 1), others on heuristic trial-and-error processing (e.g. row 2 Table 1), and still others on information exchange (e.g. row 1, Table 1). These approaches are summarized by Putnam (1990), who identifies four ways in which phases might unfold. Two of these capture the single-phase models described by Pruitt and Lewis, while two capture more complex models in which integrative and distributive phases follow each other sequentially or evolve simultaneously. The helix model that we go on to describe best fits with the idea that phases evolve simultaneously.

Our own research on the evolution of group negotiations has led us to formulate a set of models of the evolutionary process of group negotiations that we call punctuated helix models. A helix is a coil, and in our parlance can be thought of as composed of multiple strands of beads twisted together. The helix is an important element of our modeling. We do not think that a negotiating dyad or group abandons one strategic function or strategic orientation altogether and then moves on to another. Rather, we think that different strategies are dominant at different periods of the negotiation. Thus, our necklace consists not of a single strand of beads alternating in color and composition, but of multiple strands of beads, one for each strategy: integrative information, distributive information, value creation and value claiming twisted together. Within a strand beads linked together represent reciprocal sequences. Beads linked between strands indicate complementary or structural sequences. If we stretch our twisted necklace out flat on a table and look at it from above, we will see that some strategic strands are on top more often than others and at different points throughout the length of the necklace. Breakpoints, those striped macaroni shaped beads, punctuate the necklace and signal change in the dominant strand. If we lay out a set of necklaces, each representing a different group, we will see that even though they have many beads in common all the necklaces are at least slightly different and some are very different. Their differences are in terms of the micro composition of their strands (what beads are used), the macro composition of their helices (the relative frequency of links between strands, the relative dominance of different strands of strategy, and the presence or absence of their breakpoints). Some necklaces may have knots indicating that the group made forward progress, then turned back on itself, before making forward progress again.

TOWERS MARKET ILLUSTRATION

To illustrate our punctuated helix view of the evolution of negotiation in groups, we will look at our studies of Towers Market, a four-person group negotiation over whether to jointly open a market (Weingart, Bennett & Brett, 1993). Towers Market is a mixed-motive group negotiation task: Group members are motivated to cooperate in order to reach an agreement and to compete in order to do the best for themselves as possible. Five issues need to be resolved for the parties to reach a decision to open the market. Members have their own set of priorities across the five issues and there is no a priori majority coalition that cuts across all issues. All five issues must be resolved at a one-hour meeting, if an agreement is to be reached.

We videotaped the discussions of 36 groups performing the Towers Market task. We then transcribed the tapes and unitized the transcripts into subject-verb utterances to generate the behavioral building blocks for our analyses. We then assigned each behavior a tactical code. Throughout this process we preserved order and speaker's identity. We used correspondence analysis to generate the strategic typology in Table 1.

To this point our analysis has identified the set of behaviors (beads) enacted by each group. Each behavioral bead has a color indicating the strategic orientation of the tactic and a shape indicating the strategic function of the tactic. We place all the beads that are indicators of our four major strategies on separate strands. Thus, each group's necklace has four strands and each group's unique profile is indicated by the way the strands twist together into a helix.

There are two different ways of using the necklace metaphor to analyze the evolution of group negotiation. One approach divides the group's session into arbitrary time periods independently of content or frequency of strategies or sequences. The other approach uses phases, normalizing so that the length of a phase represents the percentage of the group's session that phase occupied.

Evolution of Acts and Sequences Over Time Periods

The first step in developing a time period based view of evolution is to define the length of the negotiation session. There are two ways to do this, each with different analytical implications. We can use fixed time periods, for example 10 minute segments, or we can use number of speaking turns (or elapsed time). The fixed time choice generates heterogeneity in the data in time periods toward the end of the session. Unless all groups deliberate for exactly the same amount of time, and ours did not, the fixed time periods toward the end of the session will consist of some finished groups that drop out of the period, groups finishing up, and groups still very much engaged in the negotiation. For this reason, we prefer to use number of speaking turns or elapsed time, rather than fixed time periods as the indicator of session length.

The second step in developing a time period view of evolution was to divide each group's negotiation session into a set of elapsed time periods defined independently of content. These time periods needed to be long enough to allow strands of even low frequency strategic acts or sequences to surface, but not so long as to camouflage strategic shifts in emphasis. We parsed the Towers Market negotiations into six periods based on the number of speaking turns. By creating six time periods, we could examine six potentially different twists of the helix. Researchers studying longer negotiations may want to use more time periods, and those studying shorter negotiations, fewer time periods. The rules for choosing how many time periods, while qualitative in application are logically clear: long enough to allow for important strategies to appear; short enough so that strategic shifts are not camouflaged and so that multiple twists of the necklace can be studied.

Strategic Acts Over Time

For our analysis of acts, we aggregated our data to a group by time period matrix capturing the frequency of each type of strategy within each time period. Next, we divided this frequency by the total number of speaking turns in the group's session to generate a measure of relative frequency. Finally, we used a logit transformation of the relative frequencies, as suggested by Cohen and Cohen (1983) because they were proportions.

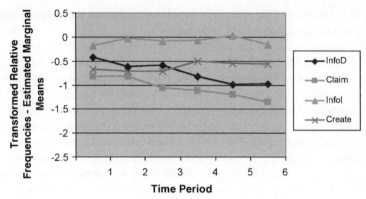

Fig. 1. Negotiation Strategies Over Time.

The results are shown in Fig. 1. A multivariate test confirmed that the use of strategies changed over time. Significant trend analyses revealed: the integrative information strategy peaked twice in time periods 2 and 5; the creating value strategy exhibited a significant increase during time period 4 and slight decreases before and after period 4, and; the distributive information and value claiming strategies decreased linearly with time.

Three of the four strategies follow the general pattern of Morley and Stephenson's (1977) rational model negotiation. Earlier periods of group deliberations were marked by greater frequencies of relative use of distributive strategies that tapered off over time, but did not disappear altogether. Later periods were marked by greater relative emphasis on value creation. However, the integrative information strategy, though it ebbed and soared, dominated all other strategies throughout the negotiation.

The interpretation of these results suggests a necklace that looks as follows: There are two core strands of large beads. The thickest and most often on top of the helix is integrative information; the strand of value creation gets thicker and is on top of the helix more often toward the end of the negotiation as members focus on proposals for agreement. Distributive information and value claiming strands never really dominate the helix, and these beads get smaller over time, ultimately becoming quite hidden in the necklace.

Sequences Over Time
Frequencies tell only part of the story of the evolution of group process. Particularly in a group negotiation setting, some members may get and hold the floor longer than others (Kern et al., 2003). This may bias the picture of the evolution of negotiation

based on frequencies. Sequences overcome this bias because they represent group process at the level of interaction between parties.

Different sequences provide different ways of viewing the group process. The choice of which sequences to study should be theory-driven. Here we are interested in how strategic function shifts over time, because evolutionary theories of group development and negotiation process are primarily functional. So, we have chosen to analyze the reciprocal sequences and the complementary sequences. Had we been primarily interested in the development of strategic orientation over time, we would have analyzed the reciprocal and structural sequences.

We constructed a group by time period matrix capturing the frequency of each reciprocal and complementary sequence within the time period. Next, we divided the sequence frequency by the total number of interacts in the group's session to generate a measure of relative sequence frequency. Finally, we used a logit transformation of the relative sequence frequencies, as suggested by Cohen and Cohen (1983) because they were proportions. The results are in Figs 2 and 3.

Figure 2 illustrates the evolution of reciprocal sequences. A multivariate test showed that reciprocity changed over time. The only sequence that was not time related was integrative information. Integrative information was more likely to be reciprocated than were tactics from any other strategic group and this pattern persisted throughout the evolution of the group process. Distributive information and value claiming exhibited significant negative linear trends over time, indicating that by the second half of the negotiation tactics from these strategic groups were even less likely to be reciprocated than earlier in the evolution of the process. The trend for creating value revealed a significant mid-process transition, possibly akin to the transitions that Gersick found in group deliberations over time (1988, 1989). The tactics in the value creating category are proposals for agreement that

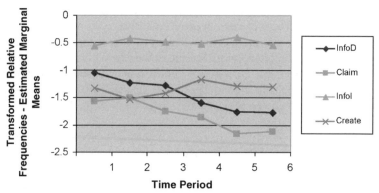

Fig. 2.   Reciprocal Sequences Over Time.

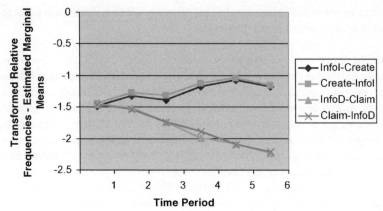

Fig. 3. Complementary Sequences Over Time.

typically refer to multiple issues and take the concerns of others into account. The increase in the level of reciprocation of such tactics over time and the decrease in the reciprocation of value claiming (which promotes self-interests) indicate that by the middle of their process group members had recognized their interdependence and were working cooperatively with each other to compose an agreement.

The resemblance between the act data in Fig. 1 and the reciprocal sequences data in Fig. 2 indicates that changes in frequencies of acts over time are supported by changes in reciprocity over time. The reciprocal sequences reveal that group negotiation behavior reveals a structured pattern of social interaction. The patterns in Fig. 1 are not due to the behavior of one group member, rather they reflect an underlying social structure of reciprocity.

Figure 3 illustrates the evolution of complementary sequences over time. Complementary distributive behavior decreases over time, whereas complementary integrative behavior largely increases over time, with a bit of a slowdown after the initial increase (time period 3). Also interesting is that the directionality of complementarity within strategic function (information to action or action to information) within a strategic orientation (integrative or distributive) does not differentiate how complementarity changes over time. For example, the sequences integrative information to create value and create value to integrative information have almost identical patterns.

The complementary patterns appear to reinforce the reciprocal patterns. Complementary responses to distributive strategies decrease over time the same way that reciprocal responses decrease over time. Complementary responses to integrative strategies increase at the beginning and midpoint of the group's deliberation, reflecting the early increase in reciprocity of integrative information and later increase in reciprocity of value creating. These results again point to the underlying structure of group processes.

Phase Analyses

Summing across groups as we did for the analysis of acts and sequences generates sufficient data to evaluate trends, but hides between-group differences. To evaluate between-group differences we have to open the lens a little further and study phases. Our phase analyses also require that we look at all the acts that occurred in a group, not just the ones that are of theoretical interest. This required that we included process and closure strategies that we believe serve as breakpoints, and a general "other" category of behavior.

We used WinPhaser (Holmes & Sykes, 1993) to generate phase maps for each group. We used single acts to define phases because we wanted to use the phase analysis to investigate breakpoints, too. Our theorizing about events that serve as breakpoints suggests that such events are likely to be single isolated acts. These choices mean that in our analysis a phase lasts for as long as group members use the same strategy and ends when they change strategies. We normalized maps to the same scale to take into account sessions of different lengths and to be able to make comparisons between groups.

Figures 4a though 4c present phase maps for three different groups. In these maps, the length of the phase represents the percentage of the total session occupied by that phase. The left side of each figure breaks the session into 10 periods based on phases. The white space between phase lines provides a visual indication of how long the phase lasted. The boxes to the right in each figure provide visual results of the gamma analysis we ran to identify evolutionary patterns within each group (Pelz, 1985; Poole & Roth, 1989a). The gamma analysis established phase precedence, or the general order in which phases occurred, and revealed within group patterns of sequences. It also indicated the degree of separation among the phases, that is, whether the session consisted of a few long phases or of many short phases. The gamma analysis made it possible to construct a prototype sequence of phases based on when in the session phases occurred and the distinctiveness of their temporal location. Solid boxes in the right column of the figures indicate that phases were well differentiated from each other; dashed boxes indicate phases that were less differentiated. The order of boxes indicates phase precedence.

Group 62 in Fig. 4a has the most differentiated phase structure of the three groups. This group began with other or off task discussion, and then moved to sharing distributive information. The phase map indicates this discussion was punctuated by process, at several points beginning just before the midpoint of the negotiation (50th percentile) and continuing through the 70th percentile

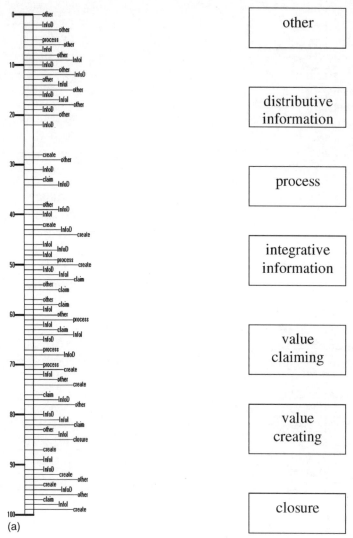

Fig. 4. Phase Map for (a) Group 62, (b) Group 78, and (c) Group 36.

of discussion. Note that integrative information became more dominant in the second half of the negotiation, followed by value claiming and value creating and closure. Group 62 reached an agreement, but it had to manage its process to do so, transforming what began as a distributive negotiation into an integrative one.

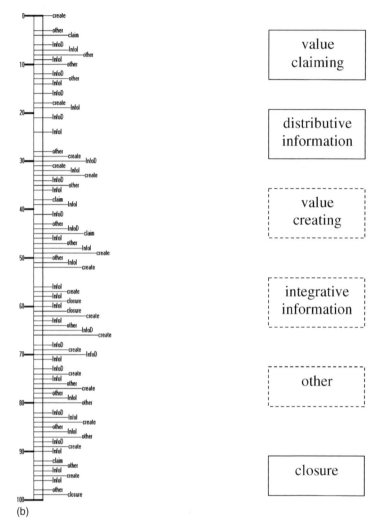

(b)

Fig. 4.   (Continued)

The gamma results (not shown) revealed the following sequences characteristic of this group: distributive information was followed almost equally often by value creating acts as value claiming acts; value claiming acts led to closure, and; consistent with our theorizing about breakpoints, process led to creating value.

Group 78 in Fig. 4b illustrates a group with a moderately well differentiated phase map. This group also reached an agreement, but its path was rather different from the path taken by Group 62. Group 78 opened with value claiming, followed

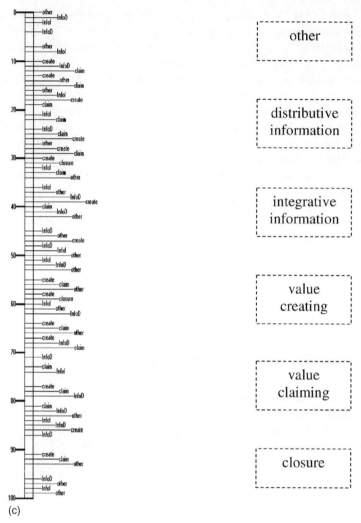

Fig. 4. (*Continued*)

by distributive information, then entered a middle period of undifferentiated value creating and integrative information sharing, and ended with closure. The gamma statistics indicated that value claiming was followed by integrative information and value creation, not vice versa, suggesting, the members of this group were actively trying to reorient the group behaviorally. Note this group did not discuss process at all.

Group 36 in Fig. 4c illustrates the phase map of a group with a poorly differentiated phase structure. Group 36 did not appear to have developed systematic social interaction. It also had no process intervention breakpoints. Perhaps not surprisingly, this group did not reach an agreement.

Across all the groups that we studied, information (both integrative and distributive) and value creation phases occurred more frequently than value claiming. What accounted for group differences was how these three phases were inter-woven. In some groups' necklaces, the dominant strand of beads was integrative information; in other groups it was distributive information, and, in others, value creation dominated the necklace. The strand of value claiming beads was less dominant and more prone to being broken up by longer strands of other strategies.

We also observed that phases focusing on the negotiation process or moving the group to closure acted, as predicted, like breakpoints. These phases occurred infrequently and intermittently throughout the groups' sessions. We noticed that process breakpoints occurred during the first half of the session in some groups and appear to have helped negotiating groups move away from distributive strategy. A second type of process breakpoint occurred toward the end of some groups' sessions and seemed to function to focus these groups on the need to reach agreement.

CONCLUSION

Our analyses of the evolution of group negotiations, whether based on the frequencies of acts and sequences or the occurrence of phases, do not reveal the pattern of the rational model. These group negotiation sessions do not begin with distributive bargaining, move to problem solving, and end with decision-making (Morley & Stephenson, 1977). The correspondence analysis that generated the typology in Table 1 split distributive bargaining and problem solving into information and action functional categories. The act and sequence frequency analyses over time in Figs 1 and 2 indicate that groups primarily discuss integrative information throughout their sessions. Integrative information does not get turned on after the groups reach impasses trying to use distributive information and value claiming to reach agreement. It is true that groups exchange more distributive information early in the session than later, but even the early stages of these group negotiations were not dominated by distributive bargaining. Value creation, the action aspect of integrative strategy, does increase in importance as the session develops and the second half does seem to be dominated by integrative bargaining that continues to be dominated by integrative information sharing. The phase analyses provide an even more nuanced picture of the evolution of negotiating groups' process. These results revealed even more clearly than the act and sequence frequency data that group negotiations did not follow a smooth evolutionary process, but twisted and turned as different phases took over from one another. Some groups did struggle between distributive and integrative strategy, where process and closure strategies served as breakpoints reorienting the negotiation. Other groups appeared to use sequences to avoid conflict spirals and impasse. Groups that did neither had difficulty reaching agreement.

These results suggest that our helix model is a much better representation of the evolutionary process of a negotiating group than the rational model or the lazy model. Our helix model, however, needs a modification to fit the data well. The strand of integrative information beads dominated the helix of negotiating groups. These beads are simply bigger than the beads representing other strategies. When all the strands of strategy are woven together, the larger integrative information beads stand out.

The helix model fits the data from group negotiations over time better than the rational or lazy models proposed by prior theorists. With its twisted strands of strategy, the helix model does not require groups to evolve along lines of functional determinism. The helix model and the data imply that groups do develop stable patterns of social interaction, however, those patterns do not exhibit the functional determinism predicted by the rational model. Across groups, the major strike against functional determinism comes from the overall dominance of the strategy of sharing integrative information. Within groups, the phase analysis results indicate that social interaction is sometimes a struggle for strategic dominance, and that different patterns emerge in different groups.

The helix model can be applied to groups not engaged in mixed motives. Just because their task may be easier than Towers Market, we see no reason to suppose that group members will not develop an evolutionary process that is revealed by the pattern of group members' social interaction. Nothing in the previous research on group decision development suggests that such groups will display a pattern of social interaction that reflects rationality (Poole & Roth, 1989a, b). While researchers studying such groups will want to develop a strategic typology that is appropriate to their research question, we think they can use the acts, sequences, phases, and breakpoints framework for analysis.

In addition, we believe that the helix model can be applied to negotiating dyads. It is possible that stable patterns of social interaction develop more quickly in negotiating dyads than groups because of turn taking. In a dyad, one either reciprocates the other's strategy or not, but in a group, one has to get the floor before reciprocating, and someone else may get there first, taking the group in a different strategic direction. Nevertheless, nothing in the previous research suggests that negotiating dyads meet the standard for rational decisions (Neale & Bazerman, 1991). Why then should their evolutionary process follow a rational pattern?

Our framework – conceptualizing behavioral units into acts, sequences, phases, and breakpoints – and our helix model are amenable to a variety of research initiatives in the context of negotiating groups, cooperative decision-making groups, and negotiating dyads. One approach would be to determine how individual differences (e.g. differences in social motives) affect the development of a group's helix. Another approach would be to determine how situational factors affect the patterns of acts, sequences, phases or breakpoints. Okhuysen and Eisenhardt (2002), for example, show that simple interventions, like basic instruction about how to share information, increased the number of interruptions in task execution, focused the group on the group's secondary agenda (i.e. process) and improved knowledge integration.

It is time to set aside rational and lazy models of the evolution of group process and develop a nuanced understanding of the myriad of ways that groups can reach decisions. Our framework of behavioral units organized as acts, sequences, phases and breakpoints provides the tools for doing so. Our helix model provides an alternative to the rational model as a standard against which to evaluate the evolution of group process.

REFERENCES

Bales, R. F. (1953). The equilibrium problem in small groups. In: R. Parsons, R. Bales & E. Shils (Eds), *Working Papers in the Theory of Action* (pp. 186–269). New York: Free Press.

Bales, R. F., & Strodtbeck, F. L. (1951). Phases in group problem-solving. *Journal of Abnormal and Social Psychology, 46*, 485–495.

Baxter, L. A. (1982). Conflict management: An episodic approach. *Small Group Behavior, 13*, 23–42.

Brett, J. M., Shapiro, D. L., & Lytle, A. L. (1998). Refocusing rights- and power-oriented negotiators toward integrative negotiations: Process and outcome effects. *Academy of Management Journal, 41*, 410–424.

Cohen, J., & Cohen, P. (1983). *Applied multiple regression/correlation analysis for the behavioral sciences*. Hillsdale, NJ: Lawrence Erlbaum.

DeDreu, C. K. W. (in press). Motivation in negotiation: A social psychological perspective. In: M. Gelfand & J. M. Brett (Eds), *Culture and Negotiation: Integrative Approaches to Theory and Research*. Palo Alto, CA: Stanford University Press.

Dewey, J. (1910). *How we think*. Boston: D.C. Heath.

Donohue, W. A. (1981). Development of a model of rules in negotiation. *Communication Monographs, 48*, 106–120.

Donohue, W. A., Diez, M. E., & Hamilton, M. (1984). Coding naturalistic negotiation interaction. *Human Communication Research, 10*, 403–425.

Druckman, D. (1986). Stages, turning points, and crises. *Journal of Conflict Management, 30,* 327–360.

Druckman, D. (2001). Turning points in international negotiation: A comparative analysis. *Journal of Conflict Resolution, 45,* 519–544.

Gersick, C. J. G. (1988). Time and transition in work teams: Toward a new model of group development. *Academy of Management Journal, 31,* 9–41.

Gersick, C. J. G. (1989). Marking time: Predictable transition in taskgroups. *Academy of Management Journal, 32,* 274–309.

Gulliver, P. H. (1979). *Disputes and negotiations: A cross-cultural perspective.* New York: Academic Press.

Hall, E. T. (1976). *Beyond culture.* Garden City, NY: Anchor.

Holmes, M. E., & Sykes, R. E. (1993). A test of the fit of Gulliver's phase model to hostage negotiations. *Communication Studies, 44,* 38–55.

Jett, Q. R., & George, J. M. (in press). Work interrupted: A closer look at the role of interruptions in organizational life. *Academy of Management Review.*

Janis, I. L. (1982). *Victims of groupthink* (2nd ed.). Boston: Houghton-Mifflin.

Kern, M. C., Brett, J. M., & Weingart, L. R. (2003). Getting the Floor: Persistence, Motives, Strategy, and Individual Outcomes in Multi-party Negotiations. Northwestern University. Dispute Resolution Research Center Working Paper No. 233.

March, J. G., & Olsen, J. P. (1976). *Ambiguity and choice in organizations.* Oslo: Universitetsforlaget.

McGrath, J. E. (1984). *Groups: Interaction and performance.* Englewood Cliffs, NJ: Prentice-Hall.

Morley, I. E., & Stephenson, J. M. (1977). *The social psychology of bargaining.* London: Allen & Unwin.

Neale, M. A., & Bazerman, M. (1991). *Cognition and rationality in negotiation.* New York: Free Press.

Okhuysen, G. A., & Eisenhardt, K. M. (2002). Integrating knowledge in groups: How simple formal interventions help. *Organizational Science.*

Olekalns, M., & Smith, P. L. (2000). Negotiating optimal outcomes: The role of strategic sequences in competitive negotiations. *Human Communications Research, 24,* 528–560.

Olekalns, M., & Smith, P. L. (2001a). *Social motives in negotiation: The relationship between dyad composition, strategy sequences and outcomes.* Cergy, France: International Association of Conflict Management.

Olekalns, M., & Smith, P. L. (2001b). Metacognition in negotiation: The identification of critical incidents and their role in shaping trust and outcomes, Melbourne Business School Working Paper 2001–15.

Olekalns, M., Brett, J. M., & Weingart, L. R. (2002). In-phase, out-of-phase: Temporal patterns in negotiators' interactions. Paper to be presented at International Association of Conflict Management, Park Cities, Utah.

Olekalns, M., & Smith, P. L. (in press). Testing a three-way relationship among negotiators' motivational orientations, strategy choices, and outcomes. *Journal of Experimental Social Psychology.*

Pelz, D. C. (1985). Innovation and complexity and the sequence of innovating stages, Knowledge: Creation, Diffusion. *Utilization, 6,* 261–291.

Poole, M. S. (1981). Decision development in small groups I: A comparison of two models. *Communication Monographs, 48,* 1–24.

Poole, M. S. (1983a). Decision development in small groups II: A study of multiple sequences in decision making. *Communication Monographs, 50,* 206–232.

Poole, M. S. (1983b). Decision development in small groups III: A multiple sequence model of group decision development. *Communication Monographs, 50,* 2321–2341.

Poole, M. S., & Roth, J. (1989a). Decision development in small groups IV: A typology of group decision paths. *Human Communication Research*, *15*, 323–356.

Poole, M. S., & Roth, J. (1989b). Decision development in small groups V: Test of a contingency model. *Human Communication Research*, *15*, 549–589.

Pruitt, D. G. (1981). *Negotiation behavior*. New York: Academic Press.

Pruitt, D. G., & Lewis, S. A. (1975). Development of integrative solution in bilateral negotiation. *Journal of Personality and Social Psychology*, *31*, 621–633.

Putnam, L. L. (1990). Reframing integrative and distributive bargaining: A process perspective. *Research on Negotiation in Organizations*, *2*, 3–30.

Putnam, L. L., & Jones, T. S. (1982a). Reciprocity in negotiations: An analysis of bargaining interaction. *Communication Monographs*, *49*, 171–191.

Putnam, L. L., & Jones, T. S. (1982b). The role of communication in bargaining. *Communication Monographs*, *49*, 262–282.

Thompson, L. L. (2001). *The mind and heart of the negotiator* (2nd ed.). Upper Saddle River, NJ: Prentice-Hall.

Walton, R. E., & McKersie, R. B. (1965). *A behavioral theory of labor negotiation: An analysis of a social interaction system*. New York: McGraw-Hill.

Weick, K. (1969). *The social psychology of organizing*. Menlo Park, CA: Addison-Wesley.

Weingart, L. R., Bennett, R. J., & Brett, J. M. (1993). The impact of consideration of issues and motivational orientation in group negotiation process and outcome. *Journal of Applied Psychology*, *78*, 504–517.

Weingart, L. R., Brett, J. M., & Olekalns, M. (2002). Conflicting social motives in negotiating groups. Paper to be presented at Academy of Management, Denver, Colorado.

Weingart, L. R., Hyder, E., & Prietula, M. J. (1996). Knowledge matters: The effect of tactical descriptions on negotiation behavior and outcomes. *Journal of Personality and Social Psychology*, *70*, 1205–1217.

Weingart, L. R., Prietula, M. J., Hyder, E., & Genovese, C. R. (1999). Knowledge and the sequential processes of negotiation: A Markov chain analysis of response in kind. *Journal of Experimental Social Psychology*, *35*, 366–393.

Weingart, L. R., Thompson, L. L., Bazerman, M. H., & Carroll, J. S. (1990). Tactical behavior and negotiation outcomes. *The International Journal of Conflict Management*, *1*, 7–31.

PART II:
SYNCHRONIZING GROUP ACTIVITIES OVER TIME

HOW PROJECT TEAMS ACHIEVE COORDINATED ACTION: A MODEL OF SHARED COGNITIONS ON TIME

Josette M. P. Gevers, Christel G. Rutte
and Wendelien van Eerde

ABSTRACT

This chapter addresses how project teams achieve coordinated action, given the diversity in how team members may perceive and value time. Although synchronization of task activities may occur spontaneously through the nonconscious process of entrainment, some work conditions demand that team members pay greater conscious attention to time to coordinate their efforts. We propose that shared cognitions on time – the agreement among team members on the appropriate temporal approach to their collective task – will contribute to the coordination of team members' actions, particularly in circumstances where nonconscious synchronization of action patterns is unlikely. We suggest that project teams may establish shared cognitions on time through goal setting, temporal planning, and temporal reflexivity.

INTRODUCTION

As a result of growing competition and new technologies, many projects must be performed in shorter time intervals. Moreover, meeting deadlines is increasingly

Time in Groups
Research on Managing Groups and Teams, Volume 6, 67–85
Copyright © 2004 by Elsevier Ltd.
All rights of reproduction in any form reserved
ISSN: 1534-0856/doi:10.1016/S1534-0856(03)06004-3

regarded as an important measure of project success (Freeman & Beele, 1992; Waller, Conte, Gibson & Carpenter, 2001). Nevertheless, Lientz and Rea (2001) have indicated that over half of all system and technology implementation projects overrun their budget and schedule by 200% or more. Although many factors may play a role in the delay of projects, Lientz and Rea have suggested that many problems experienced in these projects are related to the diversity in team members' knowledge and working procedures in cross-functional teams.

In collaborative action, timeliness of performance requires that members of the project team have synchronized actions. On the one hand, team members need to structure their efforts to the deadline; on the other hand, they also need to adapt to each other's actions in order to coordinate individual contributions (McGrath & O'Connor, 1996). Team members may, however, have very different ideas about how to use their time when working on a collective task, for example, when people from different organizational units or fields of expertise are brought together in a cross-functional project team. These differences in temporal habits may stem from differences in the throughput and process priorities of such units, and from the time spans associated with their goal accomplishments (Rastegary & Landy, 1993). Not only functional background may lead to differences in deadline salience and responses to progress feedback (Waller, Conte, Gibson & Carpenter, 2001), but also individual differences in time perception and experience (Bartel & Milliken, 2004); differences in personal temporal tendencies (Blount & Janicik, 2001, 2002); and time urgency (Conte, Landy & Mathieu, 1995). Moreover, taking into consideration that individual team members often work in multiple projects, they may have competing pulls on their time use, which may induce different norms and values about deadlines, schedules, and other time-related issues. Such mismatches in team members' temporal perspectives may cause group conflict or may impede the group's ability to coordinate individual actions effectively, thereby endangering the timeliness of group performance.

The foregoing raises an interesting question: How do project teams – given the diversity in how members may perceive and value time – manage to achieve the coordinated action required for meeting deadlines? In this chapter, we propose that project teams may reach coordinated action either through the process of entrainment (a nonconscious tendency toward behavioral synchrony) or through more explicit group processes aimed at the development of cognitive congruence in team members' perceptions of the appropriate timing and pacing of actions in task execution. For this purpose, we introduce the concept of shared cognitions on time as the extent to which team members agree on the team's temporal approach to the collective task. We will argue that shared cognitions on time contribute to the coordination of team members' actions, particularly in circumstances where nonconscious synchronization of action patterns is unlikely. Finally, we will provide insight into the possible antecedents of shared cognitions on time and discuss how goal setting, temporal planning, and temporal reflexivity may help project teams to develop a common view on the temporal approach to their task or project. We will illustrate our theoretical notions with samples from interviews with members of project teams in the Information Technology business.

COGNITIONS ON TIME

According to Blount and Janicik (2001, 2002), individuals organize their time at work based on two sets of cognitions regarding time in the work place. First, every individual has his or her personal temporal tendencies, for example: temporal orientation (Bartel & Milliken, 2003; Waller, Conte, Gibson & Carpenter, 2001); level of time urgency (Conte, Landy & Mathieu, 1995; Landy, Rastegary, Thayer & Colvin, 1991); polychronicity, or the preference to work at different tasks at the same time (Slocombe & Bluedorn, 1999); and pacing preferences, that is, preferences for a particular speed and duration of activities (Blount & Janicik, 2002). Personal temporal tendencies are assumed to affect the anticipation of certain events and outcomes. Some individuals are naturally more attentive to time; they always keep a close eye on upcoming deadlines and frequently schedule their activities. Others seem unconcerned with time and tend to procrastinate. Some people like to work fast and juggle multiple tasks at once, while others work slowly and prefer to concentrate on one thing at a time. Although these personal temporal tendencies are relatively stable attributes of individuals, they may fluctuate across situations as a function of social and institutional forces such as the organizational environment in which the individual is working (cf. Bartel & Milliken, this volume). The second set of cognitions that influences how the individual spends his or her time at work concerns that person's perception of the organization's temporal agenda.

Blount and Janicik (2001, 2002) have postulated that a person deduces a prevailing temporal agenda from the temporal information generated by the work environment. The work environment (e.g. the organization, department, or project team) expresses how time is to be perceived, evaluated, and spent by its members through cycles and rhythms of activities, sociotemporal norms, schedules, and deadlines. Implicit cycles and rhythms of activities regulate the use of time at different organizational levels; they influence everyday routines, such as when people enter the work place, when they take coffee breaks, and whether or not they work overtime (Perlow, 1999, 2001); they structure interaction patterns between different functional subgroups (Ancona & Chong, 1999), and they direct the accommodation of strategic actions to the surrounding competitive environment (Ancona & Chong, 1999; Eisenhardt, 1989). Sociotemporal norms provide guidelines for appropriate behavior with respect to the pacing of activities, punctuality, adherence to deadlines, and trade-offs between quality and speed (Schriber & Gutek, 1987). Furthermore, managers use explicit schedules and deadlines to allocate temporal resources and to communicate plans regarding the duration of subtask accomplishment, the sequence for these subtasks to be executed, and the final deadline for completing the total work package.

Together, these cognitions on time define a person's perspective on the appropriate timing and pacing of actions in the work place. Because of the personal nature of these perceptions, individuals within the same organization, department, or project team may have different perspectives on the appropriate temporal strategy for a particular task or project. The diversity of these temporal perspectives is important to team functioning. When people work together to accomplish a certain task or project, several distinctive features of time perception may disrupt the synchronization of activities. Team members may disagree on the importance of a particular temporal milestone and/or on the pacing of activities between the current moment and a temporal milestone (Blount & Janicik, 2002). As a result, team members may disagree on the appropriate time to start working on a task, they may disagree on the appropriate pacing of activities in task execution, or they may disagree on the right moment for completing the task. Individual differences in the perception and the use of time may foster project team functioning when they balance out and team members who want to rush things are calmed down, while those who tend to procrastinate are motivated to get started. Disparate views on the appropriate temporal approach to a task could, however, cause group conflict and result in dysfunctional group dynamics. This is illustrated by the following incident, as described by one of the project managers we interviewed:

> We set up a team of software developers and graphics designers to prepare the new release of our software package, which would be presented at the annual trade fare. The software developers were to write the new software code; the graphic designers were to develop demonstration material. Because the designers needed time to prepare the graphics, the developers were to deliver the new software at least two weeks before the trade fair. Unfortunately, progress on the software development was slow, and it looked like they were not going to make it on time. The software developers did not perceive this as a problem, knowing that they could upload the final code to the internet at the last minute before the trade fair. The designers, however, now had to prepare their demonstration material based on the unfinished software. In the end, the developers were very pleased that they managed to release the final version of the software package in time for the opening of the trade fair. The designers, however, were furious: Half of their demonstration material did not function properly, because it did not match with the final version of the software.

This example shows that the temporal coordination of group members' action patterns is essential for successful group performance. Because the software developers did not recognize the importance of the deadline that was set for writing the software code, the graphics designers did not deliver the proper demonstration material, and the presentation of the new software was not nearly as successful as it could have been. To achieve effective and satisfying group functioning, team members need to adapt their behavior to the demands of the task and to other team members, while maintaining flexibility to collectively adjust actions to changing circumstances. In the following sections, we will argue that when team members are behaviorally interdependent and work in close proximity their action patterns may spontaneously synchronize through the process of entrainment. Other work conditions (e.g. when team members are merely sequentially interdependent, as the team in the example above) will require team members to pay more conscious attention to time and to reach agreement on the proper timing and pacing of activities. We expect that explicit group communication processes (i.e. goal setting, temporal planning, and temporal reflexivity) may contribute to the development of shared cognitions on time.

These processes that lead toward coordinated action are depicted in Fig. 1. The figure also shows that once coordinated action between team members is achieved, it also may influence their cognitions and communication processes. Entrainment indirectly improves cognitive congruence within a team through its facilitating effect on team coordination. We will now elaborate on these implicit and explicit processes toward project team coordinated action.

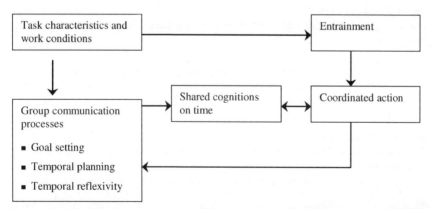

Fig. 1. Model of Implicit and Explicit Processes Toward Coordinated Action in Work Groups.

COORDINATED ACTION THROUGH ENTRAINMENT

One of the theoretical notions explaining how temporal action patterns become synchronized in groups is entrainment. Entrainment is the process by which one internal rhythmic process is captured and modified by another (internal or external) rhythmic process (Kelly, 1988). Examples of entrainment processes encountered in the biological sciences include the alignment of the human biological rhythm with the cycle of the sun, and the synchronized chirping of crickets and flashing of fireflies (cf. Blount & Janicik, 2002). At the interpersonal level, mutual entrainment refers to the synchronization of some particular behavior or pattern of action by two or more interacting partners (Ancona & Chong, 1996; McGrath & O'Connor, 1996).

The process of entrainment is typically nonconscious in nature; that is, people naturally adapt their behavior to match the rhythms of others around them without making an effort or even thinking about it. The actual system responsible for coupling these rhythmic processes remains uncertain, but it may be compared to such phenomena as social facilitation or mirroring behavior, social processes that arise spontaneously in groups. Blount and Janicik (2001) assumed that individuals may experience discomfort from being "out of synch" with others around them. They suggested that pace alignment in project teams stems from an individual level tendency to prefer the experience of feeling in-pace to that of feeling out-of-pace with others. Therefore, they argued, entrainment is most likely to occur when team members work in close proximity on a cyclical task with a high level of task interdependence.

Limitations of Entrainment: Task Characteristics and
Work Conditions

McGrath and Kelly's review of task pacing studies (1986) suggested that interacting persons show a strong tendency toward entrainment of activities. Still, automatic alignment of action patterns in project teams cannot be taken for granted. Many task activities lack the predictive and cyclical nature on which the entrainment process is based (Blount & Janicik, 2001). Task complexity and the nonroutine nature of the execution process also influence the likelihood of entrainment, as these factors affect the extent to which standard procedures can be employed to make the behavioral patterns of group members more predictable. Other work conditions of modern project teams, such as working in virtual teams or working on several projects or in different teams simultaneously, also reduce the likelihood of synchronization of individual action patterns because these practices reduce the extent of interaction between team members, and possibly also the quality of the interactions.

At the same time, we need to consider that many tasks that project teams perform do not require full synchronization of individual action patterns. While some tasks require project teams to complete the greater part of the work in close interaction (e.g. surgical teams or cockpit crews), other tasks allow team members to perform their individual subtasks alone and to collaborate periodically. Many cross-functional project teams perform these so-called "hybrid tasks" (Wageman, 2001). Rather than seeking a "state of absolute coordination" (i.e. where one unit's pace or rhythm dominates that of others), team members may seek a "state of relative coordination" (Turvey, 1990; cf. Zalesny, Salas & Prince, 1995), where each team member functions at his or her own pace, and delivers output for the team in a timely manner.

When team members only collaborate periodically, they have fewer opportunities to learn to become a team (Wageman, 2001), making them extremely susceptible to the development of disparate views of their collective goals, including their time goals. Because they perform their work individually, they are less likely to resolve process problems and to develop norms and collective strategies. Especially under time pressure, team members may be inclined to only get together to divide subtasks, and to proceed with their work individually, having little or no contact until the moment their individual contributions must be combined. Because entrainment is unlikely to occur in these circumstances, we argue that such work conditions demand that teams devote more conscious attention to time and to developing shared cognitions on time to achieve coordinated action.

COORDINATED ACTION THROUGH SHARED COGNITIONS ON TIME

In an overview of the principles underlying coordination, Turvey (1990) stated that the challenges inherent in coordination hold for perceiving as well as acting. This means that coordinated action requires shared knowledge, norms, values, beliefs, explanations, and expectations among team members (cf. Zalesny, Salas & Prince, 1995). This idea matches that of shared cognitions as important to regulating teamwork. Research on shared cognitions and team performance has involved various distinct, though related, constructs (cf. Mohammed & Dumville, 2001), including shared mental models (Cannon-Bowers, Salas & Converse, 1993; Klimoski & Mohammed, 1994), team schema similarity (Rentsch & Hall, 1994), transactive memory (Wegner, 1995), and shared understanding (Cohen, Mohrman & Mohrman, 1999).

Central to each of these constructs is the idea that cognitive congruence among team members will improve team processes and, ultimately, team performance (Cohen et al., 1999; Mathieu, Heffner, Goodwin, Salas & Cannon-Bowers, 2000; Rentsch & Klimoski, 2001). Cannon-Bowers et al. (1993) suggested that shared mental models of the task and team enable team members to form accurate explanations of and expectations about task execution, which help team members to coordinate their actions and adapt their behavior to the demands of the task and to other team members. However, research in this area has not addressed time as an explicit aspect of shared cognitions. Although individual temporal behavior is based on one's personal perspective on time and one's interpretation of the temporal agenda expressed by the work environment, we believe that sharing at least some of these cognitions on time will enhance team members' abilities to accommodate to each other's work patterns. To specify which cognitions on time should be shared, we need to consider which processes are most important for coordinated team action.

We believe that for a project team to reach a "state of relative coordination" the timing of completing, exchanging, and integrating individual contributions is important. To complete a task or project on time, team members must finish their individual subtasks on time and avoid delays in the flow of work. Schedules and deadlines provide important collective temporal reference points. They reduce temporal uncertainty by explicating the amount of time available for completing subtasks and indicating the expected flow of work among team members. As such, schedules and deadlines clarify interdependencies in the project team and set the stage for the pacing of work activities.

Schedules and deadlines also influence the timing and pacing of task activities by eliciting time pressure (Rastegary & Landy, 1993). Studies by Gersick (1988, 1989), Gladstein (1984), and Seers and Woodruff (1997) showed that groups increase their activities on a task as their deadline draws near and time pressure increases. However, individual perceptions of deadline pressures may differ considerably as a result of individual norms on time. For schedules and deadlines to result in a smooth flow of work, team members need to collectively value norms concerning punctuality, speed, and adherence to deadlines. They should agree on what these are, and should attach the same importance to complying to these norms. Janicik and Bartel (2002) provide empirical evidence that time-urgent norms that emphasize attention and adherence to schedules, deadlines, and work pace, enhance the ability of the project team to produce an appropriate temporal patterning of activities. Also, when team members collectively acknowledge that temporal issues are important, they will be less likely to get off-pace or to disturb others in their task activities.

Thus, sharing cognitions on time means first that team members agree on the temporal milestones and workflow schedules for their collective task. This will promote shared expectations for who will execute which subtasks and when these will be accomplished. Secondly, sharing cognitions on time means that team members attach equal importance to these reference points on the basis of shared temporal norms. Teams lacking shared cognitions on time are likely to experience coordination problems and process loss (Steiner, 1972), for example, because team members neglect temporal milestones for subtask completion.

We acknowledge that a group can share inappropriate perceptions of time due to groupthink or majority influence, leading them to adopt an inappropriate temporal strategy. We believe, however, that group processes that involve the explicit questioning of the way time is used in task execution will increase the likelihood that shared cognitions are appropriate.

DEVELOPING SHARED COGNITIONS ON TIME

When nonconscious synchronization of project team activities is unlikely, teams may use explicit group communication processes to align cognitions on time. By devoting explicit attention to time in goal setting, temporal planning, and temporal reflexivity, team members may develop a shared understanding of their temporal goals and task strategies, and may build shared temporal norms with respect to these goals and strategies. These group communication processes may be different, depending on the extent to which formal project planning is used. Some project teams are initiated with only a vague idea of what a collaboration of team members could offer. These project teams will have to define their own objectives with respect to time, as well as other output standards, before they can reach agreement on a collective strategy toward those objectives. Other project teams may be provided with explicit performance standards and detailed task strategies by their management. In these cases, group communication processes may be aimed more at aligning the interpretation of these goals and plans and at obtaining the commitment of the team members.

Goal Setting

In their taxonomy of team processes, Marks, Mathieu and Zaccaro (2001) identified goal specification as an important process to guide team activities toward goal accomplishment. Goal specification refers to "the identification and prioritization of goals and subgoals for mission accomplishment" (p. 365). Goal-setting theorists (Locke & Latham, 1990; Locke, Shaw, Saari & Latham, 1981) have identified goals as immediate regulators of task performance: They direct attention, mobilize effort, increase persistence, and motivate strategy development. These goal-setting effects have been identified for individual goals as well as group goals (Locke & Latham, 1990; O'Leary-Kelly, Martocchio & Frink, 1994).

In many work situations, task performance involves the concurrent attainment of multiple goals such as quality, quantity, costs, and timeliness. People ideally handle multiple goals by prioritizing them and subsequently allocating the time available according to their importance. As a result, people perform better on high priority goals (Kernan & Lord, 1990). Several authors (Cohen, Mohrman & Mohrman, 1999; Sawyer, 1992) argued that successful task accomplishment in project teams requires a shared understanding among team members of the relative importance of the various outcomes and of the trade-offs that need to be made among them. As we argued earlier, this implies that teams need to establish a shared understanding of the importance of their temporal objectives in order to accomplish their task on time.

In a cross-sectional survey study of 108 knowledge work teams, Cohen et al. (1999) found that goal-setting processes had a positive effect on team performance by contributing to a shared understanding of the purpose, priorities, and work approach within the team. Hierarchical goal-setting processes in which management set particular goals for a team had a positive effect on shared cognitions. However, this effect was relatively weak compared to the effect of the participation of team members in goal setting, which strongly predicted shared understanding within the team. In addition, group goal-setting contributed to improvements in work processes and methods.

On the basis of these findings, we propose that group goal-setting processes may also help align team members' perceptions of the importance of temporal goals. Involving team members in the goal-setting process helps them understand: (1) the importance and urgency of the temporal milestones; and (2) other performance indicators that may be compromised in order to ensure deadlines are met. Such specifications will offer direct guidelines to adjust task strategies adequately once the project team feels it cannot complete its tasks on time. Research on creative team projects (Amabile, Conti, Coon, Lazenby & Herron, 1996) suggested that if a deadline is experienced as a challenge, it may boost the team's motivation. From our interviews with project managers, we know that participative goal setting is already successfully employed in product development teams, effectively reducing the duration of product development cycles. These projects are led off with a multi-day "launch-meeting" where management and members of the project team discuss the feasibility of the project in all its aspects: scope, time, budget, resources, and risks. The purpose of the meeting is to reach an agreement, signed in a contract book, between management and project team on the project targets and the appropriate project approach before the work is begun. One IT project manager we asked about this practice said that these meetings boost awareness on what is important in a particular project, and motivate participants to contribute fully to the project. He illustrated his point by describing a project without these meetings:

> This was a project with an estimated duration of 10 months that outrun its schedule by two months. Even near the end, the atmosphere in the team remained quite relaxed. Considering the amount of work that still had to be done, you would have expected these guys to get nervous and pressure each other to make sure deadlines were met, but that kind of spirit was missing. I feel that the management team could have inspired these workers by voicing the importance of that deadline from the very start, which they did not do. I believe that is the way to shake things loose and really get people going; if you wait until things start to go wrong, you are already too late.

In conclusion, goal-setting processes, especially those in which team members define and prioritize goals, provide a team with a deeper understanding of the meaning of temporal milestones and deadlines, a shared view on how to deal with time limitations, and the motivation and commitment to keep an eye on task progress. This will enhance team efforts to adapt in response to signals that the team might not finish its project on time.

Temporal Planning

Reaching goals involves the specification of subtasks, the division of labor among team members, and the planning and implementation of activities in an efficient and effective goal-directed manner (Zalesny, Salas & Prince, 1995). According to Marks, Mathieu and Zaccaro (2001), planning consists of decision-making on *how* team members will achieve their goals. This includes discussing expectations and task-related information, and assigning roles and responsibilities to team members, while taking into consideration the situational and time constraints, team resources, member expertise, and changing nature of the environment. Empirical research showed that planning in teams resulted in better performance during periods of high workload (Gevers, Van Eerde & Rutte, 2001), primarily because it increases the degree to which team members share an understanding of each other's needs and information requirements (Stout, Cannon-Bowers, Salas & Milanovich, 1999). To harmonize team members' cognitions on the temporal demands of the task, however, we propose that project teams should also engage in a more detailed type of planning than what is usually practiced, with a particular focus on the use of time (i.e. temporal planning).

In our view, temporal planning concerns the strategy formulation on how to use time for goal accomplishment. We distinguish temporal planning from goal setting in that the former concerns a lower level of strategy development, which has to do with the operationalization of the way specified goals are to be achieved. As such, temporal planning may encompass: (a) estimating the time it will take to accomplish specific subtasks, and setting milestones for these subtasks; (b) determining the order and timing of actions, and setting up a plan for the flow of work between team members; and (c) discussing individual team members' time constraints and temporal preferences for the task.

By discussing issues of subtask duration and sequential interdependence, group members build congruent expectations for the temporal approach to the task, and explicate norms with respect to punctuality, speed, and adherence to deadlines. This will keep team members attentive to task progress – not just their own subtasks, but also the flow of work as a whole. Moreover, discussing team members' individual time constraints and pacing preferences will enhance accurate expectations and explanations for the individual pacing and timing of efforts. As such, temporal planning probably will benefit both the member-support function, and the production function of project teams (McGrath, 1990). On the one hand, temporal planning will provide team members with the opportunity to coordinate individual contributions in such a way that personal preferences can largely be met and conflicts may be avoided. On the other hand, temporal planning also will allow team leaders to take appropriate measures to safeguard task progress (e.g. deciding who should do what).

Several project managers we interviewed said that they were very careful how they allocated work among the team members, particularly with tasks that were critical to the total project duration. One project manager stated that he was well aware that some team members just could not handle more than one work package at a time: "If you give them several tasks at once, they don't know where to start, or which job to do first. So, I always take the qualities of team members in consideration when allocating tasks, just to get the best out of each of them." Another project manager said, "There definitely are differences in work pace between team members, especially when taking into account the quality of their output. Therefore, I make sure that team members who are less productive get more time, or get the easier jobs."

Although one would expect project teams to discuss time-related issues when planning strategies for task accomplishment on their own accord, several researchers have provided evidence that this is not the case. Some project teams fail to spontaneously engage in temporal planning without an external prompt from a manager (cf. Janicik & Bartel, 2002). In a study of self-managing work groups, Janicik and Bartel (2002) found that, when teams do engage in temporal planning, it assists them in establishing normative expectations about and an increased sensitivity to the ways team members manage time, leading to better team coordination and task performance.

In many project teams, planning and scheduling is the responsibility of the team leader or manager. The manager may present team members with a cut-and-dried working schedule for task execution, or may involve team members in setting the schedule by asking their personal estimates for work package duration and their ideas on the most efficient flow of work between team members. We prefer the latter approach. Participation in planning will enhance team members' commitment to the schedule and will increase the likelihood that subtasks will be completed on time. In addition, challenging group members to think about an effective flow of work will emphasize team members' interdependence and strengthen a social orientation in the team. This may reduce the likelihood that individuals fail to pass on outputs that are accomplished earlier than scheduled, just because it is not in their personal interest (Leach, 1999).

To summarize, we propose that temporal planning, established in cooperation with team members or on the basis of team members' input, will enhance shared normative expectations with respect to time, and will strengthen team members' awareness of their interdependence to reach team goals.

Temporal Reflexivity

Monitoring progress is an important team process for work groups when team members actually conduct activities directly aimed at goal accomplishment (Marks, Mathieu & Zaccaro, 2001). The extent to which group members collectively reflect upon the group's objectives, task strategies, and internal processes, and adapt to current and anticipated endogenous or environmental circumstances, is named group reflexivity (West, 1996). According to West (1996), reflexive teams have a more comprehensive and shared cognitive representation of their work that enables them to be more adaptive to and more effective in the execution of their tasks, especially when operating in uncertain and dynamic circumstances.

Research has shown that reflexivity on actions increases the likelihood that deadlines will be met (Gevers, Van Eerde & Rutte, 2001). This research suggests that, under high levels of time pressure, reflecting on time limitations, task progression, and the way plans should be adapted to meet the temporal demands will benefit timely task completion. Therefore, we propose that the extent to which teams reflect upon the temporal aspects of their task execution processes will have a strong impact on their ability to perform in a coordinated and timely manner.

Temporal reflexivity means that team members pay attention to time, monitor whether they finish tasks according to plan, and evaluate and communicate any adjustments in plans and actions needed to meet temporal milestones. Team members keep each other informed on their progress and discuss problems or unforeseen demands that might endanger the timeliness of their collective performance. They do so to determine whether it is necessary to speed up, reallocate resources, or alter schedules and milestones. Only when performance gaps are recognized at an early stage and team members collectively commit themselves to adaptive actions can a project team recover from schedule delays and bring future progress in line with initial plans.

Temporal reflexivity may be scheduled at regular intervals in project team meetings or may arise spontaneously. Unexpected events, outcomes, or inter-ruptions (e.g. the absence of essential resources, unanticipated test results, or exceeding an important temporal milestonc) are likely to cause project teams to evaluate their progress and to redirect their temporal approach to the task (cf. Waller, Zellmer-Bruhn & Giambatista, 2002). Presumably, some managers and team members will be concerned that temporal reflexivity will only waste precious time that the team could be using to take action. However, jumping to new strategies in an unstructured way will not be effective when the situation calls for adaptive actions carried by the entire team. Shifts in plans and schedules need to be supported by all team members to be effective. While project teams should not waste their time discussing every insignificant detail of their work behavior together, they should discuss essential issues that concern the entire project team, not restricting these discussions to subgroup discussions.

Thus, temporal reflexivity in project teams enables team members to guide and direct their temporal performance and to build a shared perspective on the adaptive actions required in response to performance gaps or unexpected events. Collective shifts in the timing and pacing of actions can only be accomplished when team members understand the necessity for these shifts, a condition that we expect can be established through temporal reflexivity.

DISCUSSION AND CONCLUSIONS

In this chapter we have addressed how project teams may achieve coordinated action given the differences in how team members perceive and value time. We have argued that team members working in close proximity may effortlessly reach synchronized action on the basis of entrainment processes, while more explicit attention to time is probably needed to establish coordinated action in work condi-tions where team members are merely sequentially interdependent, or when their activities are unpredictable. We have introduced the concept of shared cognitions on time as the congruence in group members' perceptions of the appropriate tim-ing and pacing of actions with respect to their collective task. These perceptions are based on shared knowledge, attitudes, and norms with respect to the temporal agenda of the task at hand. Shared cognitions on time will facilitate team members to structure their behavior to fit with external temporal demands and to adapt to each other's actions. As a result, project teams with realistic congruent cognitions on time will be better able to meet deadlines than project teams with divergent views.

We have proposed that project teams may align their cognitions on time by giving explicit attention to time in project team communication processes, such as goal setting, temporal planning, and temporal reflexivity. Our discussion of project team communication processes offers several opportunities for practitioners to increase the likelihood of cognitive congruence among team members and to enhance project team functioning. As in many projects, project management is likely to benefit from group meetings to launch time-critical projects. In these meetings, management and team members establish, prioritize, and commit to goals they agree on. Moreover, the possibilities for group members to adapt to each other's task activities will be increased when goals are translated into work schedules that provide temporal milestones for subtask duration, explicate sequential interdependencies, and emphasize normative time expectations. Similar meetings can be held during the execution of the project to evaluate task progression, team functioning, and required adaptive actions. These reflections on task progress may be scheduled or may arise spontaneously among team members who work in close proximity. Many project teams work in one large room, which facilitates communication and entrainment. However, project teams should avoid wasting valuable time on extensive discussions about small, task-specific problems. Management should be aware that these communications might interrupt and disturb the thought processes of individual team members engaged in cognitive tasks (Perlow, 1999).

We acknowledge that our reasoning in this chapter has limitations in the sense that it may be a simplification of the circumstances in which many project teams perform their tasks. Project teams do not operate in isolation; they face external demands over which they may have little or no control. Clients, suppliers, subcontractors, or related projects that are preceding or running in parallel to the project team may keep a team from performing on time despite cognitive congruence and coordinated action among its members. Moreover, coordinated action does not merely require team members to finish their tasks on time; it also demands that they attend to the quality of their work. If task quality is not properly monitored, team members may finish subtasks quickly and the flow of work may appear to run smoothly, but time will be needed to detect and restore errors – ultimately slowing down project completion. Consequently, deadlines may still be missed because of rework. In addition, projects vary in the degree of predictability of products and processes. This may limit some project teams in their ability to preplan, coordinate, and pace their actions, increasing the need for project team flexibility. Finally, individuals and project teams often have to perform multiple tasks at the same time. As a result, shared cognitions on time with respect to one task may conflict with the cognitions on time regarding another task. To address multiple tasks, project teams and their managers will need to prioritize tasks and to establish shared cognitions on time across tasks (Waller, 1997). Still, provided that project teams attend to the quality of their work and manage to deal with external dependencies satisfactorily, shared cognitions on time are likely to enhance coordinated action, and to add to the timeliness of task performance if appropriate.

While our reasoning has provided us with an interesting theoretical model of the implicit and explicit processes toward coordinated action in project teams, it should be tested empirically in future research, especially with respect to the effects of shared cognitions on time. This research may prove to be challenging in a number of ways. First, it may be difficult to determine who is to be considered part of the project team. Most projects have several parties involved, some more intensely than others. These parties may put people on or off the job, depending on the project status or circumstances. However, in most cases, a core team stays on the project from start to finish. This core team may be the best sample from a project.

Second, even in a single branch of business there may be large differences between projects in scope, complexity, and uncertainty. The diversity of projects will complicate the comparison of project outputs. How a project team completes a routine job in a small project team may have little in common with how a group finishes a large innovative project with multiple project teams working interdependently. Moreover, missing deadlines may pay off, and may lead to politics of delay. For example, projects that use total cost calculations may lead to more delay than fixed-priced projects, because total-cost projects may be able to claim the payment of extra hours from the client. Researchers should control for such project characteristics.

A final issue we would like to address here concerns the operationalization of shared cognitions on time. We gladly refer the reader to the existing literature on the measurement of shared cognitions (see Kraiger & Wenzel, 1997). However, when cognitions concern time, we have an additional matter to address. Even though cognitions on time may be shared by group members, other parties, such as a client may consider these cognitions to be incorrect. Of course, in most cases, temporal norms are explicated in contractual obligations; still, there is always the possibility that specifications have not been exhaustive and that their meaning is not interpreted in the same way by contracting parties. Consequently, team members may collectively believe that they have done a wonderful job by delivering a product right on time, while their client considers the same job to be late or incomplete. In practice, frequent communication with the external party during the project could probably help to reach a common perspective of what is "on time." If we are to measure timeliness, its evaluation by multiple parties would lead to more valid conclusions than when only the team evaluates it.

We invite fellow researchers to test our model empirically, while we encourage practitioners to address the issue of shared cognition on time in time-critical projects, and to examine whether group communication processes are helpful to improve coordinated action.

ACKNOWLEDGMENTS

We thank Robert A. Roe and the reviewers for their helpful comments on earlier versions of this chapter. The preparation of this chapter was supported by a grant from the cooperation centre Tilburg and Eindhoven Universities, The Netherlands, research project: 99-Z.

REFERENCES

Amabile, T. M., Conti, R., Coon, H., Lazenby, J., & Herron, M. (1996). Assessing the work environment for creativity. *Academy of Management Journal, 39*, 1154–1184.

Ancona, D., & Chong, C. L. (1996). Entrainment: Pace, cycle, and rhythm in organizational behavior. In: B. M. Staw & L. L. Cummings (Eds), *Research in Organizational Behavior* (Vol. 18, pp. 251–284). Greenwich, CT: JAI Press.

Ancona, D., & Chong, C. L. (1999). Cycles and synchrony: The temporal role of context in team behavior. In: R. Wageman (Ed.), *Research on Managing Groups and Teams: Vol. 2. Groups in Context* (pp. 33–48). Greenwich, CT: JAI Press.

Bartel, C. A., & Milliken, F. J. (2004). The effects of diversity in time perspectives on work group functioning. In: S. Blount, E. Mannix & M. Neale (Eds), *Research on Managing Groups and Teams: Time in Groups* (Vol. 6). Greenwich, CT: JAI Press.

Blount, S., & Janicik, G. A. (2001). When plans change: Examining how people evaluate timing in changes in work organizations. *Academy of Management Review, 26*, 566–585.

Blount, S., & Janicik, G. (2002). Getting and staying in-pace: The "in-synch" preference and its implications for work groups. In: E. A. Mannix, M. A. Neale & H. Sondak (Eds), *Research on Managing Groups and Teams: Vol. 4. Toward Phenomenology of Groups and Group Membership* (pp. 235–266). Greenwich, CT: JAI Press.

Cannon-Bowers, J. A., Salas, E., & Converse, S. (1993). Shared mental models in expert team decision making. In: N. J. Castellan, Jr. (Ed.), *Individual and Group Decision Making: Current Issues* (pp. 221–246). Hillsdale, NJ: Lawrence Erlbaum.

Cohen, S. G., Mohrman, S. A., & Mohrman A. M., Jr. (1999). We can't get there unless we know where we are going: Direction setting for knowledge work teams. In: R. Wageman (Ed.), *Research on Managing Groups and Teams: Vol. 2. Groups in Context* (pp. 1–31). Greenwich, CT: JAI Press.

Conte, J. M., Landy, F. J., & Mathieu, J. E. (1995). Time urgency: Conceptual and construct development. *Journal of Applied Psychology, 80*, 178–185.

Eisenhardt, K. (1989). Making fast strategic decisions in high-velocity environments. *Academy of Management Journal, 32*, 543–576.

Freeman, M., & Beele, P. (1992). Measuring project success. *Project Management Journal, 23*, 8–17.

Gersick, C. J. G. (1988). Time and transition in work teams: Toward a new model of group development. *Academy of Management Journal, 31*, 9–41.

Gersick, C. J. G. (1989). Marking time: Predictable transitions in task groups. *Academy of Management Journal, 32*, 274–309.

Gevers, J. M. P., Van Eerde, W., & Rutte, C. G. (2001). Time pressure, potency, and progress in project groups. *European Journal of Work and Organizational Psychology, 10*, 205–221.

Gladstein, D. (1984). Groups in context: A model of task group effectiveness. *Administrative Science Quarterly, 29*, 499–518.

Janicik, G. A., & Bartel, C. A. (2002). Talking about time: Effects of temporal planning and time urgent norms on group coordination and performance. Unpublished manuscript, Stern School of Business, New York University.

Kelly, J. R. (1988). Entrainment in individual and group behavior. In: J. E. McGrath (Ed.), *The Social Psychology of Time: Vol. 91. New Perspectives* (pp. 89–110). Thousand Oaks, CA: Sage.

Kernan, M. C., & Lord, R. G. (1990). Effects of valence, expectancies, and goal performance discrepancies in single and multiple goal environments. *Journal of Applied Psychology, 75*, 194–203.

Klimoski, R., & Mohammed, S. (1994). Team mental model: Construct or metaphor? *Journal of Management, 20*, 403–437.

Kraiger, K., & Wenzel, L. H. (1997). Conceptual development and empirical evaluation of measures of shared mental models as indicators of team effectiveness. In: M. T. Brannick, E. Salas & C. Prince (Eds), *Team Performance Assessment and Measurement: Theory, Methods, and Applications* (pp. 63–84). London: Lawrence Erlbaum.

Landy, F. J., Rastegary, H., Thayer, J., & Colvin, C. (1991). Time urgency: The construct and its measurement. *Journal of Applied Psychology, 76*, 644–657.

Leach, L. P. (1999). Critical chain project management improves project performance. *Project Management Journal, 30*, 39–51.

Lientz, B. P., & Rea, K. P. (2001). *Breakthrough technology project management*. London: Academic Press.

Locke, E. A., & Latham, G. P. (1990). *A theory of goal setting and task performance*. Englewood Cliffs, NJ: Prentice-Hall.

Locke, E. A., Shaw, K. N., Saari, L. M., & Latham, G. P. (1981). Goal setting and task performance: 1969–1980. *Psychological Bulletin, 90*, 125–152.

Marks, M. A., Mathieu, J. E., & Zaccaro, S. J. (2001). A temporally based framework and taxonomy of team processes. *Academy of Management Review, 26*, 356–376.

Mathieu, J. E., Heffner, T. S., Goodwin, G. F., Salas, E., & Cannon-Bowers, J. A. (2000). The influence of shared mental models on team process and performance. *Journal of Applied Psychology, 85*, 273–283.

McGrath, J. E. (1990). Time matters in groups. In: J. Galegher, R. E. Kraut & C. Egido (Eds), *Intellectual Teamwork: Social and Technological Foundations of Cooperative Work* (pp. 23–61). Hillsdale, NJ: Lawrence Erlbaum.

McGrath, J. E., & Kelly, J. R. (1986). *Time and human interaction: Toward a social psychology of time*. New York: Guilford Press.

McGrath, J. E., & O'Connor, K. M. (1996). Temporal issues in work groups. In: M. A. West (Ed.), *Handbook of Work Group Psychology* (pp. 25–52). Chichester: Wiley.

Mohammed, S., & Dumville, B. C. (2001). Team mental models in a team knowledge structure: Expanding theory and measurement across disciplinary boundaries. *Journal of Organizational Behavior, 22*, 89–106.

How Project Teams Achieve Coordinated Action

85

O'Leary-Kelly, A. M., Martocchio, J. J., & Frink, D. D. (1994). A review of the influence of group goals on group performance. *Academy of Management Journal, 37*, 1285–1301.
Perlow, L. A. (1999). The time famine: Toward a sociology of work time. *Administrative Science Quarterly, 44*, 57–81.
Perlow, L. A. (2001). Time to coordinate: Toward an understanding of work-time standards and norms in a multi-county study of software engineers. *Work and Occupations, 28*, 91–111.
Rastegary, H., & Landy, F. J. (1993). The interactions among time urgency, uncertainty, and time pressure. In: O. Svenson & A. J. Maule (Eds), *Time Pressure and Stress in Human Judgement and Decision Making* (pp. 217–239). New York: Plenum Press.
Rentsch, J. R., & Hall, R. J. (1994). Members of great teams think alike: A model of team effectiveness and schema similarity among team members. In: M. M. Beyerlein, D. A. Johnson & S. T. Beyerlein (Eds), *Advances in Interdisciplinary Studies of Work Groups: Vol. 1. Theories of Self-Managing Work Teams* (pp. 223–261). Greenwich, CT: JAI Press.
Rentsch, J. R., & Klimoski, R. J. (2001). Why do great minds think alike?: Antecedents of team member schema agreement. *Journal of Organizational Behavior, 22*, 107–120.
Sawyer, J. E. (1992). Goal and process clarity: Specification of multiple constructs of role ambiguity and a structural equation model of their antecedents and consequences. *Journal of Applied Psychology, 77*, 130–142.
Schriber, J. B., & Gutek, B. A. (1987). Some time dimensions of work: Measurement of an underlying aspect of organizational culture. *Journal of Applied Psychology, 72*, 642–650.
Seers, A., & Woodruff, S. (1997). Temporal pacing in task forces: Group development or deadline pressure? *Journal of Management, 23*, 169–187.
Slocombe, T. E., & Bluedorn, A. C. (1999). Organizational behavior implications of the congruence between preferred polychronicity and experienced work-unit polychronicity. *Journal of Organizational Behavior, 20*, 75–99.
Steiner, I. D. (1972). *Group processes and productivity*. New York: Academic Press.
Stout, R. J., Cannon-Bowers, J. A., Salas, E., & Milanovich, D. M. (1999). Planning, shared mental models, and coordinated performance: An empirical link is established. *Human Factors, 41*, 61–71.
Turvey, M. T. (1990). Coordination. *American Psychologist, 45*, 938–953.
Wageman, R. (2001). The meaning of interdependence. In: M. E. Turner (Ed.), *Groups at Work: Theory and Research* (pp. 197–219). London: Lawrence Erlbaum.
Waller, M. J. (1997). Keeping the pins in the air: How work groups juggle multiple tasks. In: M. M. Beyerlein, D. A. Johnson & S. J. Beyerlein (Eds), *Advances in Interdisciplinary Studies of Work Teams* (Vol. 4, pp. 217–247). Greenwich, CT: JAI Press.
Waller, M. J., Conte, J. M., Gibson, C. B., & Carpenter, M. A. (2001). The effect of individual perceptions of deadlines on team performance. *Academy of Management Review, 26*, 586–600.
Waller, M. J., Zellmer-Bruhn, M. E., & Giambatista, R. C. (2002). Watching the clock: Group pacing behavior under dynamic deadlines. *Academy of Management Journal, 45*, 1046–1055.
Wegner, D. M. (1995). A computer network model of human transactive memory. *Social Cognition, 13*, 319–339.
West, M. A. (1996). Reflexivity and work group effectiveness: A conceptual integration. In: M. A. West (Ed.), *Handbook of Work Group Psychology* (pp. 555–579). Chichester: Wiley.
Zalesny, M. D., Salas, E., & Prince, C. (1995). Conceptual and measurement issues in coordination: Implications for team behavior and performance. *Research in Personnel and Human Resource Management, 13*, 81–115.

PERCEPTIONS OF TIME IN WORK GROUPS: DO MEMBERS DEVELOP SHARED COGNITIONS ABOUT THEIR TEMPORAL DEMANDS?

Caroline A. Bartel and Frances J. Milliken

ABSTRACT

Achieving temporal synchronization may require that work groups develop shared cognitions about the time-related demands they face. We investigated the extent to which group members developed shared cognitions with respect to the three temporal perceptions: time orientation (present vs. future), time compression, and time management (scheduling and time management). We argue that group members are more likely to align their perceptions to temporal characteristics of the group or organizational context (e.g. time compression, scheduling, proper time allocation) rather than to each other's individual time orientations. Survey data collected from 104 work groups are largely consistent with these expectations. The implications of shared cognitions on time for work group functioning and performance are discussed.

INTRODUCTION

More than ever, individuals in professional and managerial jobs must work faster than they did in the past. The increased pace and complexity of work

Time in Groups
Research on Managing Groups and Teams, Volume 6, 87–109
ISSN: 1534-0856/doi:10.1016/S1534-0856(03)06005-5

highlights the importance of understanding how individuals think about and manage their time. Notably, perceptions of time and time pressure are likely to shape individuals' approach to tasks (e.g. the perceived need to rush through tasks), the quality of their interactions with other organization members (e.g. the degree to which they experience frustration when others are not producing as fast as they would like) and, ultimately, the effectiveness of their work (e.g. the quantity and quality of their work). Because individuals increasingly perform their jobs as members of one or more work groups, differences between individuals in how they perceive time and time pressure may complicate work group functioning.

Recent research on time and time pressure in work groups (Ancona & Chong, 1996; Blount & Janicik, 2002; McGrath & Kelly, 1986) has emphasized the importance of temporal synchronization, a condition in which work group members agree on the rate at which group activities should occur and align the pace at which they work to complete individual and shared tasks. Temporal synchronization plays a vital role in work groups because it promotes effective coordination, a key contributor to successful task performance (Hackman, 1987; McGrath, 1984). We suggest that a work group's ability to achieve temporal synchronization and, thus, coordinated action is partly contingent on the degree to which members hold similar perceptions about time-related variables. Examples include members' perceptions of how much time pressure the group faces, how much time their particular part of the task will take, and the importance of the group's deadlines relative to other deadlines that members face for extra-group tasks or projects.

Organizational research that has cast a spotlight on the different temporal perceptions that individuals hold has generally focused on three time-related cognitions: an individual's time orientation – present or future (Waller, Conte, Gibson & Carpenter, 2001; Zimbardo & Boyd, 1999), the degree of time pressure that individuals experience in their jobs (Perlow, 1999), and the norms about time that exist in organizations (McGrath & Rotchford, 1983; Schriber & Gutek, 1987). If it is true that temporal synchronization is important to work group functioning, then it is critical that we understand the degree to which work group members agree in their perceptions of time and the time pressures they face. Such perceptions are likely to affect the probability that a work group will be able to align the pace preferences of its members and synchronize members' actions for individual and shared tasks. In other words, achieving temporal synchronization may require that work groups develops shared cognitions about the time-related demands they face. But to what extent do work groups come to develop shared cognitions in the course of their interactions? It is this question that we explore in this chapter.

We investigated the extent to which members of work groups develop shared cognitions with respect to three temporal perceptions mentioned earlier:

time orientation (present vs. future), time compression (pressures to speed up work), and time management (organizational norms about time allocation). We expected that work group members would demonstrate more agreement for certain temporal perceptions than for others. Specifically, we have proposed that temporal perceptions that derive mainly from ongoing differences in job roles, job demands, or personality differences would be more difficult for group members to align than temporal perceptions that are more situationally determined. That is, the extent to which group members develop shared cognitions on time will vary depending on whether the temporal perspective under consideration emerges from attributes of the person or situation. We explore this proposition with survey data collected from a diverse sample of work groups in varied organizational settings.

SHARED COGNITIONS ON TIME IN WORK GROUPS

A basic principle in work group research is that coordinated action is best accomplished when individuals align their thoughts, feelings, and behavior. The classic writings of Asch (1952) advanced this position, noting that individuals who work cooperatively acquire a shared understanding of the world that enables group performance. According to Asch (1952, p. 251)

> There are group actions that are possible only when each participant has a representation that includes the actions of others and their relations. The respective actions converge relevantly, assist and supplement each other only when the joint situation is represented in each and when the representations are structurally similar.

Contemporary group research continues to embrace this idea, noting that effective coordination requires that groups develop a shared set of expectations for the actions of individual members, for determining whether their actions fit together properly, and for detecting and resolving problems that hamper progress on achieving group goals (Arrow, McGrath & Berdahl, 2000). Such expectations evolve from patterns of interaction between leaders and members that develop, stabilize, and adapt over time. The importance of shared understandings in groups is evident in recent assessments of collective mind (Weick & Roberts, 1993), shared reality (Hardin & Higgins, 1996), strategic orientations (Levine, Higgins & Choi, 2000), and transactive memory (Moreland & Myaskovsky, 2000; Wenger, 1987).

We focus on shared cognitions on time, defined as situations in which work group members hold similar views about the temporal demands they face. Group members' views of time and time pressure are likely to converge in the course of their interactions as a result of explicit communications about time. Gevers, Rutte and van Eeerde (2004) proposed that such communications are a mechanism through which shared cognitions develop; examples include a group's goal setting, temporal planning, and temporal reflection activities. For example, Janicik and Bartel (2003) showed that discussions of temporal issues, although a seemingly simple step in the initial planning process, can have lasting effects on how group members interact to accomplish their tasks. An implication of this study is that such discussions contributed to the formation of shared views that being aware of time and adhering to deadlines and schedules are important, which minimized coordination difficulties and promoted high quality group outcomes. When work groups ignore temporal aspects of the task, members may hold inconsistent expectations and preferences about time that potentially create coordination problems as their work gets underway.

Our position is that shared cognitions on time are generally beneficial in work groups. Groups in which members think about time in similar ways are in a strong position to plan how they will use their time on tasks and to coordinate their task activities (see Gevers et al., 2004). That is, work groups that develop shared cognitions on time should be best able to achieve temporal synchronization. We therefore suspect that shared cognitions on time are most important in work groups that face intense coordination demands associated with complex, interdependent tasks requiring a specific output (e.g. product, plans, decisions) by some deadline. This is due to the influence of shared cognitions on time on coordinated action.

Three Varieties of Shared Cognitions on Time

Researchers have conceptualized time and its effects on work in many different ways. We focus on three different temporal perceptions that organizational research has emphasized. These include individuals' *time orientations* (future or present), perceptions on *time compression*, and *time management*. We view these temporal perceptions as the basis of different shared cognitions on time that may exist in work groups.

Each of these temporal perceptions varies in the degree to which it derives from individual differences and situational factors. As illustrated in Fig. 1, we can array these temporal perceptions on a continuum, with one end representing perceptions of time that are shaped mostly by individual differences and the other end reflecting perceptions of time that are thought to emerge mainly from the influence of a given social context. As we describe below, the implication is that temporal perceptions arising more from individual differences and

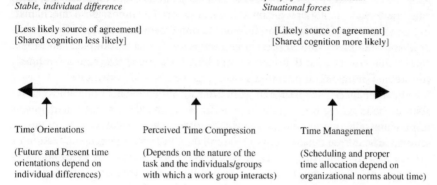

Property of the Person:
Stable, individual difference

[Less likely source of agreement]
[Shared cognition less likely]

Property of the Work Context:
Situational forces

[Likely source of agreement]
[Shared cognition more likely]

Time Orientations

(Future and Present time
orientations depend on
individual differences)

Perceived Time Compression

(Depends on the nature of the
task and the individuals/groups
with which a work group interacts)

Time Management

(Scheduling and proper
time allocation depend on
organizational norms about time)

Fig. 1.   Potential Sources of Shared Cognitions on Time in Work Groups.

less from contextual factors are likely to yield more variance among work group members.

Time Orientations

Many researchers have studied individuals' orientations towards time as if these views about time were relatively stable attributes of individuals (Mainemelis, 2001; Waller et al., 2001; Zimbardo & Boyd, 1999). The early work of Kurt Lewin (1951) proposed that a person's temporal perspective represents "the totality of the individual's views of his psychological future and psychological past existing at a given time" (p. 75). Guided by Lewin's initial thinking, Zimbardo and Boyd (1999) proposed that people tend to possess a temporal perspective that is oriented primarily towards past events, present desires, or future anticipated outcomes. These time orientations are cognitive frames that people use to interpret experienced events, and thus help give order, coherence and meaning to their personal and social experiences. Moreover, Zimbardo and Boyd (1999) argued that a person's time orientation provides the foundation on which he or she formulates expectations and goals, determines appropriate levels of risk taking, and generates judgments, decisions, and actions.

We focus on Zimbardo and Boyd's conceptualizations of present and future time orientations. According to these researchers, people with a present orientation are thought to possess a pleasure-seeking, risk-taking attitude toward time and life and to be more concerned with present enjoyment than with future consequences. Such individuals may tend to dedicate minimal energy to planning for the future, may be inclined to take substantial risks and to act impulsively, and may pay little attention to the passage of time. In contrast, people with a future time orientation emphasize planning for and achievement of future career objectives, even at the cost of present enjoyment. Such individuals are often highly organized, which may be due, in part, to feeling a need to use time carefully to accomplish tasks and attain their goals. Zimbardo and Boyd viewed present and future time orientations as dispositional characteristics, but note that larger social and institutional forces (e.g. cultural, educational, religious, and familial) also shape people's views on time.

In their recent article on time in work groups, Waller and her colleagues (2001) also focused on time orientation as an individual-difference variable that shapes perceptions of deadlines and subsequent deadline-driven behavior in work group settings. These researchers adopted Zimbardo and Boyd's conceptualization of time orientation, focusing on the role of present and future time orientations in work groups. Waller and colleagues argued that group members with a present orientation may be motivated more by immediate, rather than future, deadlines and are unlikely to see a strong need for long-range strategic planning. In contrast, group members with a future time orientation are likely to be highly goal-oriented, to consider future consequences, and to engage in long-range planning. They also are likely to be motivated to expend considerable effort today to meet future deadlines.

To the extent that future and present time orientations are relatively stable attributes of people across time and situations, then it is unlikely that members would be able to develop a shared view on time specifying the time orientation that the group as a whole will take. That is, group members may find it difficult to align their different time orientations given that they are predisposed to view and react to time differently. Because time orientations are more a property of the person than of the immediate social or task context, we propose that work groups will be characterized by persistent differences in how their members think about and value time.

Perceived Time Compression
Another perspective on time concerns the extent of perceived demands by outside parties (e.g. customers, supervisors) for timely or speedy delivery of products or services. Increasingly, work groups face pressures to deliver high quality outcomes at faster rates (Gleick, 1999; Perlow, 1999). Researchers who study time compression or "time famine" (Perlow, 1999) contend that this perception derives in large part from an individual's work context. Thus, the expectation is that individuals located in the same work context should perceive similar degrees of time compression as they are exposed to the same contextual cues. In comparison to individuals' time orientations, perceived time compression is likely to be less a property of the individual and more a property of the social or task context. When people perceive that their work context places a premium on speed of delivery, they often feel as though they are working in a state of perpetual crisis (Perlow, 1999).

Although we have emphasized contextual forces in shaping perceptions of time compression, it is also possible that personal factors are influential as well. Three factors appear especially relevant: aspiration level, perceived ability, and time orientation. First, level of aspiration refers to the level of future performance a person explicitly seeks to attain for a given task or goal. Individuals with higher aspiration levels are likely to feel that they need to accomplish more difficult and challenging goals than colleagues with lower aspiration levels. Such individuals are likely to perceive the need to do more and higher quality work relative to others (with lower aspiration levels), which could make issues of time highly salient. That is, high aspirations levels create perceptions of time compression as people feel the need to accomplish relatively more within a given time frame.

Second, a person's perceived ability to accomplish one's goals is also influential. Individuals who see themselves as highly capable are likely to believe that they can accomplish their goals easier and faster than less competent colleagues, which may make them less sensitive to time. Notably, speed-ups that occur at work may be less salient to such individuals, thereby minimizing perceptions of time compression.

Lastly, an individual's perception of time compression may be related to their time orientation. Individuals with a future orientation (Zimbardo & Boyd, 1999) may be highly sensitive to external time pressure, given tendencies to consider future consequences and to engage in long-range planning.

These considerations suggest that perceived time compression is a product of both individual and contextual factors, as shown in Fig. 1. To the extent that perceived time compression is contextually determined in part, then group members who operate in the same work environment should hold similar views about the need to accomplish a given task in less time than they (or other groups performing similar tasks) had to accomplish it in the past. This implies that there may be less variation in members' perceptions of time compression than in their time orientations (future or present), thus making perceived time compression a temporal perspective for which work groups have a high likelihood of developing shared cognitions.

Perceptions about Time Management

A third type of temporal perspective concerns one's views about proper time management within their organization. Organizational research has argued that organizational prescriptions about the proper use and allocation of time can shape such perceptions (McGrath & Rotchford, 1983; Schriber & Gutek, 1987). These "temporal norms" are defining elements of an organization's culture, helping to regulate how individuals think about and use time at work (McGrath &

Rotchford, 1983; Schriber & Gutek, 1987). Such perceptions about proper time management thus derive mainly from contextual forces.

McGrath and Rotchford (1983) argued that the dominant conception of time in modern work organizations is that time is a valuable, scarce resource. This belief necessitates that organizations actively manage three temporal problems: reduction of temporal uncertainty, managing scarce temporal resources, and resolving conflicting claims on temporal resources. McGrath and Rotchford (1983) noted that organizations can address these problems by creating schedules and deadlines and by allocating time to tasks appropriately. The function of scheduling is the reduction of temporal uncertainty, which involves enhancing accurate prediction of when specific actions or events will occur. The function of time allocation is the resolution of conflicting claims on scarce temporal resources and involves distributing time in an efficient way to maximize organizational goals. Thus, norms that organizations create about schedules and deadlines and appropriate time allocation to projects can have substantial influences on organization members.

Schriber and Gutek (1987) explored different temporal perceptions present in organizations and developed an instrument to measure the presence of temporal norms that might guide individual's perceptions about time in the workplace. Temporal norms convey appropriate ways of thinking about, reacting to, and managing time in certain situations and under certain circumstances in a given organization. Schriber and Gutek uncovered two temporal norms that correspond perfectly to McGrath and Rotchford's (1983) notions of scheduling and time allocation. "Schedules and deadlines" reflect tendencies to create clear temporal boundaries and to place value on meeting deadlines, staying on schedule, and being punctual. "Time allocation" reflects the degree to which employees perceive that there is sufficient time for tasks (e.g. schedules are not too tight, tasks do not take longer than planned, and time is not a constraint to achieving goals). We see these temporal norms as contextual forces that shape individuals' perceptions of proper time management at work.

Like other social norms, we would expect that temporal norms in organizations are a powerful means of social influence, providing information about attitudes that have a high probability of being conventional and accepted (Cialdini, Reno & Kallgren, 1990). Individuals usually are aware of norms in their organization and act in accordance with them. By observing what others are doing, members can make judicious and efficient choices about how to think about and manage time at work. Thus, organization members are likely to understand and follow temporal norms even when they are not stated explicitly (Levine & Moreland, 1998). To the extent that an organization has clear norms about schedules and the allocation of time, then we would expect work group members to hold similar perceptions about proper time management. That is, we would expect less variation in these perceptions than in group members' time orientations (future or present) or in their perceptions of time compression. As Fig. 1 shows, it seems likely that perceptions of proper time management are a temporal perspective for which group members are most likely to possess shared cognitions.

In summary, our analysis above suggests that the ease with which members agree in their views about the group's temporal demands varies across the three temporal perceptions we discussed. In the case of temporal perceptions that are assumed to be stable and enduring attributes of individuals (e.g. present or future time orientation), it should be difficult for work groups to form a shared perspective. In contrast, the idea that organizational cultures may have temporal norms about proper time management creates the possibility that work groups may cultivate a shared perspective about such issues. The next section reports the results of a preliminary test of these ideas.

ASSESSING THE DEGREE TO WHICH WORK GROUPS DEVELOP SHARED COGNITIONS ON TIME

We conducted a preliminary assessment of the degree to which members of work groups possess shared cognitions with respect to three temporal perceptions. We surveyed 126 work groups (598 individuals) that perform a wide variety of tasks in assorted organizational contexts. Work groups had to meet several criteria, based on Hackman's (1990) definition of work groups, to be included in the study: clear group boundaries (i.e. it is clear who is in the group), an appropriate group size (i.e. we arbitrarily specified a range of 4–10 members), and at least moderate degrees of task interdependence.

We used data from work groups for which we received complete surveys from all members, producing a sample of 104 work groups (504 individuals, 82% response rate) representing 92 different organizational contexts. Survey respondents included roughly equal proportions of men (54%) and women (46%), who were generally 20–29 years of age, and who had worked in their organization for an average of four years.

Work groups in our sample included internet web-site designers, creative advertising teams, retail sales teams, financial analyst teams, boards of directors, strategic planning and decision making groups, engineers, management consultants, firefighters, television news teams, and athletic groups. All groups interacted on a task and social basis regularly and generally completed their work in close proximity to each other, usually face-to face. There were no work groups in our sample where members worked remotely.

Temporal Perspective Measures

We distributed surveys to individual group members who responded to questions corresponding to each of the temporal perceptions of interest.

Time Orientation
We used Zimbardo and Boyd's (1999) instrument to measure individuals' time orientations, including only those items that had factor loadings greater than 0.50 and factor cross-loadings less than 0.25 (as reported in Zimbardo & Boyd, p. 1275). Five items assessed future time orientation (e.g. "meeting tomorrow's deadlines and doing other necessary work come before tonight's play") (Cronbach's $\alpha = 0.71$); six items assessed present time orientation ("I make decisions on the spur of the moment") (Cronbach's $\alpha = 0.82$). This is a measure of individual differences, thus the referent for the scale items was "I."

Time Compression
We measured perceived time compression with three items adapted from a measure of work group efficiency created by Denison, Hart and Kahn (1996) (e.g. "To what extent do people outside your group expect your group to cut the amount of time it takes to accomplish its work?") (Cronbach's $\alpha = 0.77$). This is a measure of the extent to which members perceive that outside parties (e.g. customers, supervisors) are pressuring the group for timely or speedy delivery of products or services. Accordingly, the referent for the items was the group.

Time Management
We used items from Schriber and Gutek's (1987) temporal norms instrument to measure perceptions on proper time management. We assessed scheduling with four items (e.g. "Staying on schedule is important in this organization") (Cronbach's $\alpha = 0.75$) and time allocation with three items (e.g. "We never seem to have enough time to get everything done in this organization") (Cronbach's $\alpha = 0.70$). This is a measure of perceptions of time management in work groups' larger organizational context, thus the organization was the referent for the scale items. Respondents used various 7-point response scales for survey items representing the different temporal perceptions.

Evidence of Shared Cognitions on Time

We used four complementary measures of within-group agreement to determine the degree of congruence in group members' time perceptions. First, significant

F values resulting from a one-way ANOVA (in which group membership served as the independent variable and the study scales as the dependent variables) represents nonindependence among observations due to group membership (Kenny & Judd, 1986). Then we computed two forms of the intraclass correlation coefficient, referred to as ICC(1) and ICC(2) (Bartko, 1976; Bliese, 2000; James, 1982), to assess between group variability by comparing between group variance to the total variance across work groups. Both coefficients provided an omnibus index of homogeneity and were calculated from a one-way random effects ANOVA where the variable of interest is the dependent variable and the group membership is the independent variable. ICC(1) is a form of proportional consistency and can be interpreted as the proportion of total variance that is explained by group membership. ICC(1) was computed as (Bartko, 1976)

$$ICC(1) = \frac{MSB - MSW}{MSB + [(k1) \times MSW]}$$

where MSB is between-group mean square, MSW is within-group mean square, and k is average group size. ICC(1) values can range from -1 to $+1$, with values between 0.05 and 0.30 being most typical (Bliese, 2000).

Whereas ICC(1) provided an estimate of the reliability of a single assessment (individual group member rating) of the group mean, the second intraclass coefficient, ICC(2), provided an overall estimate of the reliability of group means. The ICC(2) was computed as

$$ICC(2) = \frac{MSB - MSW}{MSB}$$

The closer ICC(2) is to 1.00, the more work groups can be reliably distinguished in terms of individual members' perceptions on the variable of interest. Generally, values equal to or above 0.70 are acceptable, values between 0.50 and 0.70 are marginal, and values below 0.50 are poor (Klein et al., 2000; Ostroff, 1992).

Lastly, we calculated a measure of within-group agreement, $r_{wg(J)}$, for each work group in our sample (James, Demaree & Wolfe, 1984). This procedure compared observed within-group variability to within-group expected variability and was calculated as (James et al., 1984):

$$r_{wg(J)} = \frac{J[1 - (s_{xj}^2/\sigma_{EU}^2)]}{J[1 - (s_{xj}^2/\sigma_{EU}^2)] + (s_{xj}^2/\sigma_{EU}^2)}$$

where $r_{wg(J)}$ is the within-group interrater agreement for group members' mean scores based on J items, s_{xj}^2 is the mean of the observed variances on the J items, and σ_{EU}^2 is the variance on the items if all judgments were due exclusively to random measurement error. Groups that scored above a predetermined threshold (typically 0.70) provided evidence of having developed a socially-shared cognition about some aspect of their experience (James et al., 1984; West & Anderson, 1996).

Table 1 reports our findings for each measure of within-group agreement. All temporal perceptions produced a significant F-test ($p < 0.001$), indicating that variance in respondents' reports was greater between members of different work groups than among members of the same group.

Turning to the intraclass coefficients, ICC(1) values ranged from 0.09 to 0.32. Values for time orientations (present and future) were low in comparison to time compression and time management (scheduling and time allocation), which had relatively higher values. Our findings for ICC(2) exhibited a similar pattern. Values for time orientations fell far below the low 0.50 criterion to be considered marginal, which suggests that work groups could not be reliably distinguished by individual members' responses. ICC(2) values for time compression (0.61) and time allocation (0.64) were marginal, and scheduling yielded an acceptable value (0.73). Finally, we calculated interrater agreement for each temporal perspective (James et al., 1984). As Table 1 shows, work groups exhibited a high level of interrater agreement for each temporal perspective measure, with median $r_{wg(J)}$ values ranging from 0.89 to 0.93.

Interpretation of Results

Different procedures used to justify group-level constructs can yield different conclusions, as is the case here. We found substantial agreement within each work group, as indicated by $r_{wg(J)}$, but different degrees of between-group variability as indicated by ICC(1) and ICC(2). If we had used $r_{wg(J)}$ alone, we would have concluded that our work groups had developed shared cognitions on time for each of the temporal perceptions we studied. The different pattern of results across procedures stems mainly from how random variance is defined, either in terms of an expected random distribution within a group or in terms of total (within and between group) variance. Therefore, the four procedures must be considered together.

The pattern of results for present and future time orientations provides weak evidence that members had developed shared cognitions. We found substantial agreement in group members' assessments about the degree to which they possess present and future time orientations, but these responses yielded low intraclass coefficients, suggesting that work groups could not be reliably distinguished from each other in terms of members' responses. The implication is that the individuals in our sample had similar time orientations. Even though individuals made assessments of their own unique perceptions about time, such assessments were generally similar within work groups and across work groups from different

Table 1. Aggregation Statistics, Descriptive Statistics, and Correlations[a] for all Temporal Perceptions.

	F	ICC(1)	ICC(2)	Median $r_{wg(J)}$	Individual Mean[b]	Work Group Mean[c]	1	2	3	4	5
1. Present time orientation	1.49*	0.09	0.33	0.92	4.05 (1.18)	—[d]	—	0.05	0.00	0.02	-0.05
2. Future time orientation	1.61**	0.11	0.38	0.93	4.95 (1.00)	—[d]	—	—	0.16**	0.20**	0.00
3. Time compression	2.58**	0.25	0.61	0.90	4.12 (1.42)	4.16 (0.93)	—	—	—	0.19**	-0.22**
4. Time management: Scheduling	3.29**	0.32	0.73	0.89	5.46 (1.13)	5.45 (0.80)	—	—	0.17	—	0.06
5. Time management: Proper time allocation	2.69**	0.26	0.64	0.92	4.31 (1.29)	4.27 (0.87)	—	—	-0.35**	0.09	—

[a] Correlations above the diagonal are at the individual-level, correlations below the diagonal are at the group-level.
[b] Standard deviations appear in parentheses, $N = 504$ individuals.
[c] Standard deviations appear in parentheses, $N = 104$ work groups.
[d] Insufficient evidence to justify aggregation of group members' responses.
* $p < 0.01$.
** $p < 0.001$.

organizations. We found that the individuals ($n = 504$) reported being more future oriented ($M = 4.05$, S.D. 1.00) than present oriented ($M = 4.04$, S.D. 1.18). It is also worth noting that future and present time orientations were not significantly correlated ($r = 0.05$, $p > 0.05$, $N = 504$), suggesting that these time orientations are best viewed as separate temporal perceptions (consistent with Zimbardo & Boyd, 1999) rather than opposite poles of a single perspective (Waller et al., 2001).

One interpretation of the lack of between-group variability is that a selection effect is operating: people who are attracted to working in the business world tend to be high on future orientation. Also, the organizational level and occupational title held by most people in our sample are obvious sources of homogeneity that may affect their degree of future orientation. To the extent that future orientation measures achievement orientation, our sample, thus, is likely to be at the upper end of the range on achievement orientation.

The pattern of results for time compression provides modest evidence that shared cognitions existed. Members within work groups exhibited high agreement in their assessments of the degree to which their group faces time pressures imposed by other individuals or groups with whom they interact. Moreover, the intraclass coefficients indicate that members' responses were moderately useful in differentiating the groups in our sample, suggesting that work groups across different organizational contexts differed in their perceptions of time compression. Aggregating group members' responses, we find that work groups ($N = 104$) reported moderate levels of time compression ($M = 4.16$, S.D. $= 0.93$). We had argued that perceived time compression is the result of both individual differences and situational forces, and therefore, that group members are more likely to develop a shared cognition about the time pressures they face than about time orientation. Our results provide initial support for this argument.

With respect to perceptions of time management, we found a different pattern of results for scheduling and time allocation. We had expected that work groups would be most likely to develop shared cognitions on time for these perceptions because their origins were thought to lie mainly in the organization's norms about time management (Schriber & Gutek, 1987). We found supportive evidence for this prediction with regard to the scheduling component of time management. The results strongly suggest that scheduling demonstrated group-level properties, indicating that work groups possessed a shared view about the need to create clear temporal boundaries and the value of meeting deadlines, staying on schedule, and being punctual. Moreover, work groups across organizational settings differed in their perceptions about the degree to which their organization has norms about creating schedules and deadlines. Aggregating group members' responses, we find that work groups reported that scheduling was central to their work ($M = 5.45$, S.D. $= 0.80$).

In contrast, we found only modest evidence of a shared view with respect to proper time allocation. This refers to perceptions that there is sufficient time for tasks; that schedules are not too tight, tasks do not take longer than planned, and time is not a constraint to achieving goals. Members within work groups exhibited high agreement in their responses about the degree to which their organization tends to allocate sufficient time for tasks. These responses were moderately useful in differentiating the groups in our sample, indicating that the different organizations in our sample held some similarities in their norms about time allocation.

Results Summary

In predicting the probability that shared cognitions on time would exist, we argued that work group members were more likely to align their perceptions to temporal characteristics of the group or organizational context (McGrath & Rotchford, 1983; Schriber & Gutek, 1987) rather than to each other's individual time orientations (Waller et al., 2001; Zimbardo & Boyd, 1999). Our results are largely consistent with these expectations. We expected to find agreement among group members with regard to perceptions that outside parties (e.g. customers, supervisors) were pressuring them for timely or speedy delivery of a product or service time, as well as perceptions about organizational norms about time (e.g. emphasis on schedules and deadlines and allocating sufficient time for tasks). Consistent with this expectation, we found that the emergence of shared cognitions on time is most prevalent for temporal perceptions that are partly due to situational factors (e.g. time compression, scheduling, proper time allocation).

However, the finding that work groups' responses did not vary substantially across our sample for most temporal perceptions (e.g. time orientations, time compression, proper time allocation) suggests that groups working in organizational contexts might view certain temporal issues similarly as a result of situational factors common across work groups within organizations or across organizations. For example, most organizations face increased competition from rival organizations, which may require people to develop short-term and long-term competitive goals and strategies. Such forces may have promoted greater homogeneity in time orientations among the professional and managerial employees in our sample than in the sample of undergraduate students that Zimbardo and Boyd (1999) surveyed. This may partly explain why we observed more similarities in work groups' temporal perceptions than we had originally expected.

DISCUSSION

Our objective in this exploratory study was to assess the degree to which members of work groups shared similar perceptions of time-related issues. We discovered that the degree of alignment in group members' perceptions was partly contingent on whether a given temporal perception is caused more by attributes of the person or the situation.

For example, individuals' time orientations (present or future) may be hard to align because they are enduring cognitive frames that are not highly salient to people on an everyday basis. We suspect that the time orientations of group members (present vs. future) are more likely to be determined by individual differences than by group or work-related variables. Nonetheless, members' time orientations are likely to have subtle yet pervasive effects on the group, operating as filters through which members perceive and enact their tasks. Differences in orientations towards time, like other types of individual or cultural differences, are unlikely to be noticed and discussed but, rather, operate as part of the backdrop for group functioning.

In contrast, group members are more likely to develop similar perceptions of time pressure and schedules because these views partly derive from features of the task or work environment. Such contextual influences affect all group members as a regular part of their life in the group. Consistent with the argument advanced by Gevers and colleagues in this volume, we suspect that contextual influences promote shared temporal views because they affect the nature of work group discussions. Group research has consistently shown that group members tend to share common information that is known or available to all members in discussions rather than unique information that they alone possess (Stasser & Stewart, 1992). When most group members are exposed to or are aware of certain contextual influences, such as pressures from customers to speed up delivery of services, it may infuse the group with information that may assist the development of an agreed upon set of views about its temporal demands. In this regard, our research serves as an important building block for thinking about how shared cognitions on time develop in work groups.

Moving Ahead: Directions for Future Research

We see several fruitful paths for future research on work groups' temporal perceptions. First, we focused on three temporal perceptions that are likely to be relevant for group-based work, but certainly there are others. For example, individuals may differ in their preferences for how work is paced (Blount & Janicik, 2002) – some individuals may prefer to work at a steady speed all throughout a project's lifespan while others prefer to work very little early in the project's lifespan and then work very hard as the deadline approaches. People who prefer a steady pace may have a very hard time working with people who like the adrenaline flow created by time pressure. We encourage organizational research to explore other types of temporal perceptions that are relevant for work groups; perceptions that have implications for temporal synchronization and performance seem most critical.

A second path for future research concerns the properties of work groups that make it more or less possible for members to converge in their temporal perceptions. For example, we highlighted the potential role of work group discussions in promoting shared cognitions on time, suggesting that patterns of member participation in group activities may be worthy of exploration. When widespread participation exists, it can expose similarities and differences in members' temporal perceptions either explicitly (through actual statements or assertions made by members themselves) or implicitly (through inferences members make about others). When members are inclined to share, rather than censor, their ideas, opinions, or perceptions about time, then the potential for convergence is enhanced. When members participate sporadically, there are fewer opportunities for a group to exert influence on members' perceptions and for members to gather information about other's perceptions and adjust their own views accordingly.

It is therefore worthwhile to assess that myriad factors that shape the participation levels of group members, including the number and complexity of other work and non-work responsibilities, members' motivation to engage in the task, and the group's efforts to include or exclude members from being involved. For example, an important implication of the increased pace and complexity of work may be a decrease in members' ability to fully participate in their work groups. For example, many professional and managerial employees now work in several project groups simultaneously. This fact may reduce individuals' engagement with the members of any particular work group given the competing demands on their time. In addition, the effect of having to produce products or services faster means that people are likely to spend less time together producing the product or service. Thus, the combination of multiple engagements and limited contact may reduce the probability that shared cognitions emerge in work groups.

We also recognize that external forces often lead groups to take immediate action without much discussion beforehand. Although we view shared cognitions on time as a precursor to temporal synchronization, we acknowledge that convergence in members' temporal perceptions may also emerge after group members take initial action. Attribution theories have long argued that individuals come to know their own thoughts and feelings by inferring them from their own overt behavior. Hence, structuring group tasks in response to external temporal cues can promote common temporal perceptions to the extent that members

Table 2. Type and Degree of Expected Variance in Temporal Perceptions with
Different Contributing Factors.

	Contributing Factors to a Given Temporal Perception			
	Individual Differences	Work Group Factors	Organizational Factors	Industry Factors
Degree of expected variance in temporal perception				
Variance within work groups	High	Low	Low	Low
Variance between work groups within an organization	High	High	Low	Low
Variance between work groups across organizations	High	High	High	Low

make inferences about their attitudinal states based on their actions. Thus, shared cognitions on time and temporal synchronization will likely co-occur, but causality may not be unidirectional. Rather, we see these work group properties as mutually influencing each other over time. Ultimately this is a question for future research.

Another future research opportunity might include specifying in more detail the likely sources of difference or similarity in group members' temporal perceptions. Our finding that work groups from 92 different organizational contexts exhibited modest between-group variance in perceived time compression and in perceived organizational norms about proper time allocation suggests that more "macro" aspects of an organization's environment, such as globalization and competitive pressures, may influence some temporal perceptions. This surprising degree of similarity across work groups and across organizations suggests that more work is needed to identify the origins of different temporal perceptions.

Table 2 outlines our expectations for the type and degree of variance that we would expect when a given temporal perspective originates mainly from individual differences; or work group, organization or industry factors. In this chapter, we examined the degree of variance among members of a given work group and among work groups from different organizations, but research could also examine variance among work groups within the same organization. For example, temporal perceptions that stem mainly from individuals' predispositions are likely to yield considerable variance among work group members, as well as between work groups within an organization and across work groups from different organizations. The amount of within-group variance and between-group variance though is likely to be similar when individual differences are the main driver of perceptual differences.

In contrast, temporal perceptions that emanate from members' functional responsibilities in an organization are likely to show a different type of pattern.

If a work group comprises members from a single functional area, we would expect high levels of agreement among members of a group. On the other hand, for cross-functional work groups we would expect lower levels of agreement within groups. Further, if we assessed several cross-functional work groups within a given organization, we might find that the between group variance is relatively small compared to the within group variance. Finally, for temporal perceptions that are tied to some variable in the industry environment, then we would expect little variance between individuals within a work group as well as little variance across groups in an organization or even across organizational contexts. Ultimately these are issues for future research.

Implications for Work Group Performance

We view our findings as a first step in what could be a promising stream of research on how shared cognitions on time affect work group coordination and performance. Having provided suggestive evidence that work group members can hold common views about certain temporal issues, further research could examine how the presence or absence of different shared cognitions differentially affect temporal synchronization and task performance.

We suggest that differing temporal perceptions among group members can be conceptualized as a form of diversity in work groups. The potential problems that might emerge when there are large differences in temporal perceptions among group members include higher levels of conflict (Jehn, Chadwick & Thatcher, 1997; Jehn, Northcraft & Neale, 1999) and lower levels of cohesiveness (Jackson, Brett, Sessa, Cooper, Julin & Peyronnin, 1991). The work group may become divided as members are drawn to others with similar perceptions of time and away from those members whom they believe to value and manage time differently. Such fragmentation may lead to negative stereotypes and distrust of other members that, in turn, could reduce cooperation and coordination. For example, research on differences in individuals' pacing preferences (Blount & Janicik, 2002) suggests that fast-paced people may become frustrated with slower-paced people because they perceive the slower-paced people as holding up their ability to accomplish their tasks. Groups caught in such situations therefore might need to actively manage this diversity to achieve temporal synchronization and perform well.

Notwithstanding the potential disadvantages of temporal diversity, it is possible that differences in members' time perceptions may be beneficial under certain circumstances. Thus, we suggest that the presence or absence of shared cognitions on time is not universally beneficial or harmful to work group functioning.

Future research therefore is needed to explore the circumstances under which temporal differences matter. For example, diversity in members' time orientations may prove useful for work groups that must consider short-term and long-term performance issues simultaneously. It may allow for a more complete analysis of alternative ways of approaching a task as members focus on different goals (short-term vs. long-term) and different ways of completing and ordering sub-tasks (sequential vs. simultaneous, evenly distributed over time vs. skewed). Alternatively, diversity in members' perceptions of time compression may be functional in work groups engaged in tasks requiring creativity, as time pressure is thought to interfere with the performance of creative work. When only a few members are concerned about a looming deadline, the majority of members are able to function without a sense of imminent external pressure.

Moreover, different forms of temporal diversity might differentially affect group coordination and performance. For example, diversity in terms of time compression may affect coordination less than diversity associated with proper time management through scheduling. Differences in perceived time compression may interfere little with a group's ability to actively scan and assess task requirements, negotiate a division of labor so that members have agreed upon roles, and decide how and when task related inputs and outputs may be integrated. In contrast, differences in members' beliefs about the need to create clear temporal boundaries and to honor deadlines and schedules may create coordination costs for groups in terms of creating appropriate task strategies and executing them successfully. Such differences may lead to problems in setting and meeting deadlines, staying on schedule, prioritizing activities, and estimating the amount of time required for various task activities. We encourage researchers to tease apart the differential effects that diversity in different temporal perceptions might have on work group functioning.

Concluding Remark

In closing, in this chapter we reported on a research project in which we explored the question of whether members of work groups exhibit congruence in their temporal perceptions. We assessed three types of time-related perceptions that appear relevant to a work group's ability to achieve temporal synchronization. Our intent was to place the idea of shared cognitions on time under a theoretical and empirical microscope to reveal the degree to which group members converge in their temporal perceptions and for which types of perceptions. Our analysis suggests that shared cognitions in work groups take different forms and that there are some commonalities in individuals' temporal perceptions that span group and organization boundaries. We hope the current results spark additional interest in shared cognitions on time and the differential effects that various temporal perceptions might have on group processes and outcomes.

REFERENCES

Ancona, D., & Chong, C. L. (1996). Entrainment: Pace, cycle, and rhythm in organizational behavior. In: B. M. Staw & L. L. Cummings (Eds), *Research in Organizational Behavior* (Vol. 18, pp. 251–284). Greenwich, CT: JAI Press.

Arrow, H., McGrath, J. E., & Berdahl, J. L. (2000). *Small groups as complex systems: Formation, coordination, development and adaptation.* Thousand Oaks, CA: Sage.

Asch, S. E. (1952). *Social psychology.* Englewood Cliffs, NJ: Prentice-Hall.

Bartko, J. J. (1976). On various intraclass correlation reliability coefficients. *Psychological Bulletin, 83*, 762–765.

Bliese, P. D. (2000). Within-group agreement, non-independence, and reliability: Implications for data aggregation and analysis. In: K. J. Klein & S. W. J. Kozlowski (Eds), *Multilevel Theory, Research, and Methods in Organizations* (pp. 349–381). San Francisco: Jossey-Bass.

Blount, S., & Janicik, G. (2002). Getting and staying in-pace: The "in-synch" preference and its implications for work groups. In: E. A. Mannix, M. A. Neale & H. Sondak (Eds), *Research on Managing Groups and Teams: Vol. 4. Toward Phenomenology of Groups and Group Membership* (pp. 235–266). Greenwich, CT: JAI Elsevier.

Cialdini, R. B., Reno, R. R., & Kallgren, C. A. (1990). A focus theory of normative conduct: Recycling the concept of norms to reduce littering in public places. *Journal of Personality and Social Psychology, 58*, 1015–1026.

Denison, D. R., Hart, S. L., & Kahn, J. A. (1996). From chimneys to cross functional teams: Developing and validating a diagnostic model. *Academy of Management Journal, 39*, 1005–1023.

Gevers, J. M. P., Rutte, C. G., & van Eerde, W. (2004). How work groups achieve coordinated action: A model of shared cognition on time. In: M. Neale, E. Mannix & S. Blount (Eds), *Research on Managing Groups and Teams* (Vol. 6). Greenwich, CT: JAI Press.

Gleick, J. (1999). *Faster: The acceleration of just about everything.* New York: Pantheon Books.

Hackman, J. R. (1987). The design of work teams. In: J. W. Lorsch (Ed.), *Handbook of Organizational Behavior* (pp. 315–341). Englewood Cliffs, NJ: Prentice-Hall.

Hackman, J. R. (1990). Work teams in organizations: An orienting framework. In: J. R. Hackman (Ed.), *Groups that Work (and Those That Don't): Creating Conditions for Effective Teamwork* (pp. 1–14). San Francisco, CA: Jossey-Bass.

Hardin, C. D., & Higgins, E. Tory (1996). Shared reality: How social verification makes the subjective objective. In: R. M. Sorrentino & E. T. Higgins (Eds), *Handbook of Motivation and Cognition* (Vol. 3, pp. 28–84). New York: Guildford.

Jackson, S. E., Brett, J. F., Sessa, V. I., Cooper, D. M., Julin, J. A., & Peyronnin, K. (1991). Some differences make a difference: Individual dissimilarity and group heterogeneity as correlates of recruitment, promotions, and turnover. *Journal of Applied Psychology, 76*, 675–689.

James, L. R. (1982). Aggregation bias in estimates of perceptual agreement. *Journal of Applied Psychology, 67*, 219–229.

James, L. R., Demaree, R. G., & Wolf, G. (1984). Estimating within-group interrater reliability with and without response bias. *Journal of Applied Psychology, 69*, 85–98.

Janicik, G., & Bartel, C. A. (2003). Talking about time: Effects of temporal planning and time urgent norms on group coordination and performance. *Group Dynamics: Theory, Research and Practice* (forthcoming).

Jehn, K. A., Chadwick, C., & Thatcher, S. M. (1997). To agree or not to agree: The effects of value congruence, individual demographic dissimilarity, and conflict on workgroup outcomes. *International Journal of Conflict Management, 8*, 287–305.

Jehn, K. A., Northcraft, G. B., & Neale, M. A. (1999). Why differences make a difference: A field study of diversity, conflict, and performance in workgroups. *Administrative Science Quarterly, 44*, 741–763.

Kenny, D. A., & Judd, C. M. (1986). Consequences of violating the independence assumption in analysis of variance. *Psychological Bulletin, 99*, 422–431.

Klein, K. J., Bleise, P. D., Kozlowski, S. W. J., Dansereau, F., Gavin, M. B., Griffin, M. A., Hofmann, D. A., James, L. R., Yammarino, F. J., & Bligh, M. C. (2000). Multilevel analytical techniques: Commonalities, differences, and continuing questions. In: K. J. Klein & S. W. J. Kozlowski (Eds), *Multilevel Theory, Research, and Methods in Organizations* (pp. 512–553). San Francisco: Jossey-Bass.

Levine, J. M., Higgins, E. T., & Choi, H. S. (2000). Development of strategic norms in groups. *Organizational Behavior and Human Decision Processes, 82*, 88–101.

Levine, J. M., & Moreland, R. L. (1998). Small groups. In: D. T. Gilbert, S. T. Fiske & G. Lindzey (Eds), *The Handbook of Social Psychology* (4th ed., pp. 415–469). New York: McGraw-Hill.

Lewin, K. (1951). *Field theory in the social sciences: Selected theoretical papers*. New York: Harper.

Mainemelis, C. (2001). When the muse takes it all: A model for the experience of timelessness in organizations. *Academy of Management Review, 26*, 548–565.

McGrath, J. E. (1984). *Groups: Interaction and performance*. Englewood Cliffs, NJ: Prentice-Hall.

McGrath, J. E., & Kelly, J. R. (1986). *Time and human interaction: Toward a social psychology of time*. New York: Guilford.

McGrath, J. E., & Rotchford, N. L. (1983). Time and behavior in organizations. In: L. L. Cummings & B. M. Staw (Eds), *Research in Organizational Behavior* (Vol. 5, pp. 57–101). Greenwich, CT: JAI Press.

Moreland, R. L., & Myaskovsky, L. (2000). Exploring the performance benefits of group training: Transactive memory or improved communication? *Organizational Behavior and Human Decision Processes, 82*, 117–133.

Ostroff, C. (1992). The relationship between satisfaction, attitudes, and performance: An organizational-level analysis. *Journal of Applied Psychology, 77*, 963–974.

Perlow, L. A. (1999). The time famine: Toward a sociology of work time. *Administrative Science Quarterly, 44*, 57–81.

Schriber, J. B., & Gutek, B. A. (1987). Some time dimensions of work: Measurement of an underlying aspect of organizational culture. *Journal of Applied Psychology, 72*, 642–650.

Stasser, G., & Stewart, D. (1992). The discovery of hidden profiles by decision-making groups: Solving a problem vs. making a judgment. *Journal of Personality and Social Psychology, 63*, 426–434.

Waller, M. J., Conte, J. M., Gibson, C. B., & Carpenter, M. A. (2001). The effect of individual perceptions of deadlines on team performance. *Academy of Management Review, 26*, 586–600.

Weick, K. E., & Roberts, K. H. (1993). Collective mind in organizations: Heedful interrelating on flight decks. *Administrative Science Quarterly, 38*, 357–381.

Wenger, D. M. (1987). Transactive memory: A contemporary analysis of the group mind. In: B. Mullen & G. R. Goethals (Eds), *Theories of Group Behavior* (pp. 185–205). New York: Springer-Verlag.

West, M. A., & Anderson, N. R. (1996). Innovation in top management teams. *Journal of Applied Psychology, 81*, 680–693.

Zimbardo, P. G., & Boyd, J. N. (1999). Putting time in perspective: A valid, reliable individual-difference metric. *Journal of Personality and Social Psychology, 77*, 1271–1288.

THE ROLE OF STATUS DIFFERENTIALS IN GROUP SYNCHRONIZATION

Ya-Ru Chen, Sally Blount and Jeffrey Sanchez-Burks

ABSTRACT

Drawing from findings in sociology and anthropology on time as a symbol of status, this paper examines the role that status differentials affect how group members internally align the pace of their activities over time (group synchronization). We examine the psychological process of group synchronization from the perspective of the individual, the nature of status differentials in work groups, and how one's status within a group affects a person's willingness to adjust the timing of his/her activities to match other people's timing. We then identify three types of status structures within work groups and analyze how each affects the group's ability to synchronize. We close by considering the implications of our approach for better understanding temporal dynamics in work groups.

INTRODUCTION

The control of time is a human symbol of status (Gell, 1992; Hall, 1983; Levine, 1997; Zerubavel, 1981). Across all known cultures, the control of calendars and schedules resides with the wealthy, political, and/or religious elite. Elite-controlled calendars identify feast days, harvest times, and rites of passage within individuals' lives. In more economically developed societies, they also

Time in Groups
Research on Managing Groups and Teams, Volume 6, 111–133
Copyright © 2004 by Elsevier Ltd.
ISSN: 1534-0856/doi:10.1016/S1534-0856(03)06006-7

specify the nature of work weeks, national holidays, vacation schedules and
age-based driving, voting and drinking privileges. As Levine (1997) notes, with
status comes the ability to control one's own and other people's time: "There is
no greater symbol of human domination" (p. 118).

Within work organizations, too, time and status are intimately tied. Senior
managers control the temporal goals for the firm; while mid-level managers
coordinate their subordinates' schedules to adhere to them; and lower-level
employees time their behaviors accordingly (Moore, 1963; Thompson, 1967).
Even on a perceptual level, actors with high status have been found to evoke less
negative reactions than do those with low status when they miss deadlines, take
up extra conversational "air time," and arrive late to meetings (Blau, 1986; Hall,
1983; Owens & Sutton, 2001). The implication is that higher status actors are
accorded more freedom in determining how their own and other people's time is
used within work contexts. Lower status actors are not.

Further, among high-status actors, the control of time is a vehicle commonly
used to assert one's power: "The longer people wait for you, the higher your
status" (Levine, 1997). Thus, high-level executives have been observed to keep
rivals waiting on hold before taking their phone calls, tacitly compete with their
peers to be the last to arrive to a meeting or to phone into a group conference call
– all as a means of competing for more status (Owens & Sutton, 2001).

These observations point toward a central thesis of this paper: Status differentials naturally occur in human groups, affecting group temporal dynamics.
Low-status members' time tends to be less valued than high-status members' time,
and high-status members are sometimes tempted to use a group's time to assert
their authority. As a result, understanding an individual's status within a group
and the overall status structure of a group is central to understanding the temporal
dynamics that occur within it. In this chapter, we focus on the role of status
differentials in group synchronization, that is, how group members internally
align the pace of their activities over time. We argue that status differentials
are a key mechanism affecting the process of within-group synchronization –
sometimes facilitating and sometimes inhibiting it.

Specifically, we argue that status differentials facilitate synchronization when
low-status members defer to high-status members to align the pace of their activities. For example, when work group members look to their supervisor to help them
set timeframes, identify deadlines, and establish temporal work norms, group
synchronization is enabled. Status differentials inhibit synchronization when high-
status members use the group's time to assert their authority, or when the temporal
goals of the high-status members do not reflect the group's best interests. Consider
here the manager who interrupts the flow of a group meeting to satisfy his own
timing needs. Members will be inclined to align with the manager's timing in order

to appease him. In the process, however, the group may end up working at a pace that runs contrary to the temporal needs of their task (e.g. because of the manager's interruption, group members may have to stay late into the night to complete their work). As a result, both member satisfaction and task performance can suffer.

To build our formal argument about the role of status in group synchronization, we begin by examining the psychological process of group synchronization from the perspective of the individual member. We examine both the personal (intra-individual) and social factors that influence how people naturally pace their activities. Next, we review the construct of status in groups; namely, what status is and how people get it. Third, we explore how having low vs. high status within a group influences a member's time pacing preferences. Finally, we consider how different status structures within a group aggregate to affect whether the group effectively synchronizes or not.

Individual Pacing and Group Synchronization

Conceptually, the process of group synchronization can be broken into two parts: (a) the task of aligning the group's temporal performance with that of the extra-group environment, that is, timing the group's activities to meet the deadline demands of its constituents; and (b) the task of combining individual members' activities to create a synchronized group pace, that is, internally aligning group members' paces over time. Two papers in this volume examine the phenomenon of extra-group alignment. Zellmer-Bruhn, Waller and Ancona (2003) focus on how external temporal markers influence the timing of group behavior through organizational entrainment. Bluedorn and Standifer (2003) examine how groups come to understand the temporal norms and expectations present in their surrounding environment, and how these understandings shape how the group behaves.

Two other papers consider the topic of within-group temporal alignment. Bartel and Miliken (2003) examine the broad diversity in members' temporal perspectives present in ongoing work groups. As Gevers, Rutte and van de Lien (2003) observe, all groups must overcome such differences in order to achieve co-ordinated action. They propose that both non-conscious entrainment processes and more explicit group behaviors, including goal setting and temporal planning, allow groups to develop shared cognitions about time which lead to coordinated action.

Our current paper also considers the topic of within-group temporal alignment. Similar to Bartel and Miliken (2003), we start with the premise that members will exhibit individual differences in how they perceive and value time. However, rather than examining how group-level processes influence members' perceptions (e.g. Gevers et al., 2003), we focus on how status differentials implicitly influence how group members construct their own timing preferences and consequently pace out their activities in the group context.

Individual-Level Pace

To build our argument, we begin by examining how people form preferences about the timing of their activities. We propose that people assign an implicit value (or utility) to the pace or velocity of their activities over time (Chapple, 1970, 1982; Loewenstein, 1987; Loewenstein & Elster, 1992; Varey & Kahneman, 1993). People have preferences regarding how slowly or quickly they work and how slowly or quickly their social interactions proceed across time. These pacing preferences often result in temporal goal setting regarding the velocity at which particular activities occur. For example, a person may hope to complete an editing task within an hour, or wrap-up a conversation with a colleague within 15 minutes.

Our interest is group settings, where the individual's time pacing preferences correspond to how quickly or slowly the group member seeks to perform group tasks and resolve group interactions over time. So we start with the assumption that group members often having time pacing preferences and set corresponding goals (either implicitly or explicitly) regarding the realization of group outcomes and events within specified time periods (Blount & Janicik, 2002; Carver & Scheier, 1999). Thus, Jane may want her team to complete three activities during their 2:00–4:00 p.m. meeting, and may plan for the group to spend less time on the first activity and more time on the other two. If the first activity takes longer than she wanted, Jane may experience frustration because her pacing goals for the meeting are not being met.

Note that for any group task or event, a member can have preferences regarding both how much time is allocated and how hard and intensely he works across the allocated time period. This means that people's pacing goals encompass two elements: (a) the absolute amount of time (e.g. an hour, a day, or a week) allocated to the task (duration preferences); and (b) the rate at which associated activities are spaced out across the available time (intensity preferences), that is, will the person work intensely at the beginning and then "let up," or will she work a little bit each day (Blount & Janicik, 2002).

Individual-Level Factors in Pacing Preferences

A variety of factors can influence how the individual group member forms these duration and intensity goals. These include: personal traits, prior experiences, and personal extra-group demands. A person's pacing preferences, therefore, can be thought of as a composite construct, to which a number of different individual-level factors are conceived to contribute.

The duration component of personal pacing preferences will incorporate, for example, *individual trait tendencies* toward need for closure (see Webster & Kruglanski, 1994 for a review), time urgency (see Conte, Landy & Mathieu, 1995 for a review), as well as poly- vs. mono-chronicity (i.e. the desire to pursue multiple tasks at once vs. focusing on one task at a time; Hall, 1983; Slocombe & Bluedorn, 1999). The intensity aspect will be influenced by factors such as the individual's cognitive processing speed and working memory capacity (see Conway, Cowan, Bunting, Therriault & Minkoff, 2002 for a review), as well as self-regulation and impulsive tendencies (see Baumeister & Heatherton, 1996; Rastegary & Landy, 1994 for reviews). For example, a person's innate cognitive capacities can affect how easily a person maintains focus on a task involving a high cognitive workload before needing a break.

Past research demonstrates that pacing preferences for a particular task also will be influenced by a person's *prior experience*; that is, they may be the product of habit. Kelly and McGrath (1985) demonstrated this by giving individuals a set amount of time, ranging from 5 to 20 minutes, to solve anagrams. They found that as the allotted amount of time increased, rates of work speed decreased. In subsequent rounds, when time frames were changed, people continued to work at the pace they had set during their original time limit. Thus, people's pacing tendencies at solving anagrams were shaped by how much time they had spent on a similar task in the past – even if the prior timing of that activity was arbitrarily determined.

In the group setting, the individual member's preferences regarding the pacing of group activities also will be influenced by *personal extra-group demands*, that is, personal situations outside the group that require the member's time. These extra-group demands can affect both the amount of time that the individual has available to devote to group activities and the intensity with which the individual cognitively and emotionally engages in group activities. Extra-group temporal demands can include, for example: (a) job demands made by the organization beyond the group context; (b) family and other personal life demands that limit how much time the individual has available for work (see Blount & Janicik, 2001 for a review); and (c) broader social, ethnic, and cultural influences that affect how a person understands, interprets, and allocates time for work (see Hall, 1983; Levine, 1997 for reviews). The underlying issue here is the degree to which the member perceives that he or she has temporal slack. When people have low levels of temporal slack, they will have less time available for group tasks.

In sum, we use the personal pacing preferences construct to conceptualize how individual-level trait differences, past experiences, and personal extra-group demands jointly influence how members approach the pacing of group activities. Rather than detailing the vast array of individual-level factors that might affect how members perceive and value their time in group contexts, we focus our analysis on the ways in which these factors jointly influence the individual member's pacing preferences.

In-Synch Preference

In addition to having personal duration and intensity preferences for how group activities are paced out over time, there is a great deal of evidence which suggests that people have a preference for aligning pace with others. That is, they like to feel in tempo, in rhythm when interacting with other people. Chapple (1970, 1982) provided the original foundations for this idea, and multiple lines of empirical research have provided subsequent support for it. For example, research on oral synchrony has shown that individuals speaking with each other tend to fall into cyclical rhythms (see Davis, 1982 for a review). More recently, Chartrand and Bargh (1999) and Sanchez-Burks (2002) have demonstrated that people tend to subtly and unconsciously align their behaviors with those of their interaction partners. Moreover, Chartrand and Bargh's (1999) results show that people report increased levels of liking for interactions in which their behaviors are subtly mirrored compared to when they are not mirrored. Similarly, Blount and Janicik (2002) report the results of two laboratory studies which found that people prefer interactions in which they perceive that their own and other actors' pacing goals are aligned than interactions in which they are not. Moreover, partners who perceived that they were temporally aligned performed more effectively in joint decision making tasks and liked each other better than did partners who perceived that their pacing goals were not aligned.

In sum, we suggest that members enter group interactions with two types of preferences regarding the pacing of group activities. These are: (a) their personal pacing preferences; and (b) the preference to synchronize with others, to be "in-synch." The member's personal pacing preferences represent a composite construct that combines individual-level traits, past experiences, and extra-group temporal demands to determine how long and how fast the member wants to work on group tasks and participate in group interactions. The in-synch construct, as we have suggested, represents a universal human tendency to prefer that those around us interact at a pace that matches our own.

Group-Level Pace

In discussing the implications of individual preferences for group-level dynamics, we begin with the observation that groups often have a natural pace or rhythm to their activities (e.g. Brown & Eisenhardt, 1998; Gersick, 1989; McGrath & Kelly, 1986). In fact, many researchers have theorized that, like other biological organisms, members of human groups naturally synchronize their activities through social "entrainment" (Ancona & Chong, 1996; McGrath & Kelly, 1986; McGrath & Rotchford, 1983). The central insight of biological entrainment models is that the timing of cyclical or repetitive patterns of behaviors can be heavily influenced by rhythms generated by surrounding environmental stimuli, such that the beat or cadence of groups of organisms performing related activities naturally becomes synchronized over time (see Ancona & Chong, 1996; McGrath & Kelly, 1985, for reviews). Familiar examples include the synchronized chirping of crickets and flashing of fireflies, or, alternatively, the alignment of a human body's physical systems (e.g. circulation, breathing and nervous systems).

A distinguishing aspect of physical and biological entrainment processes is that the coordinated activities occur with a high degree of reliability and their timing is determined on a non-conscious level. Organisms intuitively align the rate of their activities to match surrounding cadences and rhythms. One obvious limiting factor in applying entrainment models to human work groups is that the timely and reliable completion of a specific task by an individual in a work group cannot be taken for granted in the same way, for example, that a heartbeat can (Blount & Janicik, 2002). Individual group member's work motivation may wax and wane during a day, across a week, over months. Effort and performance variability also can arise non-motivationally, as individuals' cognitive abilities experience peaks and valleys within a day or over a week (Bodenhausen, 1990). Thus, to understand synchronization in work groups, a more complex understanding of human behavior is needed.

Consistent with entrainment theorists, we make the assumption that groups do develop their own temporal norms and rhythmic patterns as members interact together and with their environment over time. However, we suggest that groups are not as tightly prescribed as entrainment models would imply. Given the broad diversity of people's pacing preferences, asynchrony can be quite common in groups.

When one or more group members have difficulty adapting his or her pace to the group's pace, the group will experience asynchrony. This can happen when members disagree about the appropriate milestones or deadlines for accomplishing the group's work. Even if members agree about how to allocate and segment the group's time, a group can get out of synch if members disagree about how intensely to work at a particular point in time. For example, some members may want to work hard now and ease up later, while others prefer to procrastinate until later. These work style differences can lead the group to feel out-of-synch, particularly if the group tasks require on-going coordination across members (Blount & Janicik, 2002). The more that a group finds that its members' work pace preferences do not converge, the higher the degree of asynchrony. Under high levels of asynchrony, task performance can suffer. The group may miss important deadlines. Coordination failures may affect the quality of the group's outcomes, and group cohesion can fall as members experience ongoing temporal conflict (Blount & Janicik, 2002; Jehn, 1995). Simply put, asynchrony imposes costs on work groups.

Therefore, in contrast to entrainment theorists, we argue that given the natural diversity present in people's temporal preferences, asynchrony is quite normal in human groups. The more interesting question, we would suggest, is: How do groups overcome high levels of asynchrony to achieve coordinated action? As we have noted earlier, entrainment models that rely on non-conscious convergence do not accurately portray this phenomenon. Gevers et al. (2003) posit several explicit, group-level cognitive processes that can facilitate synchronization. In this paper, we consider how the status structure of a group will affect group synchronization. We begin, first, with an overview of what status is and how it affects interaction in work groups.

Status in Work Groups

Sociologists have long observed that when humans gather, status orderings naturally emerge: some members gain higher social standing than others (Blau, 1986; Fiske, 1992; Homans, 1950). When an actor is judged to be comparatively superior to oneself in an important domain (e.g. more intelligent, articulate, attractive, wealthy or athletic), he or she is perceived to have relatively higher status than oneself. Status judgments also form at the group level when one member is perceived as more esteemed by other members, based on an attribute that is valued by the group (Blau, 1986; Homans, 1961; Ridgeway, 1997). Thus, when multiple members hold a particular member in high regard, it is because they agree that that member is legitimately "better" in some way with higher organizational rank or superior technical skills (Blau, 1986; Pratto, Sidanius, Stallworth & Malle, 1994). Indeed, a key indicator of the degree to which a status structure exists within a group is whether or not shared rationales exist for how status is assigned.

In this sense, status is context-specific. The specific nature of the group and its context will determine how group members assign status. "Earning superior status in a group requires not merely impressing others with outstanding abilities but actually using these abilities to make contributions to the achievement of the collective goals of the group or the individual goals of its members" (Blau, 1986, p. 126). Thus, a group member with high task competence but low social skills will probably be accorded high status in performance-relevant contexts and relatively lower status in the group's social events.

Sources of Status

The sources of status within work groups can be categorized into three general types: performance competence, organizational power, and behavioral dominance. The performance competence perspective argues that people gain status when they demonstrate the ability to enhance the achievement of the group's and/or individual members' goals. For example, the member is seen as particularly articulate or technically competent in ways that allow the group to perform more effectively (Bales, 1950; Berger, Rosenholtz & Zelditch, 1980; Homans, 1961; Ridgeway, 1984, 1987). The literature on organizational power predicts that people will gain status in groups based on the power or authority that they hold in the broader organization context within which the work group is embedded (Pfeffer, 1992; Kramer & Neale, 1998). Here, for example, the member may hold a high rank in the organization or perhaps be well-connected with other people who do. A final perspective, offered by ethological theorists (Lee & Ofshe, 1981; Mazur, 1985), argues that status hierarchies in groups result from the innate human impulse for dominance over others. In the battle for dominance, attributes such as attractiveness, physical size, personal demeanor, and genealogical lineage are all important sources of status.

Note that unlike the performance competence and organizational power perspectives, the behavioral dominance perspective suggests that status differentials can be created independent of the group's goals. Further, these differences result from contests among individual group members who share a generalized need to gain superiority over others. Thus, the behavioral dominance perspective highlights the pervasive human tendency to create social hierarchies based on personal attributes such as size, attractiveness, and facial features, as opposed to competences directly relevant to group tasks.

Numerous authors have observed that early in the existence of any group, status orderings tend to reflect generalized means of social differentiation, such as those based on personal and social characteristics and organizational power (Berger et al., 1980; Mazur, 1985). Research also shows that once a status system has developed, it can be slow to change. This is because those who have status within the initial group hierarchy often determine the course of the subsequent group activities – both what takes place and what is seen to take place (e.g. Berger et al., 1980; Messe, Kerr & Sattler, 1991; Sidanius & Pratto, 1999). Logically, their goal is to direct these activities in such a way that they maintain their status (Fiske, 1993; Pfeffer, 1992). However, research also finds that the longer a group exists and more information becomes available about each member's actual contributions to the group, status orderings often adapt to reflect the role of actual performance competence (Goffman, 1957; Ridgeway & Erickson, 2000; Wageman & Mannix, 1998).

It is worth noting here that status, power, and influence are terms that are often used interchangeably in the psychological and management literatures (e.g. Keltner, Gruenfeld, & Anderson, in press; Kramer & Neale, 1998; Lee & Tiedens, 2001; Pfeffer, 1992). Here, we have defined status as a perception of comparative social esteem that is context-specific and consensually defined. We intentionally distinguish this definition of status from definitions of organizational power, which we define as "an individual's capacity to modify others' states by providing or withholding resources or administering punishments" (from Keltner et al., 2002). We also distinguish it from authority, which we define as derived from institutionalized roles or arrangements (e.g. hierarchies, Weber, 1947). We further distinguish our definition of status from the interactive processes of influence and persuasion that occur when people use communication to change other people's perceptions and preferences (e.g. Cialdini, 1993). Thus, in this paper, the label of high status refers to enhanced social standing that some group members have based on either their group-relevant performance competence, access to organizational power or authority, and/or behavioral dominance attributes.

Uses of Status

The presence of status differentials affects group members' willingness to cooperate with each other and the group's goals (Blau, 1986). It is well established that when people perceive status differences, they tend to defer to them (Goffman, 1957; Mazur, 1985; Ridgeway, 1997). Traditional psychological studies of cooperation in groups emphasize the role of collectivism (Chen, Brockner & Chen, 2002; Chen, Brockner & Katz, 1998; Triandis, 1995), social identification (Spears et al., 1997; Tajfel & Turner, 1986), or alternatively, prosocial value orientations (McClintock, 1977; Messick & McClintock, 1968) in cooperation. Here, we highlight the role of status deference in explaining members' willingness to cooperate with other members.

In contrast to the traditional group-based conceptions of cooperation listed above, status deference occurs when a group member yields to the wishes of a higher status group member and adopts behaviors that comply with the higher-status member's wishes. In contrast to cooperative actions that are achieved through a member's identification with the group's goals or outcomes, cooperative actions based on status deference are dyadically motivated and involve exchanges between higher and lower status actors. This cooperation occurs regardless of whether the lower status member accepts or identifies with the goals that the higher-status member espouses or is collectively motivated. The key point is that status deference induces cooperative behaviors when the higher-status actor's goals are aligned with the group's goals.

Recent research suggests that status deference can be motivated in two ways (Y. Chen, 2002). The first way is through obedience, because the low-status member fears retribution from the high-status member (i.e. cooperation is derived from the high-status actor's potential use of coercive power, reward power, etc.). The second way is through the experience of respect and the lower status member's positive regard for the high-status member (i.e. cooperation based on perception of the higher status actor's superior attributes, abilities or role legitimacy). In either case, when one group member defers to another member, that group member is agreeing: (a) to allow the higher-status member to define the group's goals; and (b) to cooperate with those goals.

Cooperative vs. Competitive Status Construal

In distinguishing between obedience- and respect-based compliance, it is important to note that there is not a single, universal way to construe status. As recent research by S. Chen, Lee-Chai and Bargh (2001) has shown, how people construe *high* status depends on their own social values (Clark & Mills, 1993). Specifically, S. Chen et al. (2001) found that people who are more exchange-oriented tend to exploit their high status in dyadic exchange relationships. In contrast, people who are more communal-oriented tend to give more weight to the needs of other actors when having high status in dyadic exchange relationships.

In fact, Y. Chen (2002) posits that how status is construed also varies across social systems (e.g. national cultures, industries, organizations, or groups) depending on the ideological beliefs, incentives, and norms embedded within these social systems. Specifically, she distinguishes between two types of status construal: *cooperative* and *competitive*. She suggests that when status differences are cooperatively construed, status is associated with differential role responsibilities rather than perceived differences in group members' "worthiness." Cooperative construals are more likely in communal social systems, in which each member's contribution is equally valued, and members share the same level of group membership regardless of status. Both those in high and low status positions bear mutual accountability toward each other and the group (King, 1991; Lunyu, 1991; Mao, 1994; Yang, 1993). High-status members work to ensure that they carry greater responsibilities for attaining group goals and show concern for lower status members' needs (Chen, Lee-Chai & Bargh, 2001; Confucius, 1938). Lower status members, in turn, work to ensure that they assist high-status members in their group efforts by showing respect and deference for the guidance from the high-status members

(Lunyu, 1991). As Y. Chen (2002) argues, in communal social systems, both high- and low-status actors share high levels of group identity and relational solidarity (Brewer & Gardner, 1996). Status differences are cooperatively construed, and status deference tends to be based on respect and esteem for high-status members.

In contrast, Y. Chen (2002) suggests that when status differences are competitively construed, high-status members of groups tend to perceive themselves as more worthy than and superior to low-status members. Competitive construals are likely in exchange and equity-based social systems, in which members compete to attain status-based rewards. In such systems, status is strongly associated with a perception of elite group membership, posing esteem threats to low-status out-group members while boosting the esteem of high-status in-group members (Fiske, 1993; Frank, 1985; Keltner et al., in press; Sidanius & Pratto, 1999). Given the transactive nature of such social systems, high-status members are more likely to construe their interactions with low-status members in an exchange manner and use rewards and punishments as influence strategies (Wilson, Near & Miller, 1996). Lower status members, in turn, are more likely to perceive social differentiation between themselves and high-status members (e.g. adopting an "us vs. them" relational schema, Kramer, 1996). They may consequently fear being exploited by the high-status members and engage in vigilant social information processing (Chen, Brockner & Greenberg, 2003; Lee & Tiedens, 2001; Van den Bos, Bruins, Wilke & Dronkert, 1999). Logically, in groups in which status is competitively construed, low-status actors will tend to obediently, rather than respectfully, defer to high-status others.

Summary

In this section, we have examined the construct of status in work groups. We have noted that status is typically defined as a perception of comparative social esteem across group members, and it is context specific and consensually defined. Status differentials are naturally occurring in groups – particularly when groups are considered within a social context, such as an organization. Further, when people perceive status differences, they tend to defer to them. Thus, status differentials can help groups to achieve cooperation and coordination among members. Finally, we described that status deference can take multiple forms. In certain groups, status will be construed more competitively and induce obedience from low-status actors. In other groups, status will be construed more cooperatively and induce respect-based compliance.

In the next section, we integrate our discussions of status and synchronization. Specifically, we examine how status differentials within a group can enhance or inhibit group-level synchronization.

Status and Synchronization

As a first step in examining how status differentials influence the group process of temporal alignment, we consider how having high or low status within a group affects an individual member's pacing preferences. Specifically, we focus on: (a) how a member's perceived social status affects how he or she constructs personal pacing preferences regarding group activities; and (b) when personal pacing preferences conflict with synchronizing, how a member's social status affects the weights that a member places on achieving his or her personal pacing preferences vs. being synchronized with the group.

The Effects of Status on Pacing Preferences

A broad body of research suggests that having high status is associated with increased perceptions of self-efficacy and control (Keltner et al., in press; Kipnis, 1972; Lee & Tiedens, 2001), and a desire to maintain the status quo (Chen, Brockner & Greenberg, 2003; Pfeffer, 1992). These findings suggest that high status group members will tend to have well-articulated personal pacing preferences, because they will know what they want temporally and will perceive that achieving their personal pacing goals in the group setting is viable. Because of their high perceived efficacy within the group, high-status members will not perceive conflicts between achieving their own pacing goals and synchronizing with the group. Instead, they are likely to expect that the group will, in fact, synchronize by adapting to their own preferences.

However, the distinction between cooperative vs. competitive status construals suggests an interesting nuance regarding how high-status member are likely to construct their preferences in different group contexts. If status is competitively construed within a group, we hypothesize that the high-status member's pacing goals will be influenced most by his/her own personal traits, experiences, and extra-group demands. When the group synchronizes, the high-status actor will prefer that it does so in line with his or her own pacing goals and will expect obedience from low-status members in order to do so (Chen, 2002; Chen, Lee-Chai & Bargh, 2001).

In contrast, when status is construed cooperatively, we posit that a strong sense of group identity and relational solidarity with low-status members will accompany the high-status role. The high-status actor will perceive the welfare of the group and its members as valuable to the self (Chen et al., 1998, Chen et al., 2002). In this case, the high-status member's own pacing goals will reflect not only his or her personal traits, experiences and extra-group demands; but also a perception of what is best for the group and its other members. Thus, when the group synchronizes, the high-status member will prefer that it does so in line with his or her own preferences, but these will be based, at least in part, on what he/she believes to be in the best interests of the group (Chen, 2002).

For those low in status positions, we hypothesize that personal pacing preferences may not be as strongly held, because having low status is associated with low levels of self-efficacy and control (Keltner et al., in press; Lee & Tiedens, 2001). Thus, low-status members may assume and expect that the group's timing demands will infringe on their personal timing preferences (e.g. they will be expected to work later or faster than they would personally prefer on behalf of the group.) Further, we hypothesize that the tendency toward status deference and the role of temporal control in conferring status will heighten this effect. The net result being that lead low-status actors will weight the in-synch preference more heavily in group interactions, particularly as compared to how they weight their own pacing preferences (Blau, 1986; Keltner et al., in press; Lee & Tiedens, 2001; Simmel, 1950).

However, just as with high-status actors, we anticipate some interesting nuances depending on how status is construed in the group context. Namely, in groups where status is cooperatively construed, a strong sense of group identity and relational solidarity with high-status members will be present. Low-status members will feel comparatively high levels of personal efficacy and identification with the group. As a result, personal pacing preferences may be formed by low-status members which reflect a collective perception of the self. Here, achieving group synchronization can be perceived as personally motivating because it meets personal pacing goals, and as socially motivating because it satisfies the general preference to synchronize. In contrast, when status is competitively construed, the personal pacing preferences of low-status actors will reflect a more individualistic perception of the self. In this case, when synchronization occurs, it is more likely to be perceived as incongruent with personal preferences and be based on obedience. Thus, when a conflict is perceived between achieving one's personal pacing goals and group synchronization, it is likely to be more acute for the low-status member in groups where status differences are competitively, rather than cooperatively, construed (Chen, 2002).

How Group Status Structures Help Synchronization
Combining these observations with our earlier points, we note that: (a) the control of time is a well-accepted symbol of status; (b) status differentials are inevitable in groups; and (c) people generally like to synchronize. Correspondingly, we posit that the status differentials within groups facilitate the internal synchronization of group members' activities because they induce temporal deference from low-status group members. That is, low-status members will place a high value on synchronizing with the group. In order to synchronize, low-status members will seek to align the pace of their activities to match the pace set by high-status members.

As entrainment models emphasize, individuals within groups intuitively look for temporal markers with which to align their activities. We posit that the behavior of a high-status group member, who feels high levels of personal efficacy and control in the group setting, provides the temporal cues that others follow.

This line of reasoning has three important implications for work groups. First, it suggests that when a member with high performance-based status establishes a temporal agenda for a group, lower-status members will perceive that agenda as credible and seek to align with it. This will be true even if group members hold divergent personal pacing preferences, as long as they acknowledge the high-status member's rank and role legitimacy. In this case, low status group members may seek to influence how the high-status member sets the agenda, but ultimately should be willing to align with the duration and intensity cues established by the higher status member's agenda.

Second, in the absence of task-relevant temporal cues (i.e. the nature of the group task does not itself engender specific temporal pacing parameters – perhaps deadlines are ambiguous or the nature of how to pace the work is unknown), the presence of a high-status member can facilitate effective group performance. This will be particularly true if that member takes a lead in setting a pace through his or her own actions, which provides a temporal structure for the group. Thus, when temporal cues are otherwise ambiguous, high-status members can provide temporal reference points and salient rhythmic cues based on their own schedules, work styles and pace. Again, if low-status members acknowledge the high-status member's rank and role legitimacy, they will tend to synchronize their activities with those cues. A salient example of this type of synchronization would be the work-hour norms set by a group leader who works from 8 a.m. to 7 p.m. everyday and, by doing so, implies that is a reasonable expectation for other members of his group. In this case, group members are likely to adopt similar hours in an effort to synchronize with him and others in the group. Here, the high-status member's personal temporal referents provide salient cues, which by virtue of his or her status gain legitimacy.

Third, in times of transition and substantial change, high-status members can provide temporal referents that allow groups to re-establish work flow more quickly. If a group finds its rhythms disrupted by unexpected events (a salient example for those of us at NYU was the events of September 11, 2001), the presence of high-status members can provide a critical "righting" function by providing new markers and pace-setting activities that allow groups to stabilize more quickly than if they were not present. Again, in the presence of ambiguity and unclear temporal markers from other sources, the presence of high-status members who clearly articulate temporal cues and ongoing rhythms can provide temporal clarity for a group.

In this sense, the presence of status differentials within a work group can be highly beneficial to temporal performance. This is because the behaviors of high-status members act as temporal cues with which other members naturally look to align and pace their own activities. Yet, as we note below, the effects of status differentials on group synchronization may not always be beneficial.

How Group Status Structures Inhibit Synchronization

Implicit in our argument, thus far, has been the assumption that a clear status hierarchy exists within the group, which delineates one group member as having legitimately higher status than the other members. In contrast to that model, we can imagine three types of status hierarchies that could inhibit, rather than facilitate, effective intra-group synchronization.

The first situation occurs when the basis used for determining status does not reflect the task-relevant capabilities of the group, a result consistent with the behavioral dominance perspective. This can happen when behavioral dominance or personal connections, rather than performance competence, determine status. Here, a high-status actor may emerge within the group who sets a temporal agenda for the group that does not reflect the true performance needs of the group. The high-status actor may be the one who is most attractive or has a well-connected social network, but lacks the temporal leadership skills that the group needs. Alternatively, if organizational power determines who has high status, but that actor, while generally competent, is over-extended and distracted by other organizational responsibilities, he or she may not be able to set the most effective temporal agenda for the group. Unless another informal leader emerges, a group can languish, and group members will have difficulties synchronizing their activities.

A second problematic situation can occur when two or more actors emerge (depending on the size of the group) as having high status. When multiple actors occupy equally high status positions, an internal status contest can emerge, particularly if one or more of the high-status actors construes status competitively and seeks domination. The temporal coordination of the group's activities can become a forum for them to engage in status contests. As numerous authors have observed, high-status actors often compete to arrive appropriately late to meetings, such that either the meeting is held up until their arrival or alternatively, the meeting is restarted when they arrive (e.g. Owens & Sutton, 2001). These types of actions can quickly impede a group's effective temporal functioning. The co-CEO model in mergers and acquisitions is another example that illustrates the difficulties inherent in such a status distribution structure (Sirower, 1997, 1999). This type of leadership model more often fails than succeeds, precisely because numerous temporal and other conflicts often emerge. If two CEOs have strong divergent pacing preferences (e.g. regarding when to make a post-merger layoff announcement), critical decisions may be delayed, slowing the realization of synergies between the two companies (Sirower, 1997).

A third type of status hierarchy that can impede the internal synchronization of group activities is an equal status structure, where group decision-making is characterized by consensus. Whether temporal consensus can be easily achieved depends on an array of factors. For example, if none or only one of the group members holds strong personal pacing preferences, then the first temporal suggestion that a particular member makes might serve as a salient anchor that sets the pace (Kramer, 1991). Such a tendency is more likely in groups where social harmony is a dominant value (Janis, 1982). Temporal consensus within an equal-status group also can be facilitated when there are salient task-related temporal cues associated with the group's work (e.g. a clear imposed deadline from an important client or a professor's due date for a group project). In contrast, when there are strongly-held, divergent personal preferences among multiple group members, temporal conflicts can emerge. Members with opposing temporal preferences might use the opportunity to compete for status in the group, and members who share similar preferences might form coalitions to collectively compete against each other (Rubin & Brown, 1975). After an internal struggle, a new status structure with a clear hierarchy might emerge. For this reason, the actual existence of an equal status distribution structure is rather rare and often relatively short-lived (Blau, 1986; Simmel, 1950).

Integration

These three examples emphasize that the role of status in group synchronization is complex. Sometimes the presence of status differentials can facilitate synchronization; sometimes they will inhibit it. Again, we posit that the degree to which different status structures inhibit synchronization also may depend on whether status is cooperatively or competitively construed within the group context. When status is cooperatively construed among all members of a group, we predict that, on average, synchronization will be less problematic because members' personal temporal goals are more likely to coincide with the group's goals. Thus, when conflicts emerge, they will be readily resolved. However, in group settings in which status is competitively construed, these issues will be more problematic. Here, the control of time will be central to how people gain standing in the group. When time-based conflicts emerge, the agreement to go along with the group can be perceived as a loss of face and lead to more contentiousness and dissension.

CONCLUSION

We began this chapter with the observation that time is a symbol of status (Blau, 1986; Hall, 1983; Levine, 1997; Owens & Sutton, 2001). We used this observation as a launching point for examining the role of status in how group members temporally align their activities. While psychologists have examined the effect of relative status on many facets of people's emotions, cognitions, and behaviors (e.g. Chen et al., 2003; Crocker, Major & Steele, 1998; Lee & Tiedens, 2001; Keltner et al., in press; Sidanius & Pratto, 1999), here we have focused on the role of status in the social process of synchronizing group members' activities. Our central thesis has been that understanding status and the status structure that exists within a group is central to understanding the temporal dynamics that occur within the group.

We developed this thesis in several stages. First, we reviewed Blount and Janicik's (2002) model of within group synchronization that posits people have both: (a) personal pacing preferences; and (b) a general preference to feel temporally in-synch in social interactions. Despite the in-synch preference, we described how individual diversity in pacing preferences presents a challenge for achieving group synchronization. We then introduced the notion of status and how status differentials within a group can both facilitate and inhibit the realization of group synchronization. Status was defined as a perception of comparative social esteem across group members that is context-specific and consensually defined. We described two ways in which people defer to status differences: obediently or respectfully (Chen, 2002). When status is construed competitively, it induces obedience from low-status actors, and when it is construed cooperatively, it induces respect-based compliance. In both instances, we have argued that status differentials matter in groups because they affect member's temporal behavior vis-à-vis group goals. Whether competitively or cooperatively constructed, we have argued that status differentials lead low status group members to align the timing of their activities with that of high-status members in order to synchronize.

When a clear status structure exists with one member holding more status than the others, group members will naturally synchronize with that actor. This situation will be good for the group as long as the high-status actor's temporal cues reflect what is best for the group. When the actor is not competent, or perhaps distracted by other activities, this type of status structure can negatively affect group temporal performance. Further, when a clear status structure does not exist, or when multiple actors are engaged in status contests, group members may be inhibited in their efforts to synchronize effectively.

Overall, we posit that the degree to which status differentials become problematic for a group will be determined by the degree to which status is cooperatively or competitively construed within the group. When status is cooperatively construed, we hypothesize that, on average, synchronization will be less problematic. This is because member's personal goals are more likely to, at least in part, reflect the group's needs. This will be true for both low- and high-status members. In contrast, in groups in which status tends to be competitively construed, personal temporal goals will tend to reflect a more individualistic perception of the self, and synchronization with the group is more likely to be perceived to be at odds with personal interests.

Status differentials across members are common to work groups, and they affect how groups internally align their activities. Low-status members' time tends to be less valued than high-status members' time, and high-status members are sometimes tempted to use a group's time to assert and confirm their existing high status. As a result, how status is distributed across members affects how readily a group synchronizes.

To effectively understand the temporal dynamics of work groups, therefore, we suggest that the following elements must be considered: (a) the underlying status structure of a group; (b) the nature of how status is achieved within the group; (c) how individual group members perceive and construe their own status; and (d) whether status is construed cooperatively or competitively at the group-level. By considering these factors, further advances can be made into the understanding of temporal dynamics of any work group. We advocate that the study of time in work groups must incorporate the study of status. Status differentials are a ubiquitous aspect of social life, and with status, comes the control of time.

REFERENCES

Ancona, D., & Chong, C. L. (1996). Entrainment: Pace, cycle, and rhythm in organizational behavior. *Research in Organizational Behavior, 18*, 251–284.

Bales, R. (1950). *Interaction process analysis*. Reading, MA: Addison Wesley.

Bartel, C. A., & Miliken, F. J. (2003). Perceptions of time in work groups: Do members develop shared cognitions about their temporal demands? In: S. Blount, E. Mannix & M. Neale (Eds), *Research on Managing Groups and Teams* (Vol. 6). Hillsdale, NJ: Lawrence Erlbaum.

Baumeister, R. F., & Heatherton, T. F. (1996). Self-regulation failure: An overview. *Psychological Inquiry, 7*, 1–15.

Berger, J., Rosenholtz, S. J., & Zelditch, M., Jr. (1980). Status organizing processes. *Annual Review of Sociology, 6*, 479–508.

Blau, P. (1986). *Exchange and power in social life*. New Brunswick, NJ: Transaction Publishers.

Blount, S., & Janicik, G. (2002). Getting and staying in-pace: The "in-synch" preference and its implications for work groups. In: E. A. Mannix, M. A. Neale & H. Sondak (Eds), *Research on Managing Groups and Teams: Vol. 4. Toward Phenomenology of Groups and Group Membership* (pp. 235–266). Greenwich, CT: JAI Elsevier.

Bluedorn, A. C., & Standifer, R. (2003). Groups, boundary spanning, and the temporal imagination. In: S. Blount, E. Mannix & M. Neale (Eds), *Research on Managing Groups and Teams* (Vol. 6). Hillsdale, NJ: Lawrence Erlbaum.

Bodenhausen, G. V. (1990). Stereotypes as judgmental heuristics: Evidence of circadian variations in discrimination. *Psychological Science, 1*, 319–322.

Brewer, M. B., & Gardner, W. (1996). Who is this "We"? Levels o collective identity and self representations. *Journal of Personality and Social Psychology, 71*, 83–93.

Brown, S. L., & Eisenhardt, K. M. (1998). *Competing on the edge: Strategy as structured chaos.* Boston: Harvard Business School Press.

Carver, C. S., & Scheier, M. F. (1999). Control theory: A useful conceptual framework for personality-social, clinical, and health psychology. In: R. F. Baumeister (Ed.), *The Self in Social Psychology: Key Readings in Social Psychology* (pp. 299–316). Philadelphia, PA: Psychology Press.

Chapple, E. D. (1970). *Cultural and biological man: Explorations in behavioral anthropology.* New York: Holt, Rinehart & Winston.

Chartrand, T. L., & Bargh, J. A. (1999). The chameleon effect: The perception-behavior link and social interaction. *Journal of Personality and Social Psychology, 76*, 893–910.

Chen, S., Lee-Chai, A. Y., & Bargh, J. A. (2001). Relational orientation as a moderator of the effects of social power. *Journal of Personality and Social Psychology, 80*, 173–187.

Chen, Y. (2002). How one experiences and uses status depends upon how one gets it: Differences in the effects of status in cooperative vs. competitive social systems. Working Paper.

Chen, Y., Brockner, J., & Chen, X. (2002). Individual-collective primacy and ingroup favoritism: Enhancement and protection effects. *Journal of Experimental Social Psychology, 38*, 482–491.

Chen, Y., Brockner, J., & Greenberg, J. (2003). When is it "a pleasure to do business with you?" The effects of status, procedural fairness, and outcome favorability. Manuscript under review.

Chen, Y., Brockner, J., & Katz, T. (1998). Toward an explanation of cultural differences in group favoritism: The role of individual vs. collective primacy. *Journal of Personality and Social Psychology, 75*, 1490–1502.

Cialdini, R. B. (1993). *The psychology of influence and persuasion.* New York: Quill.

Clark, M. S., & Mills, J. (1993). The difference between communal and exchange relationships: What it is and what it is not. *Personality and Social Psychology Bulletin, 19*, 684–691.

Confucius. (1938). *The analects*, Trans. D. Hinton. Washington, DC: Counterpoint.

Conte, J. M., Landy, F. J., & Mathieu, J. E. (1995). Time urgency: Conceptual and construct development. *Journal of Applied Psychology, 80*, 178–185.

Conway, A. R. A., Cowan, N., Bunting, M. F., Therriault, D. J., & Minkoff, S. R. B. (2002). A latent variable analysis of working memory capacity, short-term memory capacity, processing speed, and general fluid intelligence. *Intelligence, 30*, 163–183.

Crocker, J., Major, B., & Steele, C. M. (1998). Social stigma. In: D. T. Gilbert, S. T. Fiske & G. Lindzey (Eds), *The Handbook of Social Psychology* (4th ed., Vol. 2, pp. 504–554). New York: Oxford University Press.

Davis, M. (1982). *Interactional rhythms: Periodicity in communicative behavior.* New York: Human Sciences Press.

Fiske, A. P. (1992). The four elementary forms of sociality: Frameworks for a unified theory of social relations. *Psychological review, 99*, 489–723.

Fiske, S. T. (1993). Controlling other people: The impact of power on stereotyping. *American Psychologists, 48*, 621–628.

Gell, A. (1992). *The anthropology of time: Cultural constructions of temporal maps and images.* Oxford, Providence: Berg.

Gevers, J. M. P., Rutte, C. G., & van de Lien, W. (2003). How work group achieve coordinated action: A model of shared cognitions on time. In: S. Blount, E. Mannix & M. Neale (Eds), *Research on Managing Groups and Teams* (Vol. 6). Hillsdale, NJ: Lawrence Erlbaum.

Gersick, C. J. (1989). Making time: Predictable transitions in task groups. *Academy of Management Journal, 32*, 274–309.

Goffman, I. W. (1957). Status consistency and preference for change in power distribution. *American Sociological Review, 22*, 275–288.

Hall, E. T. (1983). *The dance of life: The other dimension of time.* Garden City, NY: Anchor Press/Doubleday.

Homans, G. C. (1950). *The human group.* New York: Harcourt, Brace.

Homans, G. C. (1961). *Social behavior: Its elementary forms.* New York: Harcourt Brace Jovanovich.

Janis, I. (1982). *Victims of groupthink* (2nd ed.). Boston: Houghton-Mifflin.

Jehn, K. (1995). A multi-method examination of the benefits and detriments of intragroup conflict. *Administrative Science Quarterly, 40*, 256–282.

Keltner, D., Gruenfeld, D. H., & Anderson, C. (in press). Power, approach, and inhibition. *Psychological Review.*

Kelly, J. R., & McGrath, J. E. (1985). Effects of time limits and task types on task performance and interaction of four-person groups. *Journal of Personality and Social Psychology, 49*, 395–407.

King, A. Y. (1991). Kuan-shi and network building: A sociological interpretation. *Daedalus, 120*, 63–84.

Kipnis, D. (1972). Does power corrupt? *Journal of Personality and Social Psychology, 24*, 33–41.

Kramer, R. M. (1991). The more the merrier? Social psychological aspects of multiparty negotiations in organizations. In: M. H. Bazerman, R. J. Lewicki & B. H. Sheppard (Eds), *Research on Negotiation in Organizations: Handbook of Negotiation Research* (Vol. 3, pp. 307–332). Greenwich, CT: JAI Press.

Kramer, R. M. (1996). Divergent realities and convergent disappointments in the hierarchic relation: Trust and the intuitive auditor at work. In: R. M. Kramer & T. R. Tyler (Eds), *Trust in Organizations: Frontiers of Theory and Research* (pp. 216–245). Thousand Oaks, CA: Sage.

Kramer, R. M., & Neale, M. A. (1998). *Power and influence in organizations.* Thousand Oaks, CA: Sage.

Lee, M. T., & Ofshe, R. (1981). The impact of behavioral style and status characteristics on social influence: A test of two competing theories. *Social Psychology Quarterly, 44*, 73–82.

Lee, F., & Tiedens, L. Z. (2001). Is it lonely at the top: The independence and interdependence of power holders. *Research in Organizational Behavior, 23*, 43–91.

Levine, R. B. (1997). *A geography of time.* New York: Basic Books.

Loewenstein, G. (1987). Anticipation and the value of delayed consumption. *Economic Journal, 97*, 666–684.

Loewenstein, G., & Elster, J. (1992). *Choice over time.* New York: Sage.

Lunyu (1991). *New interpretations of Lunyu.* Taipei: Sa Ming Book Company.

Mao, L. R. (1994). Beyond politeness theory: "Face" revisited and renewed. *Journal of Pragmatics, 21*, 451–486.

Mazur, A. (1985). A biosocial model of status in face-to-face primate groups. *Social Forces, 64*, 377–402.

McClintock, C. (1977). Social motives in settings of outcome interdependence. In: D. Druckman (Ed.), *Negotiations: Social Psychological Perspective* (pp. 49–77). Beverly Hills, CA: Sage.

McGrath, J. E., & Kelly, J. R. (1986). *Time and human interaction: Toward a social psychology of time.* New York: Guilford.

Messe, L. A., Kerr, N. L., & Sattler, D. N. (1991). But some animals are more equal than others: The supervisor as a privileged status in group contexts. In: S. Worchel & W. Wood (Eds), *Group Process and Productivity* (pp. 203–223). Thousand Oaks, CA: Sage.

Messick, D. M., & McClintock, C. G. (1968). Motivational bases of choice in experimental games. *Journal of Experimental Social Psychology, 4*, 1–25.

Moore, W. E. (1963). The temporal structure of organizations. In: E. A. Tiryakian (Ed.), *Sociological Theory, Values, and Sociocultural Change: Essays in Honor or Pitirim A. Sorokin* (pp. 161–170). New York: Free Press.

Owens, D. A., & Sutton, R. I. (2001). Status contests in meetings: Negotiating the informal order. In: M. E. Turner (Ed.), *Groups at Work: Theory and Research* (pp. 120–135). Mahwah, NJ: Lawrence Erlbaum.

Pfeffer, J. (1992). *Managing with power: Politics and influence in organizations.* Boston, MA: Harvard Business School Press.

Pratto, F., Sidanius, J., Stallwaorth, L. M., & Malle, B. F. (1994). Social dominance orientation: A personality variable predicting social and political attitudes. *Journal of Personality and Social Pschology, 67,* 741–763.

Rastegary, H., & Landy, F. J. (1994). The interactions among time urgency, uncertainty, and time pressure. In: O. Svenson & J. Maule (Eds), *Time Pressure and Stress in Human Judgment and Decision Making* (pp. 132–147). New York: Plenum Press.

Ridgeway, C. L. (1984). Dominance, performance, and status in groups. In: E. J. Lawler (Ed.), *Advances in Group Processes* (Vol. 1, pp. 59–93). Greenwich, CT: JAI Press.

Ridgeway, C. L. (1987). Noverbal behavior, dominance, and the basis of status in task groups. *American Sociological Review, 52,* 683–694.

Ridgeway, C. L. (1997). Where do status value beliefs come from? New developments. In: J. Szmatka, J. Skvoretz & J. Berger (Eds), *Status, Network, and Structure* (pp. 137–158). Stanford, CA: Stanford University Press.

Ridgeway, C. L., & Erickson, K. G. (2000). Creating and spreading status beliefs. *American Journal of Sociology, 106,* 579–615.

Rubin, J. Z., & Brown, B. R. (1975). *The social psychology of bargaining and negotiation.* San Diego, CA: Academic Press.

Sanchez-Burks, J. (2002). Protestant relational ideology and (in)attention to relational cues in work settings. *Journal of Personality and Social Psychology, 83,* 919–929.

Sidanius, J., & Pratto, F. (1999). *Social dominance theory: An intergroup theory of social hierarchy and oppression.* New York: Cambridge University Press.

Simmel, G. (1950). *The sociology of Georg Simmel.* Glencoe, IL: Free Press.

Sirower, M. L. (1997). *The synergy trap: How companies lose the acquisition game.* New York: Free Press.

Sirower, M. L. (1999). One head is better than two. *Wall Street Journal,* Oct 18, A48.

Slocombe, T. E., & Bluedorn, A. C. (1999). Organizational behavior implications of the congruence between preferred polychronicity and experienced work-unit polychronicity. *Journal of Organization Behavior, 20,* 75–99.

Spears, R., Doosje, B., & Ellemers, N. (1997). Self-stereotyping in the face of threats to group status and distinctiveness: The role of group identification. *Personality and Social Psychology Bulletin, 23,* 538–553.

Tajfel, H., & Turner, J. C. (1986). The social identity theory of intergroup behavior. In: S. Worchel & W. G. Austin (Eds), *Psychology of Intergroup Relations* (pp. 7–24). Chicago: Nelson-Hall.

Thompson, J. D. (1967). *Organizations in action.* New York: McGraw-Hill.

Triandis, H. C. (1995). *Individualism and collectivism.* Boulder, CO: Westview Press.

Van den Bos, K., Bruins, J., Wilke, H. A. M., & Dronkert, E. (1999). Sometimes unfair procedures have nice aspects: On the psychology of the fair process effect. *Journal of Personality and Social Psychology, 77,* 324–336.

Varey, C. A., & Kahneman, D. (1993). Experiences extended across time: Evaluations of moments and episodes. *Journal of Behavioral Decision Making, 5,* 169–185.

Wageman, R., & Mannix, E. A. (1998). Uses and misuses of power in task-performing teams. In: R. M. Kramer & M. A. Neale (Eds), *Power and Influence in Organizations* (pp. 261–186). Thousand Oaks, CA: Sage.

Weber, M. (1947). *The theory of social and economic organization*. A. M. Henderson & T. Parsons (Trans.). New York: Oxford University Press.

Webster, D., & Kruglanski, A. (1994). Individual differences in need for closure. *Journal of Personality and Social Psychology, 67*, 1049–1062.

Wilson, D. S., Near, D., & Miller, R. R. (1996). Machiavellianism: A synthesis of the evolutionary and psychological literatures. *Psychological Bulletin, 119*, 285–299.

Yang, K. S. (1993). Chinese social orientations: An integrative analysis. In: L. Y. Cheng, F. M. C. Cheung and Char-Nie (Eds), *Psychotherapy for the Chinese: Selected Papers from the First International Conference* (pp. 19–56). The Chinese University of Hong Kong.

Zellmer-Bruhn, M., Waller, M. J., & Ancona, D. (2003). The effect of temporal entrainment on the ability of teams to change their routines. In: S. Blount, E. Mannix & M. Neale (Eds), *Research on Managing Groups and Teams* (Vol. 6). Hillsdale, NJ: Lawrence Erlbaum.

Zerubavel, E. (1981). *Hidden rhythms: Schedules and calendars in social life*. Chicago: University of Chicago Press.

THE EFFECT OF TEMPORAL ENTRAINMENT ON THE ABILITY OF TEAMS TO CHANGE THEIR ROUTINES

Mary Zellmer-Bruhn, Mary J. Waller
and Deborah Ancona

ABSTRACT

This chapter examines the relationship between team routines and temporal entrainment. While the process of entrainment generally reinforces the routines that teams follow temporal entrainment also creates opportunities for externally focused teams to change their routines. Entrainment creates team rhythms that include pauses in activity that can act as triggers to change. These pauses alone are not enough to impel teams to change; managers must also employ temporal design to make use of these opportunities for change. Both the rhythms of temporal entrainment and the pauses that accompany them are part of a team's task environment. By uncovering key rhythms, as well as by managing the pauses, managers can both reinforce desired routines and change problematic ones.

INTRODUCTION

Organizational teams rarely exist in isolation of their context, but rather operate within, and are at times enmeshed with, nested systems that can include departments, divisions, organizations, and industries. Such teams are externally

Time in Groups
Research on Managing Groups and Teams, Volume 6, 135–158
© 2004 Published by Elsevier Ltd.
ISSN: 1534-0856/doi:10.1016/S1534-0856(03)06007-9

focused teams because they rely on external parties for resources such as information and funding, and external parties are dependent on team outputs such as decisions, products, and services. These external parties and contexts both enable and constrain teams' work. The importance of considering the general external environment of teams has been noted in previous research (Ancona, 1990; Ancona & Caldwell, 1992). In this paper we examine one specific aspect of the team environment, the temporal context, by detailing the ways in which temporal entrainment affects team routines. In doing so, we provide detail to existing theory about the routine-enhancing role of entrainment, present the additional idea that entrainment creates opportunities for changes in team routines, and build on a growing body of literature that demonstrates the important role time and timing may play in instigating change (Ancona & Chong, 1996; Eisenhardt, 1989; Gersick, 1988, 1989, 1994; Staudenmayer, Tyre & Perlow, 2002; Van de Ven & Polley, 1992).

Much of the previous literature on temporal entrainment in groups focuses on entrainment as a force that maintains routines (e.g. Gersick & Hackman, 1990; Kelly, Futoran & McGrath, 1990; Kelly & McGrath, 1985). We agree with this view, but we also develop the idea that temporal entrainment creates *opportunities* for externally focused teams to change their routines by providing regular pauses in activity. However, more than just the occurrence of a pause is required to overcome the routine-reinforcing effects of entrainment. The focus here is on developing an understanding of the specific characteristics of entraining forces, and how these characteristics can either lock teams more tightly to their routines or help them change them. At the crux of this argument are the questions: How does entrainment both solidify routines and provide opportunities to break the routines? How can we design organizations to best make use of these opportunities for change?

The next two sections describe temporal entrainment and routines and provide some important definitions and boundary conditions. The third section details reasons why temporal entrainment may reinforce existing routines. Next, the conditions are identified under which entrainment, through entrained pauses, may prompt teams to change their routines, with specific emphasis on the need for temporal design. The chapter closes with directions for future research and concluding comments.

ENTRAINMENT

Entrainment is "the adjustment of the pace or cycle of an activity to match or synchronize with that of another activity" (Ancona & Chong, 1996, p. 258).

Entrainment occurs when endogenous routines within teams become synchronized with external pacers. Pacers are *outside* the team, and *internal* routines align with external cycles. For example, new product development groups pace new product development routines to match the timing of the external cycle of industry new product introductions (e.g. major trade shows) (Blount & Janicik, 2002). The new product development team has endogenous routines such as conducting materials analysis, creating and testing prototypes, and modifying production designs. In the absence of the deadlines created by industry new product introduction cycles, these endogenous routines may have a markedly difference pace and duration. Research on entrainment indicates that externally focused teams are entrained to outside temporal rhythms or pacers, and over time match their activity to external temporal forces (Ancona & Chong, 1996; Kelly & McGrath, 1985; McGrath & Kelly, 1986).

Previous research on entrainment emphasized two key components: pace and cycles of activity. Pace concerns the rate at which work is accomplished (Levine, 1988). Teams may become entrained to the pace of activity occurring in other parts of the organization or other levels of the team context. For example, sales teams may work at a particular pace because of external deadlines resulting from seasonal customer demand. Alternatively, cycle is "a single complete execution of a periodically repeated phenomena" (Ancona & Chong, 1996, p. 253, 1998; McGrath & Rotchford, 1983). Examples of cycles include fiscal years and quarters, academic semesters, and industry product introduction cycles linked to events such as annual trade shows. As these cycles are repeated, teams and other organizational actors over time line up their activities to coincide with them. The repetition of cycles creates temporal rhythms, and these rhythms act as "metronomes" for the activity of teams entrained to them (Staudenmayer, Tyre & Perlow, 2002).

In addition to pace and cycles, the rhythms created by entrainment involve pauses between cycles or parts of a cycle. Many pauses are preceded by interruptions or "triggers" that motivate groups to at least momentarily stop their routinized, automatic activity (Langer, 1989; Louis & Sutton, 1991; Staudenmayer, Tyre & Perlow, 2002). For example, a product development group may be interrupted by a summons from management to present an update of its progress. Similarly, a group's regular, routinized task activity may be interrupted by the introduction of new technology. A group may also be interrupted while performing its routinized work when its completed work reaches the end of a phase of work. Airline flight crews, for example, experience a natural interruption of their routines as they complete the take-off phase of flight and move into the cruise segment of flight (Waller, 1999).

While groups' routinized task work may be interrupted by countless events, not all interruptions motivate pauses of discernable length. Some interruptions emanate from the natural flow of work within groups, such as those created by moving from one endogenous phase of work to another. For example, in a creative task, one sub-set of tasks surrounds the generation and evaluation of alternatives. Once complete, the team turns attention to implementation. This transition often occurs in a seamless fashion. Therefore, such interruptions are less salient to groups and thus less likely to create pauses that result in breaks from routinized activity, as compared to those interruptions that emanate from external entraining forces. We therefore differentiate *internal pauses* from *entrained pauses*. Our focus is not on internal pauses that are precipitated by breaks in task phases that are a natural part of the team tasks or development. Our focus is on entrained pauses that are precipitated by interruptions external to groups and that are created by multiple parts of the organization and multiple teams aligning their activities to a common rhythm. This common interruption imposes communal pauses on all entities that are entrained to it. For example, one organization identifies a week when the operating committee reviews plans for all ongoing projects; during that week, organizational attention collectively pauses to focus on the direction of the company. Such entrained pauses are created by multiple parts of the organization and multiple teams that align their activities based on temporally entrained rhythms. However, the timing of internal pauses is a characteristic of teams that may affect the influence of entrained pauses on team adaptation of routines. Little attention has been paid to the role of pauses in entrainment, but it is these pauses that are the key to unlocking the routine-destroying nature of entrainment.

TEAM ROUTINES

Routines exist across all levels of an organization, including teams. Routines have been described as "a fact of life in groups" (Gersick & Hackman, 1990, p. 69). A substantial literature exists concerning organizational routines and related constructs, with a wide array of definitions and assumptions surrounding routines (e.g. Betsch, Fiedler & Brinkman, 1998; Edmondson, Bohmer & Pisano, 2001; Feldman, 1989; Gersick & Hackman, 1990; Levitt & March, 1988; March & Simon, 1958; Miner & Mezias, 1996; Nelson & Winter, 1982; Pentland & Rueter, 1994; Simon, 1947; Weick, 1992, 1993; Weiss & Ilgen, 1985; Winter, 1996). A number of common characteristics exist across definitions of routines, which can be summarized as: (a) routines involve behaviors and concern processes and action; (b) routines are sets of behaviors and must include more than a single behavior; (c) routines involve collective action and coordination, involving either multiple actors or multiple behaviors within a single actor; and (d) routines occur more than once. Clearly a wide variety of team actions can be classified as routines. Team routines are defined here as coordinated team practices that are enduring and occurring regularly. This definition follows others who consider processes and practices as interchangeable with routines (Pentland & Rueter, 1994; Szulanski, 1996).

An example of a routine team practice was described by members of a medical product sales and service team with which we are familiar. These teams, typically consisting of about 10–15 members, work to provide coordinated sales and service for many complex medical devices such as Magnetic Resonance Imaging (MRI) machines to hospitals, clinics, and research centers. These teams typically field and distribute service calls using various methods across teams. In one team, calls go directly from the customers to individual team members. If the fielding team member cannot handle the call, he or she forwards it to another team member. In another team, a member is appointed as a central clearinghouse for such calls. This person follows certain rules when parsing out the calls. Both of these practices are routines and constitute the repetitive way that incoming service calls are handled. While these routines are internal or contained within the team's boundaries, other practices may extend beyond the boundaries of a team. For example, new product development teams may have specific practices for managing the hand-off of a design to manufacturing, or iterations between design and production engineers. In this way, routines can be either fully contained within the team or may be enmeshed with other parts of the organization.

Team routines are persistent and may be functional or dysfunctional. Teams quickly develop routines that guide their collective action (e.g. Dougherty, 1992; Gersick, 1988, 1989; Gersick & Hackman, 1990; Kelly & McGrath, 1985). Routines become more persistent over time. For example, the longer a decision-making group is together, the less members experiment with new approaches to work (Ancona, 1990). Routines are functional for groups in that they improve efficiency by reducing uncertainty and by saving time by eliminating the need to deliberate over appropriate action (e.g. Allison, 1971; Cyert & March, 1963). By reducing uncertainty and providing predictability to member behavior, routines also contribute to members' comfort within their group (Gersick & Hackman, 1990). Without routines, teams would not be efficient structures for collective action (March & Simon, 1958). Taken together, the literature demonstrates the positive effect of routines on collective action in teams.

Routines, however, can also have dysfunctional consequences. They can reduce the likelihood of innovation and adaptation, and they are likely to result in performance decrements if applied in situations that have changed (Gersick & Hackman, 1990). A routine may be functional for a time, but if a performance circumstance changes, its continued use may result in undesirable outcomes (e.g. Langer, 1989). Furthermore, in the same way individual decision-makers have been demonstrated to "satisfice" (March & Simon, 1958), teams may use routines to settle for the first acceptable solution as opposed to searching for the optimal solution and "to use existing repertoires of performance programs whenever possible rather than developing novel responses" (Scott, 1992, p. 104). Routines developed early in a team's life may be satisfactory but not optimal. If this is the case, maintaining a routine even under stable conditions may limit a team's performance. Furthermore, many teams face dynamic environments necessitating changes in their routines over time to maintain or improve performance. Therefore, in many cases it may be necessary and desirable for teams to change their routines.

While it may be desirable for teams to change routines, implementing such change remains a challenge because the processes by which organizations and teams change routines are relatively under-explained in the literature (Edmondson, Bohmer & Pisano, 2001, p. 685). Routines prove quite resistant to change. Even obvious problems with existing routines do not always induce change. Furthermore, previous research has generally not considered the more complex ways that interdependence with the environment may influence team routines (Gersick & Hackman, 1990), though notable exceptions exist (e.g. Edmondson et al., 2001; Staudenmayer, Tyre & Perlow, 2002). Many team routines are interdependently linked with actors external to the team and as such team often need to synchronize their routines with actions and events occurring in these external actors (McGrath & O'Connor, 1996). For example, Staudenmayer and her colleagues (2002) describe software development teams that are interdependent with marketing. In order for the software developers to complete their work, they depend on the timing and availability of information from marketing about market shifts. If market information gathering routines are not synchronized with product development routines, inferior product choices are made.

While there may be a number of different mechanisms involved in the adaptation of routines, more attention has been paid recently to the role of time and timing in changing routines. Previous work has examined the role of deadlines (Gersick, 1988, 1989) and temporal shifts (Staudenmayer, Tyre & Perlow, 2002) in prompting changes in routines. In this paper we examine the role of the temporal context of the team, using an entrainment lens, in order to better understand the effect of entrainment on the ability and likelihood of teams to change their routines.

Routines are embedded within team processes, and can become influenced by and linked to exogenous rhythms in teams' external environments (Ancona & Chong, 1996; Blount & Janicik, 2002; McGrath & Kelly, 1986). The influence of external rhythms becomes more pronounced the more interdependent the team is with its external environment and the more permeable its boundaries. In other words, the more externally focused a team is, the more likely that entrainment will influence team routines.

TEMPORAL ENTRAINMENT AS
ROUTINE-REINFORCING

Conceptual work on team routines suggests that temporal entrainment enhances and reinforces existing routines (Gersick & Hackman, 1990). Routines are inherently difficult to change (Edmondson, Bohmer & Pisano, 2001). This resistance to change becomes magnified if routines are also entrained or modified to match the rhythm of a powerful pacer and if routines are interdependently linked with other teams, units, or organizations. By definition, entrainment involves the repetition of activity cycles. This repetitive, cyclical nature provides predictability to the team environment, which in turn supports the development of routines.

The paucity of empirical research that does examine entrainment in groups supports the idea that entrainment reinforces routines. For example, Kelly and McGrath (1985) provide an example of the persistence of entrained rhythms and the way that such rhythms may reinforce the pace of existing team routines. Pace concerns the rate at which work is accomplished. When pace is entrained, the rate at which teams work is aligned with, and becomes driven by, external temporal demands such as deadlines. In the Kelly and McGrath study, groups completed a series of tasks (solving anagram puzzles) across different deadline conditions. In the first work period, groups had either 5, 10, or 20 minutes to solve as many puzzles as possible. Groups then completed the task again twice. Groups with initially short time limits had increasingly longer time limits over the next two trials, and groups with initially long time limits had increasingly shorter time limits over the next two trials. Results indicated that groups entrained their pace of work to the length of time they were given to complete a task in their first trial (in all cases the deadline was externally set by the researchers). More specifically, in subsequent trials, the groups maintained the initially entrained pace of task performance, even if their time allotment was increased or decreased. Groups with shorter time limits in the first trial set a faster pace in their first trial and then maintained a faster pace in subsequent trials, even though they had more time to complete their task. Conversely, groups with longer time limits in the first trial set a slower pace in their first trial and maintained this slower pace in subsequent trials, even though they had less time in those subsequent trials. Other similar research indicates that in addition to pace of activity, patterns of interaction also persist across trials (Kelly, Futoran & McGrath, 1990). These results suggest that entrainment can cement routines and, once cemented, these routines will be difficult to change, even if other conditions change.

How does entrainment reinforce routines? While previous literature does not overtly delineate the processes, we suggest at least three mechanisms: (a) entrainment focuses periodic repetition, which reinforces the repetitive nature of routines; (b) entrainment links team routines to larger inertial systems; and (c) entrainment focuses team attention on certain aspects of the task and away from others that may require adaptation or signal the need for adaptation.

If routines have temporal characteristics that are linked to exogenous rhythms, these routines may be more difficult to change than routines not so linked. The first mechanism of entrainment "represents repeated patterns of activity" (Ancona & Chong, 1996, p. 278) and, therefore, the emphasis is on repetition, not innovation. Given this repetitive nature, temporal entrainment may act to reinforce existing routines – routines that involve both coordinated activities and time are more entrenched. For example, some faculty members have class sessions that are so routinized that they literally repeat the same jokes at exactly the same point in the lecture year after year. Knowing that the class will be repeated for the same number of hours for the same number of weeks year after year reinforces the practice of using the same notes and saying the same thing. Think what might happen if the professor was told that the next semester the class was being held in nine sessions instead of fifteen!

In the second mechanism, temporal entrainment reinforces routines not only because it creates repetition, but also because entrainment is a system-wide process. As a result, the team gets pulled into an interdependent temporal web. Thus, the team cannot change without changing other entrained rhythms; it is locked into a routinized *pattern*. Because of the systemic ties that entrainment creates for teams, entrainment has been identified as akin to inertial forces (Gersick & Hackman, 1990). In other words, in an interdependent temporal web, one team may not be able to alter its routines because it must depend on the availability of other parties to make changes. As a result change becomes more difficult without coordinated action across multiple interdependent entities.

For example, consider a set of healthcare teams created to develop and implement a complex redesign of the scheduling process, called "open access," in a group of medical clinics. Currently, patients typically cannot obtain an immediate appointment with their primary care physician, but must schedule the appointment further in the future than desired, resulting in a back-log of patient visits. To serve customers (patients) better, teams were created in each clinic to redesign the process to allow any patient to expect to obtain a "same day" appointment. The scheduling process consists of many enmeshed routines and is contingent on many things, including doctor availability, room availability, type of appointment, medical records, nursing staff, and laboratory demand. In one clinic, the team worked for several months on the process redesign, attempting to change the scheduling routine in August. This month, however, has a historically high demand for physician vacations, thus it is a recurring (annually) period where a substantial number of physicians are out of the office simultaneously, and, therefore, a period of low supply of appointments. Because the scheduling team was externally dependent on the physician availability, it was unable to change the existing routine. This example illustrates the way in which entrainment as a system-wide process may act to restrain a team's ability to change its routines.

Finally, the third mechanism by which entrainment reinforces routines is by linking teams to *particular* entrained pacers and, therefore, particular entities. For example, a team may be entirely focused on the product development cycle and its inherent technology. Such entrainment focuses attention on that pacer and entity and may preclude a focus on other pacers and entities (e.g. the customer). This capturing of attention through entrainment may be particularly strong when alternative pacers operate at different cycles and are never even "seen." For example, if the product development cycle ends in February, while the customer buying cycles occur in December, then the development company may have completely missed key opportunities for sales.

An interesting example of how routines get reinforced through entrainment in general, and the mechanisms of repetition and focus in particular, was provided on National Public Radio in July 2002. A call-in listener wanted to know why the major television networks could not stagger the introduction of new shows. Why, he asked, do networks start all the new shows in September when the audience is overwhelmed with new offerings? With HBO, he argued, the audience has time to get into one program before the next new one is introduced. The guest explained that the networks must get paid advertising and this has to be done in the spring. Along with spring funding comes the commitment to start in the fall. A number of attempts to change this cycle have been unsuccessful. As this situation illustrates, the entrained pattern across actors and organizations can become so strong and enmeshed that little can be done to create innovative practices. In the case of the networks, the cyclical pattern of developing shows for a simultaneous introduction date serves to lock-in this pattern of the same deadlines and cycle every year. Furthermore, advertising sales have been entrained to spring, thus reinforcing the timing of content development. In essence, this cycle places greater focus on advertising sales than on creative content development and consumer demands.

These mechanisms of repetition, enmeshed with larger temporal systems and focused attention on certain task elements at specific times, are ways in which entrainment may serve to reinforce routines. Previously, this reinforcing nature of entrainment has been the primary focus of discussions linking entrainment to routines. While the mechanisms we detailed clearly indicate that temporal entrainment may reinforce existing routines, previous research has overlooked the interesting paradox presented by entrainment – that it also may provide "moments" where changes in routines may be more possible. The routine-destroying potential is dependent, however, on what managers do at these moments.

TEMPORAL ENTRAINMENT AS ROUTINE-DESTROYING

Changing routines requires a switch of focus from automatic to active cognitive processing (Louis & Sutton, 1991), situational awareness, and a variety of other mechanisms (Gersick & Hackman, 1990; Langer, 1989). In addition to the routine-reinforcing effects described, entrainment may also support focused switches necessary for teams to change their routines. In other words, the cycles and rhythms to which routines are connected create certain points in time where change becomes more possible and thus more likely. In this sense, a routine may be connected to an exogenous temporal rhythm that has natural pauses.

Pauses are created by slowed activity, or when there are breaks in entrained cycles, or there are periodic interruptions that allow teams to "stop and think" about their work progress (Ancona & Chong, 1996; Okhuysen, 2001; Okhuysen & Waller, 2002). Such interruptions in the regular performance of work may make it more likely that groups adopt new routines. For example, Zellmer-Bruhn (2003) found in one study that teams that experienced more interruptive events in a month also reported greater attention to their routines, as well as more adoption of new routines. Entrained rhythms that share pauses also "line up" multiple elements in an organization. When teams are interdependent with external parties, and when their routines are thus interlocked with other parties, the pauses created by entrained rhythms provide "crossing points" (Ancona, Okhuysen & Perlow, 2001) at which many interdependent parties may be aligned in critical phases of their task progress, and therefore more able to change routines that require complementary changes made by other organizational units. Therefore, entrainment may provide opportunities for teams to change their routines, particularly if the routine is part of a larger network of interdependent routines.

In sum, entrained pauses are important opportunities for changing routines because they are stopping points for reflection, and they are moments to link with other parts of the organization. In this sense, temporal entrainment creates an opportunity for change, but does not guarantee that it will happen. Entrained rhythms and their corresponding pauses often become routine themselves. Thus, the interruption created by the entrained pause may not result in changes. If, by definition, the entrained pauses themselves are not novel events, what factors increase the likelihood that teams will engage in adaptive behavior during (or as a result of) the pauses created by entrainment? We suggest that temporal design is crucial to efforts aimed at tipping the entrainment balance toward creating routine changes rather than contributing to the inertia reinforcing routines. That is, the manager needs to manipulate temporal parameters to enhance the probability of innovative behavior. The temporal design factors that are the most important in this regard are:

(1) recognizing that entrainment occurs;
(2) setting up an organizational rhythm with entrained pauses;
(3) creating the appropriate meaning of time;
(4) pairing change triggers and entrained pauses;
(5) creating appropriate crossing points; and
(6) linking internal and external pauses.

It is important to note that temporal design occurs at both the organizational and the team level, even when the objective is to shift routines at the team level. As noted, an external view of teams (Ancona, 1990; Ancona & Caldwell, 1992) emphasizes that teams exist in a context that has important effects on team processes and performance. Using the entrainment lens we have seen how team routines become entrained to larger rhythms in the external environment, thus change has to come from that external environment as well.

Setting Up an Entrained Rhythm with Pauses

After recognizing that entrainment occurs, managers within the organization or subunit need to map the major external rhythms and cycles that are most relevant to it and to create a plan of action. Key activities might include prioritizing the important external rhythms and cycles. For some units the customer and top management team cycles may be the most important while for others supplier rhythms dominate the priority list. Then it becomes necessary to capture the key deadlines, windows of opportunity, and external events associated with those rhythms and cycles (Ancona & Chong, 1998). For example, in the publishing business, books need to be written by certain dates in order to reach customers when they are ready to buy.

The organization then needs to create an internal rhythm of product development, sales, manufacturing, etc., that entrains to those external demands. An important aspect here is to operate at the pace, of in conjunction, with key cycles in the environment. Also key is coordinating the work within the organization. It is within this internal rhythm that entrained pauses are created. Examples would include all product development teams being reviewed for resource allocation every four months or all university faculty being reviewed for tenure in the fall.

Pauses become the arenas where routines can be enhanced or changed. But first pauses must be created, and this requires greater awareness on the part of managers for temporal design. For example, in a study of the temporal interruptions created by changes in technology, Staudenmayer, Tyre and Perlow (2002) found that engineers and managers did not recognize that interruptions in production might be consciously exploited. Once an entrained rhythm with pauses has been identified or established, managers must attend to what occurs during the pause to capitalize on the opportunity for change it provides.

Creating the Appropriate Meaning of Time

As we have emphasized before, the mere creation of a pause does not assure that a routine that is entrained to that pause will change. To set the climate for change, the pause period needs to be imbued with the expectation of change. Managers must create the very meaning of time. Pauses can be framed as opportunities (Dutton, 1993), and thus by emphasizing what to do with the pause and accentuating the need for a shift in attention focus at the pause (Louis & Sutton, 1991), expectations held by the larger organization about innovation and temporal norms impact the meaning of time in the organization and the efficacy of entrained pauses in stimulating team adaptation of their routines.

The organizational context in which a team is embedded sets expectations about how time will be used by teams and, thus, how pauses will be used. Organizations vary in the degree to which they emphasize a need for change and innovation. Existing norms and beliefs may dictate that entrained pauses are times where change is expected. In organizations that emphasize innovation, entrained pauses are more likely to result in team adaptation than in organizations with less relative emphasis on innovation. For example, at 3M, a predetermined amount of one's time must be set aside for work on innovative, out-of-the-box ideas. In another organization, managers are required to leave time at the end of a project to catalog new things that were learned. One manager has the task of passing on the new ideas to newly formed teams.

When organizations create a context in which change and innovation are emphasized, teams within those contexts are more likely to be reflexive. In other words, when prevailing norms about *what to do with time* suggest that teams ought to use time to seek change and innovation, teams are more likely to use pauses to "collectively reflect on the group's objectives, task strategies, and internal processes, and adapt them to current or anticipated endogenous or environmental circumstances" (Gevers, van Eerde & Rutte, 2001; West, 1996, p. 559). Reflexive teams are more likely than non-reflexive teams to reflect on their relationships with their external environment, and to actively attempt to structure their activities and the way they interact, adapting them over time (West, 1996). Reflexive teams are likely to have a more developed temporal imagination, or "the ability to understand the intersection of one's own temporal behavior with that of the larger timescape" (Bluedorn & Standifer, 2002, p. 7). As a result, a reflexive team is more likely to take advantage of pauses for innovative action, thus increasing the probability that entrained pauses will be routine-destroying as opposed to routine-enhancing (Feldman, 2000). The degree to which teams use pauses to be reflexive is directly related to the extent to which managers consciously and explicitly send messages about the use of such pauses as opportunities for change, and set expectations about using pauses to change (Staudenmayer, Tyre & Perlow, 2002).

In addition to expectations about change and reflexivity, organizations and teams have varied temporal norms (Bluedorn, 2000; Schein, 1992; Schriber & Gutek, 1987; Zellmer-Bruhn, Gibson & Aldag, 2001). Organizations place varying emphasis on temporal elements such as speed, punctuality, polychronicity, work pace, time allocation, and awareness of time use. To the extent that the very meaning of time becomes associated with change (e.g. "every moment is a chance to improve"), teams will be more likely to act on the opportunity provided by entrained pauses to make changes in their routines. Without this emphasis, the pause itself is likely to become routinized and lack the requisite novelty to prompt change. In sum, organizational expectations about innovation and time infuse the organization and teams with concrete practices and also infuse the very meaning of time.

Pairing Change Triggers and Entrained Pauses

Entrained pauses are viewed as "windows of opportunity" (Tyre & Orlikowski, 1994) for teams to change their routines, but not necessarily as triggers to change in and of themselves. Gersick and Hackman (1990) and others (Langer, 1989; Louis & Sutton, 1991) have identified several triggers to changing routines. Entrained pauses will be more potent if they are paired with change triggers. That is, the fourth step in temporal design is to pair triggers and pauses; to use the trigger at the appropriate moment. Here we focus on the triggers of incentives, feedback, and technology, all of which have been associated with change at multiple levels of analysis.

Incentive
Incentives to change associated with an entrained pause can increase the probability that teams will make changes to their routines. In one organization we have observed, the entrained pause was a time for evaluating new product ideas and making budget decisions. If an innovative product idea was introduced by a team, the result could be an increased budget, becoming a strategic product, getting additional personnel, or exposure to top management. As such, these pauses are a time of new ideas from multiple teams. Innovative organizations pair deliverables associated with change to a pause.

Feedback

It is well known that change is facilitated through a feedback process; giving information about how one is doing propels them to act on that information (Ammons,
1956; Erez, 1977; Nadler, Cammann & Mirivs, 1980). Here we argue that it is
even more effective if there is a temporality to feedback. Entrained pauses become
more potent in shifting routines to the extent to which they contain feedback. If the
entrained pause contains feedback about "how we are doing" it may be more likely
to result in changes to routines. In another organization we have observed, product
development teams had to take a week off – a pause – following a particular phase
of product development to determine how they would move forward. Teams
received progress reports at this time evaluating along defined parameters their
performance. These reports helped the teams to focus their changes on the areas
most in need of improvement. Thus, if organizations want to change, then pauses
need to contain feedback that signals that they either keep moving with their
current practices or that they give up and move on to something else.

Technology

If the entrained pause is paired with a change in technology it will be more likely
to result in teams changing their routines. The implementation of new technology
has been noted as a trigger for changing organizational routines (e.g. Barley, 1986,
1988; Edmondson, Bohmer & Pisano, 2001; Szulanski, 2000; Tyre & Orlikowski,
1994; von Hippel, 1994). The period surrounding the installation of a technology
is often a period of high activity of adaptation and acquisition of routines (Tyre &
Orlikowski, 1994). Edmondson and colleagues (2001) provided an example of how
the introduction of new technology prompted changes in team routines. Their study
examined the implementation of a new cardiac surgery technique by teams in several hospitals. Installation of a new technology interrupts routine work and prompts
a period of active search for information and adaptation of routines. In several of
the teams in Edmondson's study, surgery teams changed interaction routines as a
result of the new technology. For example, the previous technology was consistent
with top-down commands from the surgeon. The new technology required much
more interdependent decision-making and, as a result, most teams changed their
communication routines after the technology was introduced. Even so, technology
is an inconsistent catalyst for change; even in the face of a technology change,
changing routines is a struggle and may not occur (Edmondson et al., 2001).

In the case of a team facing a technological change, there is likely to be
interdependence among team members, and in the case of externally oriented
teams, between team members and parties outside the team. Edmondson et al.
(2001) suggest that new team routines are developed through a process of team
learning that is dependent on leadership and the corresponding authority structure,

and psychological safety. To this, we add the timing of technology changes. Pauses provide temporal coordination points for interdependent team members. As a result, if the pause contains changes in technologies, teams will be more likely to change their routines at that time.

To summarize, the fourth step of temporal design is to explicitly pair event-based change triggers with time-based changes (for an explanation of event-based change triggers and time based changes, see Gersick, 1994; Staudenmayer, Tyre & Perlow, 2002). In particular, when entrained pauses contain incentives to change, performance feedback, or coincide with the introduction of new technology, those pauses are more likely to trigger changes in team routines.

Creating Appropriate Crossing Points

Teams may still find it difficult to change routines – even if incentives and feedback are right – because of the web of entrained and interdependent behaviors that characterize externally focused teams. Indeed, Staudenmayer, Tyre and Perlow (2002, p. 21) noted that "most change in complex organizations must be a concerted effort on multiple fronts" and such effort requires synchronization across multiple teams and actors. Thus, an entrained pause may be more likely to trigger changes to routines to the extent that the pause encompasses the multiple players engaged in an entrained rhythm. Entrained pauses have been previously identified as potential crossing points (Ancona, Okhuysen & Perlow, 2001). Crossing points temporally link multiple parts of the organization. Some crossing points may be temporally wide (i.e. the pause is shared by a large number of organizational units and levels), many of which have different internal temporal patterns. Wide crossing points permit changes in routines that are enmeshed across teams and organizational subunits. In an academic setting, summer break is a wide crossing point because most academic units within a specific university, as well as across many universities, share the timing of this pause. In the absence of a wide crossing point, teams may be unable to change routines that require corresponding, temporally synchronized changes in other parts of the organization. Thus, the fifth step in temporal design is to create at least some pauses that are wide crossing points.

Linking Internal and External Pauses

Thus far our steps of temporal design have involved organization-level initiatives. The sixth step involves linking team and organizational pauses. In one organization we studied as part of a recent data collection effort, top management initiated a major organizational shift and took the entire organization out of the office for an offsite meeting to initiate the change – a pause. Unfortunately, this event was seen as a major interruption for the teams who were in the middle of major work periods. Actual change did not start for four additional months when teams finished their work and were "ready" for new activities (Ancona, 1990). This initiative would have been more successful and would have resulted in more routines changing if the organizational pause had been linked in time to actual pauses in team work rhythms.

Research has shown that there are certain moments in a team's life when change is more likely to occur. These include the start of a team, the mid-point, the end, and other milestones in internal task performance (Gersick, 1988; Gersick & Hackman, 1990). These moments are also associated with different stages of development. We argue that the sixth step in temporal design is to link these moments with external pauses.

The linking of team and organizational rhythms can be accomplished at either level. An earlier example shows that had the head of the organization meshed the change with existing team rhythms it would have had more momentum. Linking can also occur at the team level. In one of the organizations, most of teams set their task deadlines to coincide with periodic product development evaluation meetings. The one team that did not align with this cycle was unable to gain legitimacy and funding.

One way to enhance the likelihood of appropriate linking of internal and external pauses is to address the degree of the *boundedness* of teams. Group researchers have noted that teams differ in the extent that their boundaries are permeable (Alderfer, 1977; Louis & Yan, 1999). Some teams are more likely to cross their boundaries and be open to input from outside the boundaries than are others. Other teams focus much more inwardly and tend not to engage in boundary-spanning activities (Ancona & Caldwell, 1992). Such teams may be at risk to become overbounded; they may be unable to recognize ways in which external temporal patterns interact with their routines, creating an inability to engage in change at a pause. For teams to engage in change at a pause, they must be able to identify when a pause is occurring, determine what the requirements of the pause are, and find a way to appropriately respond to those requirements. All of these activities require interaction across a boundary. To further support this idea, Gersick and Hackman (1990) identified high cohesion in groups as a factor in maintaining routines. As a result, groups that have very strong norms and are highly cohesive may be less likely to attend to the external signals created by an entrained pause. As a result, these teams may not experience the entrained pause as reason to facilitate change.

Teams with more permeable boundaries are able to assess external demands, figure out what is needed, and deliver it (Ancona, Bresman & Kaeufer, 2002). Adaptive organizations need externally oriented, adaptive teams that are able to

Table 1. Creating Routine-Destroying Temporal Design.

1. Identify critical rhythms
2. Set up an entrained rhythm with pauses
3. Create the appropriate meaning of time
4. Pair change triggers with entrained pauses
5. Create appropriate crossing points
6. Link internal and external pauses

align internal pauses with entrained pauses and take advantage of these moments. Team must be able to fit their internal rhythms to the overall beat of the organization. If team members are cocooned within their teams, they are more likely to maintain an entrainment to internal rhythms, and the team as a whole is likely to lack the capacity to fit a broader pattern of external entrainment. Unless the pause is very potent, the incentive or push for change provided by the pause will not even reach the team and therefore not offer the opportunity for routine change.

Summary

Entrained pauses create opportunities for change for teams with an external focus. These teams are typically dependent on their external environments for resources and outputs. Given the web of interdependencies around these teams, it is likely to be more difficult for them to change their routines because many of these routines are linked to external parties, and changing them would require synchronized changes by the external parties as well. Entrained pauses create moments in which multiple, interconnected parties can change. However, the opportunity for change created by entrained pauses is not likely to be realized unless other characteristics are present. Temporal design can increase the likelihood that entrained pauses trigger changes in team routines. Thus, entrainment may also facilitate change. Table 1 summarizes the steps involved in routine-destroying temporal design.

DISCUSSION

This chapter illustrates the value of focusing an entrainment lens on research concerning team routines. The temporal nature of routines, particularly the effect of larger temporal patterns on team routines, provides clues to the reasons why team may have difficulty changing their routines. However, the true fruitfulness of combining routinization and entrainment can only be realized if both routine-reinforcing characteristics and the routine-destroying potential of entrainment are considered. Managers may, at various times, wish to emphasize reinforcement over change and vice versa. The key to managing both sides of the entrainment-routine link is temporal design.

Applying the entrainment lens to team routines suggests that entrainment is a powerful force by which routines are captured and maintained. In particular, there are three mechanisms by which entrainment acts to reinforce existing routines: (a) repetition; (b) linking the team to larger external cycles; and (c) focus. The routine-reinforcing nature of entrainment can be very beneficial because routines provide comfort, security, and predictability to team members. Managers, however, must understand that entraining forces will reinforce functional as well as dysfunctional routines. By understanding temporal design, managers can act to reinforce desired routines. Entrainment can serve to reinforce routines when the routines are inten-tionally linked to key rhythms that place greater emphasis on certain aspects of the team's task and on certain stakeholders. For example, in the HBO vs. networks ex-ample given earlier, if managers wanted to emphasize routines for creative content development based on viewers interests, they could relax the demand that the show be developed according to advertising sales schedules and instead link the develop-ment to viewer-based schedules. Even if, on the balance, desirable routines rather than undesirable routines are linked to entraining forces, the powerful combination of entrainment and routines suggests that teams and organizations become incred-ibly inertial when left to their own devices. If not managed, undesirable routines may be unwittingly reinforced by entrained rhythms.

As organizations face increasingly dynamic and fast paced environments, change and innovation become increasingly important. A key part of organiza-tions' ability to change resides in teams' ability to change their routines, and thus to break out of the inertial forces of entrained routines. In this chapter, we point out that managers have at their disposal a powerful tool, temporal design, to aid in the creation of innovation and change. Temporal design expands the focus from tra-ditional emphasis on structural design to add a focus on *when*, how often, for how long, and in conjunction with which external cycles things occur. Temporal design enables managers to create and structure pauses to create innovation when it is most needed.

Managing temporal design to destroy existing routines involves a number of key steps. First, as with reinforcing routines, managers must identify important rhythms in the team's environment and subsequently link team routines to desired rhythms and pauses. Entrained pauses act as interruptions to team routines and provide the potential for adaptation. Next, managers must actively manage the meaning of time in their organizations. To enhance the routine-destroying poten-tial of entrained pauses, team members must view pauses as a time for change, resulting in greater reflexivity about their routines. Furthermore, pauses should be linked with other known triggers of change such as incentives, feedback, and technology. Timing powerful change triggers with the moments ripest for change – pauses – improves the chances that teams will change their routines. The pause, however, must encompass the right parts of the organization. If changes in team routines are not synchronized with interdependent players, the desired change will be impeded. Finally, temporal design aimed at destroying routines will be more effective if crucial internal pauses are aligned with entrained pauses. This effectively aligns endogenous moments with ripe external moments. Active management of all of these aspects of temporal design provides managers with a powerful set of tools.

While this chapter is an important first step in detailing the potential benefit of linking research on team routines and entrainment, many questions remain. For example, future research should consider how balance between reinforcing and destroying routines is best achieved. Several options are possible. First, a manager can create two sets of teams, one organized to maintain existing routines and the status quo, and the other set focused on destroying routines and change. Second, teams may be set up to maintain routines but have an overarching rhythm that shifts to routine destruction after some set time interval. For example, the same curriculum might be taught five years in a row, but every sixth year there is a curriculum change. In this instance the pauses in this sixth year may need to be designed differently. A third option is to maintain ongoing, continuous change through regular pauses that are designed for change.

In addition to questions about tipping the balance from maintenance to change, our arguments in both cases rest on managers' ability to detect crucial rhythms in the team and organizational environment. This diagnosis includes how often pauses should occur, how many and how large/long the pauses ought to be, and whether they should be aligned with areas inside or outside the organization. Future research needs to more fully explore the tools managers may use to detect key entraining forces. Also, there are likely to be multiple, nested, and often contradictory cycles in a team's environment, which present a need to understand which entraining forces are most important to a given team/routine pair. How many rhythms can or should a team be entrained to while maintaining a reasonable pace and rate of change?

Another interesting question is whether pauses need to be managed differently if evolutionary change or revolutionary change is desired. Does the timing and length of pauses need to vary depending on the type of change desired? Can some regularly occurring pauses be identified for use for evolutionary change, but then at certain times be identified as moments for radical change?

Beyond issues of the entraining rhythms and pauses themselves, additional theoretical development is needed in terms of differential effects of temporal design on various types of team routines. Clearly, routines are not uniformly alike. Routines vary in terms of length, duration, frequency, repetition, and number of actors involved, to name just a few dimensions. Some have suggested, for example, that frequently executed routines are particularly difficult to change (Edmondson, Bohmer & Pisano, 2001; Gersick & Hackman, 1990). Teams also vary in the degree to which their work is dominated by a single or small number of routines or characterized by multiple, interdependent routines. Some routines are repeated sequentially; when one cycle is finished, the routine is begun again. Other routines are performed with less regularity. Which routines are important? Which are most crucial to link to prevailing rhythms and pauses? Future research should examine the ways in which temporal design can match pause and cycle across varied types of routines.

Finally, future research must examine changes in the entrained rhythms themselves. In this chapter, we have largely stayed within existing rhythms to show how a greater understanding of existing rhythms can result in routine reinforcement as well as opportunity for change, but others (Staudenmayer et al., 2002) demonstrated the power of *shifting* deadlines and rhythms to achieve change, and the need to consider the effects of shifting timelines on team adaptation (Waller, Zellmer-Bruhn & Giambatista, 2002). Future research should examine when and why it may be appropriate to use existing rhythms and pauses to facilitate change, and when and why it may be appropriate or necessary to invoke temporal design to prompt change by creating new pauses and corresponding rhythms.

CONCLUSION

This chapter illustrates the value, both theoretical and practical, of combining temporal entrainment with team routines, to understand adaptation in teams. In so doing, we answer the call for more attention to an external view of teams – taking into consideration the relationship between teams and their contexts. We extend the literature on temporal entrainment and team routines to consider the potentially *positive* effects of temporal entrainment on team adaptation of routines. Finally, we point out potential leverage points for managers to consider when they want to prompt and encourage changes in team routines. The insights provided by the entrainment lens further reinforce the need to include an external perspective in the study of team routines.

We hope readers are left with the sense that routines are linked to temporal patterns and patterns within patterns. These patterns are linked to pauses, which are opportunities for change. Both entrainment and the corresponding pauses are a natural part of a team's task environment, and we argue that by discovering key rhythms, as well as by engineering the pauses and what occurs during a pause, managers have additional control over both reinforcing desired routines and changing those that are problematic.

REFERENCES

Alderfer, C. P. (1977). Group and intergroup relations. In: J. R. Hackman & J. L. Suttle (Eds), *Improving Life at Work* (pp. 227–296). Palisades, CA: Goodyear.

Allison, G. T. (1971). *Essence of decision*. Boston: Little, Brown.

Ammons, R. B. (1956). Effects of knowledge on performance: A survey and tentative theoretical formulation. *Journal of General Psychology, 54*, 279–299.

Ancona, D. G. (1990). Outward bound: Strategies for team survival in an organization. *Academy of Management Journal, 33*, 334–365.

Ancona, D. G., Bresman, H., & Kaeufer, K. (2002). The comparative advantage of X-teams. *Sloan Management Review, 43*(3), 33–39.

Ancona, D. G., & Caldwell, D. F. (1992). Bridging the boundary: External activity and performance in organizational teams. *Administrative Science Quarterly, 37*, 634–665.

Ancona, D. G., & Chong, C. L. (1996). Entrainment: Pace, cycle, and rhythm in organizational behavior. *Research in Organizational Behavior, 18*, 251–284.

Ancona, D., & Chong, C. (1998). Cycles and sychrony: The temporal role of context in team behavior. In: E. Mannix & M. Neale (Eds), *Research on Managing in Groups and Teams* (Vol. 2). Greenwich, CT: JAI Press.

Ancona, D. G., Okhuysen, G. A., & Perlow, L. A. (2001). Taking time to integrate temporal research. *Academy of Management Review, 26*(4), 512–529.

Barley, S. R. (1986). Technology as an occasion for structuring: Evidence from observations of CT scanners and the social order of radiology departments. *Administrative Science Quarterly, 31*, 78–108.

Barley, S. R. (1988). On technology, time and social order: Technically induced change in the temporal organization of radiological work. In: F. A. Dubinskas (Ed.), *Making Time: Ethnographies of High Technology Organizations* (pp. 123–169). Philadelphia: Temple University Press.

Betsch, T., Fiedler, K., & Brinkmann, J. (1998). Behavioral routines in decision making: The effects of novelty in task presentation and time pressure on routine maintenance and deviation. *European Journal of Social Psychology, 28*, 861–878.

Blount, S., & Janicik, G. (2002). Getting and staying in-pace: The "in-synch" preference and its implications for work groups. In: E. A. Mannix, M. A. Neale & H. Sondak (Eds), *Research on Managing Groups and Teams: Vol. 4. Toward Phenomenology of Groups and Group Membership* (pp. 235–266). Greenwich, CT: JAI Elsevier.

Bluedorn, A. (2000). Time and organizational culture. In: N. Ashkanasy, C. Wilderom & M. Peterson (Eds), *Handbook of Organizational Culture and Climate*. Thousand Oaks, CA: Sage.

Bluedorn, A. C., & Standifer, R. (2002). Groups, boundary spanning, and the temporal imagination. Groups, boundary spanning, and the temporal imagination. In: S. Blount, E. Mannix & M. Neale (Eds), *Research on Managing Groups and Teams: Time in Groups* (Vol. 6). Greenwich, CT: JAI Press.

Cyert, R. M., & March, J. G. (1963). *A behavioral theory of the firm*. Englewood Cliffs, NJ: Prentice-Hall.

Dougherty, D. (1992). Interpretive barriers to successful product innovation in large firms. *Organization Science*, *3*, 179–202.

Dutton, J. (1993). The making of organizational opportunities: An interpretive pathway to organizational change. In: L. L. Cummings & B. M. Staw (Eds), *Research in Organizational Behavior* (pp. 195–226). Greenwich, CT: JAI Press.

Edmondson, A., Bohmer, R. M., & Pisano, G. P. (2001). Disrupted routines: Team learning and new technology implementation in hospitals. *Administrative Science Quarterly*, *46*, 685–716.

Eisenhardt, K. M. (1989). Making fast strategic decisions in high-velocity environments. *Academy of Management Journal*, *32*(3), 543–576.

Erez, M. (1977). Feedback: A necessary condition for the goal-setting performance relationship. *Journal of Applied Psychology*, *64*, 533–540.

Feldman, D. (1989). Careers in organizations: Recent trends and future directions. Special Issue: Yearly review of management. *Journal of Management*, *15*(2), 135–156.

Feldman, M. S. (2000). Organizational routines as a source of continuous change. *Organization Science*, *11*, 611–629.

Gersick, C. J. G. (1988). Time and transition in work teams: Toward a new model of group development. *Academy of Management Journal*, *31*(1), 9–41.

Gersick, C. J. G. (1989). Marking time: Predictable transitions in task groups. *Academy of Management Journal*, *32*(2), 274–309.

Gersick, C. J. G. (1994). Pacing strategic change: The case of the new venture. *Academy of Management Review*, *37*(1), 9–45.

Gersick, C. J. G., & Hackman, J. R. (1990). Habitual routines in task-performing groups. *Organizational Behavior and Human Decision Processes*, *47*, 65–97.

Gevers, J. M. P., van Eerde, W., & Rutte, C. G. (2001). Time pressure, potency, and progress in project groups. *European Journal of Work and Organizational Psychology*, *10*(2), 205–221.

Kelly, J. R., Futoran, G. C., & McGrath, J. E. (1990). Capacity and capability: Seven studies of entrainment of task performance rates. *Small Group Research*, *21*(3), 283–314.

Kelly, J. R., & McGrath, J. E. (1985). Effects of time limits and task types on task performance and interaction of four-person groups. *Journal of Personality and Social Psychology*, *49*, 395–407.

Langer, E. J. (1989). Minding matters: The mindlessness/mindfulness theory of cognitive activity. In: L. Berkowitz (Ed.), *Advances in Experimental Social Psychology* (pp. 137–171). New York: Academic Press.

Levine, R. B. (1988). The pace of life across cultures. In: J. E. McGrath (Ed.), *The Social Psychology of Time: New Perspectives* (pp. 39–92). Newbury Park, CA: Sage.

Levitt, B., & March, J. G. (1988). Organizational learning. *Annual Review of Sociology*, *14*, 319–340.

Louis, M. R., & Sutton, R. I. (1991). Switching cognitive gears: From habits of mind to active thinking. *Human Relations*, *44*(1), 55–76.

Louis, M. R., & Yan, A. (1999). The migration of organizational functions to work unit level: Buffering, spanning, and bringing up boundaries. *Human Relations*, *52*, 25–47.

March, J. G., & Simon, H. A. (1958). *Organizations*. New York: Wiley.

McGrath, J. E., & Kelly, J. R. (1986). *Time and human interaction*. New York: Guilford.

McGrath, J. E., & O'Connor, K. M. (1996). Temporal issues in work groups. In: M. A. West (Ed.), *Handbook of Work Group Psychology* (pp. 25–52). New York: Wiley.

McGrath, J. E., & Rotchford, N. L. (1983). Time and behavior in organizations. In: L. L. Cummings & B. M. Staw (Eds), *Research in Organizational Behavior* (Vol. 5, pp. 57–101). Greenwich, CT: JAI Press.

Miner, A. S., & Mezias, S. J. (1996). Ugly duckling no more: Pasts and futures of organizational learning research. *Organization Science, 7*(1), 88–100.

Nadler, D. A., Cammann, C., & Mirvis, P. H. (1980). Developing a feedback system for work units: A field experiment in structural change. *The Journal of Applied Behavioral Science, 16*(1), 41–62.

Nelson, R. R., & Winter, S. G. (1982). *An evolutionary theory of economic change.* Cambridge, MA: Harvard University Press.

Okhuysen, G. A. (2001). Structuring change: Familiarity and formal interventions in problem-solving groups. *Academy of Management Journal, 44,* 794–808.

Okhuysen, G. A., & Waller, M. J. (2002). Focusing on midpoint transitions: An analysis of boundary conditions. *Academy of Management Journal, 42*(5), 1056–1066.

Pentland, B. T., & Rueter, H. H. (1994). Organizational routines as grammars of action. *Administrative Science Quarterly, 39*(3), 484–510.

Schein, E. H. (1992). *Organizational culture and leadership* (2nd ed.). San Francisco: Jossey-Bass.

Schriber, J. B., & Gutek, B. A. (1987). Some time dimensions of work: Measurement of an underlying aspect of organizational culture. *Journal of Applied Psychology, 72*(4), 642–650.

Scott, W. R. (1992). *Organizations. Rational, natural and open systems* (3rd ed.). Englewood Cliffs, NJ: Prentice-Hall.

Simon, H. A. (1947). *Administrative behavior: A study of decision making processes in administrative organization.* New York: Macmillan.

Staudenmayer, N., Tyre, M., & Perlow, L. (2002). Time to change: Temporal shifts as enablers of organizational change. *Organization Science, 13*(5), 583–597.

Szulanski, G. (1996). Exploring internal stickiness: Impediments to the transfer of best practices within the firm. *Strategic Management Journal, 17*(Winter Special Issue), 27–43.

Szulanski, G. (2000). The process of knowledge transfer: A diachronic analysis of stickiness. *Organizational Behavior and Human Decision Processes, 82,* 9–27.

Tyre, M. J., & Orlikowski, W. J. (1994). Windows of opportunity: Temporal patterns of technological adaptation in organizations. *Organization Science, 5*(1), 98–118.

Van de Ven, A. H., & Polley, D. (1992). Learning while innovating. *Organization Science, 3*(2), 92–116.

von Hippel, E. (1994). Sticky information and the locus of problem solving: Implications for innovation. *Management Science, 40,* 429–439.

Waller, M. J. (1999). The timing of adaptive group responses to non-routine events. *Academy of Management Journal, 42,* 127–137.

Waller, M. J., Zellmer-Bruhn, M. E., & Giambatista, R. C. (2002). Watching the clock: Group pacing behavior under dynamic deadlines. *Academy of Management Journal, 42*(5), 1046–1056.

Weick, K. E. (1992). *The social psychology of organizing.* Reading, MA: Addison-Wesley.

Weick, K. E. (1993). The collapse of sensemaking in organizations: The Mann Gulch disaster. *Administrative Science Quarterly, 38*(4), 628–652.

Weiss, H. M., & Ilgen, D. R. (1985). Routinized behavior in organizations. *Journal of Behavioral Economics, 14,* 57–67.

West, M. A. (1996). Reflexivity and work group effectiveness: A conceptual integration. In: M. A. West (Ed.), *Handbook of Work Group Psychology* (pp. 555–579). Chichester, UK: Wiley.

Winter, S. G. (1996). Organizing for continuous improvement. Evolutionary theory meets the quality revolution. In: M. D. Cohen & L. S. Sproull (Eds), *Organizational Learning* (pp. 460–483). Thousand Oaks, CA: Sage.

Zellmer-Bruhn, M. E. (2003). Interruptive events and team knowledge acquisition. *Management Science, 49*(4), 514–528.

Zellmer-Bruhn, M. E., Gibson, C. B., & Aldag, R. J. (2001). Time flies like an arrow: Tracing antecedents and consequences of temporal elements of organizational culture. In: C. L. Cooper, S. Cartwright & P. C. Earley (Eds), *The International Handbook of Organizational Culture and Climate* (pp. 21–52). New York: Wiley.

GROUPS, BOUNDARY SPANNING, AND THE TEMPORAL IMAGINATION

Allen C. Bluedorn and Rhetta L. Standifer

ABSTRACT

The temporal imagination is the understanding of the intersection of one entity's timescape with the larger timescapes of which that entity is a part. We examine in detail what the temporal imagination is, complemented with a discussion of the related timescape idea, and why the temporal imagination is necessary to function in any timescape. We also discuss group attributes that will likely affect the development of the temporal imagination and its use and how its use in group boundary spanning efforts affect both the groups and the larger organization.

INTRODUCTION

The temporal imagination is the ability to understand the intersection of one entity's timescape with the larger timescapes of which that entity is a part. The entity can be an individual, a group, or an entire organization, but this chapter focuses on boundary spanning groups and their parent organizations. Several attributes of boundary spanning groups that are likely to influence the quality of the group's temporal imagination are then presented and analyzed (group diversity, shared mental models within the group, longevity, and autonomy).

Two generations ago, C. Wright Mills' wrote *The Sociological Imagination* (1959), which ever since has provided an enduring description of the enterprise

Time in Groups
Research on Managing Groups and Teams, Volume 6, 159–182
ISSN: 1534-0856/doi:10.1016/S1534-0856(03)06008-0

of social science as defined by the concept in the book's title. According to Mills, "The sociological imagination enables us to grasp history and biography and the relations between the two in society" (p. 6). Further, the sociological imagination allows people "to understand what is happening in themselves as minute points of the intersection of biography and history in society" (p. 7). Thus it would be fair to say that the sociological imagination is the ability to understand the intersection of history and biography, and in that understanding to comprehend the effect each has on the other.

It is impossible, however, to understand that intersection completely without an understanding of the temporal dimensions of both biography and history, such an understanding being the proper focus of the *temporal imagination*. The term "temporal imagination" has been used sparingly in a variety of disciplines, including literature (Barth, 1991; Weitzel, 1999), sociology (Nock, 1998), and political science (Chowers, 1998). To the best of our knowledge, it has not been used previously in the organization sciences.

What is the temporal imagination? Why is it necessary to function in any timescape? How does its use in group boundary spanning efforts affect both the groups and the larger organization? These will be the fundamental questions addressed and developed in this chapter. We will begin by considering the concept of the temporal imagination itself, complemented with a discussion of the related timescape idea, followed by a discussion of group attributes that will likely affect the development of the temporal imagination and its use.

THE TEMPORAL IMAGINATION

Cervantes died on April 23, 1616. Shakespeare also died on April 23, 1616, which leads without much thought to the conclusion that both bards died on the same day – an erroneous conclusion. For the date of Cervantes' death is the date according to the Gregorian calendar, which came into use in Spain in 1582 (Richards, 1998, p. 248), whereas the date of Shakespeare's passing is the date according to the Julian calendar (details about Cervantes and Shakespeare from Whitrow, 1988, p. 119), which was still in use in England at the time and would continue to be used there until 1752 (Richards, 1998, p. 248). Thus Shakespeare actually lived ten days longer than Cervantes because the date of Shakespeare's death on the Gregorian calendar would be May 3, 1616 (Whitrow, 1988, p. 119).

The Gregorian calendar was instituted by Pope Gregory XIII in 1582 because the Julian calendar was falling out of step with the seasons, leading Easter to head into parts of the year the church felt were undesirable (Bluedorn, 2002, pp. 160–161). However, Gregory was a pope, so Anglican England did not adopt the reformed calendar until 1752, thereby creating the false impression that Cervantes and Shakespeare died on the same day.

In this example, it would be fair to say that anyone who saw the two dates and concluded that these two giants of Western literature had perished on the same day was using a limited temporal imagination. To reach the proper conclusion about their two deaths, at a minimum one would need to know the following: (1) the calendar used throughout much of the world in the 21st century for secular matters was instituted in the late sixteenth century (1582); but (2) its adoption was a slow process, especially outside Catholic countries, and that process of adoption would continue well into the twentieth century. In particular, one would need to know that England did not adopt the Gregorian calendar until 1752, well after Shakespeare's death. Without this knowledge, it would be natural to assume that the dates given for both men's deaths were dates on the same calendar, hence that both deaths had occurred on the same day. For time and things temporal tend to be cultural matters, and they often reside in the deepest parts of culture, at the level Schein labeled basic underlying assumptions (1992, pp. 16–22). As such, it is easy to take physical manifestations of culture, like the calendar, for granted and to assume that they have always been in use in their current forms.

The calendar – be it Gregorian, Julian, Hebrew, Chinese, or Mayan – serves as an example of one component of a *timescape*. Although others had used the term earlier (e.g. Benford, 1980/1992), Barbara Adam (1998) developed the concept of timescape, writing:

> Where other scapes such as landscapes, cityscapes and seascapes mark the spatial features of past and present activities and interactions of organisms and matter, timescapes emphasise their rhythmicities, their timings and tempos, their changes and contingencies. A timescape perspective stresses the temporal features of living. Through timescapes, contextual temporal practices become tangible. Timescapes are thus the embodiment of practiced approaches to time (p. 11).

The calendar and calendar system that a society uses are one part of that society's "practiced approaches to time," hence a part of its timescape. When such practices are combined mindfully with a broader understanding of the timescape to consciously affect decisions and actions, it is appropriate to say that the temporal imagination is being employed. Thus we define the temporal imagination – a derivative of the sociological imagination (understanding the intersection of history and biography) – as *the ability to understand the intersection of one's own temporal behavior (i.e. timescape) with that of the larger timescape.*

Temporal imaginations promote the functioning and survival of individuals and groups. At times, such an imagination, if used properly, can provide a competitive advantage leading to particularly high performance. Given such potential impacts, developing a strong temporal imagination seems imperative. Developing a powerful temporal imagination begins by learning what characteristics and dimensions to look for in other timescapes – as well as in one's own. Thus, a necessary condition for developing an insightful temporal imagination is the ability to discern a timescape's temporal dimensions. Toward the end of promoting such discernment, we identify six universal dimensions of timespaces in the following discussion.

EXPLORING THE TIMESCAPE

We believe that every timescape will have its unique attributes, if for no other reason than that every socio-cultural phenomenon will have a unique history, hence its development will have produced idiosyncratic forms and characteristics. Nevertheless, there are fundamental temporal phenomena that will occur in any timescape. The ability to identify these phenomena and understand their roles in the specified timescape are requisite abilities for a well-functioning temporal imagination.

Adam suggests several fundamental temporal phenomena in her general description of timescapes, emphasizing "their rhythmicities, their timings and tempos, their changes and contingencies" (1998, p. 11). Rhythmicities and their timings and tempos are important temporal phenomena that combine to form portions of a timescape, as is indicated in Adam's terms "timings" and "contingencies." Bluedorn (2002) identified some of the same fundamental temporal phenomena that Adam suggested, also emphasizing rhythms and the relationships among rhythms.

Both researchers also identified how rapidly things are done as an important temporal characteristic, albeit Adam uses the term "tempo"; Bluedorn, "speed." Bluedorn identified polychronicity, temporal depth, temporal focus, and punctuality as fundamental temporal phenomena as well.

Polychronicity is the extent to which people: (1) prefer to be engaged in two or more tasks or events simultaneously and are actually so engaged (the preference strongly implying the behavior and vice versa); and (2) believe their preference is the best way to do things (Bluedorn, 2002, p. 51). Anthropologist Edward Hall developed the concept of polychronicity and was the first to use it to explain human behavior (see Bluedorn, 1998; Hall, 1959/1981, 1983). Hall used the concept to describe and explain both individual and cultural differences, and Bluedorn (2002, p. 48) described it as "a fundamental strategy for engaging life." Polychronicity is an essential element in any well-developed temporal imagination because it describes a fundamental temporal characteristic of individuals and their timescapes as well as of a collectivity such as an organization and its timescape.[1] Thus those seeking to develop an insightful temporal imagination should certainly examine the timescape to note its level of polychronicity – just as people developing a temporal imagination should note the timescape's characteristic temporal depth and focus.

Social scientists have identified "time orientation" (e.g. Kluckhohn & Strodtbeck, 1961, pp. 13–15) as a fundamental way to describe how individuals and cultures differ in their beliefs and emphases on time, the term tending to refer to the relative emphasis placed on the past, present, and future (see Bluedorn, Kaufman & Lane, 1992, p. 26). More recently Bluedorn (2000, 2002) has pointed out that this single concept often masks two independent constructs: one having to do with which general temporal region (past, present, or future) a person or culture tends to emphasize; the other having to do with how far into the past and the future people and cultures tend to look when they are thinking about things. The former he termed temporal focus; the latter, temporal depth. Therefore, we suggest that these are important temporal aspects of entities and the timescapes in which they reside. They are best considered as two distinct temporal phenomena rather than one.

Finally, following the work of Levine (e.g. Levine, 1997; Levine, West & Reis, 1980; Levine & Wolff, 1985), Bluedorn (2002) indicated that punctuality – how important it is to be on time and what is defined as being on time – is a fundamental temporal phenomenon, and as such, like the other temporal phenomena inventoried so far, it can properly describe both entities and their timescapes.

To summarize, we have identified six fundamental temporal characteristics that would seem to be properties of all timescapes: rhythmicities/rhythms, tempo/speed, polychronicity, temporal depth, temporal focus, and punctuality. Given that they are reasonably well established in the time literature as such, they are likely to be found in all timescapes, albeit other temporal characteristics are likely to be found in timescapes too. Further, the temporal imagination can now be recast as *understanding the intersection of two or more timescapes* because the entity, including individuals, will have regular practiced approaches to time, thus allowing us to speak of an individual, group, or organization's *internal* timescape as well as of the timescapes of the larger systems of which the entities are a part. Knowing, however, which fundamental temporal properties a timescape possesses is not enough to fruitfully employ the temporal imagination; other knowledge and behaviors are necessary too.

DEVELOPING THE TEMPORAL IMAGINATION IN GROUPS

To develop and use the temporal imagination effectively, one must identify and develop knowledge about one's internal timescape as well as the larger timescapes of which one is a part. For groups and organizations to do so, knowledge is required about the potential advantages of groups and of how groups and other collectivities interact with their environments.

Groups Advantages

Given finite time and other limited resources, the individuals who compose a group should be able to see more aspects of a timescape's reality than any solitary individual, *ceteris paribus*. Further, such an advantage will accrue only when the members of the group attempt to process their knowledge to build a more accurate and larger overall picture of that timescape reality, rather than when the group's members argue that their observations are the only correct descriptions of the timescape. The group will need to see its goal as producing a larger, more accurate and complete description of the timescape, but a description that is always subject to revision and additional development. Thus, the argument should never be about issues such as: Is the elephant more like a wall, a spear, a snake, a tree, a fan, or a rope? – the debate carried on by the six blind men in John Saxe's (1892) famous poem. Rather, the discussion of how to interpret the observations should focus on what information each observation provides about the reality in question. To get the group to operate in this fashion and with this orientation is where knowledge of organizational behavior and group dynamics can truly inform this task, as will be demonstrated shortly. But before exploring further the inner workings of groups that might enhance their ability to use temporal imaginations, the relationship between groups and other collectivities with their environments needs to be addressed, especially one strategic aspect of that relationship.

Actors are Parts of Their Own Timescapes

Gareth Morgan (1997, p. 258) has noted, "Many organizations encounter great problems in dealing with the wider world because they do not recognize how they are part of their environment." Implicit in our analysis is the premise that the larger timescapes that a group or organization participates in are crucial aspects of their environments. A critical – albeit subtle – point for any temporal imagination to recognize is that the actor itself is a part of the larger timescape in which it exists, which means that to understand the intersection of the actor with its timescape requires much more comprehension than simply noting the fundamental temporal characteristics of both the actor and the timescape and how they are similar and different.

As basic as these points are to an adequate temporal imagination, they form but the foundation upon which truly imaginative temporal insights are based. Once these basics are understood, the next step is to proceed to a deeper understanding of the intersection of actor (e.g. individual, group, or organization) and timescape. Namely, how do specific actions that actors take affect/change the timescape, and in turn, how do those subsequent timescape changes affect the actor? Morgan (1997, p. 260) provides examples of how organizations, sometimes acting as an entire industry, make decisions and take actions with only the short-term future in mind. Considering only short-term consequences, this implies, however, that had longer-term futures and other possible impacts on both the environment and their consequences for the organization been considered, other decisions might have resulted.

If we consider an example focusing on the temporal aspects of both the organization and its timescape, we may see the type of thinking the temporal imagination might employ to identify such effects and consequences. The example is the development of the emphasis on speed that is at the heart of the organizational strategy known as time-based competition (Blackburn, 1991; Stalk & Hout, 1990). Let us consider: (1) this strategy from the perspective of a single focal organization; (2) the impact this organization might have on its timescape if it adopts this strategy; and (3) the likely subsequent impacts these timescape changes might have on the organization itself.

Assume that the organization's strategic management team is considering the option of time-based competition, that is, of altering its way of operating so that it can develop, produce, and bring to market new products faster than its competitors (see Stalk & Hout, 1990, p. 29). Making these changes will create costs for the organization as well as potential benefits, so the strategists would need to consider the ratio of the two, as well as the feasibility of making the changes and the probability that the strategy will work (i.e. will produce the minimal acceptable benefits and do so with an acceptable cost-benefit ratio). Such traditional thinking is likely to focus on the results for the organization, and to focus on them in terms of profitability.

Let us now add thinking directed by the temporal imagination to this decision and see some of the issues it might highlight. First, what are some of the organizational changes regarding temporal matters that a shift to a time-based strategy might require or produce? Time-based strategies require, virtually by definition, an emphasis on speed, on doing things faster. Thus one of the immediate challenges for the organization will be a change in the temporal portion of its culture, of its internal timescape, to value and practice doing things faster. This will be necessary because no strategy can be implemented optimally when it is incompatible with the organization's culture (Bluedorn & Lundgren, 1993). Clearly, this culture-change effort will be easier the closer the organization's timescape already is to values and "practiced approaches" emphasizing the importance of doing things fast. This is an easy observation, one that does move beyond just basic descriptions of timescape features – the internal timescape in this case – but one that does not overly stretch the developing temporal imagination.

More challenging are the next two questions: (1) What effect will the shift to this strategy have on the larger timescape in which the organization functions? and (2) What effect might those changes to the larger timescape have on the organization? First, let us assume that the focal organization is an industry leader, or that if it was not before the change, that it became one after the shift to the time-based strategy. (We will beg the question of causality here and simply assume an empirical association with organizational success.) Institutional forces such as mimetic imitation (DiMaggio & Powell, 1983) will likely lead other organizations operating in the same timescape to adopt versions of time-based strategies themselves. Assuming they do, this will directly change at least one fundamental dimension of the timescape: the extent to which doing things fast is valued. Compared to the moments before the focal organization adopted the time-based strategy, the entire timescape will now place a much greater emphasis on speed, on doing things fast. Other temporal dimensions of the timescape are likely to be affected too, but those effects are more difficult to anticipate.

Second, the focal organization's original time-based strategy will no longer confer the same degree of competitive advantage it once did, if at this point it will confer any competitive advantages vis-à-vis the competition at all. This suggests the temporal imagination would reveal that the competitive advantage conferred by the initial version of the time-based strategy will be finite rather than indefinite, and that subsequent competitive advantages will have to come by either enhancing the time-based strategy, that is, by doing things even faster, or by seeking competitive advantages in other areas.

To follow through with this example, let us assume the focal organization's strategists decide to enhance the time-based strategy in response to the timescape's changes, that they make further changes so that their organization values and practices doing things even faster. As would be expected, the other organizations in the timescape would respond as they did before, by enhancing their own time-based strategies, and the entire timescape comes to value and practice doing things even faster still. But as only the most creative temporal imagination might anticipate from this spiral of positive feedback loops, at some point further enhancements could well become counterproductive, that things would be done *too* fast. For example, at one point in the history of the Japanese computer industry, product changes and improvements were being developed and brought to market so quickly that customers were delaying purchases in anticipation of yet better machines being available later. This led to a conscious effort to actually reduce the rate of product development in this industry (Ancona & Chong, 1996, p. 262).

This example demonstrates that organizations are not only part of their own timescapes, but also how the temporal imagination is important. We will now see in more detail how that imagination can be developed and enhanced in a particular type of group.

GROUPS AND BOUNDARY SPANNING

We stated earlier that given the finite time and resources usually available to organizations, groups are better suited to the development of a robust temporal imagination than individuals because of the aggregated vision that comes from multiple perspectives. In this regard, all groups (and their organizations) benefit from this collective perspective; but particularly useful are those groups that engage in boundary spanning activities on behalf of their organizations.

Boundary spanners and boundary spanning groups establish and maintain relationships between the organization and external social networks, providing a primary conduit of information about these networks that the organization uses to make decisions. Therefore, groups engaged in boundary spanning activities interpret the external environment to the organization, as well as represent the organization back to entities in the environment. (This description is reminiscent of Likert's description of individuals performing linking functions between groups, 1961, p. 166, albeit we focus more on groups as the linking agents than individuals.) In the past, boundary spanning roles included sales representatives, recruiters, and bargaining agents (Kahn, Wolfe, Quinn, Snoek & Rosenthal, 1964). However, technology and increased interorganizational collaboration have broadened the definition of what constitutes a "boundary spanner."

Just as past researchers (March & Simon, 1958; Pennings, 1998; Thompson, 1967) have emphasized the importance of organizational boundaries and the boundary spanner's role as a conduit of information from a traditional perspective, we believe it is equally important to the temporal viewpoint. By gathering and assessing information from outside the organization and by using that information to aid the organization in its decision making, the boundary spanning group develops an understanding of its own internal timescape, that of its organization, and of the relationships of both to the larger timescapes in the environment. It also addresses the issues of how to "link" itself and the organization to the environment so that the environment and organization are each represented to the other, thereby enriching the group's and the organization's temporal imagination. Therefore, we will restrict our discussion of groups to those whose primary purpose is to perform boundary spanning activities and part of whose mission is the development and understanding of the timescape and hence the temporal imagination of the group and the organization.

As mentioned previously, timescapes are formed by practiced approaches to time. For groups functioning within an organizational framework, these practiced approaches can include multiple calendars (society's, the fiscal year, etc.), deadlines imposed within (or upon) the group, meetings, the methods of synchronizing member schedules, seasonal cycles, and the various idiosyncrasies of the industry in which the group functions. The ways in which boundary spanning groups address these temporal practices can change, depending upon the attributes or characteristics of the group. In other words, the characteristics of a group affect the way in which that group confronts or handles practiced approaches to time, creating the group's unique timescape. Likewise, attributes of boundary spanning groups also affect the group's temporal imagination and its ability to understand and effectively use that imagination to help it and its organization manage their relationships with the larger environment.

Because of this, we shall now discuss how various group attributes can contribute to the internal timescapes of groups focused upon boundary spanning activities and the resultant effect on such groups' temporal imaginations. Although the general research on group attributes is both broad and extensive, we will focus on the following specific attributes: informational diversity within the group, temporal diversity within the group, extent of shared mental models within the group, group longevity, and degree of group autonomy.

Prior to a discussion concerning group diversity, it should be noted that researchers study many sources of diversity in groups, including gender, race, tenure, and educational backgrounds. In fact, past researchers (Guzzo & Dickson, 1996; Jackson, May & Whitney, 1995; Magjuka & Baldwin, 1991) have linked group diversity to group effectiveness, creativity, and decision-making. Given the vast scope of research on this topic, however, and with an eye toward what is particularly relevant to groups engaged in boundary spanning activities, we restrict our discussion to two types of diversity, one of which is found in the extant literature and one of our own making: informational diversity and temporal diversity, respectively.

Informational Diversity

Informational diversity is defined as differences in knowledge and perspectives among group members due to differences in education, experience, and expertise (Jehn, Northcraft & Neale, 1999). The nature and purpose of boundary spanning

groups, which often entail cross-functional group membership and/or different organizational origins (i.e. a group created for the purposes of developing an ongoing,
interorganizational relationship), increases the likelihood of such diversity within
these groups. The empirical research that examines the effects of such diversity
within groups has produced mixed results (Ancona & Caldwell, 1992; Jackson,
1992). With regard to boundary spanning groups, however, we feel greater levels of
informational diversity within such groups will provide an advantage over groups
with lower levels of such diversity, in terms of the group's timescape and temporal
imagination.[2]

One reason is that informational diversity creates a broader, richer group
timescape for boundary spanning groups. This occurs because the diverse group
of boundary spanning members gathers information and material from a greater
number of sources as individual members target the areas with which they are
familiar. Likewise, such diversity in group members provides a richer foundation
of experience from which to assess the information and material gathered over the
course of boundary spanning activities.

Groups with diverse experience can also better determine how the results of
their boundary spanning activities can best serve the temporal needs of their
own group and the organizations they represent. It is interesting to note that
we (and researchers such as Ofori-Dankwa & Julian, 2001) question whether
it is sometimes better *not* to be perfectly synched rhythmically in all ways with
external components of one's larger social system. Indeed, Ofori-Dankwa and
Julian (2001) have suggested the idea of an "entrainment quotient," meaning the
ease and speed with which individuals, groups, and organizations can adjust time
orientations to better assess the need to synchronize with outside components.
Groups whose members' diversity of experience allows the groups' timescapes
to effectively "link" to the timescape of its environment, and whose temporal
imagination is such that the group is able to detect and effectively manipulate this
link, might have a higher "quotient" than a more homogeneous group.

Later in this chapter, we will examine several caveats that are necessary when
discussing the effects of diversity in groups. However, we prefer to discuss these
notes of caution after our examination of the second type of group diversity:
temporal diversity, to which we now turn.

Temporal Diversity

Just as diversity of experience affects a boundary spanning group's timescape
and temporal imagination, the extent to which the group members differ in key
temporal dimensions also influences the group's ability to understand and develop

its own internal timescape and how the group fits within the timescape of its organization and the larger environment. We define temporal diversity as the extent to which the group exhibits variance along the key temporal dimensions discussed earlier in the chapter. These temporal dimensions would include speed and punctuality, rhythmic activity, polychronicity, and temporal focus and depth.

In the previous section, we stated that informational diversity leads to positive outcomes (e.g. a well-developed timescape and temporal imagination). However, as a study conducted by Jehn et al. (1999) illustrates, the results of diversity are not always positive. As we will see, diversity is not uniformly beneficial with regard to these temporal dimensions either.

For example, we feel that in terms of speed and punctuality, groups exhibiting higher levels of diversity will experience more problems than groups that are more homogeneous. Hence, if some members emphasize fast decision-making while other members choose to deliberate for longer periods of time, conflict (i.e. process, task, and relationship conflict) is more likely. As a meta-analysis of conflict's effect on team performance shows (De Dreu & Weingart, 2002), such conflict among group members diminishes the performance (i.e. the quality of decisions) of the group. Likewise, if punctuality is terribly important to certain members, while others are more cavalier about arriving on time, similar results should be expected.

We suggest that the group's emphasis on speed and punctuality should be dictated by the cultural rhythms and the dynamism of the environment with which the group is scanning and interacting, rather than by the individual preferences of group members. Such sensitivity to the external timescape exemplifies the importance of a well-developed temporal imagination in boundary spanning groups, as well as the importance of understanding how the timescape of the organization and the group impacts the larger environmental timescape, and vice versa. If a group has the ability to detect rhythmic patterns and practices within its external environment, and if the group is able to effectively manage its own temporal behavior to its advantage, both the group and the organization(s) it represents benefit. For instance, Eisenhardt (1989) showed that dynamic environments dictate the need for faster speed in decision making. Therefore, a boundary spanning group that understands the intersection of its timescape with those in its environment will respect the cultural norms of that environment and respond appropriately with faster speed in its temporal behavior. And to optimally benefit its parent organization, the group will not only modify its own temporal behaviors to deal with those in environmental timescapes, but it will work to produce broader temporal adjustments from other relevant parts of the organization toward a similar end.

Another temporal dimension – rhythms – presents more of a theoretical challenge. Nevertheless, we feel that the ability to detect rhythms in the environment is essential to boundary spanning groups and is likely the *sine qua non* of their temporal imaginations. Therefore, although every group member need not be a master at environmental rhythm detection, this ability is essential to the group's ability to understand timescapes and thus exercise the group's temporal imagination effectively. Organizations can, of course, help promote a group's ability to detect and interpret environmental rhythms by consciously assigning individuals who exhibit this ability to boundary spanning groups (see Bluedorn, 1997, about how to identify such individuals and for an analysis of how they detect environmental rhythms).

While the general ability to detect environmental rhythms is crucial for boundary spanning groups, we believe that boundary spanning groups whose members can detect different *types* of rhythmic patterns in the environment will be better suited to their task than groups whose members can detect only one type of rhythm. Therefore, diversity in the ability to detect different patterns is preferable among the members of boundary spanning groups. To better understand why, consider the painting by Georges Seurat, *A Sunday Afternoon on the Island of La Grande Jatte*, created using the technique of Pointillism. The portrait is made up of nothing but small dots of pure color; it is up to the eye of the viewer to mix and interpret the dots as a unified image. To truly understand the significance of Seurat's work, the person gathering the information must see and appreciate both the micro patterns of the dots as well as the unified pattern created by them.

So it is with boundary spanning groups interpreting the external timescape and relating it back to their parent organizations. This is because most temporal phenomena are either rhythms or properties of rhythms (e.g. polychronicity describes people's characteristic rhythms for engaging events and activities). And since rhythms are often subtle and can possess wave lengths with orders-of-magnitude differences (cf. Bluedorn, 2002, pp. 130, 138), individuals who vary in their characteristic temporal depths will aid the group's ability as a whole to detect and interpret a wider variety of rhythms (i.e. rhythms whose wave lengths vary widely). Thus using Seurat's painting as a metaphor for the environment, group members who stand close to the painting (i.e. who have short-term temporal depths) will be most likely to see the dots and details about them in the painting, whereas members who stand back several feet (i.e. who have long-term temporal depths) will be more likely to see the images formed by the dots. So if boundary spanning groups can access and interpret different rhythmic patterns present in the environment and their organization, doing so will promote a broader, richer temporal imagination and timescape for the group, and ultimately for the group's parent organization.

In terms of polychronicity, boundary spanning groups exhibiting relatively polychronic behaviors can be more effective in their boundary spanning alignment activity than teams exhibiting relatively monochronic behavior; therefore, polychronic behavior by the group is preferred because more group polychromic behavior is likely to generate more information and environmental scanning, and accomplish a larger variety of tasks. Polychronic groups are more likely to see more aspects of the Seurat painting.

Does this mean that there should be little diversity among group members in their own polychronic/monochronic preference? In other words, should relatively monochronic people be discouraged from boundary spanning group membership? Not necessarily, because it is the group as a whole that should exhibit polychronic behavior with regard to the goal of boundary spanning. Thus a group with five very monochronic members, each working on a different task for the group, is by definition much more polychronic *at the group level* than another group with five very polychronic members each of whom is working on the same group task. Whether or not polychronic individuals can more readily work together in a boundary spanning group, especially on the tasks of integrating and interpreting the disparate data about external timescapes, remains an open question. It would be premature to specify the desired characteristics of individual group members in terms of their positions on the polychronicity continuum.

The final temporal dimension under discussion here is temporal focus. (We previously addressed the need for diversity of temporal depths in our discussion of the Seurat painting). Just as with informational diversity and the ability to detect different types of rhythms, diversity with regard to temporal focus is preferable for groups engaged in boundary spanning activities. If a group is charged with gathering and interpreting vast amounts of information from a variety of environmental sources, it is helpful if some members focus on the past and others on the future, thereby painting a more detailed, expansive portrait of the environment and how it relates to the organization.

Cautions and an Example

Earlier, we remarked that several cautionary notes are necessary when discussing the effects of diversity in groups. Recall for a moment the discussion of Seurat's painting and the problem of observing and interpreting the reality of it. The existence (and awareness of the existence) of multiple perspectives (e.g. different perspectives due to experience, temporal focus, etc.) can aid in a clearer and fuller vision of the painting. However, for these multiple perspectives to coalesce into a complete and accurate view of the painting, the members of the group must be able (and willing) to communicate, combine, and arrange the assortment of perspectives in a meaningful way. What follows are several thoughts regarding the successful integration/utilization of multiple perspectives due to informational or temporal diversity among group members. It should be noted, however, that the successful integration of multiple perspectives in groups constitutes a large, formidable topic in and of itself. Therefore, we limit our discussion to a few suggestions particularly relevant to boundary spanning groups.

First, a diversity of perspectives creates the need for more integrating mechanisms to achieve better coordination (Lawrence & Lorsch, 1967). This could potentially make boundary spanning activities more complex for the group; however, the benefits outweigh the potential problems in this case. Promoting and maintaining a group atmosphere in which multiple perspectives are welcome should at least help reduce problems for such boundary spanning groups and increase the likelihood that such mechanisms will be encouraged and used.

Second, boundary spanning groups whose membership consists of a high degree of diversity with regard to organizational origin (e.g. cross-functional groups created for interorganizational purposes) should expect a decrease (albeit not completely) of positive results because of a lack of familiarity among members and possibly a lack of trust. One way to counteract this problem would be to allow such interorganizational groups to remain intact for longer periods of time, thereby allowing members to become familiar and comfortable with one another. (See our discussion below about group longevity for further elaboration on this point.)

Finally, we must ask: How much diversity is too much diversity? The answer is, *it depends*. For instance, greater levels of informational diversity are desirable for the development of a boundary spanning group's temporal imagination. In fact, a certain amount of informational diversity is necessary in boundary spanning groups for a rich temporal imagination to develop. However, moderate levels of diversity can cause groups to splinter into subgroups along "faultlines," causing a detrimental effect to the group and its purpose (Lau & Murnighan, 1998). Higher-than-moderate levels of informational diversity might result in better development than in groups with moderate levels of such diversity, particularly with regard to the tasks often associated with boundary spanning groups. (The strength of such an effect might depend upon the salience of differences relative to the task at hand, and whether these differences were perceived and subgroups created early in the formation of the group, Lau & Murnighan, 1998.)

The optimal level of *temporal* diversity, however, requires further consideration. As we discussed, temporal diversity involves multiple key dimensions; these dimensions can (and we expect, will) differ in terms of preferable levels of diversity. In terms of speed and/or punctuality, we expect moderate levels of diversity to cause results similar to those of informational diversity. For example, if the group is split evenly between members who are always on time and members who are always late (i.e. two groups), a faultline might emerge between the "on-time" and "late" groups, causing conflict. (Of course, if the need to be punctual is not crucial to the task, then its salience might be minimized.) If, however, there is no clear division, either because of common punctuality practices (i.e. one group) or because there is a high level of diversity (i.e. many groups) in terms of punctuality, the issue of being on time might not emerge as an issue within the group because subgroups will not appear.

With regards to other temporal dimensions, however, we suggest that moderate levels of diversity might not have such a detrimental effect. For instance, in terms of temporal focus or the boundary spanning group's ability to detect different types of rhythms, higher levels of this type of temporal diversity might have a positive effect up to a certain point. When a variety of perceptions is valuable to the task at hand (e.g. creativity and decision-making), researchers have linked diversity to positive effects in groups (Guzzo & Dickson, 1996; Jackson, 1992). We suggest that such is the case in terms of these particular types of temporal diversity. At extreme levels of such temporal diversity, however, the negative aspects will most likely outweigh any positive benefits due to increased conflict and uncertainty, such as has been suggested by other researchers (Greening & Johnson, 1997; Hambrick, Seung Cho & Chen, 1996; Williams & O'Reilly, 1998). Of course, there is little or no empirical evidence with regard to temporal diversity or the development of a group's temporal imagination at this time; as such, our discussion is preliminary to such research.

Let us now consider an example of how these forms of diversity in boundary spanning groups might influence a group's understanding of the synergistic relationship of its parent organization's internal timescape with the larger timescape of the external environment. We will return to the example of time-based competition. A boundary spanning group whose members have differing areas of temporal expertise will be more likely to develop a clearer, more accurate composite of the internal and external timescapes. This is so because, at the most fundamental level, such a group will be better suited to assess temporal differences between the organization and the environment. The fact that the group can access and interpret information from a variety of environmental sources also allows it to determine how organizational changes will alter the timescape of the environment and how, in turn, those external alterations will impact the organizational timescape. In time-based competition there is a point of diminishing returns because of the detrimental, cyclical effects as both the organization and the environment respond to the other with an ever-greater emphasis on speed. A boundary spanning group that can gather information from a wider variety of environmental sources might detect that effect faster than a group that only accesses one area of environmental information.

Likewise, differences along temporal dimensions (i.e. overall temporal diversity) affect how time-based competition might have been approached in the earlier example. For instance, a group that emphasizes speed might be able to determine the extent to which the environment embraces (or rejects) the idea of speed and whether a competitive advantage based on speed can be sustained by the organization within that environment.

Shared Group Mental Models

Another potentially influential attribute of the temporal imagination is the existence of shared mental models among group members. A "mental model" is defined as an organized knowledge structure that allows for effective interaction with the environment (Mathieu, Heffner, Goodwin, Salas & Cannon-Bowers, 2000). The idea of "shared" models of understanding dates back to the 1930s, when Mead (1934/1974) described the necessity of such shared models for teams engaged in complex activities requiring a good deal of cooperation. When a mental model is "shared," teams are better able to effectively coordinate activity and decision making (Stout, Cannon-Bowers & Salas, 1996). Shared mental models are helpful to groups engaged in complex, dynamic tasks (Mathieu et al., 2000) and have been positively linked to organizational team effectiveness (Klimoski & Mohammed, 1994). Specifically, shared mental models make it possible for groups to explain phenomena, draw inferences, make predictions of future events, and recognize relationships among environmental elements and other contextual components (Cannon-Bowers, Salas & Converse, 1993). Given this, we feel shared mental models are particularly helpful to groups engaged in boundary spanning activities.

According to shared mental model researchers (e.g. Cannon-Bowers et al., 1993; Klimoski & Mohammed, 1994), teams can use different types of mental models to achieve collaborative, cooperative goals. These models include a shared understanding of technology, mutual knowledge about procedures or environmental conditions, and collective knowledge of member roles, sources of information, and common patterns of interaction.

We would like to add another shared mental model to this list: a shared mental model that denotes a common (shared) timescape and temporal imagination. Indeed, other researchers have discussed the idea that different groups (and cultures) construct shared meanings of time (Ancona, Okhuysen & Perlow, 2001). Boundary-spanning group members who share common, practiced approaches to time (i.e. meanings related to speed, punctuality, deadlines, industry rhythms, etc.)

should experience the same benefits mentioned above that are provided by other mental models. These benefits include the ability to draw inferences, to make predictions of future events (but not to regard those predictions as certainties), and to recognize relationships found in the environment. All these benefits directly relate to a group's shared understanding of its own and other timescapes, all of which denote a broader, richer temporal imagination being employed by the boundary spanning group. Likewise, a shared temporal mental model of practiced approaches to time should aid boundary spanning groups with heterogeneous compositions (informational or temporal) in tasks such as integrating information from varied perspectives, yet still allow a creative flow of different ideas and opinions during the integrative process.

Finally, we suggest that a shared temporal mental model within a group could act as an integrating mechanism, which we recommended earlier. Ancona et al. (2001) have described the need for such a mechanism (called "temporal coordination mechanisms") to control for differences in temporal perspectives and offset potential temporal conflicts between groups and outside, environmental entities. We suggest that a shared temporal mental model within a group could act as such a mechanism and could also make other such mechanisms easier to create and implement.

Group Longevity

Organizational groups vary in the length of time they exist; some groups come together for short, project-based tasks, then separate, while other groups are created for more strategic, long-term purposes. How does this difference affect the temporal characteristics of these groups, and is one form preferable over the other when boundary spanning is the group's purpose? We suggest that both short-term *and* long-term groups are appropriate, depending upon the reason for boundary spanning, and in fact, a balance of both types of groups might be preferable within organizations. In general, a combination of long-term and short-term boundary spanning groups helps create a balance of perspectives within organizations.

On the one hand, Bluedorn and Ferris (2000) found that the longer the organization has been in existence, the longer its temporal depth would be. Therefore, it seems reasonable to suggest that when organizations need a long-range perspective, stable, long-term boundary spanning groups should be emphasized. Such groups will gather and interpret information from the environment of interest for a longer period of time as a unified body, the result of which should be a clearer picture of how their timescape relates to the external one.

For groups that are interorganizational in nature, longer group longevity might be particularly important. Such groups are composed of members that represent different (and often competitive) organizational parties. Longer tenure for these groups is necessary to ensure norms of reciprocity (Ziller, 1965), as well as feelings of trust and collaborative tendencies among members.

However, researchers also have shown the merits of short-term groups. One such virtue relates to the effect of familiarity. Researchers found that the positive effect of familiarity among group members is most significant early in the life of the group (Cannon-Bowers et al., 1995; Katz, 1982). Such familiarity allows groups to come up to speed quickly and coordinate rapidly. However, if the group remains intact over long periods of time, familiarity leads to a decrease in communication and in performance.[3] One could speculate that familiarity might push the group toward groupthink in its deliberations and decision making too.

Given the apparent benefits of both long- and short-term groups, what is best in terms of temporal issues and boundary spanning groups? We suggest that groups of varying tenure be employed to engage in boundary spanning activities. In terms of the organization's comprehension and alignment of its timescape to that of its environment, deeper, richer understandings are created by taking advantage of the strengths of groups of varying tenure. Long-term groups provide long-term experience and perspective, while short-term groups provide flexibility and faster decision-making regarding domain-specific issues. If both short- and long-term groups are in place, the organization has a greater variety of perspectives and information it can draw upon, depending, of course, upon the reason and need for the boundary spanning activity. (We should note that references to either short- or long-term groups does not imply anything about how much time group members spend with each other in boundary spanning or other activities. As with many group activities in organizations, much group work will be carried out by people acting individually. Group activities conducted by the group acting as a face-to-face whole may only occur in meetings held a few times during the year.)

Degree of Autonomy

This final group attribute concerns the degree to which boundary spanning groups are allowed the freedom to direct their own activities. Groups with autonomy usually perform tasks that are highly interdependent within the group, and are usually given the responsibility and authority to control aspects of their work related to those tasks (Guzzo & Dickson, 1996). Given the nature of their goals, we feel boundary spanning groups benefit from a sense of autonomy, particularly from a temporal standpoint.

Such autonomy allows boundary spanning groups to create their own timescape, which may (or may not) mirror the timescapes of parent organizations; in fact, the timescape of the boundary spanning group might actually be more similar to outside entities than to the organizations that created the groups. This can be a good thing. To achieve the goals of boundary spanning, these groups must be allowed to create a timescape that allows them to serve their parent organizations best, and such timescapes should reflect and integrate aspects of the larger social system with which these groups need to interact, and then interpret for their parent organizations. This is the very nature of boundary spanning. Furthermore, when the timescapes of these boundary spanning groups successfully reflect and integrate these elements, the boundary spanning group becomes a sort of lubricant between the organizations,[4] allowing an easier flow of communication and information than might otherwise occur without an ongoing, connecting entity. Without the freedom and authority to break from temporal conformity with their organizations, boundary spanning groups will be restricted in their ability to accurately scan, assess, and represent the environment to the parent organizations, and likewise, the organizations back to the external environment.

CONCLUSION

In this chapter, we have proposed the concept of the temporal imagination, not as a precisely defined theoretical construct that can be instantly operationalized to begin a program of empirical research, but like its sociological progenitor, as a sensitizing concept (Blumer, 1954). A sensitizing concept is a general idea that can point to phenomena that are potentially important (Blumer, 1954, p. 7). In this case, it points to them for time and group scholars to consider, perhaps to investigate.

The results of such consideration may reveal significant competitive advantages to any individual, group, or organization that cultivates the temporal imagination's development and integrates it into strategic deliberations. Competitive advantages accrue not just because additional data are obtained and interpreted, as an information-processing perspective would suggest (e.g. Galbraith, 1977), but because a perspicacious temporal imagination that serves individuals, groups, and organizations well is likely to result from a confluence of idiosyncratic factors such as the histories of both the imaginers (i.e. individuals, groups, and organizations) and the timescapes of which they are a part. Such idiosyncrasies will make each temporal imagination unique; indeed, each application of each temporal imagina-tion will be unique. Thus specific manifestations of temporal imaginations, being unique, will also be inimitable, and according to the resource-based theory of the firm, inimitability is a key attribute of any organizational resource that gives the firm a competitive advantage (Barney, 1986, 1991). And the more inimitable the resource, the longer-lived the competitive advantage will be – something that is likely to be true for individuals and groups, just as it is for organizations.

Regardless of whether the temporal imagination invests its practitioners with significant competitive advantages vis-à-vis others, it promises to provide its practitioners with a better understanding of their worlds. This may be the most important advantage of all.

NOTES

1. Bluedorn (2002, pp. 278–279) has demonstrated that polychronicity was an attribute of the organizations he studied by illustrating the point that polychronicity can be a characteristic of both individuals and collectivities, the former having been demonstrated in several studies (see Bluedorn, 2002, pp. 48–82). In a similar vein, individuals can obviously develop and use temporal imaginations, and when acting collectively as in a boundary spanning group, such a group can *potentially* develop practices for understanding timescapes – the group's own as well as others. This could happen if the synergies of within-group interaction produce perceptions and understandings beyond those of any individual group member. In this sense a group can be described as developing and using a temporal imagination.

2. While the focus of this discussion is the effect of informational diversity upon the group's temporal development, we feel the positive effect of informational diversity (as well as the effect of some forms of temporal diversity, which we discuss below) upon the group's timescape and temporal imagination will ultimately have a positive effect upon the group's effectiveness for the organization as a boundary-spanning entity as well. In other words, we feel that the relationship between informational (and temporal) diversity and group effectiveness is an indirect one, mediated by the richness and complexity of the group's timescape and temporal imagination.

Williams and O'Reilly (1998) maintain that the impact of diversity in groups goes beyond simple main effects. Likewise, the assertion that the relationship between group diversity and performance is an indirect one has been studied by group researchers, with mixed results. For instance, previous researchers have found a direct link between diversity and effectiveness (Bantel & Jackson, 1989; Magjuka & Baldwin, 1991); however, recent studies have found no such direct correlation (Jehn et al., 1999), stressing instead the importance of mediating constructs such as task conflict. Other researchers have suggested such mediating constructs as task complexity and the interdependence of group members. We feel that because we know the purpose of our group (boundary spanning), we can make some assumptions regarding the nature and context of these other mediating variables. Likely boundary-spanning tasks include gathering and assessing environmental information for the purposes of organizational decision making and strategizing. Such tasks are typically complex, ambiguous, and require a fair amount of interdependence among the group members. Therefore, our discussions of information and temporal diversity and their impact upon groups presumes such a task environment.

3. It is worth considering that the decrement in communication and performance in the above studies might also come from other intervening constructs – see our previous note about the impact of mediating variables upon group outcomes.

4. We would like to thank editor Margaret Neale for suggesting to us the concept of the boundary spanning group as lubricant.

ACKNOWLEDGMENTS

This chapter was written with support provided by a Summer Research Fellowship from the College of Business at the University of Missouri-Columbia. We would also like to acknowledge the suggestions and guidance provided by Margaret Neale and two anonymous reviewers, for which we are most grateful.

REFERENCES

Adam, B. (1998). *Timescapes of modernity: The environment and invisible hazards.* London: Routledge.
Ancona, D., & Chong, C. L. (1996). Entrainment: Pace, cycle, and rhythm in organizational behavior. *Research in Organizational Behavior, 18*, 251–284.
Ancona, D. G., & Caldwell, D. F. (1992). Demography and design: Predictors of new product team performance. *Organization Science, 3*, 321–341.
Ancona, D. G., Okhuysen, G. A., & Perlow, L. A. (2001). Taking time to integrate temporal research. *Academy of Management Review, 26*, 512–529.
Bantel, K. A., & Jackson, S. E. (1989). Top management and innovations in banking: Does composition of the top teams make a difference? *Strategic Management Journal, 10*(Special Issue, Summer), 107–124.
Barney, J. (1991). Firm resources and sustained competitive advantage. *Journal of Management, 17*, 99–120.
Barney, J. B. (1986). Organizational culture: Can it be a source of sustained competitive advantage? *Academy of Management Review, 11*, 656–665.
Barth, J. R. (1991). The temporal imagination in Wordsworth's *Prelude*: Time and the timeless. *Thought, 66*(261), 139–150.
Benford, G. (1992). *Timescape.* New York: Bantam Books. (Original work published in 1980.)
Blackburn, J. D. (Ed.) (1991). *Time-based competition: The next battleground in American manufacturing.* Homewood, IL: Business One Irwin.
Bluedorn, A. C. (1997). Primary rhythms, information processing, and planning: Toward a strategic temporal technology. *Technology Studies, 4*, 1–36.
Bluedorn, A. C. (1998). An interview with anthropologist Edward T. Hall. *Journal of Management Inquiry, 7*, 109–115.
Bluedorn, A. C. (2000). Time and organizational culture. In: N. M. Ashkanasy, C. P. M. Wilderom & M. F. Peterson (Eds), *Handbook of Organizational Culture and Climate* (pp. 117–128). Thousand Oaks, CA: Sage.
Bluedorn, A. C. (2002). *The human organization of time: Temporal realities and experience.* Stanford, CA: Stanford University Press.
Bluedorn, A. C., & Ferris, S. P. (2000, October 13). Temporal depth, age, and organizational performance. Paper presented in the INSEAD Strategic Management Seminar Series, Fontainebleau, France.

Bluedorn, A. C., Kaufman, C. F., & Lane, P. M. (1992). How many things do you like to do at once? An introduction to monochronic and polychronic time. *Academy of Management Executive*, 6(4), 17–26.

Bluedorn, A. C., & Lundgren, E. F. (1993). A culture-match perspective for strategic change. *Research in Organizational Change and Development*, 7, 137–179.

Blumer, H. (1954). What is wrong with social theory. *American Sociological Review*, 19, 3–10.

Cannon-Bowers, J. A., Salas, E., & Converse, S. (1993). Shared mental models in expert team decision making. In: N. J. Castellan, Jr. (Ed.), *Individual and Group Decision Making* (pp. 221–246). Hillsdale, NJ: Lawrence Erlbaum.

Cannon-Bowers, J. A., Tannenbaum, S. I., Salas, E., & Volpe, C. E. (1995). Defining competencies and establishing team training requirements. In: R. A. Guzzo & E. Salas (Eds), *Team Effectiveness and Decision Making in Organizations* (pp. 333–380). San Francisco, CA: Jossey-Bass.

Chowers, E. (1998). Time in Zionism: The life and afterlife of a temporal revolution. *Political Theory*, 26, 652–685.

De Dreu, C. K. W., & Weingart, L. R. (2002, August 9–14). Task versus relationship conflict: A meta-analysis. Paper presented at the Annual Meeting of the Academy of Management, Denver, CO.

DiMaggio, P. J., & Powell, W. W. (1983). The iron cage revisited: Institutional isomorphism and collective rationality in organizational fields. *American Sociological Review*, 48, 147–160.

Eisenhardt, K. M. (1989). Making fast strategic decisions in high-velocity environments. *Academy of Management Journal*, 32, 543–576.

Galbraith, J. R. (1977). *Organization design*. Reading, MA: Addison-Wesley.

Greening, D. W., & Johnson, R. A. (1997). Managing industrial and environmental crises. *Business and Society*, 36, 334–361.

Guzzo, R. A., & Dickson, M. W. (1996). Teams in organizations: Recent research on performance and effectiveness. *Annual Review of Psychology*, 47, 307–338.

Hall, E. T. (1981). *The silent language*. New York: Anchor Books. (Original work published in 1959.)

Hall, E. T. (1983). *The dance of life: The other dimension of time*. Garden City, NY: Anchor Press.

Hambrick, D. C., Cho, T. S., & Chen, M.-J. (1996). The influence of top management team heterogeneity on firm's competitive moves. *Administrative Science Quarterly*, 41, 659–684.

Jackson, S. (1992). Team composition in organizational settings: Issues in managing an increasingly diverse work force. In: S. Worchel, W. Wood & J. A. Simpson (Eds), *Group Process and Productivity* (pp. 138–173). London: Sage.

Jackson, S. E., May, K. E., & Whitney, K. (1995). Understanding the dynamics of diversity in decision-making teams. In: R. A. Guzzo & E. Salas (Eds), *Team Effectiveness and Decision Making in Organizations* (pp. 204–261). San Francisco, CA: Jossey-Bass.

Jehn, K. A., Northcraft, G. B., & Neale, M. A. (1999). Why differences make a difference: A field study of diversity, conflict, and performance in workgroups. *Administrative Science Quarterly*, 44, 741–763.

Kahn, R. L., Wolfe, D. M., Quinn, R. P., Snoek, J. D., & Rosenthal, R. A. (1964). *Organizational stress: Studies in role conflict and ambiguity*. New York: Wiley.

Katz, R. (1982). The effects of group longevity on project communication and performance. *Administrative Science Quarterly*, 27, 81–104.

Klimoski, R., & Mohammed, S. (1994). Team mental model: Construct or metaphor? *Journal of Management*, 20, 403–437.

Kluckhohn, F. R., & Strodtbeck, F. L. (1961). *Variations in value orientations*. Evanston, IL: Row, Peterson.

Lau, D. C., & Murnighan, J. K. (1998). Demographic diversity and faultlines: The compositional dynamics of organizational groups. *Academy of Management Review, 23*, 325–340.

Lawrence, P. R., & Lorsch, J. W. (1967). *Organization and environment: Managing differentiation and integration.* Boston, MA: Division of Research, Graduate School of Business Administration, Harvard University.

Levine, R. (1997). *The geography of time: The temporal misadventures of a social psychologist, or how every culture keeps time just a little bit differently.* New York: Basic Books.

Levine, R. V., West, L. J., & Reis, H. T. (1980). Perceptions of time and punctuality in the United States and Brazil. *Journal of Personality and Social Psychology, 38*, 541–550.

Levine, R., & Wolff, E. (1985). Social time: The heartbeat of culture. *Psychology Today, 19*(3), 28–35.

Likert, R. (1961). *New patterns of management.* New York: McGraw-Hill.

Magjuka, R. J., & Baldwin, T. T. (1991). Team-based employee involvement programs: Effects of design and administration. *Personnel Psychology, 44*, 793–812.

March, J. G., & Simon, H. A. (1958). *Organizations.* New York: Wiley.

Mathieu, J. E., Heffner, T. S., Goodwin, G. F., Salas, E., & Cannon-Bowers, J. A. (2000). The influence of shared mental models on team process and performance. *Journal of Applied Psychology, 85*, 273–283.

Mead, G. H. (1974). *Mind, self, and society: From the standpoint of a social behaviorist.* Chicago: University of Chicago Press. (Original work published 1934.)

Mills, C. W. (1959). *The sociological imagination.* London: Oxford University Press.

Morgan, G. (1997). *Images of organization* (2nd ed.). Thousand Oaks, CA: Sage.

Nock, S. L. (1998). Turn-taking as rational behavior. *Social Science Research, 27*, 235–244.

Ofori-Dankwa, J., & Julian, S. D. (2001). Complexifying organizational theory: Illustrations using time research. *Academy of Management Review, 26*, 415–430.

Pennings, J. M. (1998). Structural contingency theory. In: P. J. D. Drenth & C. J. de Wolff (Eds), *Handbook of Work and Organizational Psychology* (pp. 39–60). East Sussex, UK: Psychology Press Ltd.

Richards, E. G. (1998). *Mapping time: The calendar and its history.* Oxford: Oxford University Press.

Saxe, J. G. (1892). *The poetical works of John Godfrey Saxe.* Boston: Houghton, Mifflin and Company.

Schein, E. H. (1992). *Organizational culture and leadership* (2nd ed.). San Francisco: Jossey-Bass.

Stalk, G., Jr., & Hout, T. M. (1990). *Competing against time: How time-based competition is reshaping global markets.* New York: Free Press.

Stout, R. J., Cannon-Bowers, J. A., & Salas, E. (1996). The role of shared mental models in developing team situational awareness: Implications for training. *Training Research Journal, 2*, 85–116.

Thompson, J. D. (1967). *Organizations in action.* New York: McGraw-Hill.

Weitzel, W. C., III (1999). *The space of memory: Romanticism, modernity, and the temporal imagination.* Unpublished doctoral dissertation, Harvard University, Cambridge, MA.

Whitrow, G. J. (1988). *Time in history: The evolution of our general awareness of time and temporal perspective.* Oxford: Oxford University Press.

Williams, K. Y., & O'Reilly, C. A. (1998). Demography and diversity in organizations: A review of forty years of research. *Research in Organizational Behavior, 20*, 77–140.

Ziller, R. C. (1965). Toward a theory of open and closed groups. *Psychological Bulletin, 64*, 164–182.

PART III:
TIME PRESSURE AND GROUP
PERFORMANCE

TIME PRESSURE AND TEAM PERFORMANCE: AN ATTENTIONAL FOCUS INTEGRATION

Steven J. Karau and Janice R. Kelly

ABSTRACT

Despite the potentially vital implications of time pressure for group performance in general and team effectiveness in particular, research has traditionally neglected the study of time limits and group effectiveness. We examine the small, but growing, body of research addressing the effect of time pressure on group performance and introduce our Attentional Focus Model of group effectiveness (Karau & Kelly, 1992). We examine recent research on the utility of the model and identify selected implications of the model for how time pressure may interact with other factors such as task type, group structure, and personality to influence team performance. Finally, we discuss methodological issues of studying attention, interaction processes, and team performance.

Time limits are a central component of nearly all group tasks, and many organizational teams operate under time pressure. Given that many organizations rely heavily on teams and that this reliance has been steadily increasing over the past two decades (Devine, Clayton, Philips, Dunford & Melner, 1999; Gordon, 1992; Lawler, Mohrman & Ledford, 1995), it is vital to understand the effects of time pressure on team processes and outcomes. Indeed, time pressure

Time in Groups
Research on Managing Groups and Teams, Volume 6, 185–212
Copyright © 2003 by Elsevier Ltd.
ISSN: 1534-0856/doi:10.1016/S1534-0856(03)06009-2

may take on special relevance for project teams that must coordinate and plan complex activities. Although a host of processes and outcomes are important to teams – including interaction processes, cohesion, conflict, coordination, and satisfaction – team performance is often the critical outcome variable for work teams (Hackman, 1987). After all, teams are usually formed and designed to accomplish specific tasks and performance functions.

Despite the potentially vital implications of time pressure for group performance in general and team effectiveness in particular, research has traditionally neglected the study of time limits and group effectiveness. Therefore, although some group process and effectiveness issues have attracted literally hundreds of studies on topics such as mere presence effects (Bond & Titus, 1983), member motivation (Karau & Williams, 1993; Sheppard, 1993), polarization of attitudes (Isenberg, 1986), within-group social influence (Wood, Lundgren, Ouellette, Busceme & Blackstone, 1994), general work team performance (Cohen & Bailey, 1997), and cohesion (Mullen & Copper, 1994), much less attention has been directed to temporal influences on performance. Fortunately, however, a small but growing body of research has begun to examine time pressure and group performance, and an understanding of some key processes has started to emerge (e.g. Driskell, Salas & Johnston, 1999; Karau, 2003; Karau & Kelly, 1992; Kelly & Karau, 1999; Kelly & Loving, in press; Parks & Cowlin, 1995).

In recent years, we have developed and tested various facets of an Attentional Focus Model of group effectiveness (Karau & Kelly, 1992) that has special relevance to time pressure. We believe that this model provides a useful framework for understanding and integrating existing research on time pressure and group performance, and poses a number of testable hypotheses for future work. In the current chapter, we seek to: (a) introduce the Attentional Focus Model and highlight its relevance to time pressure and team performance; (b) examine recent research on the utility of the model; (c) identify selected implications of the model for how time pressure may interact with other factors such as task type, group structure, and personality to influence team performance; (d) discuss some methodological issues central to studying attention, interaction processes, and team performance; and (e) draw some conclusions for future research and practice in the area of time pressure and team performance.

THE ATTENTIONAL FOCUS MODEL

The Attentional Focus Model (AFM; Karau & Kelly, 1992) is the organizing framework for our research program on time pressure and group effectiveness. The model represents an integration of prior individual-level research on time pressure and performance with more recent group-level research on interaction process and performance. The key features of the model are shown in Fig. 1. The AFM suggests that time limits and other situational factors interact with task features, group structural variables, and individual differences to influence group members' attentional focus and information processing objectives, which in turn affects the content of the group interaction. Interaction processes congruent with task demands are likely to lead to good performance, whereas interaction processes that are poorly matched with task demands are likely to lead to poor performance.

In the case of time limits, the AFM suggests that time pressure serves to narrow group members' focus to the most salient features of the group interaction and task. As time pressure increases, features that appear most central to completing the key demands of the task become more salient, whereas features that appear less immediately relevant or central to task completion become less salient. The features that appear most central to task completion likely vary as a function of the task and situation, but will typically include things such as key information and arguments, opinions of key individuals, simplifying heuristics, and decision rules and information processing strategies conducive to completing the task rapidly. As the time available to complete the task increases, a wider range of task and situational factors beyond mere task completion are likely to become salient. These differences in group members' attentional focus and interaction objectives are likely to produce related differences in the discussion content and information processing strategies adopted by the group, thereby affecting resulting group performance.

A central implication of the AFM is that time pressure can either enhance or reduce performance depending on the requirements for successful task performance and the nature of the most salient environmental cues. If time pressure leads groups to focus on an optimal amount of information that is truly relevant and diagnostic, decisions might actually be improved. However, for many tasks – especially those that are complex, require a high degree of member coordination, or demand systematic consideration of a large amount of information – time pressure is likely to restrict either the amount of information considered or the thoroughness with which information is processed, thereby reducing decision quality. The logic of the AFM also suggests that for most tasks and situations there is an optimal time limit or level of temporal stimulation. When the time limit is optimally matched to the demands of the task, group performance should be highest. Hence, there is likely to be a curviliner relationship between time pressure and team performance such that increases in time pressure up to and including the optimal level should enhance performance, but additional increases in time pressure beyond this point should reduce it (cf. Easterbrook, 1959; Yerkes & Dodson, 1908; Zajonc, 1980).

However, temporal influences are not likely to operate in isolation. Hence, the AFM also states that a variety of input factors interact to determine group

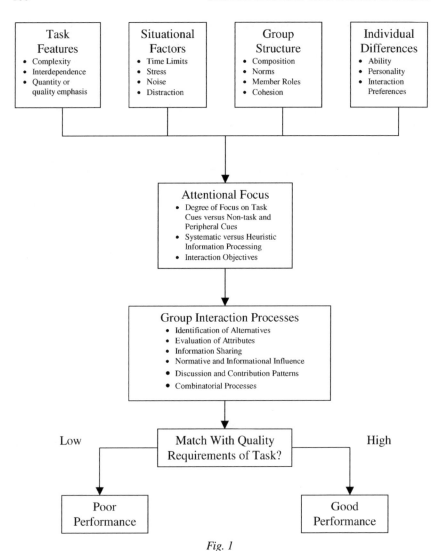

Fig. 1
Key Attributes of the Attentional Focus Model (AFM; Karau & Kelly, 1992). *Note:* Bulleted
lists provide examples of classes of variables subsumed within each construct. These lists
are not intended to be all-inclusive.

members' attentional focus and information processing objectives. These input factors include situational factors other than time limits, such as stress, noise, and distraction; group structural variables, such as norms, composition, role relationships, and cohesion; task characteristics, such as complexity, information load, and optimizing-versus-maximizing emphasis; and individual differences in group members' skills, abilities, and personalities (Karau & Kelly, 1992).

The AFM is consistent with a number of theories stating that arousal and stress lead individuals to attend to an increasingly narrow range of cues (e.g. Baron, 1986; Easterbrook, 1959; Kruglanski & Webster, 1996) in a manner that may influence information processing and decision making (e.g. Cohen, 1978; Craik & Lockhart, 1972; Petty & Cacioppo, 1986). The AFM also is consistent with a number of theories suggesting that processing objectives influence the content of the group interaction, in turn influencing group performance (e.g. Hackman & Morris, 1975; Hirokawa, 1988) and that task attributes influence these relationships (e.g. Baron, 1986; Hackman, 1987). Hence the AFM is grounded in a long tradition of cue utilization and group process-group performance theories. The AFM is unique, however, in identifying how time pressure interacts with a range of other input factors to enhance or reduce group performance via interaction processes that are influenced by individual members' attentional focus and cognitive processes.

RESEARCH CENTRAL TO THE DEVELOPMENT OF THE AFM

The central logic of the AFM was based on a number of consistent patterns in previous research and theory on the effects of time pressure, stress, distraction, and heuristic processing on performance. This research has shown that time pressure and other factors that may constrain processing capabilities lead to a narrowing of attention, and also often lead to faster rates of work, but reduced quality. For example, research examining the effects of time pressure on both individual and group behavior has found that it typically leads to increased work rates (e.g. Davis, 1969; Kelly, Futoran & McGrath, 1990; Locke & Latham, 1990; Yukl, Malone, Hayslip & Pamin, 1976), a greater emphasis on actions necessary to task completion (Kelly & McGrath, 1985), and decreased performance quality (Kelly & McGrath, 1985). Two studies with qualitative dependent variables also suggest a curvilinear relationship such that moderate time pressure enhances quality but high time pressure reduces it (Isenberg, 1981; Pepinsky, Pepinsky & Pavlik, 1960). High levels of time pressure have also been found to lead individuals to process information less thoroughly and to consider a narrower range of decision alternatives (e.g. Christensen-Szalanski, 1980; Luchins, 1942;

Zakay & Wooler, 1984). Similar findings have emerged from studies examining situational variables that may be expected to reduce processing capability in a manner similar to time pressure, such as stress (Lanzetta, 1955), threat (Lanzetta, Haefner, Langham & Axelrod, 1954), and noise (e.g. Hygge & Knez, 2001). Taken as a whole, these findings are consistent with a narrowing of attention under time pressure and stress, and to an increased focus on task-central features.

RESEARCH TESTING KEY ASPECTS OF THE AFM

Since we developed the AFM about ten years ago, we have conducted several studies testing key facets of the model. In addition, a number of studies by other researchers have examined hypotheses central to the major assumptions of the model. In our first AFM-driven study (Karau & Kelly, 1992), we asked triads to work on planning tasks under low, moderate, or high levels of time pressure. Each group's written solution to a common problem was coded on quality, and group discussions were videotaped and coded for process features central to performance using the TEMPO system (Futoran, Kelly & McGrath, 1989). Time pressure was strongly and positively related to an increased focus on task activity and inversely related to interpersonal activity and other actions that did not advance the task. Participants also reported that their attention was focused more directly on completing the task rapidly when time pressure was high, providing strong initial support for the attentional focus and group interaction implications of the AFM. Moderate, but not high, levels of time pressure enhanced the creativity and adequacy of written solutions, consistent with an attentional focus that was well matched to the demands of the task. In addition, we found that interaction process was a more potent predictor of group performance when either too much or too little time was provided for the task in contrast to when an optimal time limit was provided.

An interesting study by Parks and Cowlin (1995) also provided support for the interaction process implications of the AFM. Groups were asked to make decisions under low, moderate, or high levels of time pressure. Groups increased their rates of activity and were less likely to repeat previously mentioned information when working under high time pressure. Parks and Cowlin concluded that these effects were entirely consistent with a narrowing of attention and a focus on task-focused action under time pressure.

Kelly, Jackson and Hutson-Comeaux (1997) examined influence processes during group discussion under time pressure. They found that groups working under time pressure engaged in relatively more normative influence, whereas groups not working under time pressure engaged in more informational influence. This indicates a decreased reliance on systematic processing of information during time pressure, consistent with the AFM.

In another recent study of group decision making (Kelly & Karau, 1999), we examined the effects of initial preferences and subjective time pressure on discussion content and final decision quality. Information provided to members of triads about two decision alternatives was distributed such that some information was shared (provided to all three members) and some was unshared (provided to only one member). The information distribution was such that the sheets received by each person either favored the correct choice, slightly favored the incorrect choice, or strongly favored the incorrect choice. Thus, communication and sharing of information was more important when the initial decision preferences were likely to be in error. We used the logic of the AFM to reason that initial preferences would serve as a salient cue during group discussion and would thus have strong effects on final decisions, and that this influence would be enhanced under time pressure. Results provided partial support for these predictions. Initial preferences had large effects on both interaction process and performance, such that both discussions and final decisions were biased in favor of initial preferences. Discussion content was also strongly related to final decisions. These results provide strong support for the process-performance and information salience facets of the AFM. Results for subjective time pressure were less clear. Consistent with the AFM, time pressure led to a faster work rate and higher self-reports of task-focused attention. Time pressure also tended to enhance the impact of initial preferences on group decisions, but only in the correct and mildly incorrect preference conditions. Notably, time pressure's enhancement of initial preferences in the correct preference condition actually improved decision quality, consistent with the interaction process-task match implication central to the AFM. Time pressure also enhanced the tendency to bias discussions in favor of initial preferences, consistent with the model.

A study employing a similar paradigm (Karau, 2003) was designed to examine the joint effects of time pressure and awareness of expertise on group discussion and decision making. Groups were asked to choose between two decision alternatives for which they were provided information sheets containing both shared and unshared information. Groups worked under either high or low time pressure (created by time limits pre-tested to produce either high or low levels of time pressure), and group members were either aware or unaware of which specific facts relevant to the decision were shared or unshared. Results provided strong support for several key elements of the AFM. Specifically, time pressure reduced decision quality, but this decline in performance was only significant when group members were not aware of which information was shared and unshared. Hence, awareness of expertise might serve as a buffer against time pressure by encouraging experts to share their unique information with the group. In addition, groups that worked under time pressure discussed information at a much faster rate and were less likely to repeat non-diagnostic facts, consistent with a narrowing of attentional focus under time pressure. The content of the group interactions was strongly related to actual group decisions, supporting the model's logic that performance is enhanced by interaction processes that are well matched to task demands. Finally, examining discussion patterns within those groups that were aware of which information was unshared revealed that self-censorship activity took place during many of the discussions (cf. Janis, 1982). Namely, members chose not to reveal some important unshared facts, even though the information was clearly relevant to the decision, and members knew that they were the only ones with access to these facts. Interestingly, the level of self-censorship was higher under time pressure. In relation to the AFM, time pressure may serve to inhibit introduction of information that would detract from a quick decision, even when such information is highly relevant and may prevent a flawed choice.

Kelly and Loving (in press) explored more directly some of the cognitive processes underlying the time pressure effects predicted by the AFM. Specifically, they examined whether the focus on a restricted range of task relevant cues was due to differential encoding of task relevant cues at the time that information is learned (a process they referred to as "encoding") or to differential contribution of information to the group discussion (a process they referred to as "filtering"). Either effect is consistent with the AFM. Furthermore, both processes may occur simultaneously, or even perhaps differentially operate for different situations or types of tasks. They once again used an information sharing task, similar to the ones described above, such that group members were given positive, negative, and neutral information about three decision options. Fairly strong support was found for a filtering effect. That is, no encoding differences were found for groups working under conditions of subjective time pressure compared to groups not working under conditions of subjective time pressure (e.g. both groups recalled a similar amount of information and similarly valenced information). However, time pressure groups were less likely to contribute neutral information, and more likely to contribute valenced information to the group discussion, compared to no time pressure groups. Consistent with prior research, groups worked at a faster rate of performance when working under time pressure. Furthermore, when directly assessing task goals, there was some evidence that members of time pressure groups were more likely to endorse goals related to task completion, whereas members of non-time pressure groups were more likely to endorse non-task (e.g. interpersonal) goals.

Finally, several recent studies have examined additional aspects of group process and performance relevant to the AFM. First, Driskell and Salas (1991) found that, contrary to prior research showing a tendency for authority to centralize in hierarchical organizations experiencing stress (e.g. Staw, Sandelands & Dutton, 1981), leaders and members of small groups become more receptive to crucial task-relevant information when working under stress. Consistent with the AFM, stress and time pressure may lead to an enhanced focus on information when such information is central to the demands of the task. Second, Zaccaro, Gualtieri and Minionis (1995) found that teams that were high in cohesion based on shared commitment to the task were better equipped to cope with time pressure. Specifically, time pressure reduced performance quality, but only for teams low in task cohesion. Teams high in task cohesion also devoted more time to planning and communicated task-relevant information more frequently than teams low in task cohesion. In terms of the AFM, a shared commitment to a team task could serve to direct attention to task functions crucial to performance, thereby buffering the impact of time pressure on performance. Third, Waller, Giambatista and Zellmer-Bruhn (1999) found that the presence of individuals who engaged in time-oriented behavior increased group activity and enhanced performance on their primary assigned task and reduced polychronic (or multi-task) behavior directed to multiple competing secondary tasks. Consistent with the AFM, these findings may suggest that member actions that focus attention on time constraints can lead groups to emphasize those actions most central to completing the key functions of their primary task. Fourth, Driskell, Salas and Johnston (1999) found that stress, created from a combination of noise, time pressure, and distraction, led to a narrowing of team perspective such that individuals become more focused on their own actions and outcomes relative to group outcomes under stress. This suggests that stress may serve to narrow attention to central features within the interpersonal domain as well as the task domain. Finally, Gevers, van Eerde and Rutte (2001) found that both planning and reflexivity (i.e. the degree to which the group actively regulates its processes and strategies in relation to its progress and to environmental cues, West, 1996) assisted project groups in successfully meeting a deadline. In addition, the effect of time pressure on project progress was moderated by perceptions of group potency. In terms of the AFM, planning and coordination activities may serve to direct attention to key task-relevant attributes, and potency and other perceptions related to feels of group efficacy may serve to cue actions that move the task forward to completion.

In sum, there is converging support for the central tenets of the AFM that time pressure and other input factors interact to influence attention and information processing objectives, and that these attentional differences influence the content of the group interaction and subsequent group performance. Hence, groups working under time pressure work at a faster rate of performance and engage in more task-oriented and less interpersonally-oriented and non-task activities (Karau, 2003; Kelly & Karau, 1999; Kelly & Loving, in press; Kelly & McGrath, 1985), focus on a reduced set of cues (Driskell, Salas & Johnston, 1999; Karau, 2003; Kelly & Karau, 1999), are less likely to repeat previously mentioned information (Karau, 2003; Parks & Cowlin, 1995), focus on cues that appear highly relevant to the task (Driskell & Salas, 1991; Karau, 2003; Kelly & Karau, 1999; Kelly &

Loving, in press), engage in more self-censorship of information that contradicts the group consensus and that might work against reaching a decision quickly (Karau, 2003), and engage in more heuristic processing of information (Kelly, Jackson & Hutson-Comeaux, 1997) to a higher degree than do groups that work without time pressure. These processes in turn may lead to either enhanced or reduced performance and decision quality depending on the match between the group's interaction processes and the quality requirements of the task (Karau, 2003; Kelly & Karau, 1999). In addition, the presence of cues that enhance attention to important, diagnostic information and behaviors necessary for the task can enhance some aspects of group performance (Gevers, van Eerde & Rutte, 2001; Waller, Giambatista & Zellmer-Bruhn, 1999), can serve to buffer the effects of time pressure on performance (Zaccaro, Gualtieri & Minionis, 1995), and may even lead to enhanced performance under time pressure in some conditions (Kelly & Karau, 1999).

SELECTED IMPLICATIONS OF THE AFM

The AFM states that temporal influences do not exist in isolation, but interact with other factors to influence attention and information processing orientations. Indeed, our review of relevant research above shows that a host of factors have been found to influence the nature of time pressure's influence on interaction process and performance. These factors include initial decision preferences, prediscussion distributions of task relevant information, stress, noise, distraction, planning activity, group members' time-oriented behaviors, and shared commitment to the team's task. We now explore in greater detail selected implications of the AFM for the interaction of time pressure with other important performance-related variables. Due to page constraints we cannot explore all such possible linkages and implications. Hence, we focus on three key classes of variables – task type, group structural variables, and individual differences – that are likely to play particularly important roles in influencing the impact of time pressure on attention, interaction, and performance.

Task Type

Group dynamicists have long recognized that it is vital to consider task characteristics when attempting to predict or explain group performance or specify the likely relationships between interaction process and performance (e.g. Hackman & Morris, 1975; McGrath, 1984; Steiner, 1972). Consistent with this traditional emphasis, the effects of time pressure on attention, process, and performance are likely to be heavily reliant on task characteristics. In general, we would expect time pressure to enhance performance when the available time is optimally matched to the number of task-relevant cues, amount of interaction, and amount of coordination required for good performance on the task. Similarly, we would expect time pressure to reduce performance when the available time is insufficient to allow the group to properly attend to important task relevant cues, interact sufficiently to reach a reasoned judgment, and coordinate necessary group processes relevant to the task. Given that time pressure typically enhances attention to salient cues, the nature of the cues that are made salient by the task and situation also is likely to be very important. If the salient cues are diagnostic and provide a good understanding and representation of the problem being considered, time pressure may well enhance performance. But if the salient cues are not diagnostic or are unrepresentative, time pressure is likely to reduce performance. With these general guidelines in mind, a large number of likely time pressure by task interactions are probably best understood by a more detailed consideration of the implications of various task typologies for time pressure and performance.

Two key aspects of the task concern complexity and information load. On relatively simple tasks with low information loads and clear, relevant data, time pressure may help matters by focusing attention on the matter at hand, reducing unnecessary discussion and procrastination, and encouraging individuals to finish the task or problem efficiently. However, on complex tasks involving a high information load and requiring careful consideration of a range of alternatives and attributes of those alternatives, time pressure is likely to create a resource problem such that the group cannot adequately attend to and process all task-relevant information. A similar problem may occur on tasks that require a great deal of communication, coordination, social influence, or conflict management in order to determine the best course of action and reach agreement on it (e.g. Hirokawa, 1988; Stasser, Kerr & Davis, 1989). In such situations, the communication and coordination demands on the group exceed the available temporal resources. There are two main logical alternatives that can be followed to resolve this dilemma. The group could either consider each piece of information (or each verbal utterance or other contribution of a group member) for a shorter amount of time, or the group could exclude some data from consideration and discuss or process only the information that appears most central to the task at hand (such as information with clearly positive or negative implications or information that is presented by experts or opinion leaders).

We propose that increasing the rate of information processing is most likely when the information does not appear to differ much qualitatively. When some information is clearly more vivid, salient, or relevant than other information, groups might be more likely to focus on the information that appears more relevant to the exclusion of apparently trivial or peripheral information. Member contribution rates could be altered in a similar way. If some members have more status or authority, are better liked, or are better respected than others, their thoughts and inputs might take on special weight relative to the inputs of other members (Isenberg, 1981; Janis, 1982). Alternately, if status or expertise levels are relatively equal, each member may seek to edit the length of his or her own contribution so that all group members contribute more facts and opinions per unit time. Of course, these represent two ends of a group discussion continuum ranging from high centralization of information and contribution to more rapid, but more evenly balanced discussion and consideration of information. In summary, discussions and interaction under time pressure are likely to focus on a restricted range of information and cues that appear, at the surface, to be more relevant and diagnostic to the current task or decision.

Similarly, communications may focus on contributions that move the task forward to completion and may inhibit contributions that require detailed scrutiny or that take momentum away from consensus formation. This latter conclusion is consistent with the results of an interesting study by Kruglanski and Webster (1996). Namely, when groups were asked to discuss an emotionally laden issue with a clear majority preference, the tendency to react negatively to opinion deviates was enhanced both under time pressure and in the presence of environmental noise. Thus, consistent with discussions of groupthink (Aldag & Fuller, 1993; Janis, 1982), a drive toward consensus within a group can inhibit free discussion and lead to poor decisions when members become hesitant to disrupt the momentum and cohesion of the group under stress.

The nature of the task with respect to the product or process the group is trying to create also is likely to interact with time pressure to influence attention, process, and performance. For example, Hackman and Morris (1975) identified three classes of performance-related tasks: (a) production tasks that require the group to generate ideas or images; (b) discussion tasks that require the group to evaluate an issue, and; (c) problem-solving tasks (also called planning tasks by some researchers) that require the group to devise a plan of action that could be followed to solve a specific problem. When working under time pressure, groups are likely to focus on generating ideas and products more rapidly on production tasks, but are likely to focus instead on the pros and cons of an issue or on devising a plan on discussion and planning tasks. Hence, time pressure is likely to lead to faster performance and communication rates but to fewer qualitative changes when groups work on production tasks. However, when groups work on discussion and problem-solving tasks, the actual content of the interaction is more likely to change to facilitate more rapid consensus and agreement on a course of action, whereas faster rates of performance may or may not occur depending on the number, complexity, salience, and apparent relevance of information and other cues.

Therefore, regarding social influence processes, time pressure is likely to enhance reliance on normative influence and reduce reliance on informational influence on discussion and problem-solving tasks (Kelly, Jackson & Hutson-Comeaux, 1997).

In his especially influential task typology, Steiner (1972) distinguished between optimizing tasks that focus on quality and maximizing tasks that focus on quantity. Time pressure is likely to enhance work rates without regard to quality on maximizing tasks, but will not necessarily lead to faster work rates and may instead lead to greater attention to salient cues or to more careful processing of key attributes on optimizing tasks. However, many tasks may have some properties of both optimizing and maximizing tasks. For example, most group decision making tasks have partially conflicting demands such that the group must balance the desire to make the best decision possible with the need to reach consensus on the decision before time expires. When opinion differences exist within the group, these goals are contradictory. Which goal takes precedence may depend on the degree to which there is a clearly best alternative rather than a choice between several relatively equally desirable alternative. Laughlin (1980) has proposed that group tasks can be placed on a continuum ranging from judgmental to intellective. On intellective tasks, a correct answer can be identified and demonstrated to be superior. On judgmental tasks, there is no single demonstrably correct or superior alternative. Under high time pressure, judgmental tasks might be more readily influenced than intellective tasks by consensus pressure and social influence processes. In addition, perceptions of task attributes on the judgmental-intellective dimension may in some cases be as potent as objective task attributes, such that subtle differences in the way identical tasks are framed and perceived by group members could influence which features become most salient under time pressure.

Steiner also classified tasks with respect to how individual inputs are combined into group products. Among these latter types are additive tasks – in which individual inputs are added into a group total, disjunctive tasks – in which the best performing member determines group performance, and conjunctive tasks – in which the worst performing member determines group performance. Provided that group members understand the nature of the task and its combinatorial properties during their activities, we might expect time pressure to lead groups to increase their work rates across the board on additive tasks, to allocate more time and attention to the most able group member on disjunctive tasks, and to allocate more time and attention to the least able group member on conjunctive tasks.

In summary, the effects of time pressure on group and team performance are likely to depend on the nature of the task. As highlighted in the earlier literature review, time pressure and group performance research has examined a variety of tasks – including decision making, planning, problem-solving, production, discussion, and project completion. So far the results appear to be consistent with the logic of the AFM that time pressure is most likely to impair performance on highly complex tasks that require a lot of communication and coordination of group activities. However, some studies point to a greater degree of complexity in task influences. For example, the degree to which cues are diagnostic may be more important then the number of cues in influencing time pressure-performance effects (e.g. Karau, 2003; Kelly & Karau, 1999; Kelly & Loving, in press), and specific task feature may well interact with one another (cf. Hackman & Morris, 1975; Parks & Cowlin, 1995). Thus, more work employing a wider variety of tasks is needed for a more complete understanding of time pressure and performance effects. Studies that examine the effects of time pressure across several different tasks and settings would be especially useful.

Group Structural Variables

Group structural variables, such as norms, role relationships, and communication networks, also are likely to have a strong influence on how time pressure affects attention, interaction process, and performance. Specifically, these structures could influence both what general cues (i.e. task relevant cues vs. non-task or peripheral cues) the group attends to during its interaction and what pieces of information (i.e. task-relevant information and attributes of decision alternatives) the group notices and discusses. Group structures that direct members' attention to important, relevant, or diagnostic features of the task would be likely to enhance performance under time pressure. In contrast, group structures that direct members' attention to non-task cues or to non-diagnostic and unrepresentative information about decision alternatives would be likely to impair performance under time pressure.

The prevailing normative environment within the group is one such structural variable that may interact with time pressure to influence attention, interaction, and performance. Broadly speaking, we can place groups on a continuum ranging from "open" (i.e. receptive to a range of opinions and actions) to "closed" (i.e. rather intolerant of opinion differences and deviant behavior). Due to differences in factors such as developmental histories, culture, individual member personalities and preferences, and the nature of shared group objectives, groups may differ in the degree to which dissent is either tolerated or encouraged, conformity is either expected or optional, and norms are either harshly enforced or used only as rough guidelines for behavior that can be adjusted as the situation demands (e.g. Feldman, 1984; Moreland, Levine & Cini, 1993). In groups with a closed environment in which disagreements are discouraged and members are encouraged not to "rock the boat," high time pressure could serve as a cue to agree with others, look to formal or informal leaders for information as to the preferred opinion, suppress disagreements, and seek to voice agreement with the group consensus (cf. Aldag & Fuller, 1993; Janis, 1982). In groups with a more open environment in which disagreements are respected and idiosyncrasies are tolerated and perhaps even celebrated, high time pressure could instead serve to lead the group to seek information quickly from all group members in an attempt to rapidly discern the key aspects of the decision (cf. Driskell & Salas, 1991; Nemeth, 1986).

Cohesiveness also could influence the operation of normative influences on time pressure-performance relationships. Highly cohesive groups typically exert greater influence on members to adhere to norms than do less cohesive groups (e.g. O'Reilly & Caldwell, 1985; Schachter, Ellertson, McBride & Gregory, 1951). If these norms are conducive to high performance, time pressure could enhance member motivation to perform well on the task and could enhance actual performance, provided that the group is aware of the performance requirement of the task and that the information load and coordination requirements are within an acceptable range for the given time limit. However, if the group norms are conducive to inefficient communication or to valuing social activity over task performance, time pressure would likely reduce performance (e.g. Zaccaro, Gualtieri & Minionis, 1995).

Another potentially important group structural variable involves the communication network and hierarchy within the group. If the default mode of communication and information processing within the group becomes habitual and is followed routinely, reliance on the central features of existing networks – especially those conducive to rapid communication – could be enhanced under time pressure (cf. Gersick & Hackman, 1990). If the network is centralized in nature, it may become even more centralized under high time pressure to accommodate rapid task completion or decision making. For example, Isenberg (1981) found that the tendency for some group members to make more verbal contributions than others was enhanced when groups worked under high time pressure. Similarly, role relationships also could become more rigidly defined under time pressure (Staw, Sandelands & Dutton, 1981) as group members rely on cues such as status, authority, and expertise as simplifying strategies to cope with information overload (cf. Petty & Cacioppo, 1986).

Communication modality and technology also are likely to interact with time pressure to influence attention, interaction, and performance within groups and teams. Although most prior research on groups has focused on face-to-face discussion with all members present, groups can also accomplish their work by combining the inputs of individuals or subgroups over time, or through asynchronous communication. In addition, modern teams have an array of available communication modalities and technologies to choose from, including face-to-face discussion, written communication, video and audio teleconferencing, groupware, and group decision support systems. The AFM suggests that communication modalities and technologies that facilitate attention to important, task relevant, diagnostic cues should enhance performance under time pressure. In contrast, communication modalities and technologies that are either inappropriate to the task, do not facilitate timely coordination of member activities, or make peripheral or non-diagnostic cues salient should reduce performance under time pressure.

Consistent with the logic of the AFM, a number of studies have found that performance suffers when the communications technology employed is poorly matched to the demands of the task (e.g. Hollingshead, McGrath & O'Connor, 1993; Kiesler & Sproull, 1992; Siegel, Dubrovsky, Kiesler & McGuire, 1986; Straus & McGrath, 1994; Valacich & Schwenk, 1995). For example, in a study of computer-mediated vs. face-to-face groups, Straus and McGrath (1994) found relatively small differences in quality, but large differences in quantity in favor of face-to-face groups. More important, performance differences between technology conditions increased for tasks that required greater coordination.

Relative to computer-mediated groups, face-to-face groups are typically more effective, take less time to complete tasks, and generate greater satisfaction among group members (for a review see Baltes, Dickson, Sherman, Bauer & LaGanke, 2002). Thus, we might conclude that media that allow for more efficient transmission of information and social cues would generally lend themselves to more efficient operation under time pressure, perhaps enhancing effectiveness on many tasks that require coordination and interaction. However, the logic of the AFM suggests that it may be possible to design technology specific to the task and situation in a way that could enhance performance under some conditions.

For example, computer mediated communication could be used as a tool for reducing or eliminating process losses commonly associated with face-to-face discussion (e.g. Steiner, 1972), such as production blocking and poor coordination among speakers. Indeed, research on brainstorming has found that the tendency for interacting groups to produce fewer ideas than nominal groups can be eliminated and sometimes even reversed when a computer-based idea generation system is used to allow group members to contribute ideas continuously throughout the session (e.g. Gallupe Dennis, Cooper, Valacich, Bastianutti & Nunamaker, Jr., 1992; Valacich, Dennis & Connolly, 1994). As another example, if the task requires a frank discussion of divergent opinions, groupware designed to allow members to make anonymous contributions may mitigate against an enhancement of consensus pressures under time pressure, although this benefit may be offset by an increased possibility of failure to reach a decision before the deadline. Groupware can also be used to allow for the efficient storage and sharing of task-relevant information across team members and geographic locations in a way that can speed efficient processing of diagnostic information. Such communication could potentially enhance performance under time pressure relative to traditional discussion, considering the logistical barriers frequently posed by attempting to schedule and coordinate face-to-face communication in the modern world.

In summary, a variety of group structural variables may interact with time pressure to affect attention, interaction process, and performance. To date, very little time pressure research has examined these structural factors. Hence, a promising area for future work is to conduct studies that measure or manipulate both time pressure and structural factors such as cohesion, salient group norms, communication modality, technology, and role relationships among members.

Individual Differences and Personality

Group members' attentional focus and interaction preferences also are very likely to be influenced by individual differences in skills, abilities, and personality characteristics. Generally speaking, we would expect time pressure to enhance attention to salient features of the task and to member characteristics that are either dominant or that have special relevance to task completion. Hence, group performance is likely to be highest when there is an optimal match between the central characteristics of individual members and the key demands of the group's task. These individual difference variables also are likely to interact with situational and group structural variables to influence attention and interaction processes. For example, the task-relevant personality traits of leaders, high status members, and members in central positions within the communication network may come to the fore under many time pressure situations.

In the realm of skills and abilities, group members are likely to attend to those features of group tasks that fall within their own areas of interest, expertise, and skill. For example, research on transactive memory has shown that group members may pay particular attention to processing and storing information within areas for which they have a high degree of relative expertise within the group (e.g. Hollingshead, 1998, 2000; Wegner, Erber & Raymond, 1991). Similarly, group members have been found to devote more effort to group tasks that are high, rather than low in personal relevance (Brickner, Harkins & Ostrom, 1986). Groups that work under time pressure may benefit from process interventions, communication networks, or structures that facilitate a relative increase in contribution levels from members whose expertise, skill, or personality traits are well suited to the demands of the task. In the absence of such processes, it is possible that time pressure could enhance attention to high status members or frequent past contributors, possibly reducing the ability of members who possess the most task-relevant knowledge and skill to resolve the issue efficiently.

With respect to personality, some individuals may be predisposed to focus their attention on time constraints and to perceive time as inherently limited. For example, individuals high in time urgency (e.g. Conte, Mathieu & Landy, 1998) may be especially sensitive to time cues and the passage of time. With respect to interaction preferences, this orientation could lead individuals to play a pace-setting role by making the group aware of deadlines and the relative progress of the group toward task completion and other goals. Time urgent individuals also may prefer a fast pace and rapid rate of progress. Similarly, Type A individuals (Strube, Deichmann & Kickham, 1989) are likely to place emphasis on efficiency, while also viewing time-wasting situations and goal-blocking obstacles as particularly frustrating.

The relative emphasis placed on short vs. long-term consequences (i.e. time perspective) also distinguishes some individuals from others. Specifically, impulsive individuals (e.g. Eysenck & Eysenck, 1969), those with a time orientation focused on the present rather than the future (e.g. Zimbardo & Boyd, 1999), and those with a low ability to delay gratification (e.g. Rodriguez, Mischel & Shoda, 1989) may have difficulty engaging in consistent task-orientated behavior over time within groups and teams. In contrast, individuals who carefully consider future consequences in their decisions (e.g. Strathman, Gleicher, Boninger & Edwards, 1994), have a future time orientation (e.g. Nuttin, 1985), or have a high level of achievement motivation (e.g. Cassidy & Lynn, 1989) are likely to engage in consistent, goal-directed behavior over an extended period of time. These individual differences within group members are likely to influence both group interaction processes and related performance (e.g. Waller, Giambatista & Zellmer-Bruhn, 1999). For example, groups with a short-term orientation may be well equipped for resolving issues within a single session, but may have a hard time planning and coordinating member efforts over time. Differences among group members on time perspective also could create either balance or conflict. For example, if a group were to match task responsibilities with members' time perspectives (e.g. assigning an individual with a short-term emphasis to a pacesetter role and assigning an individual with a long-term emphasis to a planning role), performance might actually be enhanced. But performance would likely be reduced if the level of conflict about deadlines and group activities was excessive or personalized (e.g. Amason, 1996).

Individual differences and situational factors related to personal task preferences also may influence which settings activate task-focused behavior under time pressure due to intrinsic interest and the potential value of performance on such tasks for self-evaluation. For example, individuals who are high in need for cognition (e.g. Cacioppo, Petty, Feinstein & Jarvis, 1996), who are working on a task that is high in personal involvement or self-relevance, or who are accountable for their decisions, may be less likely to have their attention diverted from information that is diagnostic and relevant to high-quality performance. Finally, from the perspective of time pressure serving as a source of stress, optimists, individuals high in self-esteem and in task-relevant self-efficacy, and other individuals who perceive time pressure as a challenge may respond with fairly adaptive behavior to time pressure, whereas those who perceive time pressure as an insurmountable threat may respond to time pressure in a less constructive manner (e.g. Folkman & Moskowitz, 2000).

In summary, a host of individual differences in skills, abilities, and personality characteristics are likely to influence group members' attentional focus and interaction preferences. Following the logic of the AFM, we would expect time pressure to narrow attentional focus to the most salient traits of group members and the most salient attributes of the group task. Group performance under time pressure should be enhanced to the degree that the group is able to rapidly identify and deploy group member resources that are optimally suited to key task demands. Conversely, group performance under time pressure should be reduced if the salient traits of group members are not well matched to task demands or if the group is not able to identify the most task-relevant skills, abilities, and dispositions of group members in a timely fashion. One implication of this logic is that it is important for groups that are likely to face time pressure to develop a high level of awareness of specific group members' attributes, as well as the strengths and weaknesses of those attributes for various tasks and situations. Another implication is that groups that are likely to face time pressure may benefit from developing informational infrastructures, communication capabilities, and other support systems that allow them to identify key task attributes and relevant member capabilities quickly and with little advance warning (cf. Okhuysen & Eisenhardt, 2002). Future research is needed to determine more precisely the conditions under which groups composed of members with specific combinations of skills, abilities, and personality characteristics are most and least successful when working under time pressure.

METHODOLOGICAL IMPLICATIONS

Studying Attention in Groups

Central to the Attentional Focus Model, and to other conceptualizations concerning the consequences of time pressure and other sorts of external stressors (e.g. Easterbrook, 1959) is the notion of a narrowed focus of attention to salient aspects of the task environment. However, to date, these attentional processes have been merely inferred from questionnaire data, patterns of group interaction, and performance outcomes. Further refinement of the AFM will require further specification and measurement of these underlying attentional processes.

One strategy for identifying suitable techniques is to borrow from the individual level literature on attention. Direct techniques often are fairly simple and straightforward. For example, one might study the attention given to a particular stimuli simply by recording the amount of time that the subject spends reading, thinking about, or gazing at that particular stimulus, or by recording preference for one stimulus over another when a choice is provided. However, direct translations of these techniques to the more complicated multi-member multi-stimuli group situation may prove too difficult.

Indirect measurement techniques also have been used at the individual level. For example, recall is sometimes used as a measure of attention on the assumption that an item is more deeply encoded and more likely to be recalled as attention to that item increases. On-line "think aloud" protocols, where subjects simply verbalize their ongoing thoughts during a task, also can be used to give an indication of the direction of thought. Although these measures are somewhat imperfect reflections of attentional processes, it may be easier to identify group level analogs.

The group itself also may provide a rich source of information about attentional processes. For example, the amount of time spent in group discussion on a particular topic seems to be a fairly straightforward measure of group attention to stimuli. These and other measures are described more fully below. First, however, it should be noted that some of the relevant variables are measured at the individual level, some are measured at the group level, and some may be assessed at both group and individual level. For example, recall of items can be assessed at both individual and group levels, whereas content coding of a group discussion is a group level measure only.

Indirect Methods: Recall, Self-Reports, Thought-Listing, and Reviewing Videotapes

As mentioned above, a number of indirect techniques have been used at the individual level to assess attentional processes, and most of these techniques have group level parallels. For example, after the group discussion, members may be asked to recall all pertinent items of discussion or to recall as many facts as possible that were contributed to the discussion. Presumably, items that were attended to more would have a greater chance of recall than less attended to items. Recall could be assessed at the individual level, or at the group level in order to assess the group transactive memory system (Wegner, 1986). It is interesting that pre-discussion recall has been used in a number of studies in order to confirm that equal attention had been given to sets of items (e.g. shared vs. unshared information), rather than that differential attention had been given to certain items types (Stasser & Titus, 1985; Kelly & Karau, 1999).

Thought listing is frequently used as an indicator of attention at the individual level. Individual level researchers look at both the number of thought listed and the content of those thought as indicators of attention. For example, the number of thought listed about one particular decision alternative vs. another might be used as an indicator of the relative attention provided to each.

A thought listing technique was recently applied to the group level in order to assess changes in group goals that might have occurred as a function of time pressure (Kelly & Loving, in press). Group members, some of whom were working under time pressure conditions, were interrupted several minutes into their discussion and asked to list all of their salient thoughts with respect to the group interaction and the task that they were thinking of at that moment. These thoughts were then coded into categories, some of which reflected a focus on task completion (a goal that presumably would be more salient under conditions of time pressure), and some of which reflected a focus on non-task or more interpersonal concerns. Thus, the relative number of thought that reflected each goal could be used to infer the direction of attentional focus.

A somewhat more straightforward technique might involve asking individual group members or the group to simply list or rate the amount of attention that they gave to certain items during the group discussion. For example, if the group is choosing between decision alternatives, they could be asked to divide 100 attention points among the possible choices, or to rate each pieces of information on how attentive the group was to it. This technique would be more applicable to situations where either the amount of information available to the group or the number of decision alternatives were finite and known. As an alternative, group members might also be asked, as individuals or as a group, to review videotaped sections of the group discussion and to either list or make ratings of items of information that were being attended to throughout the group discussion.

Direct Methods: Coding of Group Discussion (TEMPO Cycles)

Attentional focus also could be measured directly by coding aspects of the group discussion. For example, as in Karau and Kelly (1992), the group interaction could be coded in terms of the underlying processes involved in the group discussion (e.g. task-oriented vs. social-emotional processes). These processes might be used to infer the general interaction goals of the group, such as task completion or non-task concerns, that might arise from time pressure.

Attentional focus also could be measured by coding the actual content of the group discussion. Indices such as the number of words or sentences contributed to the group discussion that pertains to a particular issue could be developed to provide a quantitative index of how much of the group's attention is being devoted to that issue. Although a number of systems exist for coding interaction processes (e.g. the Bales IPA or Symlog), the TEMPO system developed by Futoran, Kelly, and McGrath (1989) includes a number of features that might be particularly applicable to assessing content. Briefly, when using the TEMPO system, each sentence uttered by a group member is coded into one of several categories that reflect task-oriented activities (e.g. contributing a new idea, evaluating an idea already proposed). Other categories of the system are used for coding sentences that reflect a non-task focus. However, in addition to providing a content code to each sentence, the TEMPO system also includes a coding category for a "cycle" that roughly corresponds to a discussion topic. For example, statements that reflect a discussion of the same decision alternative might each be given the same "cycle" code and the number of sentences receiving that cycle's code vs. a second cycle code (one that reflects a discussion of a second decision alternative) would reflect the relative attention given to each. Since TEMPO users also are instructed to code for the duration of verbal utterances as well as their content, an index of time spent on each cycle, determined by adding up the durations of all sentences given a particular cycle code, also could be used as a measure of the group's attention to each cycle topic.

Manipulations of Attentional Focus

A final method of assessing attentional focus relies on manipulations of variables and inferences from subsequent patterns of data. These manipulations might take one of two directions. First, the group might be provided with information that varies on dimensions that are relevant to task completion, such as how diagnostic the information is for completing or solving the task. To the extent that the group focuses on one subset of information over another (e.g. if group discussion is dominated by one type of information rather than another), we can infer that the group is focusing on that subset of information. This technique was employed by Kelly and Karau (1999). Group members were provided with information about each of two decision options. The information was either positive, negative, or neutral. That is, some of the information was more diagnostic or salient for task solution (the valenced information), whereas other information was less diagnostic or salient (the neutral information). In their study, groups working under conditions of time pressure were more likely to discuss the valenced rather than the neutral information, indicating that their attentional focus was on information more central for task completion. Second, a manipulation might involve direct instructions to focus on particular subsets of information. That is, rather than infer that groups are focusing their attention on particular subsets of information as a function of time pressure, groups could be directly instructed, for example, to focus their attention on information most central to task completion.

In summary, studying attentional processes within groups is a daunting task and little research has been devoted to this activity. However, as the preceding sections point out, there are a variety of tools that can be exploited to collect data at the individual, within-group interpersonal, and group- or team-as-a-unit levels that may shed light on attention, discussion, and performance features central to the study of time pressure effects in general and the AFM in particular. As a general rule, indirect techniques may be more appropriate for studying internal processes (what the individual group members are thinking about), whereas direct techniques may be more appropriate for assessing group interaction. For example, the Kelly and Loving (in press) study demonstrates how thought listing can be used to assess individual level goals for the group interaction. Creative methodologists and statisticians are likely to develop additional tools as the demand for research that is sensitive to process-performance relationships increases over time.

CONCLUSION

Time limits are central features of nearly every group task, posing an important and pervasive challenge for many work teams in organizations. Although researchers have traditionally neglected studying the effects of time pressure on team performance, within the past decade a number of researchers have taken on this challenging topic. We have presented a model – The Attentional Focus Model – that we believe can successfully account for existing research on time pressure and group effectiveness and that poses a number of testable hypotheses for future research, as well as a number of potentially important implications for organizational work teams. The model is grounded in classic research and theory on the effects of stress and time pressure on attention and cue utilization, as well as on well-regarded viewpoints on process-performance relationships that influence general group effectiveness. However, it goes beyond those foundations to clarify situations under which time pressure should be expected to either enhance or reduce performance as a function of attentional processes and information processing strategies, and the impact that those factors have on group interaction process and resulting performance. Though the model is at an early stage of development and empirical testing, a number of initial studies support its key tenets and suggest that it may have value for driving additional research on temporal factors and team effectiveness.

Our analysis of the logic of the model in relation to existing research evidence highlights a number of potentially profitable areas for future research. First, additional studies are needed that assess what specific features of the task and environment individual team members attend to when working on various tasks across differing situational contexts under both high and low time pressure. A more refined understanding of the determinants of attentional focus across settings would clarify the likely impact of those settings on group interaction process and performance. Second, future research could examine more of the time pressure interactions with other input factors that we highlight in this chapter. Given that the AFM suggests that time pressure can either help or hinder decision quality depending on the degree of match between interaction process and the quality requirements of the task, it is vital to identify the moderating variables and limiting conditions of time pressure effects. For example, manipulations of low, moderate, and high time pressure could be crossed with task attributes such as complexity, information load, method for combining individual inputs (additive, conjunctive, or disjunctive), or quantity vs. quality emphasis of the task. Similarly, various levels of time pressure could be manipulated along with factors such as group norms, communication networks, or modality of communication (such as face-to-face, electronic, teleconferencing, or video communication). Third, it would be compelling to explore the degree to which variables such as time pressure, noise, arousal, stress, and mood can be understood as different operationalizations of the same underlying construct of information processing contraints and the degree to which these factors have unique motivational, information processing, and performance implications within team contexts. Finally, an especially pressing need is to examine the time pressure implications of the AFM within intact groups and within organizational work teams to determine whether the findings documented primarily among ad hoc groups generalize beyond the laboratory. Some field studies of teams may pose unique internal validity challenges due to the likely presence of uncontrolled variables. Yet such research would enhance the ability to make confident conclusions about applications and to study factors such as socialization processes, changes in group membership, cohesion and identification levels, and long-term tasks with high personal involvement. Regardless of the path that future investigations take, we hope that the AFM will become a useful tool in stimulating and organizing additional research on time pressure and team performance.

REFERENCES

Aldag, R. J., & Fuller, S. R. (1993). Beyond fiasco: A reappraisal of the groupthink phenomenon and a new model of group decision processes. *Psychological Bulletin, 113*, 533–552.

Amason, A. C. (1996). Distinguishing the effects of functional and dysfunctional conflict on strategic decision making: Resoling a paradox for top management teams. *Academy of Management Journal, 39*, 123–148.

Baltes, B. B., Dickson, M. W., Sherman, M. P., Bauer, C. A., & LaGanke, J. (2002). Computer-mediated communication and group decision making: A meta-analysis. *Organizational Behavior and Human Decision Processes, 87*, 156–179.

Baron, R. S. (1986). Distraction-conflict theory: Progress and problems. In: L. Berkowitz (Ed.), *Advances in Experimental Social Psychology* (Vol. 19, pp. 1–40). New York: Academic Press.

Bond, C. F., & Titus, L. J. (1983). Social facilitation: A meta-analysis of 241 studies. *Psychological Bulletin, 94*, 265–292.

Brickner, M. A., Harkins, S. G., & Ostrom, T. M. (1986). Effects of personal involvement: Thought-provoking implications for social loafing. *Journal of Personality and Social Psychology, 51*, 763–770.

Cacioppo, J. T., Petty, R. E., Feinstein, J. A., & Jarvis, W. B. G. (1996). Dispositional differences in cognitive motivation: The life and times of individuals varying in need for cognition. *Psychological Bulletin, 119*, 197–253.

Cassidy, T., & Lynn, R. (1989). A multifactoral approach to achievement motivation: The development of a comprehensive measure. *Journal of Occupational Psychology, 62*, 301–312.

Christensen-Szalanski, J. J. (1980). A further examination of the selection of problem solving strategies: The effects of deadlines and analytic aptitudes. *Organizational Behavior and Human Performance, 25*, 107–122.

Cohen, S. (1978). Environmental load and the allocation of attention. In: A Baum, J. E. Singer & S. Valins (Eds), *Advances in Environmental Psychology: The Urban Environment* (Vol. 1, pp. 1–29). Hillsdale, NJ: Erlbaum.

Cohen, S. G., & Bailey, D. E. (1997). What makes teams work: Group effectiveness research from the shop floor to the executive suite. *Journal of Management, 23*, 239–290.

Conte, J. M., Mathieu, J. E., & Landy, F. J. (1998). The nomological and predictive validity of time urgency. *Journal of Organizational Behavior, 19*, 1–13.

Craik, F. I. M., & Lockhart, R. S. (1972). Levels of processing: A framework for memory research. *Journal of Verbal Learning and Verbal Behavior, 11*, 671–684.

Davis, J. H. (1969). Individual-group problem solving, subject preference, and problem type. *Journal of Personality and Social Psychology, 13*, 362–374.

Devine, D. J., Clayton, L. D., Philips, J. L., Dunford, B. B., & Melner, S. B. (1999). Teams in organizations: Prevalence, characteristics, and effectiveness. *Small Group Research, 30*, 678–711.

Driskell, J. E., & Salas, E. (1991). Group decision making under stress. *Journal of Applied Psychology, 76*, 473–478.

Driskell, J. E., Salas, E., & Johnston, J. (1999). Does stress lead to a loss of team perspective? *Group Dynamics: Theory, Research, and Practice, 3*, 291–302.

Easterbrook, J. A. (1959). The effect of emotion on cue utilization and the organization of behavior. *Psychological Review, 66*, 183–201.

Eysenck, H. J., & Eysenck, S. B. G. (1969). *Personality structure and measurement*. San Diego, CA: Knapp.

Feldman, D. C. (1984). The development and enforcement of group norms. *Academy of Management Review, 9*, 47–53.

Folkman, S., & Moskowitz, J. T. (2000). Stress, positive emotion, and coping. *Current Directions in Psychological Science, 9*, 115–118.

Futoran, G. C., Kelly, J. R., & McGrath, J. E. (1989). TEMPO: A time-based system for the analysis of group interaction process. *Basic and Applied Social Psychology, 10*, 211–232.

Gallupe, R. B., Dennis, A. R., Cooper, W. H., Valacich, J. S., Bastianutti, L. M., & Nunamaker, J. F., Jr. (1992). Electronic brainstorming and group size. *Academy of Management Journal, 35*, 350–369.

Gersick, C. J., & Hackman, J. R. (1990). Habitual routines in task-performing groups. *Organizational Behavior and Human Decision Processes, 47*, 65–97.

Gevers, J. M. P., van Eerde, W., & Rutte, C. G. (2001). Time pressure, potency, and progress in project groups. *European Journal of Work and Organizational Psychology, 10*, 205–221.

Gordon, J. (1992). Work teams: How far have they come? *Training, 29*, 59–65.

Hackman, J. R. (1987). The design of work teams. In: J. W. Lorsch (Ed.), *Handbook of Organizational Behavior* (pp. 315–342). Englewood Cliffs, NJ: Prentice-Hall.

Hackman, J. R., & Morris, C. G. (1975). Group tasks, group interaction process, and group performance effectiveness: A review and proposed integration. In: L. Berkowitz (Ed.), *Advances in Experimental Social Psychology* (Vol. 8, pp. 45–99). New York: Academic Press.

Hirokawa, R. Y. (1988). Group communication and decision making performance: A continued test of the functional perspective. *Human Communication Research, 14*, 487–515.

Hollingshead, A. B. (1998). Retrieval processes in transactive memory systems. *Journal of Personality and Social Psychology, 74*, 659–671.

Hollingshead, A. B. (2000). Perceptions of expertise and transactive memory in work relationships. *Group Processes and Intergroup Relations, 3*, 257–267.

Hollingshead, A. B., McGrath, J. E., & O'Connor, K. M. (1993). Group task performance and communication technology: A longitudinal study of computer-mediated vs. face-to-face work groups. *Small Group Research, 24*, 307–333.

Hygge, S., & Knez, I. (2001). Effects of noise, heat and indoor lighting on cognitive performance and self-reported affect. *Journal of Environmental Psychology, 21*, 291–299.

Isenberg, D. J. (1981). Some effects of time-pressure on vertical structure and decision making accuracy in small groups. *Organizational Behavior and Human Performance, 27*, 119–134.

Isenberg, D. J. (1986). Group polarization: A critical review and meta-analysis. *Journal of Personality and Social Psychology, 50*, 1141–1151.

Janis, I. L. (1982). *Victims of groupthink* (2nd ed.). Boston: Houghton Mifflin.

Karau, S. J. (2003). *Group discussion and group decision making: Effects of time pressure and awareness of expertise*. Manuscript submitted for publication.

Karau, S. J., & Kelly, J. R. (1992). The effects of time scarcity and time abundance on group performance quality and interaction process. *Journal of Experimental Social Psychology, 28*, 542–571.

Karau, S. J., & Williams, K. D. (1993). Social loafing: A meta-analytic review and theoretical integration. *Journal of Personality and Social Psychology, 65*, 681–706.

Kelly, J. R., Futoran, G. C., & McGrath, J. E. (1990). Capacity and capability: Seven studies of entrainment of task performance rates. *Small Group Research, 21*, 283–314.

Kelly, J. R., Jackson, J. W., & Hutson-Comeaux, S. L. (1997). The effects of time pressure and task differences on influence modes and accuracy in decision making groups. *Personality and Social Psychology Bulletin, 23*, 10–22.

Kelly, J. R., & Karau, S. J. (1999). Group decision making: The effects of initial preferences and time pressure. *Personality and Social Psychology Bulletin, 11*, 1342–1354.

Kelly, J. R., & Loving, T. J. (in press). Time pressure and group performance: Exploring the underlying processes of the attentional focus model. *Journal of Experimental Social Psychology*.

Kelly, J. R., & McGrath, J. E. (1985). Effects of time limits and task types on task performance and interaction of four-person groups. *Journal of Personality and Social Psychology, 49*, 395–407.

Kiesler, S., & Sproull, L. (1992). Group decision making and communication technology. *Organizational Behavior and Human Decision Processes, 52*, 96–123.

Kruglanski, A. W., & Webster, D. M. (1996). Motivated closing of the mind: "Seizing" and "freezing". *Psychological Review, 103*, 263–283.

Lanzetta, J. T. (1955). Group behavior under stress. *Human Relations, 8*, 29–52.

Lanzetta, J. T., Haefner, D., Langham, P., & Axelrod, H. (1954). Some effects of situational threat on group behavior. *Journal of Abnormal and Social Psychology, 49*, 445–453.

Laughlin, P. R. (1980). Social combination processes of cooperative problem-solving groups on verbal intellective tasks. In: M Fishbein (Ed.), *Progress in Social Psychology* (pp. 127–155). Hillsdale, NJ: Erlbaum.

Lawler, E. E. III, Mohrman, S. A., & Ledford, G. E., Jr. (1995). *Creating high performance organizations: Practices and results of employee involvement and total quality management in Fortune 1000 companies*. San Francisco: Jossey-Bass.

Locke, E. A., & Latham, G. P. (1990). *A theory of goal setting and task performance*. Englewood Cliffs, NJ: Prentice-Hall.

Luchins, A. S. (1942). Mechanization in problem solving. *Psychological Monographs, 54*, 1–95.

McGrath, J. E. (1984). *Groups: Interaction and performance*. Englewood Cliffs, NJ: Prentice-Hall.

Moreland, R., Levine, J., & Cini, M. (1993). Group socialization: The role of commitment. In: M. A. Hogg & D. Abrams (Eds), *Group Motivation: Social Psychological Perspectives* (pp. 105–129). New York: Harvester Wheatsheaf.

Mullen, B., & Copper, C. (1994). The relation between group cohesiveness and performance: An integration. *Psychological Bulletin, 115*, 210–227.

Nemeth, C. (1986). Differential contributions of majority and minority influence. *Psychological Review, 93*, 23–32.

Nuttin, J. R. (1985). *Future time perspective and motivation: Theory and research method*. Hillsdale, NJ: Erlbaum.

Okhuysen, G. A., & Eisenhardt, K. M. (2002). Integrating knowledge in groups: How formal interventions enable flexibility. *Organization Science, 13*, 370–386.

O'Reilly, C. A., & Caldwell, D. F. (1985). The impact of normative social influence and cohesiveness on task perceptions and attitudes: A social information processing approach. *Journal of Occupational Psychology, 58*, 193–206.

Parks, C. D., & Cowlin, R. (1995). Group discussion as affected by number of alternatives and by a time limit. *Organizational Behavior and Human Decision Processes, 62*, 267–275.

Pepinsky, P., Pepinsky, H., & Pavlik, W. (1960). The effects of task complexity and time pressure upon team productivity. *Journal of Applied Psychology, 44*, 34–38.

Petty, R. E., & Cacioppo, J. T. (1986). The elaboration likelihood model of persuasion. In: L. Berkowitz (Ed.), *Advances in Experimental Social Psychology* (Vol. 19, pp. 124–205). New York: Academic Press.

Rodriguez, M. L., Mischel, W., & Shoda, Y. (1989). Cognitive person variables in the delay of gratification in older children at risk. *Journal of Personality and Social Psychology, 57*, 358–367.

Schachter, S., Ellertson, N., McBride, D., & Gregory, D. (1951). An experimental study of cohesiveness and productivity. *Human Relations, 4*, 229–238.

Sheppard, J. A. (1993). Productivity loss in performance groups: A motivation analysis. *Psychological Bulletin, 113*, 67–81.

Siegel, J., Dubrovsky, V., Kiesler, S., & McGuire, T. W. (1986). Group processes in computer-mediated communication. *Organizational Behavior and Human Decision Processes, 37*, 157–187.

Stasser, G., Kerr, N. L., & Davis, J. H. (1989). Influence processes and consensus models in decision making groups. In: P. B. Paulus (Ed.), *Psychology of Group Influence* (2nd ed., pp. 279–326). Hillsdale, NJ: Lawrence Erlbaum.

Stasser, G., & Titus, W. (1985). Pooling of unshared information in group decision making: Biased information sampling during discussion. *Journal of Personality and Social Psychology, 48*, 1467–1478.

Staw, B. M., Sandelands, L. E., & Dutton, J. E. (1981). Threat-rigidity effects in organizational behavior: A multi-level analysis. *Administrative Science Quarterly, 26*, 501–524.

Steiner, I. D. (1972). *Group process and productivity*. New York: Academic Press.

Strathman, A., Gleicher, F., Boninger, D. S., & Edwards, C. S. (1994). The consideration of future consequences: Weighing immediate and distant outcomes of behavior. *Journal of Personality and Social Psychology, 66*, 742–752.

Straus, S. G., & McGrath, J. E. (1994). Does the medium matter? The interaction of task type and technology on group performance and member reactions. *Journal of Applied Psychology, 79*, 87–97.

Strube, M. J., Deichmann, A. K., & Kickham, T. (1989). Time urgency and the Type A behavior pattern: Time investment as a function of cue salience. *Journal of Research in Personality, 23*, 287–301.

Valacich, J. S., Dennis, A. R., & Connolly, T. (1994). Idea generation in computer-based groups: A new ending to an old story. *Organizational Behavior and Human Decision Processes, 57*, 448–467.

Valacich, J. S., & Schwenk, C. (1995). Devil's advocate and dialectical inquiry effects on face-to-face and computer-mediated group decision making. *Organizational Behavior and Human Decision Processes, 63*, 158–173.

Waller, M. J., Giambatista, R. C., & Zellmer-Bruhn, M. E. (1999). The effects of individual time urgency on group polychronicity. *Journal of Managerial Psychology, 14*, 244–256.

Wegner, D. M. (1986). Transactive memory: A contemporary analysis of the group mind. In: B. Mullen & G. R. Goethals (Eds), *Theories of Group Behavior* (pp. 185–208). New York: Springer-Verlag.

Wegner, D. M., Erber, R., & Raymond, P. (1991). Transactive memory in close relationships. *Journal of Personality and Social Psychology, 61*, 923–929.

West, M. A. (1996). Reflexivity and work group effectiveness: A conceptual integration. In: M. A. West (Ed.), *Handbook of Work Group Psychology* (pp. 555–579). Chichester, UK: Wiley.

Wood, W., Lundgren, S., Ouellette, J. A., Busceme, S., & Blackstone, T. (1994). Minority influence: A meta-analytic review of social influence processes. *Psychological Bulletin, 115*, 323–345.

Yerkes, R. M., & Dodson, J. D. (1908). The relation of strength of stimulus to rapidity of habit formation. *Journal of Comparative and Neurological Psychology, 18*, 459–482.

Yukl, G. A., Malone, M. P., Hayslip, B., & Pamin, T. A. (1976). The effects of time pressure and issue settlement order on integrative bargaining. *Sociometry, 39*, 277–281.

Zaccaro, S. J., Gualtieri, J., & Minionis, D. (1995). Task cohesion as a facilitator of team decision making under temporal urgency. *Military Psychology, 7*, 77–93.

Zajonc, R. B. (1980). Compresence. In: P. B. Paulus (Ed.), *Psychology of Group Influence* (pp. 35–60). Hillsdale, NJ: Erlbaum.

Zakay, D., & Wooler, S. (1984). Time pressure, training and decision effectiveness. *Ergonomics, 27*, 273–284.

Zimbardo, P. G., & Boyd, J. N. (1999). Putting time in perspective: A valid, reliable, individual-differences metric. *Journal of Personality and Social Psychology, 77*, 1271–1288.

IS A MEETING WORTH THE TIME? BARRIERS TO EFFECTIVE GROUP DECISION MAKING IN ORGANIZATIONS

Victoria Husted Medvec, Gail Berger, Katie Liljenquist and Margaret A. Neale

ABSTRACT

Time pressure impacts the information that emerges in a group discussion. Executives need help managing the challenges posed by time pressure to arrive at the best decisions. In particular, we address two common biases that impact the group decision making process: the confirmation bias and the common information effect. Strategies are presented for overcoming these two biases, particularly the advantage of privately collecting information from group members within a meeting to surface unique information and disconfirming information. We also acknowledge that an executive's goal may not always be to surface information; rather, an individual may be attempting to use a group meeting to push through a particular decision. We discuss the role of time in accomplishing this objective as well.

Time in Groups
Research on Managing Groups and Teams, Volume 6, 213–233
Copyright © 2004 Elsevier Ltd.
ISSN: 1534-0856/doi:10.1016/S1534-0856(03)06010-9

INTRODUCTION

Deciding how to decide. Although it may seem trivial, it is one of the biggest decisions facing CEOs. Should they proceed alone or utilize the wisdom of their people in a group meeting? *How* they make decisions is the critical first decision. Many organizations use group meetings as the default mode for making decisions. Group decision making, however, comes at the cost of significant organizational resources: Eight people meeting for 60 minutes equals one person's entire work day. Does group decision making warrant the amount of time it consumes?

While research indicates that groups outperform the average individual, they often fail to perform at the level of the member with the highest ability (Gigone & Hastie, 1997b). Yet, group decision making offers the potential advantages of greater informational exchange, increased accuracy, and increased diversity of perspectives and expertise. How can executives ensure that the decisions made by the groups they lead are the best possible decisions, particularly given the time constraints that surround today's corporate activities?

In this chapter, we examine key biases engendered by time pressure and discuss several factors that can be manipulated by discussion leaders to enhance the quality of the decisions made by their groups. While many factors impact the group decision-making process, this chapter specifically focuses on those related to time pressure in groups: how time pressure impacts the information that emerges in a group discussion. We offer advice to executives as to how they might manage the challenges posed by time pressure to arrive at the best decisions for the organizations they lead.

IMPACT OF TIME PRESSURE

A peak into the typical business meeting is likely to reveal a collection of clock-monitoring captives desperate for escape. Clearly, time is a critical factor in any group meeting. When surveyed about their primary goals upon entering a meeting, most executives will inevitably say: "To get out of the meeting." This universal focus on the end of a meeting suggests that a sense of time pressure may be created in meetings even when not intended. Furthermore, this implicit time pressure may impact the group discussion and outcome; specifically, it may influence the type of information that surfaces during the discussion, when various information surfaces, and how long different pieces of information are discussed.

A major challenge created by time pressure is that it hinders the disclosure of information during the decision process. Critical information for a board decision may not be considered because of time pressure, despite the directors' best intentions. On the other hand, some individuals may use time constraints strategically to ensure that only particular information is discussed. A CEO who wants to avoid a particular conversation may construct an agenda that intentionally reduces the likelihood that specific information will emerge. Regardless of whether the goal is to make the most informed decision or to push through a particular decision, time plays an important role in determining whether the goal can be accomplished.

Many studies have examined the impact of time on task performance, yielding mixed results. We will discuss studies that both highlight the detrimental effects of time pressure and highlight the benefits of time pressure on group performance. Using the Attentional Focus Model (AFM) developed by Karau and Kelly (1992) as well as the Yerkes-Dodson law (1908), we will attempt to resolve the inconsistencies in the prior research findings.

Urban, Weaver, Bowers and Rhodenizer (1996) investigated the impact of time pressure on groups in the context of tasks involving monitoring. Their results revealed a significant reduction in performance under time pressure that correlated with a decline in communication. This finding, in tandem with other research that reports reduced efficacy on group decision tasks under time pressure (Durham, Locke, Poone & McLeod, 2000), highlights the adverse effect that time pressure can have on group communication. More specifically, time pressure impedes the disclosure of information because discussants lack sufficient time to discuss pertinent information (Edland & Svenson, 1993), and as threat rigidity theory explains, time pressure also imposes an external threat that restricts information processing (Gladstein & Reilly, 1985). Moreover, time pressure creates a fertile ground in which biases relevant to group decision making can take root. Past research has demonstrated that biases such as confirmation bias, false consensus, group-think, group polarization, and escalation of commitment are often natural consequences of time pressure (Jones & Roelofsma, 2000).

Although a preponderance of evidence supporting the detriments of time pressure exists, some researchers' results support the notion that time pressure enhances task performance. For example, Schaab's (1997) research on aircraft monitoring supports the claims of those who say they work best under pressure; unless a certain threshold for stress was surpassed, time pressure actually improved the performance of aircraft monitors. The heightened adrenaline induced by time pressure evidently facilitated more vigilant monitoring by individuals. Schaab's findings may seem to contradict the findings of others (Durham, Locke, Poone & McLeod, 2000; Edland & Svenson, 1993; Gladstein & Reilly, 1985; Jones & Roelofsma, 2000), yet we believe that the apparent contradictions in these findings can be resolved in light of the Yerkes-Dodson Law (1908) and Karau and Kelly's (1992) Attentional Focus Model (AFM).

In Yerkes and Dodson's (1908) seminal paper about learning, the researchers demonstrated a curvilinear relationship between motivation and performance. Thus, an increase in motivation will improve performance – but only up to a point. Too much motivation can actually have a detrimental impact on performance. One can think about time pressure as a form of motivation. In essence an impending deadline will motivate a group to complete a task. Time pressure can motivate a group to perform; however, excessive pressure will impair performance.

Karau and Kelly (1992) also predict that the impact of time pressure on performance will vary. According to their Attentional Focus Model (AFM) of group performance, it is the nature of the task rather than the amount of time pressure that will lead to differing relationships between time pressure and performance. More specifically, their model suggests that time pressure can either enhance or hinder performance depending on the nature of the task. The AFM explains that when time pressure mounts, group members concentrate more on key elements of the task, while neglecting matters that seem less germane to task completion. Thus, for tasks that require a critical analysis of information, time pressure can detract from decision quality because it hinders either the amount of information considered or the degree to which it is processed (Karau & Kelly, 2004; Zakay & Wooler, 1984). On the other hand, performance on more simplistic tasks may benefit from time pressure.

In Karau and Kelly's (1992) study, groups worked on a planning task under conditions of time scarcity, optimal time, or time abundance. Groups in the time-scarcity condition focused their attention on task-relevant activities, to the relative exclusion of social and other non-task activities, whereas groups in the time abundant condition engaged in relatively more non-task activities. However, while solutions were produced more quickly in time scarcity groups, they were rated lower in creativity and originality than the solutions of groups in the optimal time and time abundant conditions. Although time pressure intensified task focus, the disciplined focus did not yield more innovative solutions.

A later study by Kelly and Karau (1999) looked at groups that were making a decision about which of two cholesterol-reducing drugs to market. Consistent with the AFM, they found that groups under time pressure worked at a faster rate and reported a higher level of task-focused attention. However, under certain conditions, time pressure enhanced the tendency for group discussions and decisions to be biased in favor of initial preferences; depending on whether the initial preference was correct or not, the time pressure either enhanced or diminished decision quality. Perhaps most important, Karau and Kelly's (1992) AFM explains that under time pressure, group members attend to task elements that seem most central to completing a task. In the case of a group decision task, this fosters a drive to arrive at a decision quickly and efficiently. Although today's organization places a premium on efficiency, speed often compromises quality. Consequently, in world of deadlines and time constraints, it is critical that decision-makers understand how to collect and discuss information in a manner that circumvents the biases that stem from time pressure in group settings.

We will discuss two of these biases below and suggest strategies for overcoming these biases within group meetings. In specific, we will highlight the confirmation bias and the common information effect and present tactics for surfacing disconfirming information and unique information within meetings.

CONFIRMATION BIAS

Due to information dependencies, effective group decision making requires a thorough examination of the information that each member possesses. More importantly, groups will arrive at superior decisions when they seek information that disconfirms their initial opinions during the decision-making process (Russo & Meloy, 2002). This is because truth seeking fundamentally involves falsification (Popper, 1959). In other words, seeking disconfirming evidence is often a necessary ingredient for effective hypothesis testing.

In spite of the importance of exploring potentially disconfirming information, time constraints and mental capacity force people to rely on heuristic biases in order to navigate an information-rich environment. As a consequence, individuals often cue into information that supports their existing opinions and preferences when making decisions. Research investigating the confirmation bias at both the individual and group level points to biased and systematic errors that stem from failure to seek disconfirming information (Klayman & Ha, 1987; Russo & Meloy, 2002; Snyder & Swann, 1978b; Wason, 1960; Wason & Johnson-Laird, 1972). Such failures can occur during both the hypothesis-generation (Russo & Meloy, 2002) and hypothesis-testing (Wason, 1960; Wason & Johnson-Laird, 1972) phases of decision making.

In 1960, Wason introduced the "2–4–6" task to examine the ways in which people test hypotheses. In the task, participants are told that a rule is being considered and that the triplet of numbers "2–4–6" follows the rule. The objective is for participants to discover the underlying "triplet" rule by proposing as many other triplets as desired. Each time a participant proposes a triplet, the experimenter informs the participant whether the proposed triplet conforms to the rule. Once the participant is confident that he or she can identify the rule, the participant may guess what it is. Although the task seems quite simple, participants guess the wrong rule the majority of the time. The reason for this is that most participants tend to identify a seemingly reasonable, but often incorrect, rule early on and then propose only sequences that confirm this preliminary conjecture. After a few confirmations, the participant feels confident and ventures an incorrect guess of the rule.

While Wason's 2–4–6 task examined the search for confirmatory information during task completion, Snyder and Swann (1978b) demonstrated that people also seek confirmatory information when testing hypotheses about other individuals. They examined the hypothesis-testing processes that people use in social interactions and found that individuals systematically formulate confirmatory strategies for testing hypotheses about other people. In four separate studies, participants were provided with hypotheses about the personal attributes of other individuals (targets). Participants prepared to test their hypothesis by choosing a series of questions to ask the targets in an upcoming interview. Regardless of whether participants were initially told that the target was an introvert or an extrovert, hypothesis-confirming questions were selected. Snyder and Swann (1978a) also showed that a confirmatory hypothesis-testing strategy can even constrain interaction in ways that cause the target to provide actual behavioral confirmation for the hypothesis being tested[1] (Snyder & Swann, 1978a). In sum, the tendency to seek only confirming information limits hypothesis generation, reduces the quality of hypothesis testing, and ultimately results in decision errors.

Numerous causes for the confirmation bias have been proposed. One set of explanations centers around the image of people as cognitive misers (Fiske & Taylor, 1991) suggesting that people use heuristics, or short-cuts, to simplify cognitive tasks. According to this line of reasoning, people fail to seek disconfirming information simply because it is easier to search for confirmatory evidence. The confirmation bias has also been attributed to the fact that people fail to recognize the value of seeking disconfirming information (Wason & Johnson-Laird, 1972). Finally, Kruglanski (1989) and Kunda (1990) posit a more motivational explanation for the bias, arguing that people strategically choose not to seek disconfirming information to accommodate personal beliefs and preferred conclusions.

Surfacing Disconfirming Information

Since people are reluctant to seek disconfirming information, it is important to consider how time constraints may further frustrate a group's efforts to discuss disconfirming data. Past research has shown that disconfirming information generally takes longer to emerge than confirming data (Russo & Meloy, 2002; Wason, 1960). Research on the "2–4–6" task (Russo & Meloy, 2002; Wason, 1960) indicates that confirming information surfaces before disconfirming information because participants consistently pose confirming triplets before they suggest disconfirming triplets. If disconfirming information naturally emerges later, the imposition of time constraints may entirely omit it from the discussion process, rendering confirming information that much more potent.

The work of Kruglanski and Webster (1991) lends support to the claim that a shortage of time exacerbates the confirmation bias. They found that the opinion of deviates was more strongly rejected when a dissenting opinion was articulated in close proximity to a group-decision deadline than when the opinion was raised at an earlier point in the discussion. This suggests that under conditions of time pressure, dissenting information may be more likely to be rejected because of a sense of an impending deadline. It would seem, then, that increasing the time available for group decision making might be an effective intervention against the confirmation bias. However, Parks and Cowlin (1996) found that even when groups were told to spend more time discussing information, they still did not share disconfirming information. Thus, increasing the time spent discussing information might be a necessary, but not sufficient, condition for disclosure of disconfirming information.

With this in mind, executives would be well advised to consider their time parameters and implement tactics that will mitigate the impact of the confirmation bias. Given individuals' preference for the confirmation rather than disconfirmation of their personal beliefs and suppositions (Klayman & Ha, 1987; Russo & Meloy, 2002; Snyder & Swann, 1978a; Wason, 1960; Wason & Johnson-Laird, 1972), this is a challenging goal. One possible remedy suggested by past research is to emphasize the importance of accuracy during a decision-making process. By increasing an interviewer's incentive to form impressions that are accurate, the interviewer is motivated to select more non-confirmatory questions, making it easier to test alternative hypotheses (Judice & Neuberg, 1998; Kruglanski & Mayseless, 1988). Furthermore, because a norm of confirmation often exists in groups, the executive who wants to surface disconfirming information will need to send a salient message to encourage the counter-normative behavior of asking disconfirming questions. The goal is to create a complementing norm of seeking disconfirmation rather than having only one or two of the same people always ask the disconfirming questions. If these questions were consistently to come from the same individuals, these individuals would be branded as nay-sayers and their input and information would likely be discounted. To encourage the norm of asking disconfirming questions across the group, one could begin by randomly assigning the role of the devil's advocate in each meeting. An executive sends a very strong message when he or she tells the person assigned this role that it is his or her job to question the group's assumptions and to identify the weaknesses in the group's arguments. Assigning this role to a different person in each meeting allows the executive to convey the clear message that he or she expects group members to provide disconfirming information.

In addition to assigning the role of devil's advocate, executives may want to consider whether the order of their meeting agenda is increasing the likelihood of a confirmation trap. If attendees have a shared goal of getting out of the meeting, then the end of the meeting may be a very salient marker; any discussion that runs into this marker may implicitly be subject to a high degree of time pressure. This can be problematic in a typical meeting because decisions are often saved to the end (as part of "new business") while reports and updates are provided at the beginning during the "old business" segment. Putting decisions at the end of the meeting may mean that these decisions will be made under time pressure and this may make them especially vulnerable to the confirmation bias; past research suggests that disconfirming information takes longer to emerge than confirming information, so a shortage of time may result in only confirming information being considered. It may be helpful to reverse the order of an agenda: Putting the decisions at the beginning and the reports and updates at the end will reduce the time constriction on the decision-making portion of the meeting and provide a greater opportunity for disconfirming information to surface.

Executives also need to attend to the subtle messages they unintentionally send that discourage disclosure of disconfirming information. For example, leaders often make a decision individually and then enter a group meeting and try to pretend that the decision is actually a group decision. While it is perfectly appropriate for leaders to make individual decisions, they should then announce this decision to the group rather than pretending to "decide" this decision. Otherwise group members are likely to perceive the leader's lack of desire for disconfirming information and this may transfer to future cases when disconfirming information is truly needed.

While the interventions discussed above may prove successful in encouraging disconfirming information, there are other types of information that also are often neglected during group discussions. Just as individuals are prone to seek confirming information and neglect disconfirming information, previous research has shown that groups are more likely to discuss information that is shared by all group members than information that is only known by one member of the group. This bias, known as the common information effect, is discussed below.

COMMON INFORMATION EFFECT

Organizations often use groups rather than individuals to make decisions because they believe that the group members each possess unique knowledge, expertise, and experience that will benefit the decision. An organization allocating resources toward group meetings is investing in the idea that the pooled knowledge of all group members will result in a better decision than any one of the members could have made alone. Therefore, when group members meet to make a decision, one goal of the meeting is to pool the unique information of individual group members. Unfortunately though, as discussed above, group discussions are rarely a balanced and systematic dialogue of all the relevant issues. Rather, group discussions tend to focus on particular issues and support a pre-existing consensus (Fisher, 1980).

Just as group members dwell on confirming information, information shared by all group members is spotlighted more than information that is possessed only by a single member of the group (Gigone & Hastie, 1997a). This tendency, known as the common information effect, presents a problem when team members redundantly discuss information that is already common to the group, while entirely bypassing unique information that could be imperative to making a high-quality decision (Stasser, 1992; Stasser & Titus, 1985).

Previous research (Stasser & Titus, 1985) suggests that during face-to-face discussions, group members will fail to disseminate unshared information. As a consequence, discussion tends to be dominated by information that members hold in common prior to the discussion, as well as information that supports members' preferences.

In a study by Stasser and Titus (1985), participants read descriptions of three candidates for student body president and then met in 4-person groups to decide which candidate was best suited for the position. Candidate "A" was deemed best because his profile contained more attributes that would be desirable in a student body president. In the shared condition, participants read descriptions containing all of the profile information about each candidate; with full information presented to each group member, groups in this condition selected candidate "A." Two unshared conditions were also created. In both, each of the four participants was only given partial information about each candidate; however, the participants could pool their information and collectively recreate the complete candidate profiles from the first condition. In these conditions, the positive information about "A" and negative information about the other candidates was distributed among the group members, but this information was unshared. Unless group members pooled their unique information, they were not likely to choose candidate "A." Therefore, in both of the unshared conditions, the partial information received by participants biased them against the superior candidate. Even though the groups could have selected the best candidate if they had produced complete composites of the candidates by pooling their individual information, groups in these conditions failed to discuss unshared (i.e. unique) information and thus decided in favor of candidate "B" or "C," whichever one was initially preferred by the majority.

While Stasser's (1992) work explains that shared information outweighs unique information due to its probabilistic advantage (i.e. numerically, there is a higher likelihood for shared information to surface than unique information), more recent research has focused on the qualities of shared information that may contribute to its dominance. One qualitative advantage of shared information stems from people's desire for mutual enhancement (Wittenbaum, Hubbell & Zuckerman, 1999). When shared information surfaces, both the communicator and recipients feel validated; the communicator perceives that his or her arguments are positively received, while the recipient feels validated because the mention of familiar information reinforces the idea that he or she possesses valuable information that is worthy of mention by other group members. Furthermore, shared information may be discussed more than unique information because it endows the possessor of the information with a greater sense of psychological safety (Edmondson, 1999) since the shared information carries more legitimacy.

Perhaps one reason why shared information is perceived as more valid is because shared information is generally confirming information. Untangling confirming vs. disconfirming information from shared vs. unique information has generally been problematic because most research has confounded the two. For example, in Stasser and Titus's (1985) study, all unshared information was disconfirming of the participants' individual preferences because the unshared information either disparaged their personal preference or endorsed an alternative candidate. Thus, it is difficult to interpret their results and determine whether unshared information was discussed less than shared information because it was unique or because it was disconfirming of the candidate that individuals perceived to be the best choice. Given the fact that people are unlikely to seek disconfirming information, it is hardly surprising that disconfirming information unknown to most group members was not discussed as much as confirming information that was shared by all group members. This leaves the unanswered question, however, of whether the propensity for unique information to be discussed would be moderated by whether the information is confirming or disconfirming of an individual's or team's original position.

Medvec, Berger, Liljenquist and Neale (2003) conducted a study to disentangle shared vs. unique information from confirming vs. disconfirming information. In Medvec et al.'s (2003) investigation, groups were asked to make a hiring decision for a consulting company. Participants were asked to assume one of three roles as a member of a three-person hiring committee for a new executive of Trafalgar & Associates, an international management-consulting firm. Participants received profiles for all three candidates under consideration for the position. In one condition, all of the participants shared an additional piece of confirming, positive information about the company-endorsed candidate, while only one participant had a piece of disconfirming, negative information about him. In a second condition, all of the participants shared the piece of disconfirming information about the preferred candidate, while only one of the participants had the extra piece of positive, confirming information.

Notable differences were observed in both how long unique vs. shared information was discussed when it was confirming vs. disconfirming and at what point in the discussion this information surfaced. Whereas past research has found that shared information is discussed more than unique information, Medvec et al. (2003) found that this was only true for confirming information. In fact, they showed that unique, disconfirming information was discussed significantly longer than shared disconfirming information. They also found that the total number of times that the disconfirming information surfaced was greater when the disconfirming information was unique than when it was shared. Again, the opposite was true for confirming information; participants discussed confirming information significantly more when it was shared than when it was unique. While Medvec et al.'s findings regarding confirming information are consistent with past research, their findings for disconfirming information provide new insights.

A further application of Medvec et al.'s (2003) research concerns the impact of individual preferences. Similar to past research, they found that the group's final choice was most often the candidate that was the prediscussion favorite of the majority of group members. Discussion rarely erodes even a minimal consensus because most groups deciding on issues of judgment or social preference seem to follow a majority-rules process (Laughlin & Earley, 1982). (For an exception, see the familiar groups of Gruenfeld, Mannix, Williams & Neale, 1996.) However, in Medvec et al.'s study, a comparison of the cases in which the prediscussion favorite was selected vs. rejected provides some insight into the power of disconfirming information on the group's decision; Medvec et al. (2003) found that disconfirming information was discussed for a greater duration when the prediscussion majority preference was overturned than when it was not. Thus, Medvec et al. (2003) emphasize that disconfirming information must be discussed in order to override prediscussion preferences.

In light of the fact that shared information generally has a larger impact on group processes and decisions than unshared information, one might conclude that groups would make better decisions if all information were shared by all group members. However, even in cases where it is possible to disseminate information to all parties involved, too much information can overload people's cognitive capabilities and reduce the quality of the group decision. Tindale and Sheffey (2002) observed this when they examined the effect of information load on group performance and discovered that groups who had partially shared information actually outperformed groups with completely redundant information. Gruenfeld et al. (1996) provided evidence that teams composed of familiar members produced better quality decisions when members had both unique and shared information. In contrast, groups composed of strangers produced higher quality decisions when all members had completely redundant information.

Surfacing Unique Information

Time pressure probably exacerbates the common information effect, but simply giving a group more time to discuss a decision does not alleviate the bias. Although such an intervention seems intuitive enough, researchers found that allowing more discussion time only increased the amount of attention devoted to shared information (Parks & Cowlin, 1996) or to non-task related information, especially among groups composed of familiars (Gruenfeld et al., 1996). Thus, more time may not be the answer for an executive who wants to facilitate discussion of unique information.

If endowing groups with entirely shared information or allowing more time for discussion does not prevent the common information effect, what other strategies might reduce the propensity for shared, confirming information to dominate group discussion? Strategies such as increasing the size of a team (Stasser, Taylor & Hanna, 1989) or making teams accountable for their decisions (Stewart, Billings & Stasser, 1998) did not mitigate the common information effect. More successful interventions involved characterizing a task as a problem to be solved rather than a judgment to be made (Stasser & Stewart, 1992), instructing groups to rank alternatives rather than choose the best alternative (Hollingshead, 1996), and directing groups to consider decision alternatives one at a time (Larson, Foster-Fishman & Keys, 1994).

Also relevant to the issue of surfacing unique information is the way in which group composition influences the type of information that emerges during group discussions. Recent work by Thomas-Hunt, Ogden and Neale (2003) suggests that *who* possesses the unique information can have a significant impact on its revelation to the group and on its perceived usefulness to the group in the accomplishment of its task. The results from their investigation of heterogeneous groups indicated that perceived experts participated more in discussions and emphasized shared knowledge and others' unique knowledge significantly more than did non-experts. Interestingly, however, there was no significant difference between perceived experts' and non-experts' emphasis of their own unique knowledge. These results, consistent with Larson et al. (1994) suggest that perceived experts assume responsibility for managing the sharing of information within the group, focusing on aggregating and emphasizing both shared and unique knowledge. Furthermore, out-group members participated more in discussions and emphasized more of their own unique information than did in-group members. At the same time, out-group members emphasized less of other team members' unique knowledge than did in-group members. It seems that the main strategy of out-group members was to bolster other members' impressions of their usefulness by emphasizing the unique contribution they could make.

Further analysis also indicated that out-group members felt more comfortable disagreeing than did in-group members. This suggests that within some heterogeneous groups, in-group members' discomfort with disagreeing may constrain their willingness to expose their own unique information. Such reluctance is consistent with (Phillips, in press) socially-connected members' hesitance to contribute information that is inconsistent with information provided by a socially-connected counterpart. Research by Phillips (in press) also indicates that group members are more irritated by divergent opinions expressed by those to whom they are similar (other in-group members) than divergent opinions expressed by those from whom they are different (i.e. out-group members). By anticipating such a reaction, in-group members may censor their divergent knowledge so as not to irritate and distance other in-group members.

This interaction between group composition and information sharing bears particular relevance for organizational decision making because executives are often faced with the dilemma of whether they should hire outside consultants or utilize in-house expertise in the decision-making process. The insights derived from the above research would suggest that although outside consultants are costly, they may enhance decision quality by effectively introducing disconfirming or unique information to group discussions and liberating others to more freely share information and ideas. A key to unlocking this potential value though, is to hire the consultant explicitly to provide this unique, disconfirming information. A leader who hires a consulting firm to tell him why he should do what he wants to do is unlikely to obtain much disconfirming information from the firm; hiring the consultants to tell him why he should not do what he wants to do may be a much better investment of resources. Once an executive possesses this disconfirming information, he or she can make a decision with more complete information and address the weaknesses in the plan.

While outside consultants may provide one opportunity for surfacing unique, disconfirming information, groups are missing critical opportunities if they cannot unlock the door to the unique information possessed by each of their own members. One avenue for accomplishing this may be to privately collect information from group members rather than solely relying on public discussion to surface information. The advantages of privately collecting information within a group meeting are discussed below.

Information Gathering

The way in which information is gathered can systematically affect the information that will emerge. Information can be gathered privately either before or during the meeting, or collected publicly through a typical public discussion. Publicly solicited information induces conformity (Asch, 1955), suggesting that the view first mention or held by the majority or the most vocal faction will sway the group's decision (Davis, Kameda, Parks, Stasson & Zimmerman, 1989). Privately collecting information allows the minority opinion to emerge and the unique and disconfirming information to surface.

As mentioned earlier, often groups are brought together to make decisions because the leader believes that each individual possesses unique knowledge and expertise. The leader's goal in the meeting is to surface all of this unique knowledge in order to make the best decision. However, research has shown that most of the time in a meeting is spent discussing the shared information that all of the participants know rather than the unique information that each individual possesses; thus unique information tends not to emerge. This problem can be overcome by privately collecting information from all of the participants at the beginning of the meeting, yet organizational leaders mistakenly believe that publicly gathering information will save time. If the leader's goal is to surface each group member's unique information, however, the private collection of information could provide a more efficient mechanism than public collection for accomplishing this goal.

A number of options exist regarding how a person can privately collect information. Information can either be solicited from each individual before the meeting or the information can be privately gathered from everyone during the meeting. If the information is collected privately at the meeting, there are a number of ways to collect this information. The leader could say, "There are currently three options that exist regarding this decision; I would like everyone to write down three additional options before we discuss this." Leaders can also ask group members to rank the options according to their personal preferences. Finally, leaders can ask the group to divide 100 points among the options. The number of points assigned to each option provides information about the magnitude of the person's opinion regarding each option.

The fact that private collection of information provides the opportunity to surface information about the magnitude of participants' preferences is a significant advantage compared to public information collection. Often people believe that they are surfacing the magnitude of a person's preferences in a public discussion based on the "passion" the individual is demonstrating or the persistence on a point, but this perceived passion and persistence is generally confounded by the person's personality and style. Imagine that a group is discussing three potential candidates for a job. A soft-spoken individual might feel very strongly about a particular candidate. Because the person is soft-spoken, however, his or her strong feelings may not be conveyed. However, if that person had privately assigned preference points to the candidate, then the opinion would have been expressed. On the other hand, an outgoing person with a slight preference toward a particular candidate may be perceived to have a very strong preference because the person talks about the candidate in an excited way for a long period of time or is the first to speak, thereby anchoring the group's discussion. Privately collecting information using a point allocation scheme allows for the detection of magnitude information that can never be as accurately surfaced in a public discussion.

While private collection of information can occur before a meeting or during a meeting, collecting information privately before the meeting can be problematic if the leader's goal is to surface as much information as possible. When a leader solicits private information before the meeting, people often assume that these private caucuses are occurring because the leader has an agenda and may begin to feel that the decision has been made before the meeting occurs. On the other hand, private information collection during the meeting sets a different tone by being a more transparent process.

If private collection of information allows both disconfirming information and unique information to emerge, what are some of the factors that prevent CEOs and managers from privately collecting information from their group members? Most often, organizational leaders mistakenly believe that private gathering of information takes too much time. In reality, if a leader wants to collect unique information from every group member, private information gathering may be much more efficient than trying to collect the unique information from each participant in a public forum.

Leaders also justify public information collection because they claim that they must know which individual is providing each piece of information. Unfortunately, they are erroneously equating private information collection with anonymity. Information can be collected privately without making it anonymous. Group members simply can write their names on the information that they submit.

Finally, sometimes leaders do not want to implement private information collection procedures because they believe that they are unnecessary given their organization's culture. In particular, these leaders may be skeptical of the need to gather information privately since they believe they have a cohesive group and a culture that encourages openness and respect. They may believe that it would be pointless to collect the information privately because they assume people would be willing to share their unique information publicly. However, even if the organization emphasizes candor and frankness, private collection of information can provide critical benefits. First, as we mentioned earlier, private information can provide a magnitude measure that cannot be obtained in a public discussion. Second, conformity pressure, and a tendency to repress unique information, will always exist. Finally, individuals can be biased by the information that other people share publicly. Even if the organization has a culture in which people feel comfortable sharing information, people will inevitably be influenced by the information that was publicly shared by others.

In conclusion, the information that emerges during a group discussion is likely to vary as function of whether the information was gathered privately or publicly. In particular, both unique and disconfirming information are more likely to be revealed if the information is collected privately. Therefore, private information collection can be advantageous. If a leader's goal is to surface as much information as possible in order to make the most informed decision, it seems important to reduce the role of prediscussion preferences on the group's decision. One possible explanation for the power of prediscussion preferences may be that group members come into the meeting and make immediate public commitments based on these preferences. Once people voice a public commitment, they may be reluctant to renege, even when objective data emerges suggesting that they are wrong. Privately collecting information either before a meeting or at the beginning of a meeting may help to reduce the impact of prediscussion preferences by surfacing more unique information, disconfirming information, and minority opinions (Gigone & Hastie, 1993). This is consistent with Gruenfeld, Mannix, Williams and Neale's (1996) advice to "poll before you pool." In their study, they found that groups composed of strangers performed better when their opinions were polled prior to group discussion; individual polling revealed personal preferences that increased conflict and discussion of diverse information, ultimately yielding superior decisions. However, it is critical to remember that the advice that we have given about private vs. public collection of information pertains to situations when the group is trying to make the "best" decision (that is one that most accurately utilizes the information available from all parties). If, however, the leader's goal is to push through a particular agenda, our advice would differ, and in fact, the suggestions would be quite the opposite, as we discuss below.

HARNESSING TIME FOR STRATEGIC ADVANTAGE: PUSHING A PARTICULAR AGENDA

The research findings highlighted in this chapter suggest many useful ideas for executives who seek to improve the group decision-making process and effectively manage time pressures. It is critical that executives recruit individuals who they believe possess information that is relevant to the decision and manage the time spent in the meeting to facilitate the surfacing of as much information as possible in order to arrive at the "best" decision.

But coming to the "best" decision is not always the goal. Sometimes an executive's goal in the meeting is not to get the best decision to emerge from the group, but rather to push a particular decision alternative. This may be because the executive believes this specific decision is best for the organization's objectives or because this decision furthers the executive's own agenda. The goal in this situation, then, is not to reveal all information, but rather to surface the particular information that endorses the preferred decision. The fact that time is a scarce and salient resource in meetings means that some individuals may try to strategically use time to suppress the emergence of divergent information and push through a particular decision. This suggests some provocative advice for agents of influence who want to undermine the possibility of dissension in group meetings.

First, to stifle potentially disconfirming information, a savvy executive might wish to manipulate the order of his agenda. By postponing discussion of an issue that already enjoys some support until the end of a meeting, executives can leverage time pressure to reduce the probability that disconfirming information will emerge. If discussion is rushed, a cursory review of information is likely to yield only information that confirms the preferences of the majority. Once the topic is under discussion, another strategy would be to propose the preferred course of action early in the discussion, thus influencing the remainder of the group in that particular direction.

If an executive's goal is to promote a personal agenda, the approach to collection of information should also be quite different than that recommended earlier. If the majority of group members favors the desired outcome, one could capture the benefit of these prediscussion preferences by having people publicly commit very early in the meeting, using a public discussion or a public vote.

The fact that unique, disconfirming information is likely to be discussed more often and for a longer duration than shared disconfirming information, suggests a somewhat counter-intuitive approach. If an executive knew that someone in the group who opposed his course of action possessed unique, disconfirming information that could harm the preferred agenda, the executive might want to share this information with all of the group members before the discussion and downplay it. Research suggests that changing unique disconfirming information to shared disconfirming information can reduce its role in the meeting (Medvec, Berger, Liljenquist & Neale, 2003). It would be important to let everyone know that others possessed the same information and then to delay discussion of this disconfirming information for as long as possible during the meeting. This would leverage pluralistic ignorance[2] (Miller & McFarland, 1987) to the executive's advantage and increase the likelihood that group members will assume that no one else in the group feels the point is worth discussing. If possible, before privately sharing disconfirming information with each group member, the executive should have supporters of the agenda reveal their preferences to reinforce those preferences and counter any negative implication that would stem from the disconfirming information.

Although this prescriptive advice extends from research findings, these ideas have not been empirically tested. Our suggestions lay fertile ground for future research that would further extend our understanding of how time impacts information discovery and discussion in group decisions.

Time is a critical factor in meetings. Regardless of whether an executive's goal is to have the group arrive at the best possible decision or to push through a favored decision, understanding how time influences the type of information that will emerge is key. In light of this, we are left wondering whether the Enron board was trying to use the time in their meetings to surface as much information as possible or whether executives within Enron were trying to use time to their advantage to push through particular agendas? Only time will tell.

NOTES

1. Behavioral confirmation, a self-fulfilling prophecy in social interaction, occurs when one person (the perceiver), having adopted beliefs about another person (the target), acts in ways that cause the behavior of the target to appear to confirm these beliefs. Behavioral confirmation has been demonstrated in several domains, including classrooms and organizations (McNatt, 2000). For example, Rosenthal and Jacobson (1968) showed that teachers led to expect particular levels of performance from students in their classrooms, acted in ways that elicit performances that confirm initial expectation.

2. Pluralistic ignorance occurs when individuals infer that the identical actions of the self and others reflect different internal states (Miller & McFarland, 1987). Thus, when disconfirming information is shared among all group members but is not discussed, a group member who believes this information is important may interpret others' failure to mention it as disregard for the information. If such an interpretation intimidates the individual, it may stifle willingness to voice personal opinions and induce self-limiting behavior. Mulvey, Veiga and Elsass (1996) found that the presence of an expert in the group, conformity pressure, and lack of self-confidence are key causes of self-limiting behavior in teams. Consequently, assigning a group member the role of "devil's advocate" may curb the effects of pluralistic ignorance and allow shared disconfirming information to emerge. If group members believe that it is their responsibility to represent alternative viewpoints, they will be less likely to allow erroneous assumptions about others' opinions limit the expression of their own views.

REFERENCES

Asch, S. (1955). Opinions and social pressure. *Scientific American, 193*(5), 31–35.

Davis, J. H., Kameda, T., Parks, C., Stasson, M., & Zimmerman, S. (1989). Some social mechanics of group decision making: The distribution of opinion, polling sequence, and implications for consensus. *Journal of Personality and Social Psychology, 57*(6), 1000–1012.

Durham, C. C., Locke, E. A., Poone, J. M. L., & McLeod, P. L. (2000). Effects of group goals and time pressure on group efficacy, information-seeking strategy, and performance. *Human Performance, 13*(2), 115–138.

Edland, A., & Svenson, O. (1993). Judgment and decision making under time pressure: Studies and findings. In: O. Svenson & A. Maule (Eds), *Time Pressure and Stress in Human Decision Making* (pp. 27–40). New York: Plenum Press.

Edmondson, A. (1999). Psychological safety and learning behavior in work teams. *Administrative Science Quarterly, 44*(2), 350–383.

Fisher, B. A. (1980). *Small group decision making: Communication and the group process* (2nd ed.). New York: McGraw-Hill.

Fiske, S. T., & Taylor, S. E. (1991). *Social cognition* (2nd ed.). New York: McGraw-Hill.

Gigone, D., & Hastie, R. (1993). The common knowledge effect: Information sharing and group judgment. *Journal of Personality and Social Psychology, 65*(5), 959–974.

Gigone, D., & Hastie, R. (1997a). The impact of information on small group choice. *Journal of Personality and Social Psychology, 72*(1), 132–140.

Gigone, D., & Hastie, R. (1997b). Proper analysis of the accuracy of group judgments. *Psychological Bulletin, 121*(1), 149–167.

Gladstein, D. L., & Reilly, N. P. (1985). Group decision making under threat: The Tycoon game. *Academy of Management Journal, 28*(3), 613–627.

Gruenfeld, D. H., Mannix, E. A., Williams, K. Y., & Neale, M. A. (1996). Group composition and decision making: How member familiarity and information distribution affect process and performance. *Organizational Behavior and Human Decision Processes, 67*(1), 1–15.

Hollingshead, A. B. (1996). The rank-order effect in group decision making. *Organizational Behavior and Human Decision Processes, 68*(3), 181–193.

Jones, P. E., & Roelofsma, P. H. M. P. (2000). The potential for social contextual and group biases in team decision-making: Biases, conditions and psychological mechanisms. *Ergonomics, 43*(8), 1129–1152.

Judice, T. N., & Neuberg, S. L. (1998). When interviewers desire to confirm negative expectations. Self-fulfilling prophecies and inflated applicant self-perceptions. *Basic Applied Psychology, 20*, 175–190.

Karau, S. J., & Kelly, J. R. (1992). The effects of time scarcity and time abundance on group performance quality and interaction process. *Journal of Experimental Social Psychology, 28*, 542–571.

Karau, S. J., & Kelly, J. R. (2004). Time pressure and team performance: An attentional focus integration. In: S. Blount, E. Mannix & M. Neale (Eds), *Research on Managing Groups and Teams: Time in Groups* (Vol. 6).

Kelly, J. R., & Karau, S. J. (1999). Group decision making: The effects of initial preferences and time pressure. *Personality and Social Psychology Bulletin, 11*, 1342–1354.

Klayman, J., & Ha, Y.-W. (1987). Confirmation, disconfirmation, and information in hypothesis testing. *Psychological Review, 94*, 211–228.

Kruglanski, A. W. (1989). *Lay epistemics and human knowledge*. New York: Plenum Press.

Kruglanski, A. W., & Mayseless, O. (1988). Contextual effects in hypothesis testing: The role of competing alternatives and epistemic motivations. *Social Cognition, 6*, 1–20.

Kruglanski, A. W., & Webster, D. M. (1991). Group members' reactions to opinion deviates and conformists at varying degrees of proximity to decision deadline and of environmental noise. *Journal of Personality and Social Psychology, 61*(2), 212–225.

Kunda, Z. (1990). The case for motivated reasoning. *Psychological Bulletin, 108*, 480–498.

Larson, C. E., Foster-Fishman, P. G., & Keys, C. B. (1994). Discussion of shared and unshared information in decision-making groups. *Journal of Personality and Social Psychology, 67*(3), 446–461.

Laughlin, P. R., & Earley, P. C. (1982). Social combination models, persuasive arguments theory, social comparison theory, and choice shift. *Journal of Personality and Social Psychology, 42*, 273–280.

McNatt, D. B. (2000). Ancient pygmalion joins contemporary management: A meta-analysis of the result. *Journal of Applied Psychology, 85*, 314–322.

Medvec, V. H., Berger, G., Liljenquist, K., & Neale, M. (2003). *Disentangling the common information effect and the confirmation bias.* Unpublished manuscript.

Miller, D. T., & McFarland, C. (1987). Pluralistic ignorance: When similarity is interpreted as dissimilarity. *Journal of Personality and Social Psychology, 53*(2), 298–305.

Mulvey, P. W., Veiga, J. F., & Elsass, P. M. (1996). When teammates raise a white flag. *Academy of Management Executive, 10*(1), 40–49.

Parks, C. D., & Cowlin, R. A. (1996). Acceptance of uncommon information into group discussion when that information is or is not demonstrable. *Organization Behavior and Human Decision Processes, 66*(3), 307–315.

Phillips, K. W. (in press). Disentangling the complex effects of diversity: The interplay of expectations, process and performance in groups. Paper presented at the 60th Annual National Academy of Management Conference, Toronto, Canada.

Popper, K. R. (1959). *The logic of scientific discovery.* New York: Basic Books.

Rosenthal, R., & Jacobson, L. (1968). *Pygmalion in the classroom.* New York: Holt, Rinehart, & Winston.

Russo, J. E., & Meloy, M. G. (2002). *Hypothesis generation and testing in Wason's 2–4–6 task.* Unpublished manuscript.

Schaab, B. B. (1997). The influence of time pressure and information load on rule-based decision-making performance. *Dissertation Abstracts International: Section B: The Sciences and Engineering, 58*(5-B), 2713.

Snyder, M., & Swann, W. B. (1978a). Behavioral confirmation in social interaction: From social perception to social reality. *Journal of Experimental Social Psychology, 14*(2), 148–162.

Snyder, M., & Swann, W. B. (1978b). Hypothesis-testing processes in social interaction. *Journal of Personality and Social Psychology, 36*, 1202–1212.

Stasser, G. (1992). Information salience and the discovery of hidden profiles by decision-making groups: A "thought experiment". *Organizational Behavior and Human Decision Processes, 52*(1), 156–181.

Stasser, G., & Stewart, D. (1992). Discovery of hidden profiles by decision-making groups: Solving a problem vs. making a judgment. *Journal of Personality and Social Psychology, 63*(3), 426–434.

Stasser, G., Taylor, L. A., & Hanna, C. (1989). Information sampling in structured and unstructured discussions of three and six-person groups. *Journal of Personality and Social Psychology, 57*(1), 67–78.

Stasser, G., & Titus, W. (1985). Pooling of unshared information in group decision making: Biased information sampling during discussion. *Journal of Personality and Social Psychology, 48*(6), 1467–1478.

Stewart, D. D., Billings, R. S., & Stasser, G. (1998). Accountability and the discussion of unshared, critical information in decision making groups. *Group Dynamics: Theory, Research and Practice, 2*(1), 18–23.

Thomas-Hunt, M., Ogden, T., & Neale, M. A. (2003). Who's really sharing? Effects of social and expert status on knowledge exchange within groups. *Management Science, 49*, 464–477.

Tindale, R. S., & Sheffey, S. (2002). Shared information, cognitive load, and group memory. *Group Processes & Intergroup Relations, 5*(1), 5–18.

Urban, J. M., Weaver, J. L., Bowers, C. A., & Rhodenizer, L. (1996). Effects of workload and structure on team processes and performance: Implications for complex team decision making. *Human Factors, 38*(2), 300–310.

Wason, P. C. (1960). On the failure to eliminate hypotheses in a conceptual task. *Quarterly Journal of Experimental Psychology, 12*, 129–140.

Wason, P. C., & Johnson-Laird, P. N. (1972). *Psychology of reasoning: Structure and content*. London: Batsford.

Wittenbaum, G. M., Hubbell, A. P., & Zuckerman, C. (1999). Mutual enhancement: Toward an understanding of the collective preference for shared information. *Journal of Personality and Social Psychology, 77*(5), 967–978.

Yerkes, R. M., & Dodson, J. D. (1908). The relation of strength of stimulus to rapidity of habit-formation. *Journal of Comparative Neurology and Psychology, 18*, 459–482.

Zakay, D., & Wooler, S. (1984). Time pressure, training and decision effectiveness. *Ergonomics, 27*, 273–284.

PART IV:
TIME IN GROUPS IN
ORGANIZATIONS

A GLOSSARY OF TEMPORAL TERMS RELATING TO GROUPS AND ORGANIZATIONS

Byron Kirton, Gerardo A. Okhuysen and Mary J. Waller

INTRODUCTION

During the conference in which this volume's chapters were presented and discussed, an important topic arose: the proliferation of terms used to describe the temporal aspects of groups and teams. Recognition of this proliferation is not new (cf. Ancona, Okhuysen & Perlow, 2001). While it is partly a reflection of the increased interest in things temporal, it is also a reflection of how we conduct work in the area of groups and organization studies for at least three reasons.

First, a variety of ideas and conceptualizations about time run through the core disciplines from which students of organizations typically draw ideas or analogs to apply to work contexts (e.g. anthropology, economics, sociology, and psychology). Each of these disciplines employs its own unique time terminology; thus, if time terms emanate from these disparate disciplines and are used together in either one work or one collection of works, many questions arise as to exactly what temporal phenomena are referred to by each term. Second, the experience of time is common to human beings, and a lay terminology about time is embedded in almost every culture. Students of groups and organizations, as participants in a variety of cultures and sub-cultures, may not only use different time terms from different cultures,

Time in Groups
Research on Managing Groups and Teams, Volume 6, 237–266
Copyright © 2004 by Elsevier Ltd.
All rights of reproduction in any form reserved
ISSN: 1534-0856/doi:10.1016/S1534-0856(03)06011-0

they may also perceive these terms to have very different meanings. Third, our interest in viewing groups and organizations through a time lens is relatively new, and established paradigms regarding research on time in organizations do not yet exist. Thus, the proliferation of time terminology and its subsequent confusion is in large part the natural result of pre-paradigmatic normal science (Kuhn, 1970).

This proliferation of time terminology can be problematic because it can prevent the advance of work in the arena of time in organizations by creating unintended confusion. This confusion can come from using two terms to describe the same construct, or from using the same term to describe two different constructs. In sum,

> ... if scientific knowledge is that knowledge that scientists agree is useful for achieving the goals of science, there must be agreement on the meaning of the statements and concepts that express scientific knowledge, and it must be possible for any scientist to compare some aspect of his theory with empirical research (Reynolds, 1971, p. 13).

Other areas of research, such as work on shared mental models, have faced similar difficulties (cf. Mohammed & Dumville, 2001). In these situations, interested authors have often made the effort to clarify the terminology used within the area, providing a synthesis of current terminology drawn from various fields that then serves as a basis for future work. This glossary is intended in the same vein. We want this glossary to capture and define terminology used in this volume to describe time in groups and organizations. The result is a list of terms with their associated meanings that can be used as a reference to those interested in pursuing work in the area of time.

METHODS

To develop this glossary, we relied on the chapters of this volume and on recent special issues on time in *Academy of Management Journal, Academy of Management Review*, and a few other articles that have appeared in management periodicals. A full list of sources is provided at the end of the chapter. We began by reading each piece and highlighting every term that was used to describe a temporal element. In each instance, we provide a definition for the term. This definition could have one of two sources. If the authors defined the term or a reference was provided to a source where the term was originally defined, that definition is provided. In cases where a definition was not provided by the authors, we provide an interpretation of the meaning of the term from the context in which it is provided. In the case of some compound terms (e.g. temporal context), the meaning of the term is also based on a dictionary definition of one of the words in the term.

These terms included some that were used to describe characteristics of time (pace, acceleration), terms used to describe the meaning ascribed to time (holidays), terms used to highlight the characteristics of the activity taking place during a time period (overtime). In addition, we also captured terms used to describe purely temporal variables, including those that tie together two temporal concepts (e.g. crossing times, temporal personality).

In our initial plan of this glossary, we intended to map the definitions to their sources. However, this proved to be a difficult problem. For example, we found that temporal terms are sometimes used in our sources but not defined. A problem arises when the same term is also used in another source, but with a different meaning. Attributing the same term to two sources, where the meanings conflict, seemed to us a recipe for increasing confusion, rather than reducing it. Thus, we have chosen to provide a general definition as a starting point for the usage of terms from here on.

As a final thought, we would like to share a small part of our experience. As we began our work on this glossary we were concerned that the task would be tedious due to the nature of the activities involved. However, we have been surprised by how much we have enjoyed the task, and by how much our own understanding of temporal matters has been clarified. The process of compiling this glossary has allowed us to build links between our work and the work of others and to increase our understanding of the work of others in a way that was unexpected. It is our sincere hope that the product will be at least as useful for others working in the field of time and organizations.

REFERENCES

Ancona, D., Okhuysen, G., & Perlow, L. (2001). Taking time to integrate temporal research. *Academy of Management Review, 26*, 512–529.
Kuhn, T. S. (1970). *The structure of scientific revolutions*. Chicago: The University of Chicago Press.
Mohammed, S., & Dumville, B. C. (2001). Team mental models in a team knowledge framework: Expanding theory and measurement across disciplinary boundaries. *Journal of Organizational Behavior, 22*, 89–106.
Reynolds, P. D. (1971). *A primer in theory construction*. New York: Bobbs-Merrill.

Glossary

Acceleration: The action of moving quicker, a rate of change for speed.

Act: A verbal or non-verbal behavior, which are components of longer interaction episodes.

Actual timetables: A list of the times at which successive things are done or happen, or the times occupied by a process. See also Timetables.

Agenda: A list of things to be done within boundaries dictated by time.

Aggregation interval: The time scale the recorded information is to be collected or grouped for theorizing or testing theory about a phenomenon.

Aggregation periods: A length of time occupied by the regular repetition of an accumulation of events or actions into one body or group.

Alignment of pace: The coordination of the rate at which work is accomplished by multiple entities acting in a joint manner.

Allocation: The action of assigning or arranging resources or responsibility into particular time frames. Allocation typically happens among different sets of activities so that the total time available is used in an efficient way to maximize the entity's goals/priorities.

Approaches to time: Viewpoints or methods of looking at or using time by entities such as individuals, groups, or organizations.

Asynchronic phase entrainment: Having two activities in an out-of-phase pattern, i.e. work on activity "a" is high while work on activity 'b' is low.

Asynchrony: A group level characteristic that emerges when the pace of activity of individual members does not match. It occurs when one or more members have difficulty adapting their individual activity or work pace to the pace of the group.

Atemporal: Not related to time; not having characteristics that are influenced or dictated by time.

Attention to time: The consideration or observation of the passage of time by entities.

Awareness of time use: The perception or cognizance of the allocation and/or passage of time by an entity.

Background cadences: The measure of a rhythm in a sequence of activities, not an obvious part of the phenomena, but instead hidden or obscured.

Boundary control: Managers' ability to affect how employees divide their time between their work and non-work spheres of life.

Breakpoint: A space that exists between different phases or activities that punctuates a particular stage, phase, or behavior. See also pause and interruption.

Breaks: Points in time that can act as a pause during an activity or to separate an activity into different moments in time.

Burn rate: The speed with which money is used, typically used in the late 1990s by internet ventures.

Cadences: The measure of a rhythm in a sequence of activities. It can also be the pace of activity.

Calendar: A mapping of time periods that specifies segmentation, order, and sequence, and around which there is a social consensus. In addition to specifying order and sequence, a calendar can also specify meaning for a given period or moment, such as the new year.

Career timetable: A list of the times at which successive things are to be done or happen in an individual's professional career.

Chronocentrism: The tendency to attribute more positive attributes to one's own times than to those of others.

Chronometric punctuation: Actions that divide or segment a plot into hours, weeks, years, and so on based on conventional clocks and calendars.

Chronophobia: The tendency to value others' temporal practices and beliefs above one's own. A fear of one's own time rather than of time in general.

Chronos: The time that is measurable; the time that can be numbered on a clock by making it a succession of points on a line, which are separable and distinct. See also clock time.

Circadian rhythm: Occurs when bodily cycles are entrained to the external light-dark 24-hour cycle of the earth. Features of physiological and behavioral functioning that appear to have cycles of about 24 hours.

Circular conceptions of time: A conception of time in which events repeat on a regular cycle.

Clock (cycle) speeds: The rate at which a single complete execution of one or more periodically repeated phenomena occurs.

Clock time map: A representation or delineation of relative positions that pertain to time. See Timelines, Timetables.

Clock time: Depicts the continuum as linear-infinitely divisible into objective, quantifiable units such that the units are homogeneous, uniform, regular, precise, deterministic, and measurable. See Chronos.

Clock: An instrument for indicating or measuring time.

Closing window of opportunity: A continually shortening period in which action is particularly appropriate or propitious. See also Window of opportunity.

Closure: A force or element that brings some activity or experience to an end.

Cohort-based generations: A set of individuals demarcated as a unique group because they share a common temporal starting point in a role that causes them to hold a particular status contemporaneously.

Collaboration: Entities working jointly on some desired goal either simultaneously, in sequence, or otherwise.

Compressed context: To condense a set of circumstances or to have less time than expected to accomplish a task.

Concert time: A harmonious or agreeable combination of activities or an agreement in a plan between entities.

Continuous time: Time viewed as a continuum rather than a succession of points. See also Clock time.

Cost curves: Graphical representations of the costs associated with different timing choices for activities or events.

Critical period: A time in an entity's life within which a particular formative experience will take effect and after which it will not.

Crossing points: Moments at which different parts of the organization interact for coordination purposes. Crossing points are necessary when different segments of the organization respond to task requirements that vary with regards to deadlines or schedules, and thus have different patterns of activity. A crossing point is wide when the number of parts of the organization that use it or participate in it is large. Typically, crossing points are understood as a small part of a larger, prescribed organizational design. See also Temporal Design.

Cycle: A single complete execution of one or more periodically repeated phenomena.

Cycles of boom: A single complete execution of one or more periodically repeated increases in business or economic activity.

Cycles of bust: A single complete execution of one or more periodically repeated decreases in business or economic activity.

Cyclical patterns: A sequence of events that is repeated over and over.

Cyclical social time: Refers to the patterns in time embedded in social processes that occur over and over (e.g. holidays).

Cyclical time: A conception of time in which events repeat over and over and where time is continuous and indefinite. See also Circular time.

Date line: A point in time in which if a goal has not been reached prior arrangements are canceled. Also viewed as a contingent termination period for an activity.

Dating systems: Programs or mechanisms that dictate when events have taken place in time and when events will take place in time, according to some agreed upon system of reckoning.

Deadline: A moment or point in time when an activity is meant to end. Also a moment when an activity is meant to begin (e.g. "the deadline came and the police went into action").

Deadline-oriented behaviors: Actions or activities that occur as a direct result of having a time specified in which a task or activity is to be completed.

Deadline perceptions: An entity's selective attention, comprehension, and judgment regarding the time by which some task is supposed to be completed.

Delay: The postponement of an event as it is moved farther away from the present or from the time when it is scheduled to occur. For example, when a deadline is pushed back.

Development time: A period where an action may have consequences but before the full benefit or cost of the action is present. A focus on development time is consistent with an increased focus on process.

Discount rates: A deduction taken from an amount due or a price in exchange for a payment that is earlier than anticipated.

Discrete time: A conception of time that presupposes that each moment can be differentiated from another, partly through the use of instruments such as clocks.

Downtime: A period of time in which there is little or no activity occurring.

Duration: A length of time, defined by a beginning and an end. See also Timespan.

Duration preferences: The predilection for the allocation of a specific duration to a task.

Dynamic deadline: A potentially changing moment or point in time when an activity is meant to end. Also a potentially changing moment when an activity is meant to begin.

Dynamic deadline conditions: The circumstances or situations that create the potential for a point in time when an activity is meant to end or begin to be subject to change.

Economicity of time: A perspective where time is viewed as a valuable resource that can be measured, used, bought, and sold.

Engrossment: The intense state of consciousness in which one's entire affective, cognitive, and physical resources are totally invested in the task on hand.

Entrained pauses: Breaks or stops in the activity of an individual or entity that coincide with the patterns of another activity or entity.

Entrained rhythms: The regular reoccurrence of activities and related elements that coincide with the patterns of another activity or entity. See also Exogenous rhythms.

Entraining forces: Pressures, explicit and implicit, internal and external, that cause an entity to adjust its activities to those of another activity or entity. Examples include pauses, pace, and rhythms.

Entrainment: The adjustment of the pace or cycle of an activity to match or synchronize with that of another activity. Entrainment typically involves the repetition of activity cycles. It is a non-conscious tendency toward behavioral synchrony. The process by which one internal rhythmic process is captured and modified by another (internal or external) rhythmic process. A spontaneous adjustment in individual behavior to match or synchronize with the behavior of another. It involves the capturing and modification of activity by various social customs, norms, and institutions.

Entrainment models: A method of describing or showing the adjustment of the pace or cycle of an activity to match or synchronize with that of another activity in written, oral, or physical form.

Entrainment patterns: A regular configuration or arrangement of events that is adjusted to match the pace or cycle of another activity or to synchronize with that of another activity.

Entrainment quotient: A measure of the ease and speed with which individuals, groups, and organizations can adjust to synchronize with other activities or entities. It can also involve an element of evaluation, where an assessment of the need to synchronize with other activities or entities is made.

Episode: An event of a given duration that is distinctive and separable while simultaneously belonging to a larger set of events.

Episodic: An event or occurrence that has the characteristics of an episode, of being distinctive and separable while simultaneously belonging to a larger set of events.

Evaluation interval: The period between when an action or process is enacted and when its consequences are evaluated or judged.

Evaluation point or interval: The moment when the success or failure of an action or process is evaluated or judged.

Event sequences: A continual or connected series of occurrences or incidents that is noteworthy.

Event time: A perspective where time is memorable because of the things that happen. In this perspective, time is not uniform.

Event time map: A drawing or representation of time that is organized principally according to when particular things happen. See Event timelines.

Event timelines: Events laid out or planned relative to other events. See Event time map.

Event-based generations: Generations that are created or emerge when a significant event causes differentiation among groups that span time frames.

Event-based pacing: Regulates people's attention through their recognition of specific events that signal when action can or should be initiated, corrections made, or endeavors considered complete.

Existence interval: The length of time needed for one instance of the process, pattern, phenomenon, or event to occur or unfold.

Exogenous rhythms: Regular reoccurrence of activities or related events which are external to the focal entity or individual. See also Entrained rhythms.

External cycles: A single complete execution of one or more periodically repeated phenomena that are outside the focal entity.

External environment: The elements outside of an entity that, together, compose the context in which the entity operates.

External pacers: An event or occurrence external to the focal entity that is used by the entity as a basis to organize activities in time.

External pauses: Breaks or stops in the activities of an entity caused by events or larger patterns in the environment. See also Entrainment.

External rhythms: The regular reoccurrence of activities or related events outside the focal entity.

External temporal marker: Moments or periods external to an individual or entity that are imbued with significance and can also work as a signal for those observing. See Temporal coordination points, Crossing point, Temporal markers, and Temporal milestones.

External temporal pacers: A particular element, external to an entity, which is used as a basis to organize work in time.

Fast: Rapid or swift action or activity. Also the advancement of time that is perceived as quicker than true time.

Fast world: A rapid or swift state of existence or a universally experienced rapid pace.

Fiscal year: A period of time usually measuring the length of a calendar year, but with a beginning and ending that are selected by organization actors.

Flow: The continuous occurrence or stream of events or activities. A state of peak performance of an activity for an individual. See Engrossment.

Foresight: The action or ability to see or predict the future. The action of looking forward into the future.

Frequency: The number of repetitions of a process or activity in a unit of time.

Frequency of sequences: The number of repetitions of a connected series of activities or events in a given unit of time.

Future: The time that is yet to be. Pertaining to time to come.

Future generation: A group that will occupy a role or place in the time to come but will not hold that position infinitely.

Future orientation: A set of beliefs and emphases that is focused on the time that is yet to be. See Future time orientation.

Future time orientation: A set of beliefs and emphases that is focused on the time that is yet to be. See Future orientation.

Gantt charts: A tool used for scheduling, budgeting, and project management. Gantt charts use straight lines on a grid to compare what is done to what was planned. See also Time chart.

Generation: A group of people that have some experience, belief, or attitude in common because they share a particular temporal characteristic, such as being born in a given period or being hired in a given year.

Generational transition: The succession of one generation for another, where one generation comes to take on the roles formerly occupied by the generation that is replaced.

Group development: The progress, over a group's life span, of members' ability to handle issues (e.g. dependency, control, and intimacy) seen as critical to their ability to work. See also Task progress model.

Group pacing: The action of trying to conform to a given rate of work by multiple entities.

Group pacing behavior: The acceleration or slowing of work by multiple entities to conform to a given rate of work.

Group synchronization: The manner in which individual members align the work they perform. See Synchronization.

Hastening: The acceleration of an event so that the event moves in time such that it will occur sooner. Also called a speed up. This occurs when deadlines are moved closer from the future to the present time.

Hindsight: The action or the ability to look into the time that has already occurred. The ability to reflect on the past to discover what needs to be done in the present or future.

Holidays: A day of festivity or recreation in which work is typically not done. A part of the calendar with socially constructed meaning.

Hyperbolic time discounting: The tendency for people to inappropriately over-value getting desired outcomes sooner rather than later. Similarly, the tendency to inappropriately undervalue receiving undesired outcomes later rather than sooner.

Incubation period or interval: The time following an event or action when its consequences are assumed to be present, but have not yet reached sufficient size, scale, or magnitude to be visible.

Industrial temporality: The nature of time as it is associated with productive or diligent labor, where a perspective of time as a fungible asset that can be traded prevails.

Industry life cycle: The series of developmental stages that an entire set of organizations performing similar or complementary work goes through. See Life cycle.

Industry rhythms: Repeated patterns of activity derived from the characteristics of a particular set of organizations that share a commonality of output or complementarities of work.

Inertia: The tendency to remain stable, unchanged, or inactive through time. The tendency to stay in action, to follow a given path already set, through time.

Inner duration: A state of consciousness lasting for a moment and then fading away, the sequence of which appears infinite because the moments permeate each other, living and disappearing within each other as a continuous and holistic flow of events.

Inner time: The qualitative time experienced at the subjective level of individual consciousness.

Inside entrainment: The adjustment of the pace or cycle of an activity to match or synchronize with that of another activity inside the focal entity.

In-synch preference: A group level predilection or inclination for the same pace of activity among individual group members.

Intensity preferences: A predilection or inclination for a given rate at which activities associated with a task are spaced out across the time available to complete it. A preference for a high intensity indicates that greater amounts of work are performed in a given period.

Interdependent temporal web: A network of time-related information that connects events and activities between dependent entities. See also Temporal information, Temporal web.

Intergenerational: Existing or occurring between different groups of people defined as a generation or involving more than one generation. See Generation.

Intergenerational allocation decisions: Decisions regarding distributions among different generations with present generations making choices on behalf of future generations.

Intergenerational behavior: The actions or conduct of entities necessary to establish a common link between different generations of people or involving more than one generation.

Intergenerational conflict: Strife occurs when a member or members of the present generation make decisions involving trade-offs between what is best for the present generation and what is best for the future generation.

Intergenerational contexts: The aspects of the subject, organization, activity, or event that have as an important element relevance to different generations.

Intergenerational decisions: Choices that are made that involve multiple generations, typically due to the long-range nature of the choices.

Intergenerational discounting: A reduction in value that occurs when individuals in one generation prefer smaller, immediate benefits for themselves over larger benefits for others in the future.

Intergenerational issues: The problems or circumstances affecting different generations.

Intergenerational reciprocity: The actions dictated by the desire for present generations to treat future generations in the same manner that the present generations were treated by earlier generations.

Intergenerational situation: The condition or state of things affecting different generations of people or entities or involving more than one generation.

Intergenerational terms: The words or expressions used to describe situations, concepts, or other elements of the relationships existing between different generations of people or entities or involving more than one generation. The notion or concept of existing or occurring between different generations of people or entities or involving more than one generation.

Internal clock: A means of measuring time that is contained within the focal entity.

Internal entrainment: The adjustment of the pace or cycle of an activity to match or synchronize with that of another activity, which is a subsystem of the same system.

Internal pauses: Breaks or stops in the activities of the focal entity due to events or actions within it.

Internal rhythms: The regular reoccurrence of activities and related elements within the focal entity.

Internal routines: A habitual or mechanical performance of an established procedure that takes place within the focal entity.

Internal temporal patterns: Regular configurations or arrangements of activities and events within the focal entity.

Interruption: A break in the uniformity or continuity of an activity, most typically caused by an entity external to the focal entity. See also Pause.

Intertemporal choice: Choice or choices made with an explicit consideration of the consequences of making the choice in the present vs. the future.

Intertemporal dimension: An individual element, internal to the focal entity, whose primary attribute is related to the passage of time from the present to the future.

Interval: A length of time or duration between events or moments in time.

Kairos: The time of human activity or opportunity, not of measurement. In contrast to Chronos, it is time as experienced.

Life cycle: The series of developmental stages that an entity or product goes through from start to eventual termination.

Lifespan: The length of time or duration of a complete task or entity, defined by the beginning and end of the task or entity. See also Longevity.

Linear conceptions of time: A perspective in which time is viewed as following a straight line. From this perspective, one views time sequentially one moment after another; time is divisible and measurable.

Links in time: The explicit organizational practices that address past, present, and future time horizons and the transitions between them.

Long term: Describing the distant future. Plans that involve the distant future rather than the near future.

Longevity: The length of time or duration in existence of an entity. See also Lifespan.

Metronome: A device for marking time that emits a regular tick at a selected rate.

Midpoint: The halfway point of an activity that is demarcated by time, such as through the use of a deadline.

Midpoint agreements: Commonality of opinion at the halfway point of a time-bound activity.

Midpoint redistribution of tasks: A reassigning or redividing of relevant tasks at the halfway temporal point of an activity.

Midpoint transition model: The design intended to explain the task transitions initiated by attention to time and occurring at the temporal halfway point.

Midpoint transitions: Task transitions initiated by attention to time and occurring at the temporal halfway point.

Milestones: Important events in the life or cycle of the focal entity.

Millenium: A time period that is 1,000 years long.

Monochronicity: The preference or desire to focus on one task at a time. See also Polychronicity.

Monotemporal: Time that can be represented in standardized, invariable, context-free units.

Monotemporalism: The common understanding as to the meaning of time among all group members.

Multiple subjective time map: An account or representation of time using more than one perspective, such as event time and clock time.

Natural pace: A rate at which work is accomplished by an entity that is not directed or imposed, but is rather an emergent property of the entity.

Natural pauses: A momentary stop in a routinized or automatic activity. An interruption in routinized work that occurs in relation to an external or "natural" stimulus. This natural stimulus may come from an entraining force (e.g. sleeping at night) or socially defined patterns (e.g. become hungry at noon).

Natural rhythm: A regular reoccurrence of activities or related events that is not directed or imposed but rather is an emergent property.

Natural time: Time as experienced when external or experimental factors are not in force. See System time.

Nontemporal: Not pertaining to time; an unlimited duration; eternal.

Objective view of time: Typically used to refer to clock time, a perspective based on a broad-based social construction of time.

Observation interval: The researcher-defined period of examination of a phenomenon.

On time: To be punctual, to occur at the appointed time.

Ongoing rhythms: The regular reoccurrence of activities or related events. See Rhythm.

Opportunity interval for action: A period where a given action is possible and which also defines when it is not.

Oral synchrony: A phenomenon where vocal communication between individuals falls into a regular pattern over time.

Organizational rhythm: Regular reoccurrence of activities or events in an organization.

Orientations to time: Perspectives that entities have regarding which part of time they emphasize (e.g. the past, the present, or the future). See Future orientation, Past orientation, Present orientation.

Outcome interval: The period when the consequences of an action or decisions are expected to be manifest.

Outside entrainment: The adjustment of the pace or cycle of an activity to match or synchronize with that of another activity that is external to the focal entity.

Overmanning: Occurs when the total amount of time available is greater than the time needed to do all the designated activities. See also Time abundance.

Overtime: The practice of working for a longer period of time than the standard. Typically this practice also includes paying more to the individuals who are working longer than the standard (e.g. "time and a half" pay).

Pace: The rate at which work is accomplished by an entity.

Pace alignment: The matching or equalization of work or activity rates of individual entities.

Pace of development: The rate at which a project, relationship, or entity goes from beginning to completion.

Pace/tempo entrainment: Alignment that occurs with another entity with a focus on speed or the rate of work.

Pacer: An event or occurrence that is used by the entity as a basis to organize work at a given rate.

Pacing: The action of trying to conform to a given rate of work.

Pacing behavior: The acceleration or slowing of work to conform to a given rate of work.

Pacing effort: The amount of work devoted to trying to conform to a given rate of work.

Pacing goals: An assigned rate of activity or work, typically assigned for the purpose of ensuring the completion of a task within a specified period of time.

Pacing mechanism: Tools or systems that dictate the rate at which work is to be accomplished.

Pacing motivator: One or more elements put in place to incite, impel, or influence individuals to achieve or conform to a given pace of work.

Pacing pattern: An arrangement of actions to achieve or conform to a given rate of work.

Pacing preferences: Predilection for a particular speed and duration of activities. Some individuals may prefer to work at a steady speed all throughout a project's lifespan while others prefer to work very little early in the project's lifespan and then work very hard as the deadline approaches.

Pacing tendencies: The rate in which an activity is usually performed by a given entity.

Past: Time that has already occurred. Time that cannot be regained. A former time, one that has gone by and ended.

Patterns of pacing: An arrangement of different rates of task completion.

Pause: A stop in activity; an interruption in routinized work.

Perceived timetables: A list of the times at which successive things are thought or expected to be done or happen or the times occupied by a process.

Period: A course or extent of time. See also Duration.

Periodic repetition: The performance of a task in a regular manner with the start of the performance matching a given point in a new time period.

Periodicity: The tendency for some activity or event to reoccur at intervals.

Perishability or shelf life: The length of time an event, action, or thing can persist without changing its character.

Personal pacing goals: The rate of activity or work that an individual takes upon him or herself for the purpose of ensuring the completion of a task within a specified period of time.

PERT: Project evaluation and review technique. A system of rules used to compute expected project timelines, as well as to evaluate progress towards completion of the goal.

Phase entrainment: Alignment that occurs with another entity with a focus on the synchronization of cycles.

Phases: Coherent segments of activity, typically following a given sequence. Stages or forms in a series or cycle of changes. Also, coherent pieces of activity that form when entities repeat behaviors or sequences.

Planning time: A time perspective that values closure as opposed to process. See Development time.

Plot: A temporal grouping that binds and interrelates elements from different points in time and forms them into a unity of action.

Pluritemporalism: The side-by-side existence of many different types of time, socially constructed out of diverse human experiences.

Polychronicity: The preference or desire to work on different tasks at the same time. The desire to pursue multiple tasks at once. The extent to which people prefer to be engaged in two or more tasks or events simultaneously, are actually so engaged (the preference strongly implying the behavior and vice versa), and believe their preference is the best way to function. See also Monochronicity.

Present: Time as it is experienced in the moment. The moment now being lived.

Present generation: A group that occupies a role or place in the current time but will not hold that position infinitely. In managerial thinking, the current team of managers.

Present time orientation: A set of beliefs and emphases held by cultures and individuals towards the moment being lived.

Pretransition period: Describes the length of time a given team is occupied with its own task phases before a pause occurs where the group changes direction.

Prevailing temporal agenda: The individual actor's perception and construal of the organization's temporal structure from his or her vantage point.

Process: Something that goes on; a continuous action or series of actions or events; a course or method of action; a procedure.

Procrastination: The act of avoiding some action or task (typically a burden or something unpleasant) and extending the start of the action or task to begin in the future.

Progress over time: Improvement, development, or completion that occurs through the passing of time.

Pseudoentrainment: A process that mimics entrainment, but is not entrainment because there is no adjustment of any periodicity or phase. It involves two activities whose pacers happen to be matched or whose cycles are coincidentally synchronized.

Punctuality: The capacity to act in a defined manner at the appointed time. To be punctual means to be carefully observant of an appointed time. Most typically, punctuality is associated with arriving or departing on time. Also, how important it is to be on time and what is defined as being on time.

Punctuated equilibrium: An alteration of inertial movement and radical change over the life course of an entity, as a group development model. Occurs when systems progress through an alternation of stasis and sudden appearance of long periods of inertia, punctuated by concentrated, revolutionary periods of quantum change. Also viewed as a task progress model, with a focus on task performance processes and progress over time.

Rate: The amount of work that is performed in a given amount of time. It can also include the speed, pattern, and duration in which an activity occurs.

Rate of innovation: The number of new ideas or processes, for example, which are introduced in a given amount of time.

Rate of learning: The amount of new knowledge and/or skill, for example, which is acquired in a given amount of time.

Rates of recurrence: How often events or institutions will emerge.

Real-time information: Information for which there is little or no time lag between occurrence and reporting. Usually involves information about a firm's operations or environment.

Recording interval: The frequency at which the values of variables are recorded or measured.

Reference point: Moments imbued with significance that can also signal observers that action is required. For example, the New Year, which can also signal the need to prepare end-of-year reports. The significance of temporal markers is socially derived and is used by different parts of an organization for coordination purposes. See Temporal coordination points, Crossing point, and Temporal milestones.

Reference point model: A design that relates the temporal information generated by the organization to the individual actor context.

Repetition: The performance or experience of an activity in a recurring manner.

Response time: The length of time it takes an entity to answer a call for some action or reply.

Responsibility interval: The time during which an actor can be held responsible for his or her actions.

Rhythm: The regular reoccurrence of activities or related events.

Rhythmic activity: Actions or events that possess a particular regularity.

Rhythmic cues: A signal, suggestion, or instruction that helps identify or guide the regularity of activities or events.

Rhythmic patterns: The arrangement of activities or events that possess a particular regularity.

Rhythmicities: The capacity for maintaining the regular reoccurrence of activities or related events.

Routine: A regular occurrence or procedure. A habitual or mechanical performance of an established procedure.

Routine inertia: A stop or rest of a regular occurrence or procedure.

Routinized pattern: A series of actions that are performed as part of a routine. See Routine.

Schedule: A plan specifying the timing and sequence of activities or events.

Scheduling: Creating a plan specifying the timing and sequence of activities or events.

Sequence: A continual or connected series of activities or events.

Sequencing patterns: A continual or connected series of activities or events that occurs in an arrangement where one activity follows another; pattern may be discernable or undiscernible.

Sequential: Successive activities, each activity occurring one after another.

Shared temporal models: General temporal perspectives that are implicitly or explicitly agreed upon in a social setting. Examples of shared temporal models include the meaning of punctuality and the value of time.

Short-term: Of the near future, as opposed to long term or distant future.

Simultaneous: Events or activities that occur at the same time.

Slow trap: A potential pathology for organizations attempting to make good decisions, where an emphasis on the quality of decisions becomes more important than the speed or timeliness of the decisions.

Slow world: A sluggish state of existence or a sluggish pace universally experienced.

Social entrainment: 'Capturing" and modification of human activity cycles by various social customs, norms, and institutions.

Social time: Refers to the patterns in time embedded in social processes.

Socially constructed time scales: Scales in which the intervals that compose them may depart from those associated with standard measurement through agreement by a group of actors.

Sociotemporal norms: Broadly accepted rules in society that prescribe how an entity should behave in relation to time. Sociotemporal norms provide guidelines for appropriate behavior regarding the pacing of activities, punctuality, adherence to deadlines, and trade-offs between quality and speed.

Sociotemporal reality: Broadly accepted understandings in society, particularly surrounding events or actions that might be ambiguous, and therefore subject to interpretation.

Speed: The rate of action or work of an entity, on a continuum with slow and fast occupying opposite ends.

Speed trap: A potential pathology for organizations attempting to make fast decisions, where an emphasis on the speediness of decisions becomes more important than the quality of the decisions.

Speedy adaptation: Modifications made in response to changes in the environment and which occur in a fast manner.

Stability: The characteristic of remaining the same, with no change.

Stable deadline: A moment or point in time when an activity is meant to end and which does not change. Also a moment when an activity is meant to begin, and does not change (e.g. "the deadline came and the police went into action").

Strategic pacing: The action, at a high level in an organization, of trying to arrange activities and events in a manner that will enable a particular outcome at a given time.

Structuration theory: Individuals' sequences of activities draw on both the social and the temporal contexts in which they are situated, which in turn enable them to constrain the sequences of activities that result.

Subjective time: The individual's temporal experience, as determined by the internal-clock-state and stimulus-rate match.

Subjective view of time: A perspective that suggests that time gains significance only through human interpretation.

Synchronic phase entrainment: Having two activities (a and b) whose cycles come to have an in-phase pattern (i.e. a similar phase state at the same time).

Synchronize: To arrange events or cycles so that they occur at a given point in time in relation to a different event or activity; in a complementary manner.

System time: Time as experienced when external or experimental factors are not in force. See Natural time.

Task pacing: A rate assigned for a work group with the purpose of ensuring completion of the relevant work in the allotted time.

Task pacing behaviors: Actions that a work group engages in to ensure that a rate of work is adopted that will enable completion of the relevant work in the allotted time.

Task progress model: Model of group work that emphasizes task completion as the critical outcome of the group, rather than group development. See Midpoint transition model.

Tempo: The rate of activity. See Pacing, Speed.

Temporal action patterns: An arrangement of activity dependent on time.

Tempo entrainment: The entraining of pace.

Temporal: Pertaining to time; a limited duration rather than eternal.

Temporal agenda: Items that need to be addressed or tasks to be completed within a time frame. This could be the order in which the items are to be addressed or the time in which the items are to be completed.

Temporal alignment: Agreement as to timing of activities between entities, or of activities between entities and external sources. See also Shared temporal models.

Temporal approach: Preferences concerning the rate at which work should be accomplished.

Temporal aspects: Those parts of a situation or event that describe how time influences their development or unfolding. See also Temporal characteristics.

Temporal behavior: Conduct displayed by an entity; influenced or dictated at least in part by time or the perception of time.

Temporal boundaries: References to the elements that specify the beginning or ending of an interval (e.g. deadlines).

Temporal boundary objects: A tangible thing used by a collective to indicate and denote important coordination moments across work departments (e.g. timeline charts and personnel schedules).

Temporal capability: The ability to comprehend various opposite conceptions that pertain to time, change and dimensions and to discriminate among them.

Temporal character: A distinctive trait of an activity or event that is based on how time influences it or is influenced by it. See also Temporal personality.

Temporal characteristics: Those parts of a situation or event that describe how time influences their development or unfolding.

Temporal clarity: A precise understanding of relevant features in a situation that are related to time.

Temporal complexity: The existence of multiple interrelated aspects of time in a situation or event making its understanding and explanation more difficult.

Temporal concepts: Ideas or thoughts related to explanations and understandings of time.

Temporal concerns: When time is a matter of interest or in relation to an activity.

Temporal conflict: Disagreement between entities or between entities and environments in terms of the appropriate temporal norms, such as an appropriate pace or the meaning of punctuality. See Socio-temporal norms, Temporal congruence, and Temporal consensus.

Temporal congruence: Agreement between entities or between entities and environments in terms of the appropriate temporal norms, such as an appropriate pace or the meaning of punctuality. See also Socio-temporal norms, Temporal alignment, Temporal conflict, and Temporal consensus.

Temporal consensus: Agreement between entities or between entities and environments in terms of the appropriate temporal norms, such as an appropriate pace or the meaning of punctuality. See also Socio-temporal norms, Temporal alignment, Temporal congruence, and Temporal conflict.

Temporal constructs: Concepts and theories used to integrate in a comprehensive manner data on the nature of time.

Temporal context: The aspects of the subject, organization, activity, or event that pertain to time.

Temporal continuity: The absence of interruptions or breaks in the performance of an activity such that connections within the task are never broken.

Temporal control: The ability of an entity to regulate processes by focusing on how they impact time and how time impacts them.

Temporal convergence: Agreement regarding the timing of activities between entities or between entities and environments. See also Temporal alignment, Temporal congruence, and Temporal consensus.

Temporal coordination: Agreement between entities on the order of when activities or events should take place.

Temporal coordination mechanisms: Tools used to form or shape activities and their relationships on the basis of how they impact time and how time impacts them. See also Crossing points.

Temporal coordination points: Moments at which different parts of the organization interact for planning or management purposes. See also Temporal marker, Crossing points.

Temporal crossing points: Moments defined on a timeline at which different parts of the organization interact for coordination purposes. See Crossing points and Temporal design.

Temporal cues: Prompts, signals, hints, or indicators that specify an element of an activity related to time, such as its starting point, end, or pace.

Temporal customs: Common or accepted views on the use of time within an organization or society. See Socio-temporal norms.

Temporal cycle: A single complete execution of one or more periodically repeated phenomena that have time as a core or defining characteristic.

Temporal deference: The act of one entity yielding to and assimilating the timing preferences of a greater entity.

Temporal demands: Situations that call for action from a given entity that reduces the time available for other activities.

Temporal depth: The distance into the future that entities tend to look when they plan or think about the future. Also considered a cultural attribute, with some cultures looking further into the future than others. See Temporal focus.

Temporal design: An approach to plan an organization and its attributes on the basis of characteristics related to time. Some examples of characteristics related to time include the life cycle of products and the duration of research and development activities.

Temporal development: To set forth or to make clear the matters pertaining to time. To make active or to promote the growth of time-related matters.

Temporal dimension: An individual element whose primary attribute is related to time, such as the duration of an activity or the timing of an event.

Temporal diversity: Differences in preference with regard to a task that are related to time, such as when, how fast, and for how long to work on it. Also, differences in the temporal perspectives of members of a group or organization. See Temporal Elements.

Temporal dynamics: The changing relationships between elements of an activity related to time. For example, the change in timing of an activity, due to pacing, rates, and punctuality of an entity.

Temporal effects: Consequences that are brought about through the action of time, or more accurately, through the passage of time.

Temporal elements: Individual components of activities or events related to time, such as speed, punctuality, and work pace. See Temporal dimension.

Temporal evaluation: The judgment of progress made on a task or series of tasks based on the amount of time that has passed or the amount of time remaining to a deadline.

Temporal expectations: The set of views regarding the temporal context that is personally or collectively seen as proper or necessary. See Temporal context.

Temporal experience: The act of living through an event or period in which a person has personal involvement and the effect that the personal involvement has on the person.

Temporal expertise: Special knowledge or skills that relate to matters of time, such as pacing or synchronization.

Temporal focus: The distance into the past that entities tend to look when they are remembering the past. Also considered a cultural attribute, with some cultures looking further back than others. See Temporal Depth.

Temporal functioning: The way in which the actions or operations of an entity are organized or executed within time.

Temporal goal: An objective to be accomplished by a specified point in time.

Temporal halfway point: The moment at which, in the completion of the task, one half of the allocated time has passed and one half remains. It can be distinguished from other halfway marks, such as the halfway completion mark, when one half of a task has been completed and one half remains.

Temporal heterogeneity: The extent to which the group exhibits variance along key temporal dimensions.

Temporal imagination: The ability of an entity to understand the intersection of its own temporal behavior with that of the larger environment surrounding it, especially the environment's timescape. Also the ability to understand the intersection of two or more timescapes. See Timescape.

Temporal information: Communicated knowledge that informs members of an organization or entity, or others that have ties with the organization or entity, of the time elements (e.g. rates, pace, and punctuality) of the organization or entity.

Temporal insights: An intuition that is developed regarding the rates, pace, and punctuality of activities or of customary practice in an entity or organization.

Temporal interruption: A break in the uniformity or continuity of an activity, most typically caused by an entity external to the focal entity. See Interruption, Pause, and Temporal punctuation.

Temporal leadership: The ability to provide direction for a group or organization in matters related to time, such as the creation of schedules, or the development of temporal design.

Temporal lens: The use of time as an artifact through which to examine organizational phenomena. In particular, the raising of time and issues related to time to the foreground of analysis.

Temporal limits: The edge or boundary, defined in time, for an activity or an event.

Temporal locations: Moments in time; denoted as special through the attribution of meaning, such as holidays. See Temporal punctuation.

Temporal marker: Moments that are imbued with significance, which can also work as a signal for those observing that action is required (e.g, the New Year, which can signal the need to prepare end-of-year reports). See Temporal coordination points, Crossing point, and Temporal milestones.

Temporal meaning: What is signified or intended by the use of particular temporal characteristics, such as a fast pace or a strict deadline.

Temporal midpoint: The halfway mark in a period that is allocated for the completion of a task. See Midpoint transition; Temporal halfway point.

Temporal milestone: A specific moment or point in time, which has significance as it approaches, when it occurs, and when it passes. See Temporal marker.

Temporal mode: A way or acting or behaving, described by its temporal characteristics, but which is separate from the substance or nature of the entity.

Temporal model: A preliminary representation of actions or events, described with an emphasis on time.

Temporal nature: The essential character of an action, an event, or an entity, which is described by its temporal characteristics and which makes something what it is.

Temporal need: A deficiency on the part of an individual or organization related to time, such as a timing requirement or demand. It may include requirements as diverse as the need for concrete deadlines or for meetings to begin on time.

Temporal norms: Commonly accepted views about the use of time and about standards of conduct related to time (e.g. the meaning of punctuality or the acceptability of taking long lunch breaks).

Temporal objectives: Goals that are defined by temporal characteristics, such as a deadline in product introduction. See Temporal goals.

Temporal ordering: The arrangement of events or activities, typically defining coordination such as synchronization or succession.

Temporal orientation: A set of beliefs and emphases on time held by cultures and individuals, the term tending to refer to the relative emphasis placed on the past, present, and future. See Time orientation.

Temporal pacer: A particular element on a calendar or schedule that is used by the entity as a basis to organize work in time. See Pacer.

Temporal pacing: The use of time as a metric and punctuation device to evaluate and motivate work groups.

Temporal pacing behavior: The actions taken to use time as a metric and punctuation device to evaluate and motivate the rate of work (e.g. attention to deadlines, attention to production goals).

Temporal pacing parameters: Specifications for the rate or speed with which a task should be performed.

Temporal parallel: The division of a very large task into separate parts.

Temporal parameters: Influences related to time that govern the way a task is performed. For example, specifications for how tasks should be done within a time frame.

Temporal pattern: A regular arrangement of events or activities that emerges when organized around time. Also, a guide or sample of how a task should be performed with regards to time, such as when tasks should be performed.

Temporal perception: To develop an awareness, mental grasp, or comprehension of time-related phenomena, such as the pace an organization keeps, or the deadlines an organization is expected to make. See Time perception.

Temporal performance: An evaluation of whether an objective related to time is achieved. For example, whether the rate, pace, and punctuality of tasks is appropriate. See Temporal goals; Temporal objectives.

Temporal personality: The characteristic way in which an actor perceives, interprets, uses, allocates or otherwise interacts with time.

Temporal perspective: A specific point of view on matters related to time. This point of view differs in the importance it places on the past, the present, or the future. The temporal perspective is the foundation on which individuals formulate expectations and goals, determine appropriate levels of risk taking, and generate judgments, decisions, and actions. See Time perspective, Temporal viewpoints.

Temporal phenomena: Events or experiences related to time that could be perceived (e.g. urgency).

Temporal planning: A scheme or program to take action based on time-related aspects of the task, such as the rate, pace, and temporal boundaries of an activity or activities. See Temporal strategy.

Temporal preferences: The predilection or inclination of an individual or entity for a given set of parameters related to time and action. Temporal preferences may include pacing preferences, deadline preferences, and temporal orientations.

Temporal problems: Difficulties faced by organizations because of the way time is viewed in the culture in which they are embedded.

Temporal processes: Procedures or sets of actions that rely on time in a meaningful way for their execution. Examples include starting a routine after midnight and increasing the rate of production to meet a deadline. See Time-dependent processes.

Temporal progression: A set of events or activities brought together by their succession.

Temporal punctuation: An alteration of inertial movement that takes occurs because a given moment in time has been given special meaning, such as a deadline or a holiday.

Temporal reference points: Specific moments or points in time used to determine or judge the coordination of group activities or the pacing of activities. See Temporal markers, Temporal milestones.

Temporal referents: Specific aspects of the passage of time, such as moments or cycles, that are used to determine or judge the coordination of group activities or the pacing of activities. See Temporal markers, Temporal milestones.

Temporal reflection: Means that individuals use to pay attention to time by thinking seriously, contemplating, and recollecting experiences. Temporal reflection is used to monitor whether tasks are proceeding according to plan and to communicate any adjustments in plans and actions needed to meet temporal milestones.

Temporal region: Specific place in the time continuum. The most common separations for temporal regions are the past, the present, and the future.

Temporal regularity: The conforming of an event or activity (or a series of events or activities) to a fixed principle. Typically used in describing the recurrence of events.

Temporal reliability: The level of confidence or dependability found in specific matters related to time.

Temporal resources: A help or aid that is derived from or anchored in time. For example, a deadline can be a resource to help establish the rate or pace necessary to complete a task according to a schedule.

Temporal responsiveness: The ability of organizational actors to adapt the timing of their activities to unanticipated events.

Temporal rhythm: The regular reoccurrence of activities or related events coordinated through the measurement of time.

Temporal routines: A regular occurrence or procedure that has as its core component a concern with time and work elements related to time such as pacing and deadlines. See Routines, Temporal work routines.

Temporal sensemaking: The need to create a meaningful pattern or Gestalt out of what would otherwise be a series of disconnected events.

Temporal shifts: A change in an organization or task that is related to time, such as changes in rate, pace, or punctuality.

Temporal signature: An action's defining, distinctive, or characteristic temporal embodiment. Indicates how a process or action should or can be expected to unfold over time.

Temporal slack: The time, as a measurable resource, that is available in excess of that necessary to complete a task.

Temporal stimulus: A factor derived from time that causes motivation, irritation, or change in an entity. For example, a missed deadline may cause an organization to work at a faster pace to prevent another missed deadline.

Temporal strategy: Coordination or planning used to determine the rate, pace, and temporal boundaries of an activity or activities with the objective of completing them in the most efficient manner. See Temporal design, Temporal planning.

Temporal structure: Rules or guidelines that dictate parameters related to time and events or activities, such as the rate, pace, and punctuality of activities, within an organization (e.g. daily or hourly production quotas).

Temporal style: Different ways to understand, explain, and react to time.

Temporal suggestion: Proposed or recommended, but not required, guidelines for matters related to time, such as rate, pace, and punctuality within an organization.

Temporal synchronization: The arrangement of events or cycles so that they occur at a given point in time in relation to a different event or activity, in a complementary manner. See Synchronize.

Temporal system: An arrangement of temporal elements that make up a larger organization. See Temporal design.

Temporal tasks: Actions or behaviors of an entity that are dictated, at least in part, by characteristics related to time (e.g. starting times and urgency pressures).

Temporal tendencies: Inclination towards certain time-related parameters, such as pacing preferences, temporal goals, and scheduling.

Temporal transition: The passage from one condition to another initiated by a concern for time as a resource. The movement from one type of behavior to another after attention is brought to bear on the time available to the group. See Time-triggered task transitions.

Temporal uncertainty: Situations in which the future activities or tasks are unpredictable or undependable due to certain time-related features of the environment.

Temporal understanding: Having a special grasp of issues related to matters of time, such as the ability to understand multiple timelines or the intersection between personal and situational characteristics related to time.

Temporal variable: Characteristics related to time that possess the ability to change; to increase or decrease in magnitude (e.g. preferences or attributes).

Temporal view: A specific perspective on matters related to time. See Time perspective, Temporal perspective.

Temporal web: A network of time-related information that connects events and activities. See Temporal information.

Temporal work routine: A regular occurrence or procedure that has as its core component a concern with time and work elements related to time, such as pacing and deadlines. See Routines.

Temporal zone: Any part of an organization that is considered separate or distinct on the basis of how it uses time. For example, research and development staffs generally have a longer time horizon than marketing and sales.

Temporally aligned: The agreement or condition where a specified order or timing of one or more activities takes place.

Temporally aligned sequences: Agreement of a specified order in which one activity follows another within an entity, between entities, or between entities and external sources.

Time: A nonspatial continuum in which events occur in apparently irreversible succession from the past through the present to the future.

Time abundance: A situation that occurs when the total amount of time available to an organization or an individual is enough or more than enough to do the designated set of activities.

Time allocation: The distribution of time, as a limited resource, among the different activities that must be completed. It also reflects the degree to which employees perceive that there is sufficient time for tasks.

Time awareness: The realization by an individual or group of the passage of time.

Time chart: A chart using straight lines on a grid to compare what was done with what was planned over time. See Gantt chart.

Time compression: Pressures to deliver high quality outcomes at faster rates.

Time concern: To have time or time use as one's responsibility or obligation.

Time constant of the transition: The abruptness with which a pause occurs and how it affects the manner in which the team is able to respond.

Time-dependent processes: Procedures or sets of actions that rely on time in a meaningful way for their execution. Examples include starting a routine after midnight and increasing the rate of production to meet a deadline. See Temporal processes.

Time dimensions: The different views of the phenomenon of time, including, for example, experiential views, socially constructed views, and fungible views. These dimensions are related to each other and together represent the full nature of time.

Time distortion: The recognition that, during the state of engrossment, one has been operating according to the rhythms of the activity while unaware of time.

Time-driven interruptions: A break in the uniformity or continuity of an activity motivated by attention to time as a diminishing resource, such as an approaching deadline or a midpoint evaluation of the work. See Pause and Time-triggered task transitions.

Time experience: The relationship between events and time as they are lived or remembered by the individual. For example, time flows slowly when executing a boring task; similarly, busy times are remembered as longer in duration than quiet times.

Time famine: A severe shortage of time as a resource to complete the required task. It is a severe form of undermanning.

Time frame: A period during which specific events may take place or be required to take place. For example, a time frame for completion is a period during which a task may be planned to end.

Time horizon: A marker placed in time at some point in the future where an artificial separation is made between two different periods of time, one which ends and one which begins at the marker.

Time in passing: When individuals judge the passage of time as it takes place in the present.

Time in retrospect: When individuals remember the passage of time that took place in the past.

Time lag: A change forward or backward in time from the point in which an event or an activity was to occur. Also used to describe the time between an action and the effects of that action.

Time management: The process of using time as a resource, typically through processes of allocation, scheduling, and synchronization.

Time orientation: A set of beliefs and emphases on time held by cultures and individuals, the term tending to refer to the relative emphasis placed on the past, present, and future.

Time-paced evolution: Change is keyed to the passage of time, not the occurrence of particular events.

Time pacing: The act of measuring the rate at which work is accomplished by an entity on the basis of the passage of time (e.g. the number of units completed in an hour). Alternatively, the rate of work can be measured by the occurrence of events (e.g. achieving profitability in a start up company before a public offering of shares).

Time pacing preferences: The predilection or inclination of an individual or entity for a given rate of activity.

Time perception: To develop an awareness, mental grasp, or comprehension of time-related phenomena, such as the pace an organization keeps or the deadlines an organization is expected to make. See Temporal perception.

Time perspective: A specific point of view on matters related to time. This point of view differs in the importance it places on the past, the present, or the future. See Temporal perspective, Temporal viewpoint.

Time pressure: The force exerted by the passage of time that influences mind and will. For example, the force exerted on individuals or groups when task deadlines approach and the task is still incomplete, or the force exerted on individuals or groups when the amount of time available is less than the amount of time required for the completion of a task. See Time stress and Undermanning.

Time-related statements: Written or oral communication that notes some element of the passage of time, such as an approaching deadline or the passage of a season.

Time relocation: Needing to have one or more of the conflicting events extracted from its context and rescheduled (e.g. videotaping a program to watch later).

Time resources: Time is viewed as a means to achieve an objective to supply a want or deficiency. It is also seen as a stock or reserve on which one can draw when necessary.

Time scales: The size of the intervals of time of different lengths.

Time stress: The overpowering – and, typically, adverse – pressure placed on an individual by some force or influence related to time. For example, the pressure placed on an individual when a deadline approaches and work remains to be done.

Time-triggered task transitions: The passage from one condition or task to another. The passage is motivated by attention to time as a diminishing resource, such as an approaching deadline or a midpoint evaluation of the work.

Time urgency: The quality of requiring fast or immediate action.

Time-urgent norms: Commonly accepted views of time that emphasize attention and adherence to schedules, deadlines, and work pace under situations of time scarcity.

Time zones: In an organization, specific areas of work (e.g. departments or divisions) that are different from others on the basis of their temporal concerns. For example, research and development departments may have a much longer time horizon for their activities than sales and marketing departments.

Timeless organizational vision: A mental image of an organization, including all of its characteristics, except a time for its realization.

Timeless vision: A mental image of a situation or an event, but which does not contain a time for its realization.

Timelessness: An experience in which one's total involvement in an activity results in the loss on consciousness and the sense of time.

Timeline: A graphical representation of temporal units punctuated by "tasks", "events", or "milestones." See Gantt charts, PERT, and Milestone charts.

Timeliness: The act of something taking place in a prompt, punctual, or opportune manner.

Timescape: Conceptualizations of past and present activities and interactions of organisms and matter that emphasize rhythmicities, timings and tempos, changes and contingencies. A timescape perspective stresses the temporal features of living. Through timescapes, contextual temporal practices become tangible. Timescapes are thus the embodiment of practiced approaches to time and they stand in contrast to other scapes such as landscapes, cityscapes, and seascapes, which mark spatial features.

Timespan: A length of time, defined by a beginning and an end. See Duration.

Timetable: A list of the times at which successive things are to be done or to happen; the times occupied by a process.

Timing: The regulation of activities on the basis of time. Following a rhythm or pace. Measurement of activities with relation to time, as with a clock.

Timing demands: Situations that call for action from a given entity specifically on the basis of time or the passage of time.

Timing norms: Broadly accepted rules in society that prescribe how activities are regulated on the basis of time.

Timing optimality curves: Figures that graphically display the probable success of a decision or action in achieving its purpose as a function of when the decision is inserted into an ongoing plot.

Timing preferences: Predilection or inclination to pace an activity or process, or when to start and when to complete a task.

Transition: The passage from one condition to another, the movement from one type of behavior to another in a group or individual.

Trigger: An action or event that releases a pent-up demand on an individual or group; initiating behavior or setting in motion a series of events to satisfy that demand.

Undermanning: A situation that occurs when the time available to an organization or to an individual is less than the time required to do the designated set of activities.

Urgency: A force that impels action or that insists on the importance or need for action.

Validity interval: The interval that defines the time scale over which the theory holds.

Window of opportunity: A period of time when action is particularly appropriate or propitious.

Work pace: The rate at which work is accomplished by an entity. See Pace.

FIVE ISSUES WHERE GROUPS MEET TIME

Kathleen M. Eisenhardt

INTRODUCTION

I was surprised and delighted to be asked to write the final chapter of a book on groups. I certainly thought of myself as a "groups person," but I was never quite sure that anyone else did. My research image is much more tied to organization theory and strategy. But the reality is that much of my work – from strategic decision making and product development to acquisitions and cross-business synergies – often does deal with groups. Although these more macro-level topics are in the foreground, groups are very often the backdrop.

Groups are, of course, where much of the work of organizations gets done. In comparison with individuals, groups typically possess more points of view, more thorough and insightful analysis of ideas, and enhanced implementation. The Desert Survival Exercise (and its moon and jungle equivalents) makes clear the efficacy of groups over individuals in countless Organizational Behavior classes every year. Over the years, research on groups has been enormously productive. But apart from models of group development that often seem overly lock-step, there has been surprisingly limited interest in time. Yet, if my own research experience is any guide, organizational members are frequently stumbling into situations where time is crucial to understanding the phenomenon in question.

My argument is not the clichéd "everything is moving faster and faster." Rather, it is simply that time is inescapable. I may, of course, be biased because most of my

Time in Groups
Research on Managing Groups and Teams, Volume 6, 267–283
© 2004 Published by Elsevier Ltd.
ISSN: 1534-0856/doi:10.1016/S1534-0856(03)06012-2

research is field work in organizations operating in high-velocity environments. In these contexts, pace is a signature characteristic. But, most groups and their organizations really do operate in environments that are pluralistic, turbulent, competitive, and irregular in their pace, ambiguity, and uncertainty. So, as groups research (whether conducted in the lab or the field) becomes increasingly reflective of real life experience, it will necessarily become more time-oriented.

The purpose of this chapter is to sketch a point of view on the current state of research where groups intersect time, note the significant contributions from the authors of this volume, and suggest a few future research directions. It is a particular pleasure to be involved in a volume where so many others share the view that time is fundamental. It is also encouraging to note the progress that they and others have made in understanding temporal issues within groups. My "view" draws somewhat idiosyncratically from my own research and that of others, many of whom have contributed to this volume. It no doubt reflects the fact that, to some extent, I bridge the "structural holes" among the "small worlds" of groups, organization theory, and strategy research. Nonetheless, I hope that I have leavened my discussion of five issues in temporal research on groups with the insights of "real" groups people.

To preview the conclusions, there is significant research convergence on the importance of specific temporal phenomena such as time vs. event pacing, interruptions, and synchronization. More subtle, *emotional* aspects of groups (e.g. strategies for speed that deal with confidence, effects of temporal pacing on how time is experienced, the relationship of psychological safety to the potency of interrupts) are emerging as surprisingly pivotal for understanding temporal facets of group behavior. Yet, contemporaneous with this convergence, controversy and confusion exist regarding issues such as the appropriate conceptualization of time-relevant traits of group members, the effectiveness of heterogeneity vs. homogeneity in the temporal aspects of group composition, and the existence (or not) of a speed vs. quality trade-off in group decision making. These issues, coupled with fresh time-relevant methods that open up Input-Process-Output models of group behavior, are likely to shape a compelling future research agenda.

PROCESS: GRANULARITY AND TRULY TEMPORAL CONSTRUCTS

Some of the earliest process research focuses on the progression of time in group development models. These models attempt to delineate the stages or phases that groups experience. For example, Bales (1950) and his colleagues developed a set of categories for tracking group behavior that examined the tension between instrumental and expressive concerns. They posited a model of how the tension played out over time. Similarly, Tuckman (1965) formulated a phase model of group development, the familiar "forming- storming-norming-performing." Additional development models have been proposed for other group processes such as negotiation.

Juxtaposed to this research is the Input-Process-Output tradition. This large body of work includes a wide range of studies that consider factors such as demographic conceptions of team inputs, aggregate measures of process variables such as conflict and communication, and a number of outcome variables including satisfaction and effectiveness (e.g. Ely & Thomas, 2001; Jehn, 1995; Pelled, Eisenhardt & Xin, 1999; Polzer, Milton & Swann, 2002; Williams & O'Reilly, 1998). This research approach overcomes some of the drawbacks of the group development research such as inattention to performance and lack of relevance for ongoing groups. By collapsing process variables into simple aggregate measures, however, research within this paradigm frequently destroys any real sense of the processes of groups over time.

Recent work both extends and combines these two traditions by carefully examining how patterns of behavior unfold over time and linking those patterns to performance (e.g. Gersick, 1988; Jehn & Mannix, 2001; Waller, 1999). Thus, this research ties a granular understanding of process to significant group outcomes. In addition, like the related and rich (but rarely cited by groups researchers) tradition of organizational decision making research (Hickson, Butler, Cray, Mallory & Wilson, 1986; Mintzberg, Raisinghani & Theoret, 1976; Nutt, 1984), it does not force a rigid set of sequenced phases. Rather, it enables iterative, circular, and non-linear paths to emerge.

I experienced the value of this approach first-hand in work with Gerardo Okhuysen. Our research (Okhuysen & Eisenhardt, 2002) centered on understanding how simple formal interventions improve group performance within problem-solving teams. Using an integrative problem-solving task, we explored this issue with a control group plus three simple interventions: share information, ask others to share their information, and manage time. We tracked the progress of these laboratory groups using videotape, and identified the content of their discussion using fine-grained (30 second), temporal increments.

If we had ignored the longitudinal details of the process, we would have simply known that two interventions, ask others to share information and manage time, were associated with high performance. But, we would not have understood why. Indeed we were puzzled by the initial Input-Output results. One intervention (i.e. manage time) that seemed particularly *un*related to task performance in this non-time pressured situation was effective, while a second intervention (i.e. share your information) that seemed very task-related was less effective than even the control. By tracking the content of the groups' discussions at 30-second intervals, we were able to observe that the other-directed character of the effective interventions triggered group members to bunch their collective attempts to re-strategize the direction of the groups into fresh avenues for problem-solving. Group members mostly attended to the task at hand, but occasionally engaged in significant, well-defined strategic re-directions in which they collectively changed topics, speakers, approach and so on. This rarely occurred in the ineffective conditions. Indeed, the granular, temporal process results were so striking that we could observe them in longitudinal plots using *no* statistical analysis. Even our colleagues, who were completely uninvolved in the study, could simply stand several feet away from wall hangings of these plots, and pinpoint the striking non-linear patterns and emergent paths in the results.

Two chapters in this volume contribute to this emergent stream of research that combines a granular and open view of process with performance. Mannix and Jehn (2004) present two such empirical studies. The first looks at the temporal nature of conflict by examining problem solving groups. As such, it takes a traditional topic in Input-Process-Outcome research (i.e. relationship of conflict to performance), but measures conflict (i.e. task, relationship, process) at three points in time. The findings suggest that high performance groups have a much different temporal pattern of conflict than low performers. Obviously then, measuring conflict at a single point in time or as an aggregated measure for the entire process would have given very incomplete or even misleading results. The second study is even more ambitious in its attempt to push the implications of a temporal view of process. Going beyond simply measuring well-known process constructs like conflict at multiple points, this study involves using new kinds of variables that are more temporally relevant. In particular, this study uses a negotiation-related task to examine emergent team state variables (i.e. variables that change with group interaction) such as trust and respect. The results suggest that input and process variables combine to affect these emergent states which, in turn, influence performance. Taken together, these studies make the point that a longitudinal and even moderately granular view of process that incorporates unique aspects of time can significantly add to understanding of groups.

Brett, Weingart and Olekalns (2004) move even further from traditional group process research towards creating deeply time-sensitive method and theory. They categorize process into different types of units like acts, sequences, and break points through the metaphor of a necklace with different types of beads (units) and colors (content differences). Although the empirical results discussed are limited to a few examples of the technique, they nonetheless suggest its promise for understanding commonality and difference among the temporal processes of groups.

Overall, it is clear that more granular process research will yield important new insights including non-linearities and complex interactions that were not apparent in previous work. Several chapters in this volume show the value of such granularity in traditional research topics such as the linkage between conflict and performance (Mannix & Jehn, 2004), and in novel temporal-specific topics such as the sequencing of interactions (Brett, Weingart & Olekalms, 2004). Going forward, there is likely to be continued benefit in studying process with granularity and greater use of uniquely temporal ideas.

COMPOSITION: TRAITS AND THE HETEROGENEITY VS. HOMOGENEITY PUZZLE

Composition is, of course, another classic topic in groups research. As is well-known, this research centers on demographic factors such as age, gender, and functional background and/or a variety of individual traits such as risk taking. It often includes interest in the effects of heterogeneity and homogeneity of group composition on process and/or performance as well. Yet while there is some understanding of important individual-level time characteristics such as polychronicity, time orientation, and pacing preferences (Bluedorn & Standifer, 2004), they are often poorly defined and/or measured. Not surprisingly then, only a handful of studies have looked at group composition from a time perspective.

My own introduction to the temporal aspects of group composition was an early empirical project, a study of strategic decision making by top management teams in twelve entrepreneurial companies (Bourgeois & Eisenhardt, 1988; Eisenhardt & Bourgeois, 1988). Jay Bourgeois and I began this project as a counterpoint to the extant research in organizational decision making that focused on non-profit organizations such as governments, hospitals, and schools. We thought that it was time to study decision making in for-profit organizations operating in competitive environments.

In the course of data collection, we gathered descriptive adjectives for each top management team member and descriptions of each of their behaviors during a particular strategic decision that we studied in depth at each firm. As a result, we obtained rich profiles of each executive along the individual trait dimensions that they and their peers found relevant. Perhaps because of the rapid pace of the environment in which they worked, these executives frequently provided descriptions using time-related characteristics. Two time traits emerged from the data (Eisenhardt, Kahwajy & Bourgeois, 1997). One was time orientation which referred to the time horizon or period in which the executive was most often thinking. Some of these executives were considered visionaries, who were largely occupied by trends and potential events well into the future. Others were much more grounded in the here and now, interested in today's sales or engineering results. The second dimension was pacing. Some executives were eager to quickly take bold action while others preferred to proceed more incrementally in order to engage in more analysis or wait for information to unfold.

The data suggested that the highest performing executive teams were heterogeneous with regard to these time-based traits. In other words, *dis*similar teams were more effective. This dissimilarity appeared to capture the ongoing tensions between short vs. long term considerations and between acting immediately vs. waiting for more information that characterize high-velocity environments. Thus, diversity in temporal perspectives gave voice to the inherent tensions within the environment, and led to superior performance.

Bartel and Milliken (2004) suggest an alternative view. While some diversity may be valuable, similarity is typically more important, especially when coordinated action is key. Groups in which members have similar pacing and time orientation will typically be effective because groups that must coordinate diverse time models of their members experience process losses. The authors also suggest that a shared model of time is particularly valuable in a fast changing market because it accelerates coordination. Yet surprisingly, when the authors examined over 100 diverse groups, they found limited evidence for within or across group variation for several temporal constructs, including sense of time compression, time orientation, and time allocation. On the one hand, these results suggest the pervasiveness of time pressure in the workplace. On the other hand, they raise questions regarding the measurement of temporal constructs, especially time orientation. For example, the Zimbardo and Boyd (1999) time orientation scale assumes that future-oriented people emphasize planning and are well-organized, while present-oriented people are pleasure-seekers and risk-takers. While such a scale may reflect meaningful differences for undergraduate subjects, it is unclear how these characteristics such as being organized or seeking pleasure are closely related to time. As Bartel and Milliken (2004) note, this may more accurately measure some form of goal orientation.

Gevers, Rutte and van Eerde (2004) also suggest the importance of shared cognition on time among team members to superior performance. In particular, their focus is on how people with diverse orientations toward time create a coordinated approach to a collective task. The authors argue that teams should engage in deeper understanding of their own temporal approach in order to limit and cope with differences in how members perceive and value time. This alignment should occur through communication activities such as goal setting, temporal planning, and temporal reflection.

Overall, research on temporal group composition is just emerging. Although Kirton, Okhuysen and Waller (2004) have importantly improved the definitions of many temporal constructs, precise understanding of which individual-level constructs are crucial and how they should be measured remain unclear. The Zimbardo and Boyd (1999) time orientation scale, for example, may not effectively capture important, time-relevant traits of members of ongoing work groups. There is also lack of clarity surrounding when heterogeneity vs. homogeneity of temporal group composition is valuable. It seems likely that the temporal *heterogeneity* of individual group members can be effective in situations such as dynamic environments and uncertain tasks (Eisenhardt, 1989; Eisenhardt, Kahwajy & Bourgeois, 1997). Such diversity may reflect inherent tensions in effective task performance in these situations. It also seems likely that these same temporally diverse teams are more effective when they have some basic agreement about process issues such as schedules and conflict resolution (Bartel & Milliken, 2004; Gevers, Rutte & van Eerde, 2004). In other words, process *homogeneity* may be valuable. Indeed, in my work on top management teams mentioned above, the most effective teams were temporally diverse (as noted above), but they also agreed (as Gevers et al. recommend) on the timing of decisions and the use of a "consensus with qualification" process to pace the actual making of the choice (Eisenhardt, 1989).

SPEED: ALTERNATIVE STRATEGIES AND THE TIME-QUALITY TRADE-OFF

The previous two issues (process and composition) are, in some sense, simply the "time" version of traditional topics in groups research. The next three issues (speed, pace, and temporal structure) are, however, quintessentially time-oriented. Consider speed.

I first stumbled across speed in the study of strategic decision making mentioned above. The original intent of the study was to examine conflict, power and status. For me, however, these issues soon paled in comparison to speed. Virtually every executive in the study emphasized speed. They used catch phrases such as "snooze, you lose," "the worst decision is no decision at all," and "you can't be late for the train." The decisions themselves were striking. For what was sometimes ostensibly the same decision (e.g. forming a strategic alliance or making a critical technical choice), some management teams spent about six weeks while others dragged out the choice process for over a year (Eisenhardt, 1989).

Several counterintuitive characteristics distinguished the fast from the slow (Eisenhardt, 1989). For example, fast teams used *more* information, not less, than the slow ones. The fast decision makers relied on real-time information, both internal and external, about the operations of the business. Indeed, their actions resembled playing a video game, plenty of real-time information, not static snapshots. It appeared that these teams spotted problems and opportunities sooner, frequently engaged in rehearsal of group responses, and honed intuition. Another unexpected finding was that fast teams considered *more* alternatives, not fewer. Multiple alternatives seemed to accelerate the cognitive processing of group members, perhaps because comparison is cognitively efficient. As important, multiple alternatives created confidence in the choice, a recognition that suggested that controlling emotions like anxiety and fear is central to speed. In addition to these two tactics, fast teams relied on counselors, a more complete integration of their decision with other decisions, and consensus with qualification as the choice process. In contrast, slow teams engaged in deep analysis of single alternatives in series (not parallel) and sought consensus. Ironically, these slow teams often panicked, making snap decisions in the face of looming deadlines. Overall, fast teams had higher conflict, made more high quality decisions, and were more effective (Eisenhardt, 1989). Perlow, Okhuysen and Repenning (2002) further explored the existence of speed traps and their potentially mirrored *slow* traps.

In subsequent research, Behnam, Tabrizi and I examined alternative ways that groups achieved speed. We reasoned that groups might have different strategies. Our setting was roughly 70 product development teams (Eisenhardt & Tabrizi, 1995). Some of the teams operated in slow-moving environments, while others were players in fast-moving ones (as measured by the product life cycle). In both types of environments, speed was associated with competitive advantage. The key finding was that fast teams used fundamentally different strategies for accelerating pace, depending upon the pace of their environment. In the more slowly moving environments, fast teams used what we termed a "compression" strategy of squeezing together tasks by overlapping and automating them. In the faster moving environments, they used a fundamentally different "experiential" strategy that included frequent communication, experimentation, and prototyping. This latter, more improvisational approach more closely matched the findings of the fast decision making study (Eisenhardt, 1989).

Given the positive perspective on speed that I had seen plus the results of studies such as that by Waller (1999) on the effectiveness of group speed, I was surprised by the Medvec, Berger, Liljenquist and Neale (2004) and Karau and Kelly (2004) articles. I and others had studied groups that appeared to overcome the speed vs. quality trade-off, and gain superior performance. These authors had not. For example, Medvec et al. (2004) argue that speed sacrifices quality. Time pressure lowers communication and exacerbates several decision biases. Shortening deadlines may accentuate the tendency of groups to fix on their first option, and so to succumb to confirmation bias. In addition, groups under time pressure may be at even greater risk of the information bias in which group members are more likely to share their common information at the expense of the unique. In other words, speed and quality are trade-off qualities.

The resolution of these differences may be, at least in part, related to time frame and significance of the choices. As Zaheer, Albert and Zaheer (1999) note, processes at different time scales may have unique properties. More significant, effective "real life" groups (e.g. Eisenhardt, 1989; Waller, 1999) may have discovered tactics for coping with the biases that hobble groups with less mutual experience and time (e.g. Karau & Kelly, 2004; Medvec et al., 2004). For example, the fast teams in the decision making study assigned individual team members to report unique data from their particular point of expertise such as sales input or R&D milestones (Eisenhardt, 1989). This unique reporting was part of their role, and may well have mitigated the information bias that might otherwise occur. In addition, as noted above, the fast teams explicitly developed multiple alternatives. This practice may well have limited the effects of a confirmation bias. Finally, as I will discuss in the next sections, these effective groups may more effectively pace and organize their activities to mitigate the negative effects of speed.

Overall, research suggests that groups can simultaneously attain speed, quality and performance (Eisenhardt, 1989; Waller, 1999). Further, much like the gaits of a horse, there are multiple processes by which teams can accelerate that are particularly effective for given ranges of speed (Eisenhardt & Tabrizi, 1995). Nonetheless, the speed-related chapters in this book serve as a reminder that speed can be problematic when time frames are short and group members fail to cope with critical biases (Karau & Kelly, 2004; Medvec et al., 2004). Going forward, it would seem particularly useful to delineate even more sharply when groups succumb (or not) to the speed vs. quality trade-off, and how they actually gain speed. Use of temporally informed process theory and methods (Brett et al., 2004; Mannix & Jehn, 2004) would seem particularly wise.

INTERRUPTIONS: TIME TO CHANGE

Interruptions are a fact of group life. Groups often have multiple tasks and switch among them. They are disrupted by both expected events such as deadlines and unexpected events such as crises and opportunities. While these breakpoints can be counter-productive, they can also be opportunities for groups to adapt. Indeed, they are the primary time when groups change.

In the organizations literature, there have been several noteworthy studies of interruptions. Meyer (1982) conducted one of the first. He capitalized on the unexpected occurrence of a strike at California hospitals. Management teams at some hospitals used the strike as an opportunity to not only address strike-related issues, but also to revamp the hospitals in ways that were unrelated to the strike. In a related study, Barley (1986) observed the response of medical teams to the introduction of new radiology equipment. In one situation, the introduction of the equipment triggered a fundamental shift in the status order and work processes of the teams. Recently, Melissa Graebner and I (Graebner & Eisenhardt, 2003) made related observations in a study of the acquisition of entrepreneurial companies from the seller perspective. The top management teams of the seller firms only paid attention to buyer offers when they were already interrupted from their routine business activities by hurdles such as hiring a new CEO or completing a funding round. Otherwise, they were unresponsive to even very attractive opportunities to sell.

In the groups literature, Gersick (1988, 1989), Tyre and Orlikowski (1994), and Edmondson, Bohmer and Pisano (2001) have also recognized the importance of interruptions for broad-based change. In project groups with deadlines, Gersick observed that the well-known midpoint transition is an opportunity for members to make significant changes to their approach to their tasks. Tyre and Orlikowski (1994) extended this work by examining the introduction of new technology in three organizations and thirty-seven groups across Europe and North America. A striking finding was that experimentation was more likely to occur and significant changes were more likely to be implemented immediately after the introduction of the technology. Once this narrow "window of opportunity" passed, change became much less likely. Pressure to resume regular production, congealing of routines, and the press of other activities led to the end of this intense, but brief period of activity. This narrow window persisted even when groups were aware that the technology needed further adaptation. Recently, Edmondson and colleagues (2001) have further observed the importance of psychological safety in taking advantage of these pauses in their study of cardiac surgical teams.

Okhuysen and colleagues have taken our understanding of interruptions further. Extending the concept of "semi-structure" (Brown & Eisenhardt, 1997), Okhuysen and Waller (2002) argue that a variety of devices (e.g. familiarity, deadlines, and simple interventions) create a second agenda to which group members occasionally turn. When they do so, group members create interruptions in which they stop and step back to reconsider ways in which to improve their performance, much as occurs when there are externally-driven interruptions (e.g. Barley, 1986; Meyer, 1982). This secondary agenda creates a template that partially, but not completely, structures activities.

Okhuysen and colleagues observed the semi-structure properties of secondary agendas in a series of studies using laboratory groups that engaged in an integrative problem-solving task. This task required group members to combine unique and shared information in order to diagnose a fictitious food poisoning in a fast food restaurant. Familiarity among group members (Okhuysen, 2001), deadlines (Okhuysen & Waller, 2002), and other-directed, simple interventions (Okhuysen & Eisenhardt, 2002) all create secondary agendas that, in turn, trigger interruptions, and subsequently generate new task strategies, greater flexibility, and more effective performance.

Zellmer-Bruhn, Waller and Ancona (2004) go more deeply into the conditions under which an interruption or pause will lead to change. They observed that some groups take advantage of such pauses to engage in change, while others do not. They suggest that such stopping points for reflection become activated only under certain conditions. The authors argue that it is crucial for group members to recognize interruptions as opportunities, to pair triggers such as feedback or technology introductions with interruptions to stimulate change, to organize "crossing points" in which several groups pause at the same time, and to entrain pauses with externally relevant events. These actions will heighten sensitivity to the opportunities for change, and improve the likelihood that change can and will occur.

Overall, it is clear that interruptions are a primary time during which groups can change (Gersick, 1988, 1989; Okhuysen, 2001). This is among the most robust temporal findings. These interruptions provide opportunities for groups to address not only the issues immediately associated with the breakpoint, but also those beyond the scope of the driver of the interruption (e.g. Gersick, 1989; Meyer, 1982). Several chapters in this book again highlight the importance of interruptions for change and extend our sensitivity to the fact that such change is not automatic (e.g. Zellmer-Bruhn, Waller & Ancona, 2004).

PACING: CREATING A TEMPORAL STRUCTURE

Interruptions can, of course, be driven by unexpected events like hospital strikes and acquisition overtures as well as by the semi-structure of secondary agendas. But groups may also create more expansive temporal structures. These structures not only involve interruptions that may trigger change, but also involve devices for coordination with other groups, drivers of the experience of time and time horizons, and metronomes for the pacing and spacing between tasks (Staudenmeyer, Tyre & Perlow, 2001).

Several of the initial studies of pacing were conducted by Gersick. In her first studies (Gersick, 1988, 1989), she observed that effective groups with deadlines paced their progress with a major midpoint transition in which they shifted strategies in order to complete their tasks. Regardless of time allotted, effective groups overhauled their strategies in fundamental ways at this midpoint. In a longitudinal study of an entrepreneurial firm, Gersick (1994) extended understanding of pacing. She distinguished between time and event pacing. The former refers to taking action in response to some activity like a new product introduction by a competitor. The latter refers to taking action at a particular time such as at the beginning of a season or quarter. Gersick found that both types of pacing had value in maintaining momentum and effectively adapting. Sastry (1997) subsequently simulated some of these results, showing that event pacing was effective in slower-moving environments whereas time pacing was effective in faster moving situations. Event pacing in the latter situation led to excessive change and inability to focus on the task. Finally, Kelly and McGrath (1985) found that groups tended to lock into a particular pace, and so found it challenging to adjust their pace to changed circumstances.

My own work on time pacing centered on multiple product development teams. In a study with Shona Brown, we examined how product development groups routinely created an effective flow of new products (Brown & Eisenhardt, 1997). We observed several time-related phenomena within these groups. For example, the more effective groups operated simultaneously with multiple time orientations. They contemporaneously spent time on both products for current markets and experiments for future markets. We also noted that the more effective groups were time-paced. That is, they created products on a rhythmic pace such as every six months, every nine, or every eighteen months, tying present and future together in a rhythmic flow. They were, thus, not necessarily faster than other groups, but rather more temporally consistent. Time pacing appeared to help groups to coordinate across related groups such as marketing and manufacturing, and to sustain momentum. Time pacing also had an emotional effect. It created a sense of confidence and control that is highly beneficial in high-velocity environments (Brown & Eisenhardt, 1998).

Two additional ideas have further shaped notions of temporal structure. Ancona and Chong (1996) elaborated the concept of temporal entrainment. This construct captures the notion that groups (as well as individuals and organizations) often synchronize with one another or with salient features of their environments. That is, they time pace in synchronization with external actors. Entrainment is, thus, both a natural response and often an effective one. For example, Blount and Janicik (2002) observed that individuals have an "in-synch" preference with one another in negotiations, and are more effective when they do so.

Staudenmeyer, Tyre and Perlow (2002) expanded the notion of time pacing by taking a broader definition of temporal structure, and examining how temporal structures emerge. They relied on several illustrations of companies from three different empirical studies. A good example is Desktop. Here, managers inserted a buffer period to enable product development teams to re-evaluate and revise their software development programs. It was a formalized opportunity to stop and think (Louis & Sutton, 1991). As a result of this intervention, the teams' time horizons shifted from the entire project to chunks punctuated by breaks.

Their sense of time pressure was altered as well. At Ditto, managers eliminated frequent interruptions by enforcing a "quiet period" during which team members worked without interruption. This created a work rhythm, increasing members' sense of control over time and shifting time horizons from the present to both the present and future. In both of these companies, groups created more elaborated temporal structures such that they became more rhythmic, consciously paced, and effective. Again, consistent with some of the previously mentioned studies, there were also changes in the emotional experience associated with time.

Two chapters in this volume are particularly related to temporal structures. Bluedorn and Standifer (2004) took a "big picture" perspective on temporal structure. They introduced the concept of temporal imagination, which resonates with the ideas of understanding and shaping temporal structure. As the authors describe, temporal imagination is a reflection of how and how well groups understand their own timescapes as well as their intersection with the timescapes around them. This imagination is a function of factors such as group diversity, time together, and autonomy. A well-developed temporal imagination creates virtuousity in how groups understand and create temporal advantage. In addition to this concept, the authors also present a number of other time concepts such as polychronicity, time depth, and time breadth which are likely to be useful in conducting temporal research in the future.

In contrast with Bluedorn and Standifer (2004), Chen, Blount and Sanchez-Burks (2004) focus on the micro interactions among group members as they synchronize their pace with one another. Once again the positive aspects of some temporal homogeneity are argued. In particular, the authors posit that status differentials help to create synchronization within groups, which in turn fosters superior coordination. Specifically, high status people often use time as a signal of their status, while others are willing to cooperate with high status people with respect to time. Thus, a combination of status dominance and "in-synch preference" (Blount & Janicik, 2002) can lead to synchronized work groups. Deference to status enables members to cooperate and coordinate with one another, and so to align temporal activities.

Overall, research on temporal structures is a natural extension of work on interruptions. Together with studies of speed, it forms a deepened understanding of time within groups. The distinctions between time vs. event pacing are becoming clear (Gersick, 1994) as is the role of entrainment (Ancona & Chong, 1996; Zellmer-Bruhn, Waller & Ancona, 2004). Experience of time is also becoming better understood. The chapters in this volume both add new conceptual clarity to temporal structures (Bluedorn & Standifer, 2004; Kirton et al., this volume) as well as elaborate more interstitial properties (Chen et al., 2004). Taken together, the extant research suggests that temporal structures (i.e. patterns of interruptions, time pacing, and synchronization) can emerge within groups. They shape not only the timing of work, but also the emotional experience of time including its urgency, compression, and horizon.

FINAL THOUGHTS

The purpose of this chapter is to draw an admittedly idiosyncratic sketch of current research on groups and time, the contributions of this volume, and future directions. It no doubt reflects the tastes of an organizations and strategy researcher with a predilection for field studies and a fondness for groups. There are several final thoughts.

First, current research at the intersection of groups and time consists of two related streams. One stream is a natural extension of traditional groups research. It covers traditional topics such as process and composition, traditional relationships such as conflict with performance, and traditional variables such as status and communication (e.g. Mannix & Jehn, 2004). The second stream is more uniquely time-oriented (e.g. Bluedorn & Standifer, 2004). This work is often (although by no means exclusively) field-based, and centered on novel temporal concepts and related processes such as sequences, interruptions, pacing, and the experience of time. I expect that these streams will continue to converge.

Second, several robust research findings have emerged. In terms of methods, it is apparent that granular measurement of process variables has and will continue to yield an expanded, richer, and more accurate view of how group activity unfolds (e.g. Brett et al., 2004). In terms of content, it is equally clear that interruptions are pivotal for effective change within groups (e.g. Zellmer-Bruhn et al., 2004). Indeed, there is a good deal of accumulated research about how these interruptions operate. Similarly, time and event pacing represent important, distinct temporal aspects of groups with dynamics that are becoming increasingly apparent. Further, it is clear that group members naturally synchronize with one another (e.g. Chen et al., 2004), and their groups entrain with external actors. Perhaps most surprising, the emotional aspects of groups (e.g. strategies for speed that address confidence, temporal pacing that influences the experience of time, psychological safety that affects the potency of interruptions) may well be particularly crucial for understanding temporal phenomena. The importance of emotion in understanding temporal phenomena may also make studies of ongoing groups in field settings particularly informative.

Third, new research opportunities remain. There is a lack of clarity about which are the important temporal characteristics of group members, and how they should be measured. There is debate regarding heterogeneity vs. homogeneity in the temporal characteristics of teams. Some researchers argue for shared cognitive models (e.g. Gevers et al., 2004), while others suggest the value of diversity. Reality is likely to be somewhere in the middle, with heterogeneity of individual traits and homogeneity of approach to group process as effective. There is also controversy about whether a speed vs. quality trade-off exists. Some assert that it does (e.g. Medvec et al., 2004), although I argue that this view is too simplistic. Speed is more variegated than simply compromised quality would suggest. It might also be intriguing to identify the situations in which speed vs. rhythm is more crucial. Finally, a deeper understanding of the components and patterns of temporal structure of group activity is likely to emerge.

During the past decade, there has been an energizing surge of activity at the intersection of groups with time. The topic has come a long way from the smattering of pioneering group development models of the 1950s and 1960s. The next few years should see much deeper understanding of group processes, better shaping of constructs and measures, compelling methods, and an attack on the controversies and confusion surrounding how groups intersect time. My colleagues who have written for this volume have made enormous contributions to this effort.

REFERENCES

Ancona, D. G., & Chong, C. L. (1996). Entrainment: Pace, cycle, and rhythm in organizational behavior. In: B. M. Staw & L. L. Cummings (Eds), *Research in Organizational Behavior* (Vol. 18, pp. 251–284).

Bales, R. F. (1950). *Interactive process analysis: A method for the study of small groups.* Cambridge, MA: Addison-Wesley.

Barley, S. R. (1986). Technology as an occasion for structuring: Evidence from observation of CT scanners and the social order of radiology departments. *Administrative Science Quarterly, 31,* 78–108.

Bartel, C. A., & Milliken, F. J. (2004). Perceptions about time in work groups: Member agreement on time orientation, time compression, and time allocation. In: S. Blount, E. Mannix & M. Neale (Eds), *Research on Managing Groups and Teams: Vol. 6. Time in Groups.* Greenwich, CT: JAI Press.

Blount, S., & Janicik, G. (2002). Getting and staying in-pace: The "in-synch" preference and its implications for work groups. In: E. A. Mannix, M. A. Neale & H. Sondak (Eds), *Research on Managing Groups and Teams: Vol. 4. Toward Phenomenology of Groups and Group Membership* (pp. 235–266). Greenwich, CT: JAI Press.

Bluedorn, A. C., & Standifer, R. (2004). Groups, boundary spanning, and the temporal imagination. In: S. Blount, E. Mannix & M. Neale (Eds), *Research on Managing Groups and Teams: Vol. 6. Time in Groups.* Greenwich, CT: JAI Press.

Bourgeois, L. J., & Eisenhardt, K. M. (1988). Strategic decision processes in high-velocity environments: Four cases in the microcomputer industry. *Management Science, 34,* 816–835.

Brett, J., Weingart, L., & Olekalns, M. (2004). Baubles, bangles, and beads: Modeling the evolution of negotiating groups over time. In: S. Blount, E. Mannix & M. Neale (Eds), *Research on Managing Groups and Teams: Vol. 6. Time in Groups.* Greenwich, CT: JAI Press.

Brown, S. L., & Eisenhardt, K. M. (1997). The art of continuous change: Linking complexity theory and time-paced evolution in relentlessly shifting organizations. *Administrative Science Quarterly*, *42*, 1–34.

Brown, S. L., & Eisenhardt, K. M. (1998). *Competing on the edge: Strategy as structured chaos*. Boston, MA: Harvard Business School Press.

Chen, Y.-R., Blount, S., & Sanchez-Burks, J. (2004). The role of status in group synchronization. In: S. Blount, E. Mannix & M. Neale (Eds), *Research on Managing Groups and Teams: Vol. 6. Time in Groups*. Greenwich, CT: JAI Press.

Edmondson, A., Bohmer, R. M., & Pisano, G. P. (2001). Disrupted routines: Team learning and new technology implementation in hospitals. *Administrative Science Quarterly*, *46*, 685–716.

Eisenhardt, K. M. (1989). Making fast strategic decisions in high-velocity environments. *Academy of Management Journal*, *32*, 543–576.

Eisenhardt, K. M., & Bourgeois, L. J. (1988). Politics of strategic decision making in high-velocity environments: Towards a midrange theory. *Academy of Management Journal*, *31*, 737–770.

Eisenhardt, K. M., Kahwajy, J. L., & Bourgeois, L. J. (1997). Conflict and strategic choice: How top management teams disagree. *California Management Review*, *39*, 42–62.

Eisenhardt, K. M., & Tabrizi, B. N. (1995). Accelerating adaptive processes: Product innovation in the global computer industry. *Administrative Science Quarterly*, *40*, 84–110.

Ely, R. J., & Thomas, D. A. (2001). Cultural diversity at work: The effects of diversity perspectives on work group processes and outcomes. *Administrative Science Quarterly*, *46*, 229–273.

Gersick, C. J. G. (1988). Time and transition in work teams: Toward a new model of group development. *Academy of Management Journal*, *31*, 9–41.

Gersick, C. J. G. (1989). Marking time: Predictable transitions in task groups. *Academy of Management Journal*, *32*, 274–309.

Gersick, C. J. G. (1994). Pacing strategic change: The case of a new venture. *Academy of Management Journal*, *37*, 9–45.

Gevers, J. M. P., Rutte, C. G., & van Eerde, W. (2004). How groups achieve coordinated action: A model of shared cognitions on time. In: S. Blount, E. Mannix & M. Neale (Eds), *Research on Managing Groups and Teams: Vol. 6. Time in Groups*. Greenwich, CT: JAI Press.

Graebner, M. E., & Eisenhardt, K. M. (2003). The other side of the story: Seller decision-making in entrepreneurial acquisitions, Working Paper, University of Texas at Austin.

Hickson, D., Butler, R., Cray, D., Mallory, G., & Wilson, D. (1986). *Top decisions: Strategic decision making in organizations*. San Francisco: Jossey-Bass.

Jehn, K. A. (1995). A multimethod examination of the benefits and detriments of intragroup conflict. *Administrative Science Quarterly*, *40*, 256–282.

Jehn, K. A., & Mannix, E. A. (2001). The dynamic nature of conflict: A longitudinal study of intragroup conflict and group performance. *Academy of Management Journal*, *44*, 238–251.

Karau, S. J., & Kelly, J. R. (2004). Time pressure and team performance: An attentional focus integration. In: S. Blount, E. Mannix & M. Neale (Eds), *Research on Managing Groups and Teams: Vol. 6. Time in Groups*. Greenwich, CT: JAI Press.

Kelly, J. R., & McGrath, J. E. (1985). Effects of time limits and task types on task performance and interaction of four-person groups. *Journal of Personality and Social Psychology*, *49*, 395–407.

Louis, M. R., & Sutton, R. I. (1991). Switching cognitive gears: From habits of mind to active thinking. *Human Relations*, *44*, 55–76.

Mannix, E., & Jehn, K. A. (2004). Let's norm and storm, but not right now: What to do with phase models of group interaction? In: S. Blount, E. Mannix & M. Neale (Eds), *Research on Managing Groups and Teams: Vol. 6. Time in Groups*. Greenwich, CT: JAI Press.

Medvec, V. H., Berger, G., Liljenquist, K., & Neale, M. A. (2004). Is a meeting worth the time? Barriers to effective group decision making in organizations. In: S. Blount, E. Mannix & M. Neale (Eds), *Research on Managing Groups and Teams: Vol. 6. Time in Groups*. Greenwich, CT: JAI Press.

Meyer, A. D. (1982). Adapting to environmental jolts. *Administrative Science Quarterly, 27*, 515–537.

Mintzberg, H., Raisinghani, D., & Theoret, A. (1976). The structure of "unstructured" decision processes. *Administrative Science Quarterly, 21*, 246–275.

Nutt, P. C. (1984). Types of organizational decision processes. *Administrative Science Quarterly, 29*, 414–450.

Okhuysen, G. A. (2001). Structuring change: Familiarity and formal interventions in problem solving groups. *Academy of Management Journal, 44*, 794–808.

Okhuysen, G. A., & Eisenhardt, K. M. (2002). Integrating knowledge in groups: How simple formal interventions enable flexibility. *Organization Science, 13*, 370–386.

Okhuysen, G. A., & Waller, M. J. (2002). Focusing on midpoint transitions: An analysis of boundary conditions. *Academy of Management Journal, 45*, 1056–1065.

Pelled, L. H., Eisenhardt, K. M., & Xin, K. R. (1999). Demographic diversity in work groups: An assessment of linkages to intragroup conflict and performance. *Administrative Science Quarterly, 44*, 1–28.

Perlow, L. A., Okhuysen, G. A., & Repenning, N. P. (2002). The speed trap: Exploring the relationship between decision making and temporal context. *Academy of Management Journal, 45*, 931–955.

Polzer, J. T., Milton, L. P., & Swann, W. B. (2002). Capitalizing on diversity: Interpersonal congruence in small work groups. *Administrative Science Quarterly, 47*, 296–324.

Sastry, M. A. (1997). Problems and paradoxes in a model of punctuated and organizational change. *Administrative Science Quarterly, 42*, 237–275.

Staudenmeyer, N., Tyre, M., & Perlow, L. (2002). Time to change: Temporal shifts as enablers of organizational change. *Organization Science, 13*, 583–597.

Tuckman, B. W. (1965). Developmental sequence in small groups. *Psychological Bulletin, 63*, 384–389.

Tyre, M. J., & Orlikowski, W. J. (1994). Windows of opportunity: Temporal patterns of technological adaptation in organization. *Organization Science, 5*, 8–18.

Waller, M. J. (1999). The timing of adaptive group responses to non-routine events. *Academy of Management Journal, 42*, 127–137.

Williams, K., & O'Reilly, C. (1998). Demography and diversity in organizations: A review of 40 years of research. In: R. Sutton & B. Staw (Eds), *Research in Organizational Behavior* (Vol. 20, pp. 77–140).

Zaheer, S., Albert, S., & Zaheer, A. (1999). Time scales and organization theory. *Academy of Management Review, 24*, 725–741.

Zellmer-Bruhn, M., Waller, M. J., & Ancona, D. (2004). The effect of temporal entrainment on the ability of teams to change their routines. In: S. Blount, E. Mannix & M. Neale (Eds), *Research on Managing Groups and Teams: Vol. 6. Time in Groups*. Greenwich, CT: JAI Press.

Zimbardo, P. G., & Boyd, J. N. (1999). Putting time in perspective: A valid, reliable individual-difference metric. *Journal of Personality and Social Psychology, 77*, 1271–1288.